Better Aerobatics

Alan Cassidy

Freestyle Aviation Books

Copyright © Alan Cassidy

1st Edition published in the UK in 2003
by Freestyle Aviation Books

ISBN 0-9544814-0-2

Typeset by Freestyle Aviation Books
Printed by Lightning Source Inc.
www.lightningsource.com

Freestyle Aviation Books
18 Woodhurst Road, Maidenhead, SL6 8TF, England
E-mail: ACCassidy@aol.com
Website: www.worldaerobatics.com

Dedication

Better Aerobatics is dedicated to my wife Angela who has always encouraged me to follow my passion for flying.

Acknowledgements

My greatest appreciation goes to those who have inspired my aerobatic career since my first flying lesson at the age of 18. Earliest of these influences were Roger Tribe and John Shelton, shortly followed by everyone involved in the 1970 World Championship held at South Cerney, England. In the 1980s, Eric Müller's book *Flight Unlimited* provided hours of tutoring.

More recently, I have greatly benefited from the advice of a series of French World Champions: Xavier Delapparent, Patrick Paris and Eric Vazeille. For help with the preparation and proofing of the book I am indebted to, among others, Julian Murfitt, Steve Green, John Askew and Mark Walden.

My final thanks go to the many students who have sat with me in aeroplanes for the last 13 years and taught me so much.

Exculpation

In a number of places throughout the book, I have used the masculine pronoun 'he'. This does not mean that all aerobatic pilots are men, far from it, and many of the lady pilots are justifiably held in great respect. My purpose is just to make the text easier to read, without the cumbersome 'he/she' construction.

The author (right) at RAF Newton in 1969 as a member of Cambridge University Air Squadron. *Unknown photographer*

The author with the Neil Williams Daily Telegraph Trophy for the UK National Unlimited Champion, 2001. *Maidenhead Advertiser*

A Sukhoi 31 and a brace of Su-29s over the south of England in the late 1990s. The pilots, front to back, were Paul Bonhomme, Alan Cassidy and Warwick Brady.

Peter March

Pitts S1S(E), G-AZPH at Little Snoring in 1989. This aeroplane, formerly flown by Neil Williams among others, was the author's second Pitts and is now in the Science Museum. London. *Nick Wakefield*

Pitts S2A, G-STUA (formerly N13GT) in 1999. This has been the author's instructional airframe since 1991. *Austin J. Brown*

Contents

Part Five - Advanced and Unlimited Figures

Part Six - Freestyle Figures

Part Seven - Competition Flying

Better Aerobatics

Part One

General Matters

Aerobatic Contest Organisations

All air sports, worldwide, are governed by the Fédération Aéronautique Internationale (FAI), which is based in Lausanne, Switzerland. The FAI delegates powers to individual Air Sports Commissions (ASC) for the running of different air sport disciplines.

The ASC responsible for regulating international aerobatic competitions is the Commission Internationale de Voltige Aérienne (CIVA). All FAI affiliate nations are permitted to send a delegate to the annual CIVA plenary meetings which determine the evolution of regulations for aerobatic contests.

At the national level, National Aero Clubs exist to promote air sports domestically. These bodies sometimes delegate further to national clubs or associations, such as the International Aerobatic Club (IAC) in the United States of America or the British Aerobatic Association (BAeA) in the United Kingdom.

For internet searches start at:

    www.fai.org/aerobatics
    www.iac.org
    www.aerobatics.org.uk
    www.france-voltige.org

CHAPTER **1**

Introduction

What's It All About?

When I was 16, I learned that there were two kinds of mathematics: pure and applied. I found my ability at the pure sort quite limited, but eventually managed an engineering degree of a sort using the applied stuff.

When I was 18, I learned to fly. I was fortunate enough to be taught by instructors who realised that there were also two types of flying: pure and applied! Spooky, isn't it?

In fact I learned to fly twice. Firstly with civilian instructors and then with Air Force QFIs. In those days there wasn't a lot of difference between the two; most civilian instructors were ex-servicemen. Nowadays it is very different, with by far the majority of instructors coming from the purely civilian route. Unfortunately, in my view, the civilian flying training industry teaches only the very rudimentary aspects of pure flying and thereafter is obsessed with aviation of the applied sort.

Applied Aviation

In initial PPL training, you will be taught enough pure flying to taxy, take off, climb, turn, cruise, descend and land. Thereafter you will apply this limited set of skills to flying at night, in cloud, and in bigger and more complex aircraft. And you will learn to navigate over increasing distances. With this same, basic set of skills, you can become a commercial pilot, have a long career and accumulate many thousands of airborne hours.

A military pilot will have a bit more fun. He will learn a bit more pure flying in the form of basic aerobatic training. But this extra knowledge is a stepping stone to a wider range of applied flying tasks, primarily air combat but also including some 'mud moving' in the fighter ground attack role. The military exploitation of aerobatic flight is limited to those aspects that have tactical application.

Ultimately, whether you fly for an airline, for the military or even with your best mate on a day trip to the next State, you lack freedom in the air. You are bound by tasks, procedures and limitations. The romance and pure joy of the unrestrained flight of birds are missing.

Pure Flying

Pure flying involves no application. It has no purpose other than personal fulfilment. It is selfish and pointless. It is also utterly inspiring and addictive. There is no other way of squandering large amounts of money on high-tech machinery that comes close to providing the three-dimensional freedom of expression and timeless joy of limitless pure flight. Cars, boats, yachts, jets ... you can keep them all. They don't even come close.

Through a combination of desire and good fortune (and who is to say that the former does not sometimes generate the latter), I have been immensely privileged, especially over the last 20 years, to pursue and accomplish feats of pure flying in fantasy machines that are the stuff of aviation legend. I sometimes envy the 747 captain his wallet and his pension, but not in any way his form of transport.

Learning to be Free

In pure flying you never know it all. There is always more to learn and more skills to develop. It is endless because aircraft capabilities are always being driven forward. You learn slowly by teaching yourself. You learn quicker by being taught, and even quicker by teaching others. At least, this has been my experience.

But learning alone is not education. Ability without understanding is a dangerous commodity in the unforgiving environment of the air. A good pilot must not only know what to do, but why he should do it so.

Better Aerobatics

If you are a pilot, my aim in this book is to make your aerobatics better. This applies equally whether you are a student or an instructor yourself.

If you are not a pilot, and you are still reading this, then I urge you to go on. Your basic interest will hopefully be enflamed by the insight you will gain to the complexity of the subject.

Although I was greatly helped in the early days by other aerobatic books, I thought then (and I know now) that there were gaps in the explanations given. Some even contained basic errors that could have led to hours of frustration in the air. I have tried to make this book readable while, at the same time, giving as much detail as is necessary to ensure a thorough understanding of the underlying principles in all situations. I hope I have left no gaps nor, required any intelligent guesswork.

Learning from a book can never be a substitute for learning from a Master. But explanation and encouragement, even in print, is always valuable. As much to those teaching as to those learning. If you are seeking freedom in the air, then I hope my words will be of some assistance.

The Key Features

The key features of aerobatic flight are:

- flying in all attitudes
- using every permitted part of the aircraft envelope
- judging attitude by external visual reference
- exploiting all the different forces available to manoeuvre the aircraft
- removing the limitations of your own personal flight envelope.

Flying in all Attitudes

The air is a three dimensional environment. Flying is to aerobatics as swimming is to scuba diving. To explore the latter, you need first to learn the former. Expand this analogy to develop a scale of involvement and passion. The progression is exponential.

Flying a circuit is a length of an indoor pool. A cross-country flight to Spain is swimming a kilometer out to sea. Aerobatics is diving the coral reef and cavorting with dolphins.

In conventional flight, from PPL student to airline captain, you need never exceed 60° of bank, nor 20° of pitch. Rotation about the yaw axis is something to be avoided; there might even be automatic systems to prevent it. The aerobatic pilot knows no such limitation. An elementary roll and loop explore the full 360° available in the first two axes; a stall turn gets you round 180° of the third. There are figures where you can see the top of an aircraft from the ground, while it climbs and completes up to two full rotations in yaw.

The Aircraft Envelope

For the non-aerobatic pilot, maximum speed (V_{NE}) and spins are only seen during three-yearly Certificate of Airworthiness flights, and then only by approved test pilots. Stalling, if not avoided altogether, is never prolonged nor exploited.

An accomplished aerobatic pilot will be accustomed to speeds from zero to the maximum and even to going backwards from time to time. He will be comfortable flying the aircraft for brief periods at angles of attack well past the critical. He will fly close to the G limits of the aircraft, both upright and hanging upside down in the harness.

Judging Attitude by External Visual Reference

The human eye is capable of detecting attitude changes as small as 1° and the brain of assessing pictorial information with speed and accuracy. No one has yet produced aircraft instruments that are so fine yet weigh nothing and cost less.

As aerobatics is about flying in all attitudes, then piloting is about maintaining spatial orientation, which has three elements: attitude, attitude and attitude.

- what the **attitude** is ...
- how the **attitude** is changing ...
- the rate at which the **attitude** is changing.

To know the first the pilot must look where he can see both aircraft and horizon. To know the second he must look again. To know the third he must be looking at the horizon for 95% of the time.

Exploiting all the Different Forces Available

The elevator, aileron and rudder controls exert aerodynamic forces on the airframe when there is airflow over them. The propulsion system produces the aerodynamic force of thrust to overcome drag, the enemy. The propeller produces a slipstream that acts asymmetrically on the airframe.

The propeller also produces other non-aerodynamic forces that act on the aeroplane. Whenever an angle of attack is present, the propeller will produce a turning force due to the asymmetric blade effect (sometimes called p-factor). At high positive angles of attack with a right-tuning engine, the aircraft will yaw to the left as a result. Similarly, in knife-edge flight using right rudder, the propeller will produce a force to pitch the nose up.

The propeller also produces gyroscopic effects which can place very significant forces directly into the airframe through the engine crankshaft and mounting system. With a right-turning propeller, pitching down rapidly will cause a noticeable yaw to the left, while yawing rapidly to the left, as in a stall turn, will make the nose pitch up.

Most flight training manuals will describe these forces, and how to overcome them. An aerobatic training manual will also explain how to harness these forces to enhance control effectiveness and to drive the aircraft through manoeuvres that seem un-natural to the untutored eye.

Expanding Your Own Personal Flight Envelope

The flight manual will clearly state the aircraft limitations that must not be exceeded. There is, however, no such manual to express the limitations of the pilot, which are the result of his training and experience. Consequently, initial flight training constrains the pilot to operate within a very narrow personal flight envelope. The student's envelope will be certainly more restrictive than the personal envelope of the instructor which is in turn may be to be smaller than that of the aircraft itself. The purpose of aerobatic training is to push back the student's personal limitations until his personal flight envelope perfectly matches that of the aircraft.

Successful aerobatic training achieves this expansion by giving both understanding and experience. Both are needed; alone, neither is sufficient. Proficiency in a technique, without understanding how and why it works, is not enough. Theoretical knowledge on its own cannot be applied unless the pilot also has proficiency acquired through actually using the technique and sensing the aerodynamic and physiological effects.

Experience of the physiological effects is very important, as these can swamp the mind and inhibit the use of theoretical knowledge and even of technique. It might be possible to learn to fly an inverted flat spin using a text book and *Flight Simulator* software. But this is not sufficient training to remove the limitation from the personal flight envelope, such are the physiological effects! Several conclusions follow from all this:

- an aerobatic instructor must have a personal flight envelope bigger than that of his student.
- an aerobatic instructor must have a personal flight envelope as big as that of the aircraft
- if you can find aircraft and instructors with ever greater envelopes, you can carry on learning for a lifetime.

For good reason is the highest category of aerobatic competition called Unlimited. However, as you break down these limitations and enlarge your own knowledge and skill envelope, you must develop ever greater self discipline in your duty to respect the absolute limitations of your aircraft.

The Aerobatic Pilot

The aerobatic pilot is not a super-human, demi-God, sky-god or any other such fanciful notion. He, or indeed she, is just a person like any other. But some relevant characteristics can be identified and possibly developed, so here are some thoughts on the subject.

Self-Motivation

The most critical requirement for an aerobatic pilot is that he must want to do it. This may seem a statement of the obvious, but how many people out there do you know who are pushed into doing things they would really rather avoid? This is not the mental state required for developing new skills in such an unforgiving environment as the air.

Each pilot must also set his own goals. We are all different individuals. We come from different backgrounds; we have different life experiences. And we have different ambitions. All these things conspire to make life very difficult for any aerobatic guru who tries to direct the development of his proteges in any specific direction. More importantly, the developing pilot will not have the right motivation unless he has himself decided that this is the route he wants to follow and the results he wants to achieve.

Aerobatics is, above all, an individual pursuit. Formation flying may be a group activity, but only a suicidal pair would try to learn new aerobatic techniques while flying together. In formation aerobatics, it is the formation flying that is the more difficult skill; any aerobatics involved must be so familiar to the crews that they execute the manoeuvres without thinking of anything but station-keeping.

Self-Discipline

The result of ill-discipline is immediate and potentially life-threatening. If you are flying solo, there will be no-one to slap your wrist, save the Grim Reaper himself. Self-discipline is essential to survival.

The aerobatic instructor must not be a disciplinarian, because this does not teach self-discipline. But he must set a constant example of restraint and good airmanship. His students will then learn self-discipline from his example.

Self-Criticism and Self-Confidence

Without self-criticism, self-confidence will be too high. With external criticism, self-confidence will be too low. The only way to have just the right amount of self-confidence is by self-criticism.

The developing pilot must seek out both criticism and praise externally, but he must be able to measure both against his own estimation of his performance. Ultimately, you are flying to please yourself, to have fun. Set yourself challenges, but do not be too hard on yourself when they prove to be tough ones.

CHAPTER 2

Airmanship

Airmanship is all about doing 'the right thing' in every aspect of your flying. It is a combination of protocol, etiquette, common sense, self-discipline, awareness and, above all, mental attitude. Airmanship has a number of very important benefits, which I can summarise as follows. You can put these in any order of importance you want!

- Airmanship keeps you alive.

- Airmanship keeps you out of prison.

- Airmanship earns you respect.

- Airmanship keeps your maintenance bills down.

- Airmanship would keep everyone's insurance premiums down.

Airmanship is a combination of knowledge and its application. To do 'the right thing' you have to:

- know what 'the right thing' is, and

- care enough to do it.

In this chapter I cannot possibly teach you all of the 'right things', but I can emphasise those that are especially important in aerobatics. If you then adopt the right attitude, you will study and seek new answers for as long as you keep flying. Eventually, you will get the knowledge you need from innumerable sources.

Equally, I cannot make you care enough to actually do the right thing. But I can mention a few of the consequences: death, prison, disrespect, poverty etc etc ...

When you get into the chapters of the book dealing with flying the figures, you will not find me endlessly repeating instructions to 'look out' or 'throttle back to keep the engine rpm down' or 'don't exceed V_{NE}'. Instead I will put all my thoughts on airmanship here, and you can come back and read it once a year, once a month or just after you have scared yourself and see what you did wrong.

How to Stay Alive

You stay alive by respecting limitations, of which there are two types:

- aircraft limitations, and
- personal limitations.

Aircraft Limitations

Aircraft limitations are easy to study and learn. They are written in the flight manual. Read it and respect it. No aircraft is **Unlimited**, nor will one ever be. Bridges last for centuries, but they don't fly. Aeronautical engineering is different from civil engineering and, as a pilot, you should understand why.

If you don't know, ask an aeronautical engineer – there are lots of them about.

The limitations that you must know and which must observe at all times are:

- maximum g loads, positive and negative
- weight and balance envelope
- manoeuvre speed – the maximum speed at which you can apply maximum control deflections
- maximum flick speed, positive and negative
- never-exceed speed, V_{NE}, which should be self-explanatory.

This is not a long list. I could have included flap and gear limiting speeds, but this is a list concerned with aerobatics. Also, it is about staying alive and the result of exceeding gear and flap speeds is more likely to be a big bill than death.

To live long as an aerobatic pilot you must know, understand and stay within the aircraft's flight envelope.

Personal Limitations

The biggest compliment you can pay any pilot, at any stage of his career, is to say that he knows and flies within his own limitations. You have your own personal flight envelope, just like the aeroplane. The difference is that the aeroplane's envelope is fixed by design, while yours can be enlarged by proper training. You are unlikely to kill yourself if you stay within your own personal flight envelope.

The things that form the limits of your personal flight envelope are these:

- knowledge of your aeroplane's technical capabilities
- acquisition of handling skills
- understanding of safety margins
- knowing what can go wrong
- knowing what is going on around you
- appreciation of wind and weather
- medical, physical and psychological fitness.

All these things are under your control, except perhaps medical fitness. The quantity you have of each is variable. When you are young, you may be very fit, but you really know nothing. When you are really old, you may know everything but be fit for nothing.

From when you start to learn aerobatics you should get used to the idea that it is your personal responsibility to decide what you want to learn. You should set yourself reasonable goals for the short and medium terms, while you can have great ambitions for the longer term. These latter aims may change as you accomplish the shorter term ones, but you must always have a goal set if you are to structure and control the expansion of your own flight envelope.

When it comes to the acquisition of handling skills, the understanding of safety margins and knowing what can go wrong, you will make progress many times faster if you seek out and take proper instruction rather than try to teach yourself. A good instructor can sometimes be hard to find, and may appear to be an expensive luxury, but in the long term he will turn out to be more available than you expect and very, very cost effective in saving many frustrating hours of self-education. He will also teach you ways to save your life.

If you do not know what is going on around you, even though you be a world-class aerobatic pilot, sooner or later you are going to get very close to another aeroplane you did not see, or find yourself at a turning point in the middle of a glider competition, or suddenly find the windscreen full of telephone cables. "*Look out*" is the one single word pilots most associate with 'airmanship'. Make sure you do it.

If you are not certain that the weather conditions are suitable for your planned flight, they aren't. If the cloud base is a bit lower than normal one day and you think, "*I can still do it, I'll just lower my minimums for today*". Then you are showing decidedly bad airmanship. You may well succeed at this new lower level, because by the law of averages, nothing serious is likely to go wrong. But just because something is a long shot, don't think it will never happen to you.

This is reverse lottery mentality. Lots of people buy lottery tickets even though they know the chance of winning in a hundred lifetimes is really remote. Yet every week, someone wins the lottery. The chances of your engine quitting when you do a roll straight after take-off, or of getting a control restriction when you start a spin at lower level than normal, are pretty small, but certainly greater than picking the winning lottery ticket. Yet we think it can never happen to us!

Whenever you cut back on a safety margin, because of weather, ego or any other reason, you must never lose sight of the need for an escape route when the unthinkable happens. And if you want to die in bed, then there are some safety margins that you must never ignore.

Physiological Effects of G-forces

Even if you are perfectly fit, and your aircraft in excellent condition with every system on top form, you can still turn yourself 'off' or 'blow your head up' if you are reckless with the application of G forces. I am not a doctor, so I will not write a treatise here on this subject. But I have had a lot of experience of the symptoms that can occur, and I have learned some ways of mitigating them. So I must say something about them here.

Positive G

When you pull too much positive G, your brain gets short of blood and it starts to shut down. What does 'too much' mean? Well it simply means enough to make you start to lose perception in your current condition.

The G-load at which you will start to go out will vary from situation to situation. It depends on what you have eaten and drunk, what the air temperature and humidity are, the sequence of figures one after the other. And these are factors that change from hour to hour. There are longer term changes to do with how much flying you have done recently, how old you have become, how your blood pressure has changed, how much physical training you have done and so on. But I am not going to write a treatise, so …

If you pull 'too much' the first thing you will notice is that your field of vision will reduce. You will start to get 'tunnel vision'. If you don't back off the G straight away, your already narrowed vision will lose all sense of colour, then it will go altogether. At this point you will still be able to hear, both the sounds of the engine and of your own grunting, but not for long. If you ignore this complete loss of vision you will next lose consciousness altogether. Not good.

If you get into this regime and out again, even without losing consciousness, you will feel confused and disorientated. Your subsequent performance will be greatly reduced. You should immediately stop aerobatics, fly steadily back to your airfield and land taking extra caution to do everything correctly.

You will be particularly susceptible to 'blacking out' if you pull harder and for longer than normal, especially if you have had some exposure to negative G (even simply -1g straight and level) just beforehand. So you will learn to predict when in a sequence the problems might occur.

The best way to keep blood in your brain when you pull is to close down, as much as possible, the veins in your neck that carry the blood out of your head back to the heart. The muscles in your neck can do this, if you train them. You should practice tightening all these neck muscles and, at the same time, try to grunt or growl out loud so as to make the most embarrassing noise you can think of. In the aeroplane, no-one else will hear it. Even if you are flying dual, the other person will either be doing the same themselves or will be unconscious, so they still won't hear you!

Negative G

There is no such thing as 'red out'; no direct analogy to 'black out'. There is no gradual loss of perception, nor any change in colour vision unless the blood vessel that you break happens to be in your eye.

The mildest, and most common, symptom induced by negative G is 'seeing stars'. This is almost certain to happen if you apply a sudden stab of negative G after a period of lay-off. You will simply see little flashing dots of light throughout your normal field of vision. After a short while, they will go away, but will probably leave you with a bit of a headache by the time you get back to the club house for a cup of tea.

The expression 'seeing stars' is more commonly associated with being hit over the head by a blunt object, but the symptoms are just the same. This should give you an idea of why a lot of negative G can do you absolutely no benefit whatsoever. Beyond the 'starry' stage, you will start to burst blood vessels. These may be small ones below the surface of your skin, most often around the eyebrows. You will notice little red blotches just under the surface.

These, too, will go away but they take a little longer than the stars. You may burst a blood vessel in your eye, so that the white part turns a fetching shade of scarlet. This may or may not affect your vision, but will certainly affect your success rate at the post-flight disco.

If the blood vessel you burst is in your brain stem, it may well affect your sense of balance for weeks, if not months. The effect is immediate and without warning. You will just suddenly realize that you do not know which way is up. This is, to say the least, disconcerting when airborne. The world may seem to be wobbling or spinning before your very eyes, especially if you tilt your head backwards. This will certainly make a safe landing difficult; I fear that on occasion it has made one impossible. We will just never know about some of the other unexplained crashes.

If this account worries you, then that is good, for you are becoming aware of your limitations. There are, however, some things you can do to mitigate the worst effects of negative G.

If you have done no negative before, or have had a period of non-inverted flying, always spread the build up to higher levels over a period of gradual work-up. Never go straight to -3g or -4g without several precursor flights where you have kept the limit to -2g.

Beyond -4g, and some people go significantly beyond this, you must be flying to this limit several times a week to keep match fit. If you are setting up for a really hard push, squeeze the neck muscles as you would for positive G. This can help reduce the rate at which pressure builds in your head. It also seems to be beneficial to keep your chin down against your chest and to keep your head still during the peak negative period. You have to learn how to look at the wing tip by just swivelling your eyes to the left.

If you overdo the negative, the most likely persistent symptom is loss of balance; hence the expression "*getting the wobblies*" that seems to be in general circulation. The actual damage that causes these symptoms might be in the brain or in the inner ear. In the former case, the best solution is to refrain from flying for some months.

If you can't give up altogether, then certainly stay the right way up until you are completely free of vertigo. Some inner ear problems appear to be responsive to physical treatment consisting of a special pattern of head movements. There is more information about this in specialist articles in the aerobatic press, so you can look it all up on the internet when you are bored, or when you can't fly because of the brain damage!

How to Keep Out of Prison

Know the Law. Don't get caught breaking it. Different countries have different regulations regarding the legality of aerobatics – specifically where you can do it and at what height.

In Britain the rules are quite liberal, at least at the time of writing. The only place that aerobatic flight is prohibited entirely is over congested areas. You may aerobat in controlled airspace, as long as you have permission from the appropriate controller. You may fly down to the surface as long as you remain at least 500 feet, in any direction, from any person, vehicle, vessel or structure. So if it really is truly open countryside, there is no legal minimum altitude. This leaves a lot of scope for self-discipline.

In other countries, some of which pride themselves on their tradition of personal freedom, the situation is more restrictive. Quite commonly there is a blanket restriction on aerobatics below 1,500 feet, with a process of special bureaucratic paperwork to enable lower level operation at specific times and places. I cannot list all the different rules here, but you can easily find out what is applicable where you live.

So don't be lazy and break the law through ignorance. You will never get away with that as your defence.

How to Earn Respect

When flying, particularly in a circuit pattern, don't do anything that makes someone else change their plan (let alone makes them think they are in danger!).

If you are practising for an air show or competition, do only what you need to do for the practice. Resist the temptation to add in extra spectacular fly-bys or whatever just to impress someone who *may* be watching.

If they **are** impressed, then they are too impressionable and it was not worth it. If they are **not impressed** then they probably know better than you how close you just came to death.

However much you know about something, there is always someone else who knows more. He may be the one you are bull-shitting to right now. So always be prepared to listen and to change your mind. The most common cause of a broken nose is to have been talking when you should have been listening.

How to Keep Maintenance Costs Down

Treat Your Engine with Respect

The biggest bill you can get for an aeroplane, short of a complete rebuild, is an engine overhaul or replacement. If you run a certificated training aeroplane you must have this expense at the approved Time Between Overhauls (TBO). But often, aerobatic engines do not last even that long before requiring unscheduled repair.

In order to get the best out of your engine, there are certain habits you should develop. These include the following.

◆   Avoid leaving the engine for more than a month without running it up to full operating temperature, or taking off before the engine is up to minimum operating temperature.

◆   Avoid gliding descents – always descend with some power applied to prevent rapid cooling.

◆   Never exceed maximum rpm by more than a couple of hundred!

◆   At the beginning of the aerobatic part of every flight, invert the aircraft and check that the inverted oil system produces the right pressure.

If you are a professional air show pilot and earn your living with state-of-the-art gyroscopic tumbling figures, get the biggest, heaviest propeller you can, run at 105% of maximum rpm and expect to buy a new crankshaft every winter. The other 99% of readers, should do the opposite. In other words, get the smallest, lightest propeller you can and run at 95% of maximum rpm!

Another good tip is to overhaul your carburettor or fuel injector on a regular basis, certainly not less frequently than the manufacturer recommends for certificated installations, even if your aircraft is not certificated. Defective fuel control units are a major cause of engines stopping, so a little preventive spending can be a good insurance policy.

When you open or close the throttle fully, always take a little longer to do so than you really need. Sudden changes are always more stressful for the engine and fuel systems.

Keep a Clean Ship

Little snags, when ignored, turn into bigger ones. A little bit of play in a control run or a tail wheel bearing will soon become a larger amount of play. A larger amount of play will unexpectedly turn into a fracture or disconnection. Then you will have a big bill to pay.

Inspect your airframe regularly and be really pleased when you find a small snag. Be pleased because it is a small one. Then fix it, or get it fixed, straight away. A snag ignored never healed itself. It may be a while before it reminds you of its existence, but by then it might be too late for a cheap fix.

How to Keep Insurance Costs Down

You can't. Some other fool is always forcing them up. But you can try.

The single best way of doing this is never to believe your fuel gauge. Make yourself a dip stick and use it before every flight. Never close your canopy without locking it. Never. One day you will forget to double check it, I promise.

If you shut down the engine by pulling the mixture, you do not know the state of the magneto system. Immediately before this type of shut-down, at 1,000 rpm or so, you can very briefly turn the magneto switches off and then on again. The engine should just catch its breath to show that both magnetos are properly earthed. Without this check, just turning the switches off after the engine has stopped can, and eventually will, leave a warm live engine in your hangar. This has the potential to do a lot of damage before the fuel runs out.

If you need to hand-swing an engine and there is no one competent to sit inside with the stick back and the brakes hard on, then think again about whether you really **must** start the engine just at that time. You probably don't need to. If you do, the only sure way to keep it from getting away from you is to tie the tail wheel down very firmly, with a thick bit of rope to a large concrete thing set into the ground.

From Now On

Just occasionally during the rest of the book, some of these airmanship points will be mentioned again. But the fact that they do not all appear with every exercise doesn't mean that they do not apply to every exercise.

Please bear them in mind when you read on and, even more importantly, when you fly.

CHAPTER 3

Practical Theory

Energy

When an aeroplane is stationery on the ground, it is made of paper. When it is stationary, it can be said to have no energy, or at least none that can readily be used.

Types of Energy

An aircraft in motion, however, possesses energy that can be used not only to maintain terrain clearance but also to permit it to manoeuvre. For the purposes of understanding aerobatic flight an aircraft has energy in two forms, which can be considered together to represent the gross energy of the aircraft at any particular moment. These two forms are *kinetic energy*, which is proportional to the square of the aircraft's speed and *potential energy*, which is proportional to its height above the ground.

The aerobatic pilot must understand how energy is gained and lost, and how the two types of energy are interchanged during a figure. The pilot can fly in such a way as to conserve the energy, or to throw it away. Either may be a valid tactic at different times, but to manage energy in this way requires a sound understanding of its principles.

Energy Balance

A powered aircraft gains energy, from its zero state on the ground, by burning fuel and developing thrust. As long as the brakes are not on, the more fuel burnt the more energy the aircraft gains. In a glider, the energy is gained by burning fuel in the tug plane or winch engine. In a carrier borne navy aircraft the launch catapult also supplies some energy.

But in respect of our aerobatic mount, it is generally safe to assume that the more fuel we burn, the more energy we will have to play with.

Whenever the aircraft has speed, however, energy is lost through drag (Diagram 3-1). The total drag on the airframe is comprised of profile drag, which is always there and induced drag, which only occurs when the wings generate lift. Profile drag is, like kinetic energy, proportional to the square of the speed. Induced drag is dependent on the amount of lift the wing is producing, the higher the lift the higher the drag.

Diagram 3-1

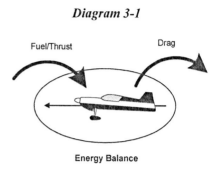

Energy Balance

If the aircraft's speed and height are not changing, then the gross energy is constant and it is a state of equilibrium. If in this condition the engine is also at maximum power output, then this is as fast as the aircraft can travel without losing energy. At the maximum level speed, drag is equal to maximum thrust. At any higher speed, drag (energy out) must exceed thrust (energy in) and so the aircraft must be losing gross energy. This is true even if the aircraft is accelerating in a dive. The speed may be increasing, but if the speed is greater than maximum level, then energy is being lost.

Conversely, if the aircraft is climbing and slowing down it can still be gaining energy as long as it is burning a lot of fuel.

During any aerobatic figure drag is constantly changing as control inputs are made to manoeuvre. In most cases drag will be increased, especially when pitching at greater than 1g but also when rolling due to aileron drag and so on.

Occasionally during figures, however, there are low drag elements, for example at less than 1g over the top of a loop, or at low speed in the vertical before a stall turn.

Energy Management Within a Figure

Different aircraft obviously have different propensities, both for generating drag and for producing thrust. Knowledge of the characteristics of the type you are flying is therefore paramount to being able to manage energy well. For example, most aerobatic aeroplanes can be looped without height loss. But depending on performance, the speed at the end may be less or more than at the beginning. In most training aircraft, I'm afraid, it will be a decrease in speed not an increase as the energy consumed in lift generation exceeds that gained by burning fuel in a relatively small engine.

As another example, consider a level turn with 60° of bank. During this figure it is necessary to generate 2g of lift. This can be achieved at an airspeed equal to the basic stalling speed multiplied by the square root of two (1.414). For an aircraft with a stalling speed of 50 knots, such a turn can be made at 71 knots. In most cases the thrust available will still exceed the drag in this configuration and so the aircraft may accelerate while turning until drag increases to match the thrust. It will then be at what we might call optimum turn speed. Energy will have been gained during the turn because the aircraft will have accelerated (kinetic energy up) while level (potential energy constant).

The same turn started from a high level speed will result in speed decaying until it reaches the optimum speed described above. In this case energy will have been lost overall because the turn was started too fast.

The best way to conserve energy within a figure, given that there is a minimum entry speed and you cannot fly slower than that, is to make sure that you do not pull or push the elevator control more harshly than you actually need to. Making tight corners is really a luxury only afforded to those with great excess energy.

The other important factor within figures is the ability to fly with the aircraft out of balance only when that is absolutely necessary. When the aircraft is out of balance, you are effectively using the fuselage to generate lift. Unfortunately it also creates drag, and the lift/drag ratio of the fuselage is always much worse than that of the wing. A little sideslip always equals a lot of drag.

Throttle Management

As burning fuel generates thrust and thus energy, flight with the throttle closed represents a lost opportunity for energy building. There are, of course, times when the throttle must be closed: to slow down for a spin entry, to reduce torque during a stall turn perhaps or when upside down in an aircraft without an inverted fuel system. At all other times, however, having the throttle closed means lost energy and, certainly if flying a sequence, finishing lower.

Yet some pilots still argue in favour of having the throttle closed on other occasions, for example on the vertical down line after a stall turn or in a similar situation after a spin recovery.

Consider the following two techniques from an energy point of view. After completing the yaw rotation at the top of a stall turn (hammerhead for American readers), you close the throttle and fly a down line for 300 feet and then pull level at 3g applying power as you pull out. Say this produces a radius of 200 feet, so that the height when you finish is 500 feet lower than at the top.

Now fly the same shape, but with power applied. The 300-foot down line will pass quicker, as you will be accelerating faster than with the throttle closed. The 200-foot radius pull-out may require 4g because of the increased speed. But it is inevitable that when you finally come level at the end of the figure, you will be going faster than had you kept the throttle closed.

If you have the same height with more speed, you have more energy, in this case because you have burned more fuel. If in a sequence, this means that the final finish height will be higher. Even if flying individual practice figures, it means less time spent climbing for height before you try something else. From an energy management viewpoint, it is wise to use every opportunity to burn fuel

There will remain concern among some readers that by maintaining power in a vertical descent they will exceed V_{NE} or the maximum G limit when pulling out. This is, of course, possible in all aircraft. So let us look at the situation another way.

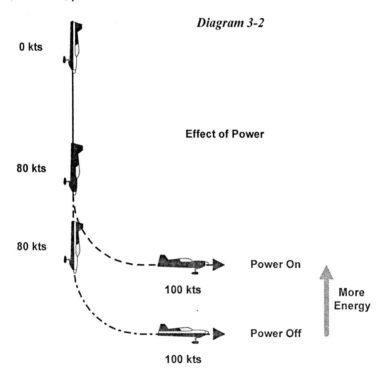

Diagram 3-2

0 kts

Effect of Power

80 kts

80 kts

Power On

100 kts

More Energy

Power Off

100 kts

Now after our stall turn we close the throttle and fly vertically down until we reach 80 knots, then we add power and pull out coming level at 100 knots, comfortably under V_{NE}. During the descent to 80 knots we lost 300 feet. Now fly the figure again and this time maintain power on the down line. When you reach 80 knots pull out as before and finish level at 100 knots.

The point is that in the second technique, getting to 80 knots takes only 250 feet, not 300. As the pull-out is the same, we have finished both figures at the same speed, but in the latter case we have saved 50 feet. At the same speed, but higher than before, we have more gross energy because we took the opportunity, albeit short, for burning fuel (Diagram 3-2).

These examples show that good energy management principles require the use of power at every opportunity. However, this means a faster work rate in some situations and more physical stress in others. In some flying, such as early training of a figure, or when carrying a non-pilot passenger, slower work rate and less stress are more important considerations than optimizing energy management. So fly according to the situation. Be prepared to be less than wholly efficient when your flying affects others.

Energy Management in an Aerobatic Sequence

When flying a sequence in the style of competition aerobatics, the pilot always inserts a visible portion of straight and level to separate the different figures. This enables the judges to follow the pattern more easily. These straight lines give the experienced pilot another opportunity to display sound energy management (Diagram 3-3).

Diagram 3-3

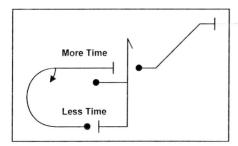 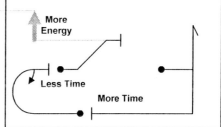

Good Energy Management   **Less Good Energy Management**

If the straight line segment is at high speed, such as at the completion of a stall turn, it is likely that the aircraft will be flying at a speed faster than it can maintain in level flight, even at full power. Therefore if the pilot flies level for an appreciable length of time the aircraft will slow down and energy will be lost. In this situation it would be better to start the next figure as soon as possible.

Some figures are finished at low speed, such as a roll-off-the-top (half loop up and half roll). In this situation, a longer period of level flight will give time for more fuel burning, with consequent acceleration and energy increase. Before flying a sequence, always take time on the ground to make an energy plan. Note the high-speed bits and plan to get from one figure to the next quickly. Remember where there are opportunities for low speed, accelerating flight and plan to maximize the time spent in this regime.

Visual References

Looking Out the Front

When driving your car, you look straight ahead for most of the time, with occasional glimpses at the instruments and mirrors. At junctions, you might look sideways. Ab-initio flight training is similar, except that you learn the principles of airmanship including 'lookout' which is a ubiquitous part of pre-flight briefings and flight exercises.

Most of the aircraft used today for PPL training have a very good view out of the front. Bank angles are usually set by reference to the horizon ahead and the top of the instrument panel. In steeper turns, bank is regularly checked by reference to the artificial horizon (AH), again drawing attention forward and into the cockpit.

The range of pitch attitudes used in normal flight is very limited – perhaps 20° nose up, 10° nose down. These attitudes can easily be set by reference to the horizon directly ahead, and confirmed inside the cockpit on the AH. Worse still, headings are most often set and maintained by reference to the gyro-stabilized direction indicator (DI).

In aerobatic training, the situation is markedly different. Pitch attitudes have to be set, and held, ranging from level to vertical up, and including vertical down, 45° up or down, inverted as well as erect. This just cannot be done by looking ahead, nor at any instrument.

Throughout this book, attitude pictures are illustrated for a range of generalized aircraft types. Diagram 3-4 shows the view ahead for three such examples: a side-by-side trainer, a tandem-seat biplane, and a low-wing single seat specialist aircraft. In all these drawings, the centre of the circle represents the centre of the pilot's field of view.

Diagram 3-4

Looking Sideways

The Navy call the Air Force 'crabs'. Something to do with walking sideways that was never really explained to me in 20 years service. I was never aware of walking crab-wise. Looking sideways, yes.

Any pitch attitude more extreme than 20° up or down, is best set and held by reference to the horizon beyond the wing tip.

Diagram 3-5

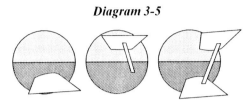

In any figure that includes looping segments of 45° or more, spend at least 75% of the time looking sideways. Always know your pitch attitude and how it is changing. Develop the ability to set, adjust and hold pitch attitudes by looking at the horizon, 90° left or right of the nose. Diagram 3-5 shows how this might look from three typical training aircraft flying straight and level. In each case, the centre of the circle is the sight line to the horizon looking 90° to the left.

To illustrate the varying benefits of looking ahead, or looking sideways, study Diagram 3-6 carefully. In the top row, the horizon is completely lost from view in four of the eight attitudes.

Diagram 3-6

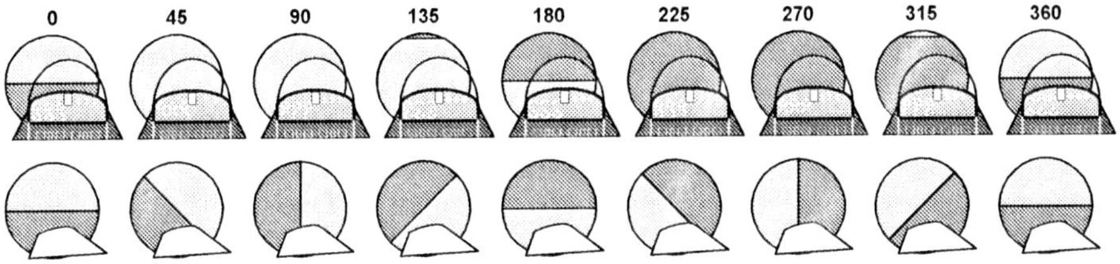

0	45	90	135	180	225	270	315	360

Diagram 3-7

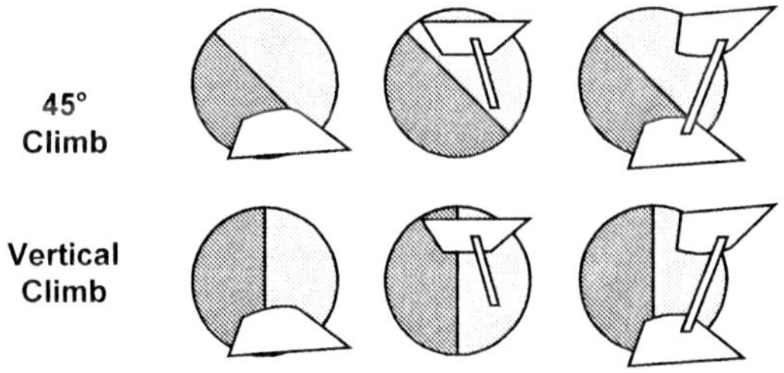

45° Climb

Vertical Climb

Only when close to inverted (180°) is it possible to gauge the pitch attitude with great accuracy. On the other hand, in the bottom row, wing tip and horizon can always be seen.

Some of the pictures are at first unusual, possibly confusing, but the required information is there.

With practice, the eye will become familiar with them and the brain able to interpret them accurately. Diagram 3-7 shows a selection of these attitudes in a greater variety of types.

Sighting Devices

Even though the lower pictures in Diagram 3-6 are a big improvement over the upper, better still is sometimes available.

Diagram 3-8

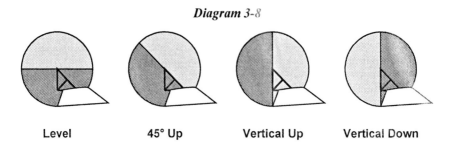

| Level | 45° Up | Vertical Up | Vertical Down |

Most modern aircraft, designed from the outset for aerobatics, come equipped with
additional sighting devices.
The CAP-10 and Pitts S-2 are
cases in point. These devices,
despite being decried by
some in the past as 'iron-

Diagram 3-9

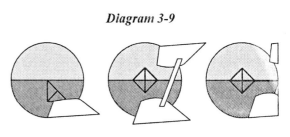

mongery', take yet another giant leap forward in promoting the ability to interpret
pitch information. Purists may still exist, but they no longer win. Every aircraft at
a modern World Championship is so equipped.

Diagram 3-9 shows typical views from a low-wing or biplane configuration. The
left-hand picture is based on a CAP-232. The centre one is typical of single seat
biplanes. The right-hand view represents the view from the back seat of a tandem
biplane, such as a Pitts S-2A. The clarity of these views in a number of attitudes
can be seen in Diagram 3-8.

Sticky Tape

The last great boon to good visual reference, and hence to accurate aerobatics, is
coloured insulating tape. Look again at Diagram 3-6 and note the position of the
horizon in the top row pictures under numbers 135 and 315. These represent,
respectively 45° climbing inverted and 45° descending upright. In both cases the
horizon is visible by looking up, but it is not close to any piece of airframe to
facilitate accurate attitude assessment.

Look at these two attitudes as they appear from a biplane (the two pictures on the
left in Diagram 3-10).

Now you can see that the horizon is close to the top wing. You can not only see that
the wing is parallel to the horizon (wings level; no roll) but you can estimate quite
accurately the distance of the top wing from the horizon and so measure pitch
attitude.

Diagram 3-10

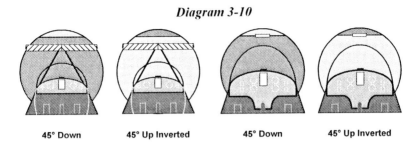

| 45° Down | 45° Up Inverted | 45° Down | 45° Up Inverted |

In the two pictures on the right in Diagram 3-10, you can see a small white mark directly over the horizon. This is a small strip of tape stuck to the inside of the canopy. This small aid is a boon as it permits accurate pitch assessment on these lines, but also lets you check heading by looking at a landmark in the far distance ahead. When sustaining these attitudes, looking ahead and also upward is not such a bad idea, as long as you have the tape in place.

Forces Generated by the Engine and Propeller

Torque

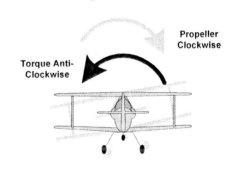

Diagram 3-11

Torque is a twisting force acting around the axis of the engine crankshaft. It turns the propeller in one direction and the engine in the other (Diagram 3-11). In a Lycoming-engined aircraft, the standard throughout this book, torque turns the propeller clockwise as seen from the cockpit. This is often called a 'right-turning engine'.

Usually unnoticed, but always present, is the torque reaction which tries to turn the airframe in the opposite direction.

Rotation of the airframe goes unnoticed on the ground because it is resisted by contact between the wheels and the earth. It usually goes unnoticed in the air because of the aerodynamic counter-force provided by the rig or trim of the aileron system. But although it is usually unnoticed it is always there, as you will forget to your discomfort in a stall turn, or in a helicopter when the tail rotor stops working.

The key thing to remember about torque is that its only effect is to roll the aeroplane. It has nothing to do with pitch or yaw and is always countered with aileron.

Diagram 3-12 Slipstream Effect

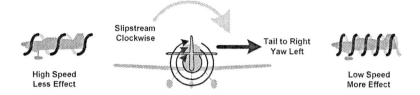

Slipstream Effect

The propeller generates a spiral slipstream which envelopes the aircraft. Because the vertical keel surfaces at the rear are predominantly above the axis of the helix, the airflow impinges primarily on the fin and rudder on the left side (reverse, of course for left-turning engines). At high speed the effect is relatively small, but at lower speeds the spiral is more compressed and exerts a greater sideways force, causing noticeable yaw to the left. This effect is always present at low speed, is independent of angle of attack and is countered with right rudder.

Asymmetric Blade Effect (P-factor)

Asymmetric blade effect is caused by, and proportional to, angle of attack. At high angles of attack and at low speed it causes a powerful yawing effect on the aircraft. Diagram 3-13 shows the source of the asymmetry by showing the different paths of the up-going and down-going blades during a half-rotation of the propeller. In the left picture, the aircraft is flying with zero angle of attack.

The paths of the two propeller blades are the same. Because of this symmetry, no p-factor is present. In the right picture the aircraft has 15° of alpha. The down-going blade (solid line) clearly has a longer path through the air than the up-going one (dashed line).

Hopefully, however, the propeller is rigid and the two blades take the same time to travel the different distances. Therefore the down-going blade travels further in the same time and so has a higher airspeed. The two propeller blades have the same angle of attack as each other, so the faster down-going blade generates more lift.

Diagram 3-13

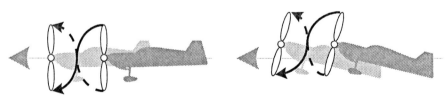

Angle of Attack = 0°, Blade paths the same   Alpha = 15°, Downward path longer

As the down-going blade of a right-turning engine is on the right side, the extra lift generated by that half of the propeller causes a yaw to the left. This force is proportional to the angle of attack and is countered with right rudder. Note that there is no p-factor at zero alpha, and that at negative angles of attack the direction of the force reverses and correction is by left rudder.

Gyroscopic Effect

Gyroscopic effects, like the other forces dealt with in this section, are taught during initial PPL training. In normal training aircraft, however, with relatively small propellers, the forces are not great and the effects are seldom noticed. Perhaps the exception to this generalization occurs in tail wheel training if the tail is lifted smartly up on take off. During an aerobatic career you are likely to fly a succession of aircraft with increasingly large engines and commensurately bigger propellers.

When flying accurate Standard category figures, you must counter the effects of the gyroscopic forces on the airframe. In Unlimited category freestyle figures you will be able to exploit the forces to your advantage and the spectators consternation. Therefore, you must understand how these forces are generated and what are their effects.

Remember that when the axis of a (propeller) gyroscope is pitched or yawed the force induced into the propeller is precessed and returned to the airframe at 90° from the original direction. One form of this effect is shown in Diagram 3-14. Note that:

• if you input a pitching motion, you get back a yaw effect

• if you input a yawing motion, you get back a pitch effect.

The detailed influence of these forces will be discussed in detail in the flight exercises for manoeuvres that are noticeably affected by them. Bear in mind, though, that if you start something with your hand, you will have to counter it with your feet, and vice versa.

Diagram 3-14

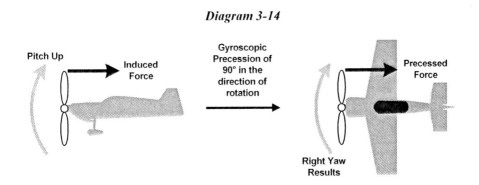

Pitch Up — Induced Force — Gyroscopic Precession of 90° in the direction of rotation — Precessed Force — Right Yaw Results

Different sized propellers produce different amounts of gyroscopic force. You should understand the reasons for this, at least in outline. The factors that affect the magnitude of the gyroscopic forces generated by a propeller are its:

- mass

- diameter

- speed of rotation.

Diagram 3-15

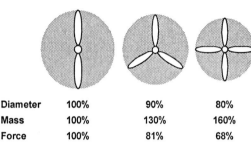

Of these, the diameter is of greatest importance. Diagram 3-15 shows three propellers, any of which might be fitted to a single aeroplane to absorb the same amount of power.

Diameter	100%	90%	80%
Mass	100%	130%	160%
Force	100%	81%	68%

With more blades, the diameter (and the noise) reduces but the weight goes up. So dominant, however, is the size factor, that the magnitude of the forces is reduced considerably despite the increasing weight.

When the CAP 230 family of aircraft was first under development, it was fitted with a 300 horsepower engine and a two-bladed metal propeller. The gyroscopic figures that could be flown with this aeroplane were astonishing, even to the experienced French test pilots. However, it wasn't long before a crankshaft broke in flight.

Patrick Paris made the landing holding the canopy open in the slipstream and looking around the oil-covered windscreen. There have been similar instances in the more distant past with Pitts and Zlin types at least.

The three-bladed propeller quickly became the standard and no more crankshafts were broken. By 2001, the standard propeller size had been reduced once again, with the introduction of a four-bladed unit. But this was done for noise abatement reasons, and the new aircraft therefore have a slight disadvantage in gyroscopic tumbling figures.

Rudder, Rudder, Rudder

The forces in the three sections above (slipstream, P-factor and gyro) can all lead to undesired yawing motion. At some times the forces act in the same sense and combine together to great effect. At others, they oppose each other and cancel themselves out.

In particularly frustrating figures they are constantly varying and the overall result is constant change. In each case rudder inputs control and mitigate their effects. This leads neatly into a general discussion on the matter of balance.

Balance

If you ride a bicycle out of balance you fall off. Aeroplanes are more forgiving. If it is not possible to fall off, then why is balance so important? There are two reasons:

- control, and
- energy.

If you want to fly the aircraft precisely at all times (and who does not) you must be in control of its balance, or something will happen other than what you want. If you want to fly in an energy-efficient manner (which you do, most of the time) you should avoid the energy-sapping drag associated with out-of-balance airflows.

There are, of course, occasions when you will fly deliberately out of balance. In a spin, for example, or when rolling straight and level, or in a vertically climbing knife-edge tumble. These are also occasions for precise rudder control. Before you learn these tricks, however, you'd best learn the subtle art of staying in balance.

Local Gravity Vector

When you sit still, the only external force acting on you is gravity. It acts downwards through your seat, even in Australia – downwards being towards the centre of whichever planet you happen to be on when reading this. When you are in your aircraft and accelerating or turning, other forces start to come into effect. Some of these work in the fore/aft direction; they do not affect balance. Others work laterally; these do.

When normal, downwards gravity is added to some external lateral force, they combine both in magnitude and direction to make the local gravity vector (LGV). In an aircraft, you control the direction of the LGV with the rudder, and to be in charge of it you also need to be aware of it.

The direction of the local gravity vector is supplied to you in two ways:

- by the slip ball.
- by the seat of your pants.

Flying by the Seat of your Pants

Diagram 3-16 shows three views of an aircraft flying level, but with increasing left rudder inputs. Ignoring for the moment the effects of roll and turn, the arrows show how the local gravity vector is controlled by the rudder.

Diagram 3-17 shows how this will appear on the slip ball and how you will feel it in your body.

27

Diagram 3-16

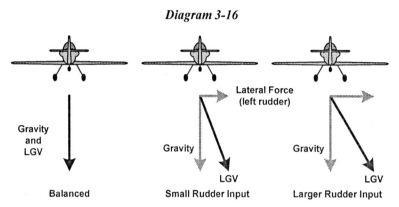

| Balanced | Small Rudder Input | Larger Rudder Input |

The force manifests itself in the friction zone between bottom and seat. The bottom is another area of the body sensitive to touch, as all sadistic school teachers knew in the old days. Feeling balance through your body is important because it keeps your eyes available for looking outside.

With practice, you will develop the ability to match what you see on the slip ball with what you feel through your pants. When this becomes automatic, you will no longer need the slip ball as you will always know where the LGV is, even without looking. When upside down, the body acts just like a pendulum in response to the LGV. This is also exactly what an inverted slip ball would do, if you had one in the aeroplane.

To know if you are in balance, just relax and feel your body. Keep looking outside. Its easy. Whichever way up you are, see which way you are leaning. If your torso has moved to your right, use right rudder, and vice versa.

The dangling pilot in Diagram 3-18 has shifted to his left, and would use left rudder to get back in balance.

Diagram 3-17

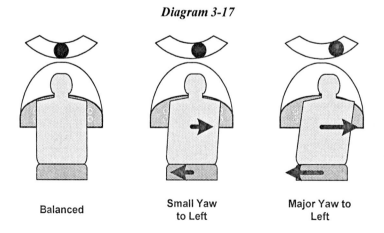

| Balanced | Small Yaw to Left | Major Yaw to Left |

When you are in the aircraft, try not to analyse the problem too much, thinking inverted is more difficult than flying it, and only comes with time. Just push with the foot that gets your body back into the centre, whichever way up you are.

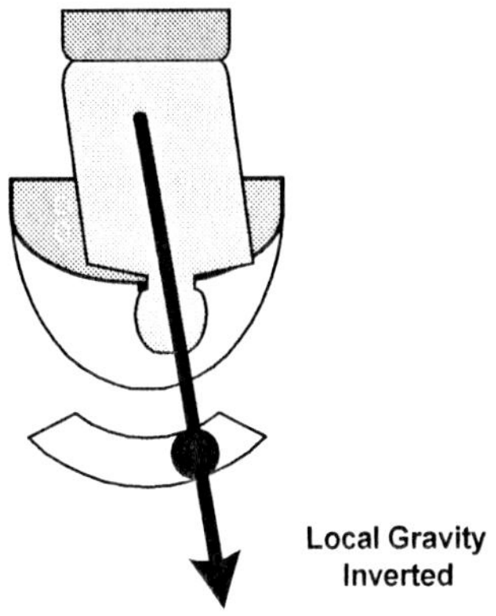

Demonstration Exercise

Try this exercise in order to educate the seat of your pants.

Diagram 3-18

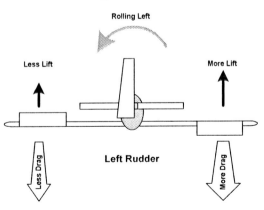

Local Gravity
Inverted

- Fly straight and level with the ball centred. Relax and feel your body centred also.

- Place a hand over the slip ball.

- Apply a small amount of right rudder, using a little aileron to keep the wings level.

- Hold the control inputs steady.

- Feel your upper body move to the left.

- Uncover the slip ball and see that it has followed your body.

- Cover the slip ball again with your hand.

- Use left rudder to centre your torso, centralize the ailerons and be steady.

- Uncover the slip ball again and check how close you got to centre.

This exercise can be done upright or inverted. The only difference in technique is which aileron you will use to hold the wings level. If upright, use left aileron with right rudder. If inverted, use right aileron with right rudder.

Adverse Yaw

Diagram 3-19

Adverse yaw is covered, in a very basic way, in the PPL syllabus. It merits further attention here for several reasons.

- It is not always there.

- When inverted it may be stronger, and you need the other rudder.

Diagram 3-19 is to refresh your memory about the cause of

Rolling Left

Less Lift

More Lift

Less Drag

Left Rudder

More Drag

adverse yaw. It depicts an aircraft flying straight and level and starting to roll in response to a left aileron input. Both wings are still producing lift in the upwards sense, but the right wing will now generate slightly more, and the left slightly less, because of the roll demand.

Lift only ever comes with a dose of drag added. So drag also increases on the right side of the aeroplane, which causes a yaw to the right. This is **adverse** to the desired roll direction.

Rolling at Zero Alpha

Diagram 3-20

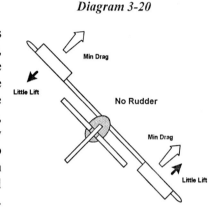

Adverse yaw, however, is not always present when you roll. To get adverse yaw, both left and right wings must be producing a fair amount of lift in the same direction. If both wings have a zero angle of attack, and are thus generating no lift, there will be no significant adverse yaw when the roll is initiated. Rolling with zero alpha occurs regularly in modern aerobatics, for example in the ballistic roll described later and in vertical aileron rolls.

Diagram 3-20 illustrates an aircraft seen from below while rolling vertically to the left. Prior to the roll starting, the wings have effectively zero alpha. When the roll input is applied, each wing generates a little lift because of the aileron deflection, but these are roughly equal amounts and are in opposite direction. A minimum of aileron drag is produced, but the drag is virtually symmetrical, even in an aircraft without a symmetrical aerofoil. Any differences that exist are too small to have a noticeable effect. No balancing rudder input is required when the roll is added.

Rolling from Negative Alpha

Diagram 3-21

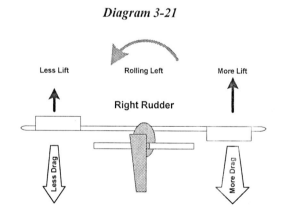

Diagram 3-21 shows a now familiar aircraft just starting to roll from straight and level inverted. At the start of the roll, both wings have a moderate negative angle of attack. Lift and drag are generated as in the first example, and rudder applied to balance the adverse yaw. Notice that this time, however, the rudder is applied by the pilot's right foot even though he is rolling left. Remember, whenever rolling with a negative alpha, adverse yaw is reversed from upright flight.

Aileron Design

Aircraft designers have known about adverse yaw for a long time, and have taken steps to minimize it. One such solution, which is built into many aerobatic training aeroplanes, is the 'Friese' aileron. This design and its operation are shown in Diagram 3-22.

Diagram 3-22

Friese ailerons

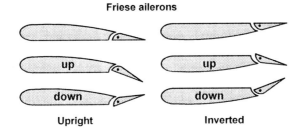

Upright   Inverted

In normal flight, when rolling, the up-going wing produces the most lift and the most drag. In the Friese design, the aileron is non-symmetrical. Its leading edge and hinge-point are chosen so that the aileron on the down-going wing produces extra drag, as the nose protrudes into the under-wing airflow. On aircraft equipped with this design, adverse yaw when rolling from upright flight is quite reduced.

Problems arise, however, when rolling from inverted. Now the up-going wing, the one producing the most induced drag also produces the extra aileron drag. Adverse yaw in this situation is actually made worse by the Friese design, and its effects are very noticeable indeed. This situation arises, for example, on the vast majority of Pitts S-2A aircraft, where the ailerons are 'Friese' despite the wing section being symmetrical.

Many modern specialist aerobatic aircraft have both wings and ailerons that have a symmetrical cross section. Diagram 3-23 shows such a wing system with typical aileron deflections of 20° up and down. Note that at full deflection the aileron gap is almost completely closed, for maximum control authority.

Diagram 3-23

Modern symmetrical wing and aileron

The symmetrical wing and aileron, however, have no way of reducing natural adverse yaw. So this effect can be quite noticeable whether upright or inverted. The main point is that it is of the same magnitude either way, so technique does not have to change significantly.

Demonstration Exercise

It is quite simple to devise a flight exercise to demonstrate the adverse yaw characteristics of any aeroplane. Flying this exercise serves not only as a demonstration, but also as a way to learn and practice the corrective rudder until it becomes second nature.

- Fly straight and level upright at normal cruise speed, towards a landmark near the horizon ahead.

- Take your feet off the rudders.

- Smoothly apply aileron, first right then left, to impart a regular rocking motion to the aircraft. Movement should be continuous, back and forth, at a steady rhythm and giving a bank angle of about 20° to 30° in either direction.

- After one or two cycles, notice that as the aileron control moves right, the aircraft nose moves left, and vice versa. With the right timing, you can make the nose swing quite significantly in either direction.

- Stop the rolling and set the wings level again.

- Put your feet back on the rudders.

- Start the wing-rocking again, but this time use rudder to correct the yaw and keep the nose pointed directly ahead, towards the landmark.

- Learn to apply the rudder in the same sense as the aileron and at the time that you start to reverse the aileron control input. Learn also that it is important to take the rudder off just before you start to reverse the aileron, or else the nose starts to follow the rudder rather than just staying still.

- If its not working properly, stop, reset level, re-engage brain and try again.

This is a useful exercise to try on any new type, as well as when you start training. It can usefully fill some of the time necessary to transit from the airfield circuit pattern to the aerobatic training area.

Advanced Training Technique

In advanced training, with an aircraft with an inverted fuel system, this exercise can be performed while flying straight and level inverted. This time, however, adverse yaw will be reversed. So as you apply right aileron, the nose will go to the right.

Left aileron and the nose goes left. So the rhythmic pattern to give wing rocks and no adverse yaw needs right rudder with left stick, left rudder with right stick.

This exercise is very useful in its own right to learn about the aircraft, but also is a very good lead-in exercise to inverted turning. The opposite aileron and rudder inputs are needed both rolling into and out of an inverted turn.

Zero Lift Axis

The Zero Lift Axis (ZLA) is a line passing through a wing seen in cross section. In this respect it is similar to the 'chord' line of the wing, but in most cases the ZLA and the chord are different lines, because wings have different cross sections. The key property of the ZLA is that it is parallel to the relative airflow when the wing is generating no lift.

Diagram 3-24 shows an exaggerated form of cross-section for a high-lift, non-symmetrical wing. In fact, if you fly a Tipsy Nipper you will realize that the exaggeration is only slight! The chord line, which joins the leading edge to the trailing edge, is shown dotted. .

Diagram 3-24

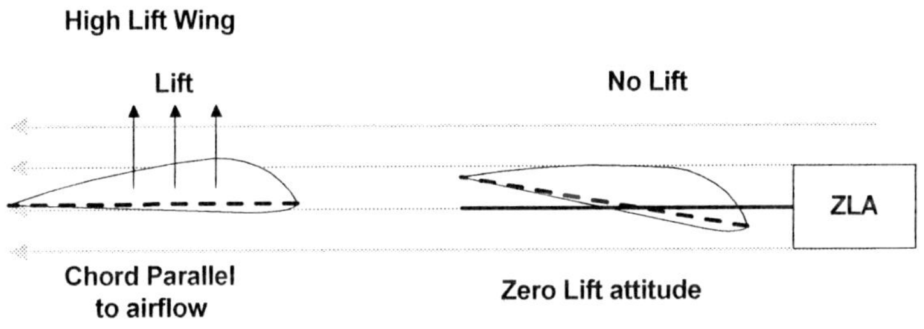

High Lift Wing

Lift — No Lift

Chord Parallel to airflow — Zero Lift attitude — ZLA

The right hand picture shows the angle this wing has to be at relative to the airflow in order to generate no lift. So now the ZLA can be drawn along the airflow arrows. The ZLA does not have a specific location; any horizontal line that cuts through some of the wing will show the principle.

If we now look at a modern, symmetrical aerobatic wing section, we will see quite a difference.

Diagram 3-25 shows such a symmetrical wing. When the chord line is parallel to the airflow, the wing generates no lift. So in this case the ZLA is the same as the chord.

Diagram 3-25

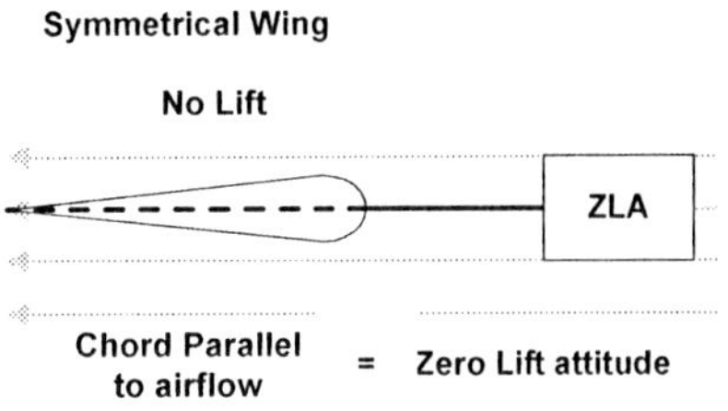

Symmetrical Wing

No Lift

ZLA

Chord Parallel to airflow = Zero Lift attitude

Level Flight

Diagram 3-26

In level flight, the wing must have an angle of attack sufficient to generate 1g of lift at the current speed. At different speeds, different angles of attack will be appropriate. The

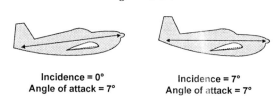

Incidence = 0°
Angle of attack = 7°

Incidence = 7°
Angle of attack = 7°

attitude of the aeroplane will be determined by the need to fly this particular angle of attack.

Let's assume for the moment that the required alpha is 7°.

Diagram 3-26 shows two aircraft flying level with 7° angle of attack on the wing. The attitude of the right hand fuselage is more nose-down, because the chord line of the wing is set at an angle of 7° to the fuselage datum axis. In the left picture, the wing chord is parallel to the fuselage datum.

This angle between wing and fuselage is called 'incidence'. You can see that for cruising you would have a much better view forward out of the aeroplane with incidence between wing and fuselage. However, as soon as you start to consider some line of flight other than level you need a different definition in order to judge accuracy.

Vertical Flight

In aerobatics we fly a lot of vertical lines. But what do we actually mean by 'vertical'?

We could define the vertical as a flight path: the line that the aircraft centre of gravity must follow. If this were the case, the pilot would have to correct for the drift suffered due to the wind. He would have to modify his attitude in both pitch and yaw, perhaps even side slip in the vertical in order to maintain a purely vertical flight path.

Unfortunately, the pilot has no reference by which he can accurately determine how close to vertical his flight path might be. In changing winds particularly, the pilot would be unable to determine his flight path from one end of a sequence to the other. This does not matter in a purely training scenario, with the student and instructor both in the aeroplane. But in a situation where the performance was being watched from the ground, as in a competition, this lack of feedback to the pilot means that no skill can be deployed in real time to fly more accurately vertical than anyone else.

So in competition flying, vertical flight (and 45° flight lines) is defined by aircraft attitude. The aeroplane is deemed to be vertical when its ZLA is vertical, and at 45° when its ZLA is at 45° to the vertical.

Diagram 3-27

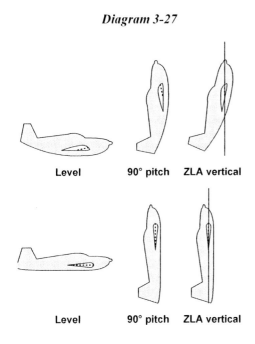

Level	90° pitch	ZLA vertical

Level	90° pitch	ZLA vertical

The implications of this approach are illustrated in Diagram 3-27. The upper row of pictures show a non-specialist aircraft that has an asymmetrical wing set at a few degrees of incidence to the fuselage axis. They show how it appears level, what it would look like pitched up 90° from this attitude and, finally, how it looks when its ZLA is vertical.

The lower row of pictures show the same things, but for an aeroplane with no incidence and a symmetrical wing section.

Just looking at the two right-hand outlines, it is easy to see how the lower aircraft might get better scores from an inexperienced judge in a vertical flight contest! This should not happen.

Judges should know the different aircraft characteristics well enough to make allowance for these intrinsic design differences. But I am not sure they always remember this. Certainly, judging of the symmetrical aircraft is much easier than the asymmetrical one, and anything that is difficult to judge will often get a lower score because of the judge's innate uncertainty.

Even among aircraft with symmetrical wings, optical illusions can occur based purely on the fuselage shape when viewed from the side in silhouette. In Diagram 3-28 a typical biplane and monoplane, both with symmetrical wings are shown with their ZLA vertical.

The biplane looks at first glance to be a little 'positive' because of its fuselage shape. Over-pitched to 95° ZLA, however, it gives a much better appearance of vertical. This attitude might get a better score, in the 'heat of battle', than the 'real' ZLA vertical attitude, although the 'cheating' pilot would have to make small adjustments to his rolling technique if a vertical roll was asked for on the same line.

Diagram 3-28

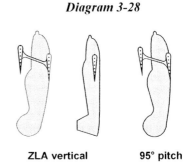

ZLA vertical	95° pitch

Most of the time, the paint scheme of an aeroplane is pretty irrelevant other than from an aesthetic viewpoint.

Unless it is low, close and illuminated by strong sunlight from behind the observer, it looks pretty much like a silhouette. But these good lighting conditions do sometimes occur, especially in competition and display flying, and so a paint scheme can be devised that makes the attitude of the aircraft easier to appreciate.

Diagram 3-29

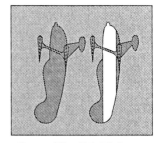

Competition Paint Scheme

Diagram 3-29 shows how the difficult-to-judge biplane can be made easier to see.

Both outlines are identical. The aeroplane is a dark shape against a 'blue' sky. However, the light colour (yellow, white or lime green are best) shows up particularly well and the observing brain will concentrate on this and ignore the low-contrast colour.

45° Flight

Diagram 3-30

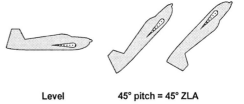

Level   **45° pitch = 45° ZLA**

On 45° lines, the symmetrical aircraft again has a distinct advantage in making the judges' task easier (Diagram 3-30). The non-symmetrical aircraft presents the judge with all sorts of problems in determining exactly what he should see when the aircraft is either inverted or on a 45° line. The row of pictures in Diagram 3-31 is pretty self-explanatory. Judging such aircraft is a nightmare!

Diagram 3-31

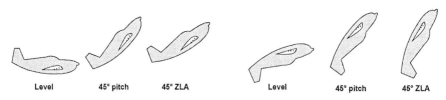

Level   **45° pitch**   **45° ZLA**   **Level**   **45° pitch**   **45° ZLA**

Terminology

In the following Chapters, I describe general technique without specific reference to symmetrical or non-symmetrical wing sections. When I talk about 'angle of attack' or 'alpha' in these situations, I am referring to generally to the angle between the relative airflow and the Zero Lift Axis, which is of much more significance than the chord line.

The Elevator and Elevator Trimming

The Elevator

Most pilots use the elevator and its trim control very naturally, but without really thinking a great deal about what they are actually doing. This is not really surprising, nor does it have any detrimental effects in normal flight. In aerobatics, however, we are striving to fly accurately through constantly changing attitudes. A lot of this manoeuvring involves prolific use of the elevator in order to make continuous changes in wing lift. Under these circumstances, accuracy requires a full understanding of the lift-generating system, of which both the elevator and its trim control are essential parts.

This section therefore amplifies the basic PPL teaching of how the elevator system works and describes its operation in terms that are of particular importance in learning how to fly aerobatic figures accurately.

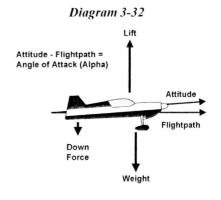

Diagram 3-32

A symmetrical wing moving through the air would always try to take the path of least drag, which would mean zero angle of attack (alpha) and no lift. The wing in flight generates lift because the elevator produces downforce that holds the wing at a non-zero angle of attack (Diagram 3-32). The elevator and the wing together form a lift generating system that we can vary and control.

When the pilot moves the elevator control, he is actually demanding a change in the angle of attack of the wing. The position of the control column, in the fore/aft sense is effectively a measure of angle of attack of the wing. The further back the stick is pulled, the greater the angle of attack becomes until the critical alpha is reached and the wing stalls. Moving the stick forward similarly demands a negative alpha until the inverted stall occurs.

There is a very important stick/yoke position in every aircraft where the tailplane and elevator effectively do nothing. The wing then has zero alpha and generates no lift. I shall call this position the 'neutral point' in reference to the elevator control.

It also follows that the same stick position will give different load factors at different speeds. In Diagram 3-33, the stick is in the same position every time, and the angle of attack is the same each time.

Diagram 3-33
Instantaneously flying a level flight path, while looping

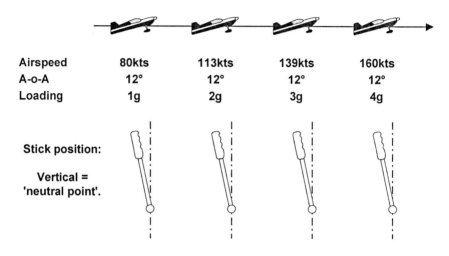

Airspeed	80kts	113kts	139kts	160kts
A-o-A	12°	12°	12°	12°
Loading	1g	2g	3g	4g

Stick position:

Vertical =
'neutral point'.

The amount of lift being generated is proportional to the airspeed squared. So each aircraft is flying under a different load condition. Also, each pilot is feeling something different through the stick, because the stick forces are different (if the trim is the same each time). The important thing to grasp is that the stick force does not tell you what the angle of attack is, but the stick position does.

Elevator trim systems are provided so that the pilot can adjust the effect of the elevator without constantly having to apply a force to the control stick/yoke. This enables the pilot to set a position of equilibrium whereby the elevator does its work without him feeling any stick 'pressure'. But please understand that the fact that there is no stick force felt does not mean that the elevator is in the neutral point.

When you trim the aircraft for level flight at a different speed, you also change the elevator position, as you have demanded a different alpha. However, there is still no stick force (Diagram 3-34).

Trimming

Suppose you are flying straight and level at a reasonably fast cruise speed with the aircraft in trim. Although you are not actually applying any manual effort to the elevator control, the elevator is still generating a downforce to maintain the required angle of attack on the wing.

So the elevator is NOT neutral, and the wing is generating 1g-worth of lift.

Diagram 3-34
Level flight path, trimmed hands off

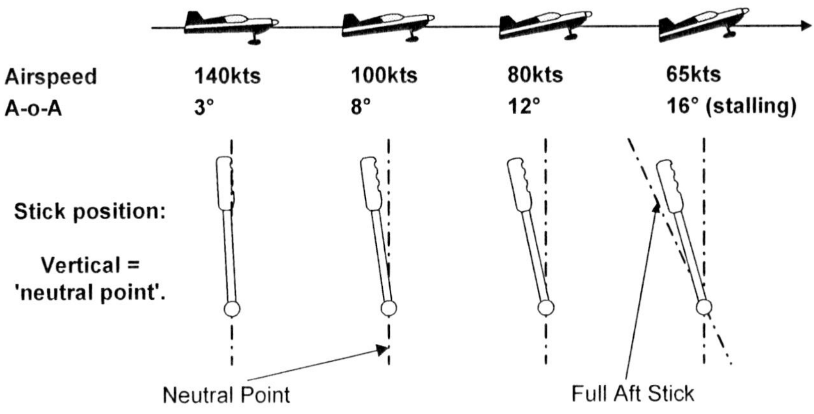

Airspeed	140kts	100kts	80kts	65kts
A-o-A	3°	8°	12°	16° (stalling)

Stick position:

Vertical =
'neutral point'.

Neutral Point   Full Aft Stick

If you now put the aeroplane into a climb and let go of the stick/yoke, the elevator position will be solely controlled by the trimmer, which will work to maintain an effectively constant angle of attack. As speed decreases, therefore, lift will also decrease and the nose will start to drop. The aircraft will level off and then start to dive, without the pilot having any input. As the aircraft descends, the speed and lift will start to increase. As the aeroplane accelerates through its original airspeed, lift will increase further and the nose will start to rise again.

This pitch oscillation will continue up and down for probably two or three complete cycles before the aircraft is again flying level at the same cruise speed, although a little lower than before.

Now suppose that before pulling up from cruise speed, you add more nose-down trim and maintain level flight by holding elevator back-pressure. After pulling up this time, you release the elevator and the nose drops faster. The time from, say, 30° nose up to 30° nose down will be less, The angle of attack will be less, and the G meter will read lower, throughout the pitch down.

In most aircraft it is possible to set the trim control position sufficiently far nose-down so that when the elevator is released the aircraft flies a parabolic flight path and the G meter reads zero. This is how weightlessness is simulated in astronaut training. With this trim condition set, a fair amount of back pressure is required on the stick to maintain level flight at cruise speed. If the stick is released it moves forward to the position where the elevator is doing no work.

This is the 'neutral point' referred to above.

It follows, therefore, that if you have set the trim control to a position where the aircraft flies level, upright hands-off, then a certain amount of forward stick pressure will be needed to reach the neutral point and to have zero alpha.

Application

There are many occasions in aerobatic flight where it is necessary to have the wings generating no lift, in other words to fly at zero alpha. These occasions include all vertical lines and both of the occasions in a straight-line roll when the wings are vertical with respect to the horizon.

The relationship between stick position and alpha is also critical in understanding how any aircraft can be flown at airspeeds much lower than the V_{S1} stall speed without actually stalling. The well-trained aerobatic pilot will be able to find the elevator 'neutral point' with ease, regardless of the elevator trim setting. How to do this is covered in the various flight exercises.

Trimming for Aerobatic Sequence Flying

It is not practical, nor is it wise, to try to change the elevator trim setting after the start of a sequence of linked aerobatic figures. So it is necessary to consider what you want and set the trim control before starting the sequence.

Where you set the trimmer is a matter for your own preference, and may vary depending on the complexity of the sequence you are going to fly. Whatever position you decide, you should make this decision based on a sound logical basis, so here are some thoughts worthy of consideration.

Some aircraft, in fact, do not have an elevator trim system adjustable from the cockpit. One such was a Pitts S-1S, G-AZPH, which I flew in the late '80s. The same is also true of production Yak-55s, although these do have a fixed tab that you can pre-set on the ground by judicious use of a calibrated thumb.

Notwithstanding these exceptions, the purpose of an adjustable trimmer is to reduce workload for the pilot. Remember that at any time when you are flying level, however briefly, at other than the trimmed speed, some stick force will be required on the elevator control to maintain the flight path. The question to ask yourself is: *"When is it most critical that the elevator looks after itself, so that I can concentrate my mind on other things?"*

Simple Sequences

If the sequence to be flown is all positive, with no vertical rolling, as you find in the **Basic** or **Sportsman** categories, then the answer is probably *"When I am flying* *very fast through the box between figures and need to think about positioning and what comes next."*

The ability to fly without having to make an elevator input will only occur when you are level at trimmed speed, so it is best to arrange this happy state for when your brain has to be quickly making other decisions. This will reduce your actual workload when you have to think fast. And the time you have to think fast is when the aeroplane is at high speed, not when it is slow.

So consider the highest speed at which you are going to be flying level during the sequence and trim for hands off at this speed. Then when you most need to think quickly about what is coming next in the sequence, you will not have to be concerning yourself also with maintaining a very accurate nose position relative to the horizon.

For example, in a **Sportsman** category sequence, the high entry speed figures are the half roll at the top of a loop, the stall turn and the half reverse Cuban eight. Very often you will be flying from one of these into the next, possibly travelling with a 20 knot tail wind and trying to remain in a restricted practice or competition area. A sensible trim setting would be that which (briefly in a low-performance craft) maintains this high entry speed in level flight.

Advanced Sequences

If the sequence to be flown includes a lot of vertical rolling, then this is the time when you need the finest elevator control. Such sequences also probably include a balance of positive and negative loops and lines. In these cases it is my strong recommendation that the trim is set to give zero G: elevator neutral point. Then vertical lines will stand a much better chance of remaining vertical when you quickly apply aileron to roll. The elevator will look after itself and you need only think about deflecting the stick sideways, not pushing slightly forward at the same time.

This is a definite recommendation for the **Advanced** and **Unlimited** categories.

My preferred method of trimming for neutral point is simply to start a climb, about 45° up, from relatively high speed, fast cruise say, then let go of the stick and look at the accelerometer.

If the trim was previously set for take-off, climb or even for cruise, the nose will slowly drop and the G-meter will read a little less than 1g. Now move the trim control nose down until the G-meter reads zero and you are effectively weightless. This is the perfect trim spot for making vertical rolls easy.

This method is also quicker and simpler than the alternative, which is to fly straight and level both upright and inverted, noting the trim positions, and selecting something half way between the two.

Now, if you fly in **Intermediate** you are on the cusp between these two recommended solutions. So you can decide for yourself which is most important to you.

'Hitting' the Vertical

Diagram 3-35

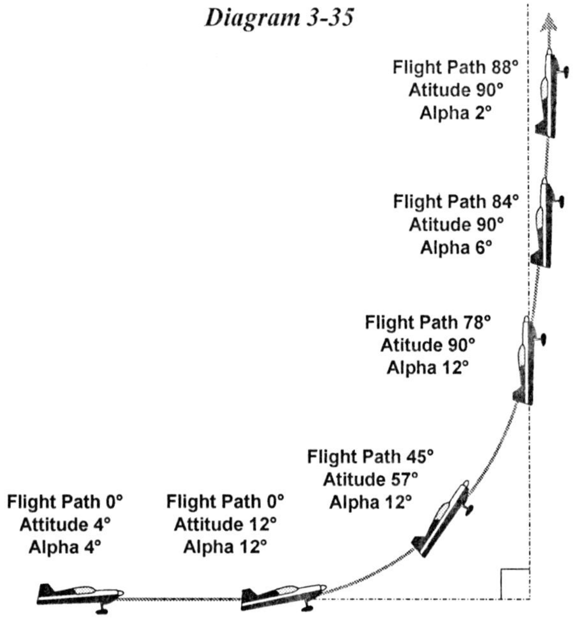

Flight Path 88°
Atitude 90°
Alpha 2°

Flight Path 84°
Atitude 90°
Alpha 6°

Flight Path 78°
Atitude 90°
Alpha 12°

Flight Path 45°
Atitude 57°
Alpha 12°

Flight Path 0°
Attitude 4°
Alpha 4°

Flight Path 0°
Attitude 12°
Alpha 12°

Assume for the moment that you have trimmed for zero G and you are flying on a calm day. You pull up for a vertical line and stop sharply as your Zero Lift Axis 'hits' the vertical. You now have a vertical flight path – right?

No, wrong! You will still have a positive angle of attack which will reduce to zero if you sustain the vertical climb for long enough.

Why? See Diagram 3-35.

At the moment that the aircraft reaches the 90° attitude it has an angle of attack (or it would have stopped looping before you got there). So although the attitude is vertical, the flight path is 90° **minus** the angle of attack.

The main point to note here is that the aim is to have constant attitude on the vertical line, but this can only be achieved if the angle of attack is slowly changing. If alpha is slowly changing, then so must the stick position.

The conclusion is that it is not enough just to stop vertical, you then have to **fly the vertical line**. If you do not pay enough attention to the visual picture, the vertical will be lost. A similar situation naturally applies when you push to the vertical, and both situations remain valid when the vertical is down instead of up.

CHAPTER **4**

Aerobatic Drawing Notation and The Aerobatic Catalogue

Pilots have always had the problem of putting down on paper an easily digestible description of their flight. Up to the 1950s there were many such individual styles, and some were beginning to be codified nationally, but there was no international agreement over any form of notation.

A Frenchman, François D'Huc Dressler, published a system in *Aviasport* and *Aeronautics* in 1955/56. This was in general use up to 1962, despite Dressler's death in 1957. But in 1961, a new book was published, the *Sistema Aresti*, of Colonel Jose Luis de Aresti Aguirre.

As the 1964 World Championship was to be held in Aresti's native Spain, this was selected by CIVA in 1963 to be the standard for that contest. This system not only used a range of basic symbols in combination to represent many thousands of possible figures, but also attributed difficulty coefficients to each figure so that a nominally objective form of judging could be undertaken. In its later forms, the *Aresti Dictionary* included upward of 15,000 figures, and became rather an unwieldy instrument.

In the mid-80s, CIVA established a working party to rationalize and simplify Aresti's work so that it was easier to use and would reflect the requirments of international competition as it had evolved to that date. This working party included members from South Africa, France, Spain, Germany, Poland, the USA, the USSR and the UK, so it was indeed an international body.

43

Their recommendations were adopted by CIVA and published in 1987 as the *FAI Aerobatic Catalogue*. This Catalogue is reviewed annually by CIVA and is maintained as an up-to-date reference, freely available to all through electronic publication, and is now used as the basis for all competitions worldwide. In 2002 it was retitled *The FAI Aresti Aerobatic Catalogue* in recognition of Colonel Aresti's major contribution to the sport of aerobatics.

Notation

Figures and Manoeuvres

These two terms are generally interchangeable in normal conversation, but they have different meanings when applied strictly in aerobatic parlance.

A figure is a complete entity that is made up of one or more manoeuvres. For example, a loop is made up of a single 360° looping manoeuvre. A stall turn, on the other hand consists of five manoeuvres: a 90° looping segment, a straight vertical line up, a 180° yaw turn manoeuvre, a straight vertical line down and finally another 90° looping segment back to horizontal flight. Further manoeuvres, such as fractions of aileron or flick rolls may be added to the stall turn to further complicate its design.

In competition flights where a pre-published sequence of figures will be flown, the figures are separated, and distinguished one from the next, by periods of level flight. This short level line is considered, from a judging point of view, to be part of the figure that follows it.

In Freestyle competition flights, the pilot's plans are not published in advance to the judges. These programmes are regulated solely by timed duration, and the various elements flown are judged, not as individual figures, but by a more general set of criteria which encompasses ideas about the synthesis of the sequence as a whole. None of the contents of this chapter is really applicable to such Freestyle flying, as the discipline of catalogue-based design is not strictly applied in that case.

Lines

Straight and curved lines are used in the notation to illustrate the flight path of the aircraft's centre of gravity. For periods when the wing is loaded with a positive angle of attack the lines are drawn continuous.

For periods when the wing is loaded with a negative angle of attack the lines are drawn dashed. In colour drawings, positive lines are conventionally shown in black while negative lines can be additionally highlighted by being in red.

The line convention is clearly illustrated in Diagram 4-1 which shows a positive, upward loop followed by a negative, downward one (not an actual combination I would like to fly often, but a good illustration).

Diagram 4-1

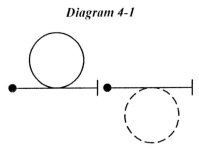

It is important to realise that the solid or dashed nature of the line shows its aerodynamic loading, not the aircraft attitude. Thus, at the top of the positive loop, the aircraft is upside down, but still positively loaded, so the line stays continuous throughout. The status of some lines is less obvious, so I'd better show some of those as well.

Diagram 4-2 shows three figures, all of which incorporate a vertical down line. There are a number of things to consider.

Diagram 4-2

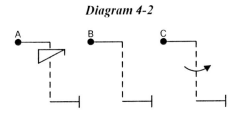

Firstly, it is not possible to go from horizontal flight to vertical flight without a curved bit in between. But because the curved section turns through less than 180° it is conventionally shown as a hard angle. This is the first instance of a kind of shorthand that simplifies the notation from a full artistic representation.

The figure labelled A also has the symbol for a one-turn upright spin (more on such symbols later). During the spin the aircraft would have a positive angle of attack, yet the vertical down line is shown as negatively loaded.

The figure labelled B has the spin removed. To get from upright level to vertical down, you have to push and perform a quarter outside loop. This is not shown because of the 'less than 180°' convention, but it results in the aircraft continuing to carry a slight negative load until the pull-out is started. Hence the dashed line.

Thus the status of the line is determined by the loading it would carry if it were flown with no rotation superimposed.

The figure labelled C has a full 360° aileron roll on the down line. In this case, the line would cease to carry its 'negative' connotation once the roll is started, but the drawn line remains dashed for simplicity.

In Catalogue figures, there is no instance of prolonged flight in knife edge, ie with sustained bank of 90°, so there are just these two sorts of line.

Pitch and Yaw Translations

Tail slides include pitch translations that are rapid and do not form part of a looping segment. Stall turns include a rapid yaw turn that also requires its own type of annotation.

Diagram 4-3 shows two tail slides and a stall turn. In the first two, the elliptical segments show the slide. Number 14 is a canopy-up slide while Number 15 is a canopy-down slide, distinguished by the dashed line.

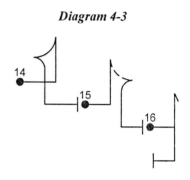

Diagram 4-3

The yaw rotation in the stall turn, number 16, is shown by the small oblique stroke at the end of the vertical line. No direction is implied by the orientation of the oblique, which could quite correctly lie on the left or right side.

Rotations

The two sections above have covered all there is about pitch and yaw changes, so that just leaves movement about the roll axis: rotation.

In the Catalogue there are two types of rotation, rolls and spins. There are also two types of roll, aileron and rudder (flick). So this means we need three types of symbol. In Freestyle flying, there is another type of rotation which is a gyroscopically-driven combination of rapid pitch generally called tumbling. No such figures occur in the Catalogue and so there is no standard symbol for such a manoeuvre.

Diagram 4-4 shows our familiar vertical down line, but this time with the full range of rotational possibilities.

Diagram 4-4

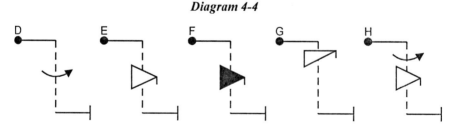

Aileron Rolls

The symbol for an aileron roll is a curved arrow (D). The curve confirms the direction of flight because it is always drawn so that it is approached from the concave side as you work your way around the figure. As well as simply conveying the requirement for an aileron roll, it is necessary to convey the extent of the rotation and whether there are to be any hesitations during the roll.

When the arrow is drawn on one side of the line only it represents a fraction. Allowable fractions are any multiple of 90°; thus ¼, ½, ¾ etc. When the extent of the continuous rotation is greater than 360°, up to the maximum permitted of 720°, two arrow symbols are drawn and linked with a short line at their tips. So in Diagram 4-5, the first three symbols from the left represent a half roll, a full roll and 1½ rolls, none with any internal hesitations or stops.

Diagram 4-5

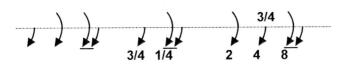

The next two symbols are also continuous rolls with no hesitations, but some numbers are added because the fraction to be specified is other than a half. For the 1¼ roll only the fraction needs definition so the text reads just '¼' not '1¼'.

The last three symbols show the further addition of text notation to indicate hesitations. The number '2' indicates two stops per revolution: a 2-point roll. The next symbol is a ¾ roll but it must have stops at the interval appropriate for 4 stops per revolution. This is in effect three consecutive ¼ rolls with evenly spaced hesitations.

The final element is 540° of rotation with stops at the rate of eight per 360°. This would amount to 12 individual roll segments of 45°each: 1½ 8-point rolls.

The difficulty coefficient of any particular aileron roll manoeuvre is the same, regardless of the line it is on being positive or negative. Thus a full level roll from upright to upright is 8K, as is the same roll when flown from inverted to inverted (Diagram 4-6).

Diagram 4-6

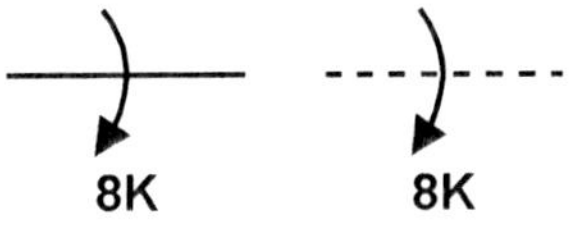

8K   8K

Rudder (Flick) Rolls

The symbol for a flick roll is an isosceles triangle (Diagram 4-4, E, F and H). At the apex of the triangle is a small tell-tale that confirms the direction of flight (in each case in Diagram 4-4, downward).

The minimum extent of rotation for flick rolls is 180°. Diagram 4-7 shows a progression of all possible degrees of rotation from half to double, with their text annotations. These are all orientated left-to-right as you look at the page. The last four are all greater than 360° and have two triangles, their tips linked by another small line.

Diagram 4-7

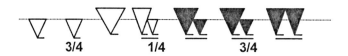

3/4   1/4   3/4

The last three are filled with solid colour, which may be red or black, to indicate that they are negative flicks (stalled with the stick forward). You may note also that the angle of the apex of the triangles is allowed to vary. This is not significant.

The difficulty coefficient for a flick roll has one of two possible values, depending on the wing loading immediately before the flick is initiated. Thus a level positive flick has a value of 11K when flown from upright to upright, but 13K when flown from inverted to inverted. (Diagram 4-8).

Diagram 4-8

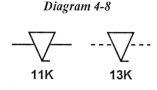

11K   13K

Spins

Spins only occur on vertical down lines at the entry to a figure. The minimum extent of rotation is 360° and the maximum, as for rolls, is 720°.

Diagram 4-9

In Catalogue based competition, positive spins are always initiated from level upright flight; inverted spins from level inverted. It is possible to enter an inverted spin from low-speed upright flight, and vice versa, but these 'cross-over' spins are no longer included in the Catalogue.

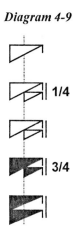

1/4

The symbol for a spin is a right-angled triangle (Diagram 4-4, G). Note that the tell-tale at the apex is always downwards and that all rotations greater than one have two triangles with the additional linking line at the tips. The black-filled symbols represent inverted spins (Diagram 4-9).

3/4

Combinations of Rotations

As well as being used singly as described above, all three types of rotation can be put together in pairs in what are known as 'Unlinked' or 'Opposite' rolls. I'll deal with combinations that include spins first, as that is the simplest section to get out of the way.

Spin Combinations

If you combine a spin with any other form of rotation, the spin must come first. This is forced on you because of the entry conditions – level entry, with vertical down finish. After you have stopped the spin, however, you can execute either an aileron or flick roll, while still on the down line, before you recover to level once again. While it might be possible to fly a second spin after the first one has stopped, there is a convention that says this should not be done in a sequence based on the Catalogue figures.

Diagram 4-10 shows a number of examples, all with a one-turn spin. In the left-hand picture, the spin is followed immediately by a one-turn negative flick. Because the two triangles have their tips on opposite

Diagram 4-10

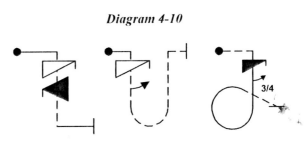

sides of the down line, these two rotations must be flown with their roll components in opposite directions. So a positive spin to the right must be followed by a negative flick with right rudder. The flick will then have a left roll component.

In the centre picture, the spin is followed by a half aileron roll and this must be in the same direction as the spin because the spin apex and the roll arrow tip are on the same side of the line.

In the right-hand picture, we have a one-turn inverted spin followed by a ¾ roll in the same direction. If the spin is executed with right rudder, its roll component will be to the left. So in that case the ¾ roll would have to be to the left also. This rotational combination is also the only one shown to include an odd quarter. As a consequence, at the exit to the figure you will be on a new heading at 90° to the original. This 'cross-box' finish to the figure is indicated by the little cross-bar at the end being horizontal instead of vertical as on the other two.

Non-Spin Combinations

Combinations that do not include a spin can be flown on vertical, 45° or level lines. In this case, both elements of the combination can be aileron rolls, or both can be flick rolls. If the two elements are, as just described, of the same type, then they must be in opposite directions.

If your combination includes a flick roll and an aileron roll, then the two elements can be in the same or opposite directions. Diagram 4-11 shows four legal combinations and one illegal one, to illustrate these principles.

Diagram 4-11

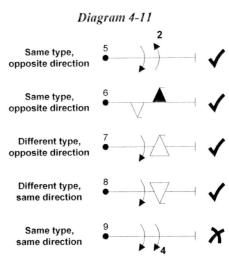

49

The FAI Aerobatic Catalogue

The FAI Aerobatic Catalogue is a pictorial guide to the full repertoire of figures that can be flown in Aresti competition sequences.

The alternative to an Aresti sequence is a Freestyle one, and for this type of programme there is no standard form of notation, primarily because the precise geometry of each figure is not defined in an agreed manner. In Freestyle sequences, much is left to the individual pilot's sense of originality and artistic composition.

The Catalogue does not simply list the figures, but also has supporting sections that summarize the conventions I have mentioned above and explain how the difficulty coefficients, or K factors, for each figure are derived. Thus, as and when new figures are added to the catalogue, their K-factors are calculated in a manner consistent with the rest of the book.

Diagram 4-12 is an example showing how a single figure is reduced to its component parts, each part evaluated and then the total divided by 10 to give an official K factor.

Diagram 4-12

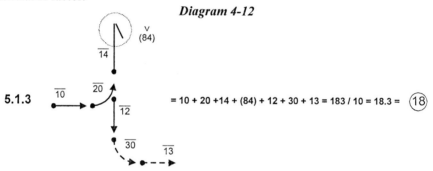

5.1.3 $= 10 + 20 + 14 + (84) + 12 + 30 + 13 = 183 / 10 = 18.3 =$ (18)

Catalogue Concepts

The main part of the Catalogue is the List of Figures. This list is sub-divided into nine Families. Families 1 to 8 can be grouped together under the general heading of Basic Shapes, while Family 9 contains all the rolls and spins.

Basic Shapes

In many instances, a basic shape can be flown, as it stands, with no rotations whatsoever. Examples would be a simple Loop, or a Tail Slide with no adornment. Such figures are sometimes referred to as 'vanilla' versions (Diagram 4-13).

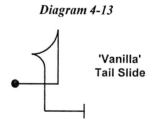

Diagram 4-13

'Vanilla'
Tail Slide

But most basic shapes can also be embellished by the addition of rotations at certain stages, while some of them cannot be flown without such roll addition. So the Catalogue also has to show where rolls may be added, or **must** be added, to the basic shape. For this reason there are specific symbols for optional rolls and also for compulsory rolls.

Rotations

Diagram 4-14

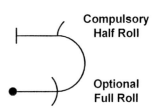

Compulsory Half Roll

Optional Full Roll

Diagram 4-14 is an example of a basic shape from Family 7 of the Catalogue. You will probably recognise it as a positive half loop upwards.

The figure starts at the round black blob and finishes at the cross-bar. Before you start the loop, you have the option to add some rolling elements.

These can be a single roll or a combination, with the sole restriction that the 'net' amount of roll must be 0° or 360° so that you are back upright when you start to pull up. Some examples are shown in Diagram 4-15.

Once the half loop is completed, this basic shape requires that you fly away to the left with the aeroplane upright once more (solid line). So at this point you actually **must** add some rolling, at least a half roll, so that you do not fly away upside down. Diagram 4-16 shows some net half rolls.

Diagram 4-15   *Diagram 4-16*

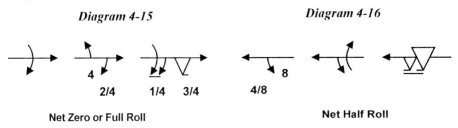

2/4   1/4   3/4   4/8

Net Zero or Full Roll   **Net Half Roll**

Note that in the Catalogue, the little arc symbols that show these roll locations do not have arrow heads. The arrow-head symbol is reserved specifically for an aileron roll whereas, in these specified locations, you can add aileron or flick rolls. These symbols also occur on 45° lines in a large number of figures. Notice that on these lines the net result must be either 0°, 180° or 360°. No odd quarter rolls can be flown as this would result in finishing on a knife-edge line.

Diagram 4-17

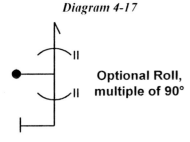

Optional Roll, multiple of 90°

When a basic shape includes a vertical line, you usually have the option to roll while in the vertical, up or down. In these situations, the net result of the rotation can be any multiple of 90°, so odd quarters are allowed.

Diagram 4-17 shows a Stall Turn, which can have optional rolls on either up or down lines, and any multiple of 90° can be used. Again, the options include combinations of opposite or unlinked rolls in addition to a single roll element.

When a figure happens to start at low speed with a vertical down line, then the Catalogue uses another character which is known as the optional spin symbol. This is the same as the optional roll symbol but with a small 'peck' on the opposite side to the double dash (Diagram 4-18). If you roll on this line, you do not have to start with a spin, but you may.

Diagram 4-18

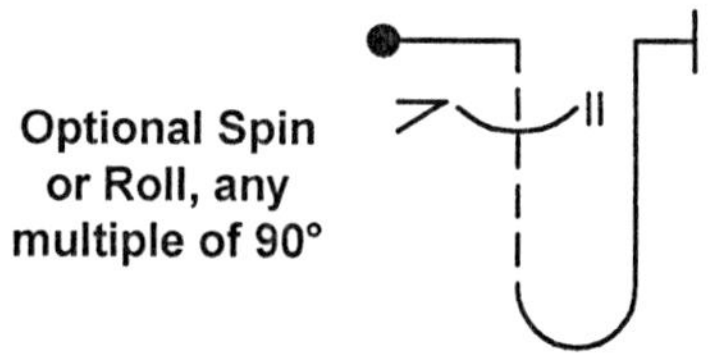

**Optional Spin
or Roll, any
multiple of 90°**

Compound Figures

You should now understand how to go about adding rotations to basic shapes to make compound figures. It is time to look at some of the different Families of basic shapes.

Catalogue Numbers

Basic Shapes

On each page of the List of Figures, for Families 1 to 8, the basic shapes are arranged in rows of four columns. Each basic shape has a unique Catalogue Number, which is made up of three components:

- Family,
- Row and
- Column.

The shaded example in Diagram 4-19 shows the derivation of Catalogue Number 8.3.3. Beside each basic shape is a small circle displaying the relevant K factor; in this case 15K.

In Families 1, 3, 7 and 8, a convention can be determined that links the different figures in a single row. The Column 1 figure always starts positive and goes upwards. Column 2 starts negative and goes upwards. Columns 3 and 4 are down-going figures, positive first, negative last. Diagram 4-20 is an illustration of this principle from Family 7, Row 10, Octagonal Loops.

Families 2, 5 and 6 have other conventions which are explained in their sections on the next pages.

In Family 9, the different rotational elements are laid out in a similar manner, except that there are up to 8 columns instead of the normal four.

Diagram 4-19

(8.) COMBINATIONS OF LINES, ANGLES AND LOOPS

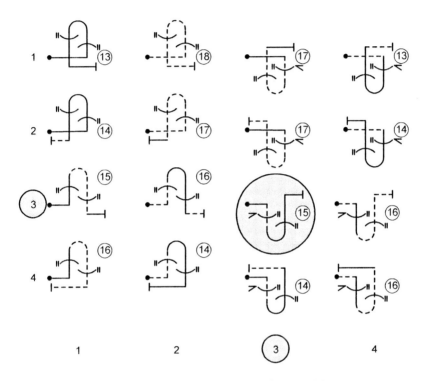

Catalogue Number 8.3.3. K factor = 15

Diagram 4-20

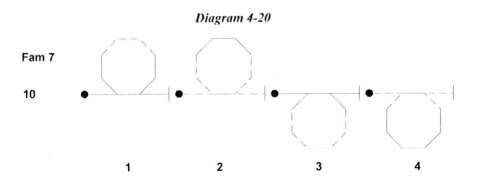

Rotations

The Catalogue Number for each rotation is made up of four components:

- Family
- Sub-Family
- Row, and
- Column.

Diagram 4-21 shows the derivation of 9.4.3.6. The sub-family '4' indicates a 4-point roll, the '3' a horizontal line and the '6' an extent of '6 quarters' or 540°. The K factor is 15. There are no K-factors in column 1 for this sub-family, because you cannot distinguish a ¼ 4-point roll from a plain ¼ roll which is included in sub-family 9.1.

Diagram 4-21

FAMILY 9.4 (4-POINT ROLLS)

(9.4)			½	¾	1	1¼	1½	1¾	2
1			9	12	15	18	20	23	25
2			7	10	13	15	17	20	22
(3)	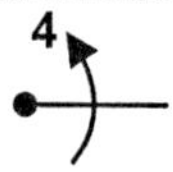		5	8	11	13	15	17	19
4			5	8	11	13	15	17	19
5			5	8	11	13	15	17	19
		1	2	3	4	5	(6)	7	8

Catalogue Families

Family 1 – Lines and Angles

Family 1 is the second largest family and contains a wide range of shapes from a simple horizontal line to complex 'N' shapes with two vertical and one 45° internal lines. All have places for added rolls and, in fact, the simple horizontal lines cannot be flown without.

The one thing they all have in common is that no single curved segment is as large as 180° so none of the shapes is drawn with a curved section.

Diagram 4-22 shows some examples.

Diagram 4-22

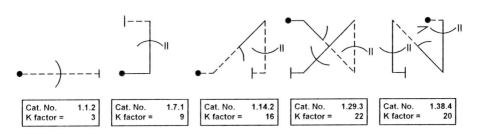

Cat. No.	1.1.2	Cat. No.	1.7.1	Cat. No.	1.14.2	Cat. No.	1.29.3	Cat. No.	1.38.4
K factor =	3	K factor =	9	K factor =	16	K factor =	22	K factor =	20

Family 2 – Turns and Rolling Turns

The unique family relationship here is obvious: this is the only family wherein all the figures involve level turning.

Turns can start upright or inverted. When rolls are included they can be to the inside or outside of the turn (Diagram 4-23), as shown by the arrow heads. To add further complication, some turns have rolls alternating between inside and outside.

In the rolling turn part of Family 2 the Column 1 figure always starts upright and the first, or all, rolls inwards. In Column 2 the start is inverted and the first roll inwards. In Columns 3 and 4 the first roll, at least, is outwards, Column 3 starting upright and Column 4 starting inverted.

Diagram 4-23

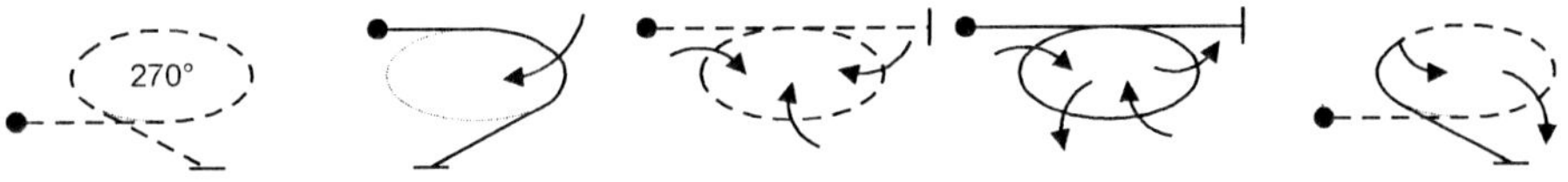

Cat. No.	2.1.4	Cat. No.	2.3.1	Cat. No.	2.9.2	Cat. No.	2.15.3	Cat. No.	2.20.4
K factor =	7	K factor =	10	K factor =	23	K factor =	24	K factor =	23

Family 3 – Combinations of Lines

Family 3 (Diagram 4-24) is very small and contains figures that are effectively parts of diamond and octagonal loops. The unique factor is that there is no place on any figure where you can add a rolling element.

Diagram 4-24

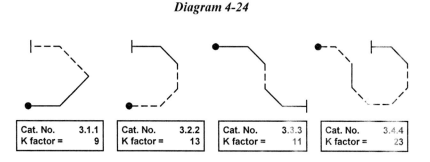

Cat. No.	3.1.1	Cat. No.	3.2.2	Cat. No.	3.3.3	Cat. No.	3.4.4
K factor =	9	K factor =	13	K factor =	11	K factor =	23

Family 4

Family 4 is now vacant. It used to contain all spins, which were only allowed on simple down lines. When spins were moved to Family 9 in 1999, these old figures were no longer needed.

Families 5 and 6

Families 5 and 6 are Stall Turns and Tail Slides.

The number of basic shapes is very small as the only variations are the entry and exit lines, positive or negative. There is just one row in Family 5, making it the smallest of all, because there is only one way to do a stall turn.

There are two rows in Family 6, because the tail slide can be canopy up or canopy down.

The column convention in these two families is concerned with the loading on the entry and exit lines. Columns 1 to 4 are, respectively, positive/positive, negative/negative, positive/negative and negative/positive (Diagram 4-25).

Diagram 4-25

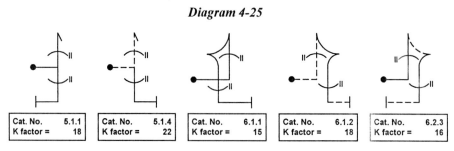

Cat. No.	5.1.1	Cat. No.	5.1.4	Cat. No.	6.1.1	Cat. No.	6.1.2	Cat. No.	6.2.3
K factor =	18	K factor =	22	K factor =	15	K factor =	18	K factor =	16

Family 7 – Loops and Eights

The key point about Family 7 is the complete absence of vertical rolls. The only vertical lines are the short sections that occur in square and octagonal loops, and there are no rolling opportunities here.

Rolling opportunities do occur, but they are generally on level or 45° lines. Rolls also occur in curved lines at the top or bottom of round loops, but these are treated as level rolls as far as the allocation of Catalogue Numbers and K-factors is concerned. Diagram 4-26 illustrates one of each basic shape together with its popular name. The number at the start of each figure gives the Catalogue row number.

Diagram 4-26

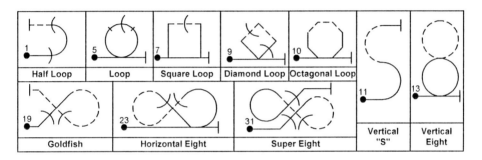

Half Loop	Loop	Square Loop	Diamond Loop	Octagonal Loop	Vertical "S"	Vertical Eight
Goldfish	Horizontal Eight	Super Eight				

Notice that where a roll is placed in the top of a loop, little demarcation lines are drawn to show that the roll has to be symmetrically placed in a roughly 60° arc.

Family 8 – Combinations of Lines, Angles and Loops

Family 8 is the largest family in the Catalogue with 72 rows of basic shapes. It is a rather amorphous group and it is not really clear why some of the shapes are not actually in Family 7. For example, Horizontal, or Cuban, Eights are in Family 7 while the familiar 'Half Cuban' is in Family 8.

I guess some day this might change. But the figures do all have one thing in common, each includes at least one looping segment of at least 180°. As for Family 7, I have illustrated one figure from each fundamental shape and give it a generic name (Diagram 4-27).

Some of these names might well be printed here for the first time. If enough copies of this book get passed around, they may become 'standard' short-hand for figures that are fairly obscure and not often flown.

Those of you with sharp eyes will notice that the 'Porpoise' includes a looping segment of just 90° that is shown as a curve, not an angle. This exception to an

Diagram 4-27

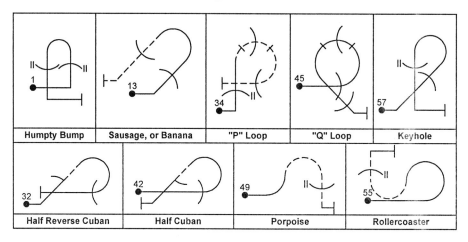

Humpty Bump	Sausage, or Banana	"P" Loop	"Q" Loop	Keyhole
Half Reverse Cuban	Half Cuban	Porpoise		Rollercoaster

otherwise firm rule is to emphasize the transition from inside loop to outside loop with no line in between.

Family 9 – Rolls and Spins

Among the aileron rolls, there are four sub-families. These are continuous rolls 2-point rolls, 4-point rolls and 8-point rolls.

Not surprisingly the sub-families are numbered 9.1, 9.2, 9.4 and 9.8. There is room to add sub-families of rolls with different numbers of points, 3 or 6 for example . These were in the original *Aresti Dictionary*, but have never been part of the FAI Catalogue.

Sub-Families 9.9 and 9.10 are positive and negative flick rolls, while 9.11 and 9.12 are upright and inverted spins.

Illustrations of these different types of rotation have been used liberally above, so I don't think I need to reproduce anything further here.

Catalogue On-line

The FAI Aerobatic Catalogue can be viewed on-line and can be down loaded for printing free of charge from the CIVA website. This is currently at:

www.fai.org/aerobatics/catalog/

CHAPTER 5

Aircraft Suitability and Performance

There is a wider variety of aerobatic aircraft available today than there has ever been. If you decide to enter seriously into the aerobatic sport/hobby then, sooner or later, you are going to ask how this type of aircraft performs in comparison with that one. Such comparisons are not simply a matter of cubic inches, as some would have you believe.

Added to the question of performance are the questions of cost, availability and suitability for the task you have in mind. With all these variables it is not surprising that newcomers to the sport find it difficult to match their ambitions with their hardware.

Your participation in this hobby is basically a selfish one. It is really about you and your desires. So you won't make any sensible decisions about which aircraft to fly or buy until you know enough about yourself: your ambitions, your ability, your budget and the time you have available to dedicate to this pursuit.

Training Aeroplanes

At first, everybody has to learn with someone else in the aeroplane. You can do this by hiring the aeroplane and instructor as a package, or by purchasing an aeroplane and then hiring an instructor.

My recommendation is strongly for the former route. As a rule of thumb, it is going to be cheaper to rent an aircraft by the hour than to own it unless you are planning to fly more than 50 hours a year. Additionally, until you have some training behind you, you really are in no state to assess your ambitions or plans. They will change rapidly early on as you develop your response to this demanding environment.

When you are training, the competence of the instructor is more important than the performance of the aircraft. However, outside of the competition field, there is no grading system for aerobatic instructors and so it is difficult to know who is cost-effective and safe. The only ways to find out are by recommendation and personal judgement. If an instructor does have experience and a successful record in competition, you can at least be sure that he knows the subject. Whether he can teach it is another matter.

This is really about aeroplanes, though, so what should you be looking for in a training aircraft? Naturally, it should be certified for all the basic aerobatic manoeuvres, but what about cost and performance? The cheapest, on an hourly basis, is not always the best choice. Below a certain minimum performance level, far too much time is wasted in transit and climbing. For example, if you were to go off for a spinning exercise and wanted to complete 12 spins, how long would it take and what, therefore, would it cost? I cannot give you an answer in print that is right for your place and time, but I can give you this very good question.

If you do have talent and dedication, you are going to want to continue to learn new things for years to come. So a training aircraft that can take you all that way, without running out of its own capability, would suit you better. On the other hand, an aircraft with too great an excess of performance will cost far too much initially and teach you far too little.

To be more specific, I would not recommend starting to learn aerobatics on an aeroplane with more performance than a Pitts S2A. To start with, choose a two-seater with a 4-cylinder engine that would be competitive at Intermediate and, perhaps, just able to get round an Advanced known. Do not start learning in a 6-cylinder aeroplane nor in a 4-cylinder aeroplane with Unlimited performance, such as the Giles G202, for cost reasons if none other.

Aeroplanes to Own

Once you are hooked on the sport and flying 50-plus hours a year, you will certainly want to consider owning at least a share of a private aeroplane. First you have to determine how much you can afford to lay out in capital. Then you can multiply that figure by two or three if you are prepared to share the ownership with some like-minded friends. If you have been active in aerobatics for a couple of years, then you probably already know who those friends might be.

Group Ownership

Group ownership lowers fixed overheads, but not in a linear manner. An increasing number of partners brings progressively less benefit and increasingly more hassle. You cannot really compare cost with hassle, but my non-dimensional, personal analysis puts the optimum group size at three partners per aeroplane, with two as a close second (Diagram 5-1).

If you have shared ownership, you need to have shared goals. You all have to be trying to get, more or less, to the same place. The benefits of mutual encouragement are then very great. A partnership will not work if the partners have different basic reasons for wanting the aeroplane and for flying it.

Diagram 5-1

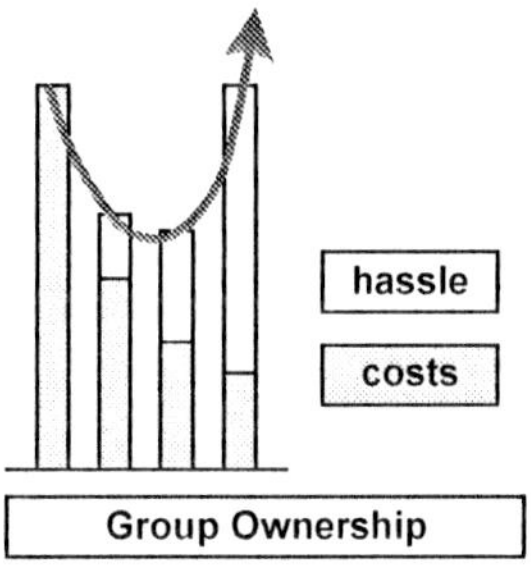

hassle

costs

Group Ownership

Configuration

Whether as an individual or a group, the next decision after budget has to be the configuration of the aeroplane: one seat, two or four. Four seats would be very unusual, but there are a couple of types out there that can do both things: carry people and go upside down, though not necessarily at the same time.

The Yak-18T and a certain type of Beech Bonanza come into this category, although their aerobatic capabilities do not extend beyond the Sportsman repertoire.

Principally, then, the choice is between one seat or two. There is no right or wrong decision here, just a number of factors to take into account. Two seaters include the following characteristics.

◆   You can teach or be taught in the dual mode.

◆   You can earn money teaching with the aeroplane if it is fully certificated.

◆   They cost more than equivalent single seaters, to buy, hangar and insure.

◆   Their performance is less than equivalent single seaters.

◆   Their extended balance envelope means they fly differently when flown solo.

◆   They can take two people to a contest, or one with a lot more baggage.

Two-seaters come with tandem or side-by-side seating, nose-wheel or tail-wheel undercarriage. Tandem seating is my preference from a viewpoint of handling niceties and visibility, while side-by-side has some advantages in early training and in cross-country flying.

For optimum solo handling, a tandem two seater should have a ballast system that allows the centre of gravity to be kept reasonably close to the aft limit.

Nose-wheel aeroplanes are most familiar to newly-qualified pilots these days, and save much time in conversion training, but their performance is generally less than equivalent tail wheel types because of the weight and drag of the wheel at the front. They also come in a range of capabilities from marginally effective (Cessna 150 Aerobat) to Unlimited-capable (Sukhoi-29, Extra 300L, Giles G202). The ratio of prices from bottom to top is probably of the order of 10 times.

Aerobatic Performance

Aerobatic performance is determined by a number of factors, some of which are not easily quantifiable. The two most difficult to pin down numerically are effort and harmony.

Effort and Harmony

The effort required to move the controls is worth considering. Heavy controls will reduce pilot performance over time. Physical effort detracts from mental effort. Aerobatics are flown through the complete aircraft speed range. Controls that are comfortable at low to medium speeds may get excessively heavy at high speeds. This will detract from pilot performance.

Rather more subtly, an asymmetric wing section may require much more control effort to fly, say, an outside loop compared to an inside one. It may also give the aeroplane a noticeably nose high attitude inverted which may detract from its ease of judging. An aeroplane with a light elevator and heavy ailerons will be difficult to roll accurately. The effort required to apply large aileron deflections will make it hard, simultaneously, to be delicate and precise with the responsive elevator.

None of these things can really be objectively quantified. What might seem heavy to one pilot might seem normal to another. But you should be aware of these characteristics which vary greatly from type to type, when you decide what to buy and fly.

Power and Weight

Power and weight commonly come together as a ratio. In so doing they give an indication of the net accelerating force that will govern and define an aeroplane's low-speed performance.

An aircraft with high power/weight will accelerate quickly level, take off in a short length of runway and have a steep climb gradient. It will regain energy quickly once it has been squandered, as long as it remains at lowish speed. It won't necessarily go especially fast, nor corner very efficiently, nor perform a great number of vertical rolls on a down line.

Drag and Speed

Classic aerobatic monoplanes of the '60s and early '70s did not have large power/weight ratios. Sequences of those days rarely contained more than three quarters of a vertical roll. But they did contain many figures and often more than one of these involved spinning. The expert pilots of the time were able to do such things in relatively heavy, underpowered aircraft like a Zlin 326 because these types had thin wings for low form drag, high aspect ratios to reduce induced drag and retractable undercarriage. These were also features of the Yak-50 in which Russian pilots won two mens' and two womens' world championships between 1976 and 1982.

Since the mid-'80s wings have become thicker and stronger (and more draggy), engines have become more powerful and undercarriages have invariably stayed 'down and welded'. Drag co-efficient, however, remains a very important ingredient of aerobatic performance. The Yak-55M and the Sukhoi-26M have very similar empty weights and the same 360 hp M-14P radial engine. The principal reason the Sukhoi has a significant performance advantage over the Yak is its more slippery airframe, giving it a higher maximum level speed and thus better energy retention through a complex sequence.

One way then to compare otherwise similar aircraft is to consider their maximum level speeds at maximum continuous power. This gives a good guide to the ability to fly sequences without undue height loss.

Rate of Roll

Rate of roll is not a valid criterion in judging aerobatic figures. You do not get a better grade for a figure just because you roll faster. However, the ability to roll fast means you can perform more rotations on any given line. As Unlimited sequences are geared to what is actually possible in the highest performance aircraft of the day, it is very difficult, nay impossible, to be competitive in an aircraft that does not roll very quickly.

The ability to roll faster has come primarily through materials technology. The traditional limit to aileron size has been the torsional stiffness of the wing. In traditional construction, if you made the ailerons any bigger, the wing would twist and the benefit would be lost.

This all changed in the late '80s and '90s with the introduction of aircraft with wings made of carbon fibre. The first such machine was the Sukhoi 26, first flown in a competition in 1984. The carbon wings were not especially light but they were, and are, very rigid, allowing large full-span ailerons to generate enormous roll rates.

Perhaps the fastest rolling aerobatic aircraft available today are the little Giles G200 and G202, together with the Edge 540. All achieve roughly 480° per second.

Personally, I have reduced the aileron throw on my G202 to just +/-18° rather than the maximum of 22°. I have found that the really fast roll rate is not always an advantage because of the resulting difficulty in stopping accurately on heading every time. Reducing the rate to about 420°/second gives more control and is still certainly fast enough.

Aerobatic Performance Index

There is currently much debate in the world aerobatic community concerning which aircraft should be allowed to compete internationally in the Advanced class. One side of the argument suggests that the 'formula' for the event should be defined by the limits put on permissible figures. For example, if more than a half roll is flown on a vertical up line, then the next element within the same figure must be a descending line, not a level fly-off. Alternatively, if more than a half roll is flown vertically down, then the recovery to level must be upright not inverted.

These regulations make it feasible to compete with G-limits of +6/-4g and a relatively low-performance aeroplane. They aim to remove any advantage that would be obtained by flying a modern Unlimited aeroplane. Thus the true test would still be one of pilot skill.

The other, more traditional approach, which also marked the introduction of these events in the late '80s, is to ban aircraft of 260 hp or more unless they are specifically agreed to be eligible by CIVA. Thus 360 hp Yaks are allowed, but not Sukhois. 300 hp Zlins are allowed but not Extras. 260 hp biplanes are allowed, but not monoplanes.

In order to aid in such policy discussion, I devised a method of combining the three quantifiable parameters of power/weight ratio, maximum level speed and maximum roll rate into a single aerobatic performance index (API). This has gained some wider acceptance and is now used as a way of comparing performance between diverse aircraft. The first step was to take an arbitrary value for each parameter and set that equivalent to unity. For example a maximum level speed of 165 knots would give a factor of 1.

If the maximum speed was just 120 knots, the index would be calculated as $120/165 = 0.73$. For power/weight ratio, the norm was set for a 260 hp Zlin 50 which happens to be 0.36 hp/kg. So an aircraft with a power of 200 hp and a contest weight (including fuel and pilot) of 650 kg would have a ratio of 0.307 and an index of 0.85.

With roll rate the 'standard' figure was set at 270°/second. Faster roll rates give an index greater than 1, but the amount of the benefit tails off above 420°/second because of the reasons outlined above.

This compound formulation allowed a ranking performance list to be devised for a wide range of current aircraft. This arrangement has been validated by the general consensus of pilots who have flown a number of the different types, so it seems to have some merit. It has not yet been put to any official use in defining standards, but it has been useful in policy discussions and bar talk alike. I publish the results of the comparison here for the first time (Diagram 5-2).

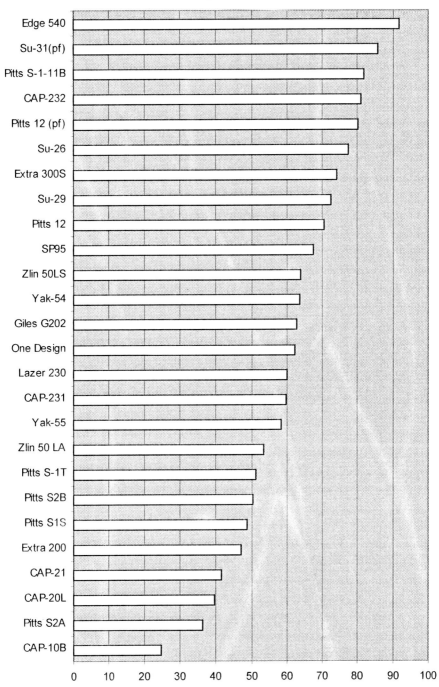

Diagram 5-2
Aerobatic Performance Index

This is only a structured model, based on data collected from a wide range of sources. Some of the claims made for certain types may be optimistic, some pessimistic. But the model overall seems fairly robust. If you have accurate data for your aeroplane, you may draw a fairly valid comparison for it with the types shown.

API Algebra

Weight = empty weight +80 kg (pilot) + contest fuel.

Contest fuel for up to 250 hp   = 40 litres (10 usg), 260 hp to 360 hp

= 60 litres (15 usg), >360 hp

= 70 litres (17.5 usg)

Power/Weight Index (PWI) = power (hp)/weight (kg)/0.36

Max Speed Index (MSI) = Max Level Speed (knots)/165

Roll Rate (RR) Index (RRI) = $\dfrac{1.6}{e^{\left(\frac{220}{RR^{1.1}}\right)}}$

API = PWI x MSI x RRI x 50

My apologies for the complexity of the roll rate index calculation, but it gives what seems to me a valid profile describing the benefit of increasing roll rate in a range of indices that compare well with ranges of the other two. This helps to give each of the three indices a similar weight in finding the overall API. As an extra matter of interest, the equation produces this graph of roll rate against RRI.

Diagram 5-3

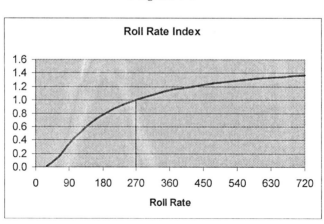

Better Aerobatics

Part Two

General Handling Exercises and Primary Figures

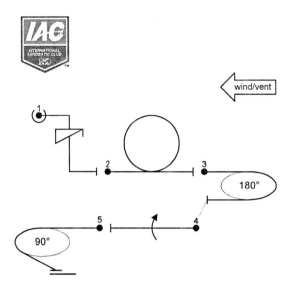

International Aerobatic Club (IAC)
Basic Known Sequence 1999

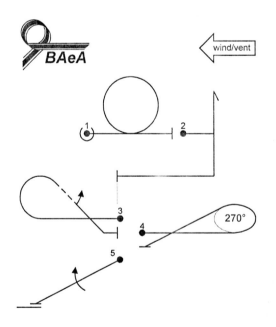

British Aerobatic Association (BAeA)
Beginners Known Sequence 2003

CHAPTER 6

Recovering Lost Control

In aerobatics, you do not have to recover from 'unusual attitudes'. Ultimately, all attitudes will be within the bounds of what you consider usual. There will be times when, in seeking to master a new attitude, you lose control over what the aircraft is doing. In these situations, you require a technique with which to get the aircraft back under control once again.

In PPL training, you will have become used to recovering from spiral dives and approaching stalls. You will also have been shown how to recover from a fully developed stall and an incipient spin. This chapter is concerned primarily with loss of control at low speed and, usually, with a high nose attitude.

The aim of the flight exercises is to instill confidence through the knowledge that control can always be recovered after it has been lost, given a sensible minimum height for exploring new attitudes and manœuvres.

Airmanship

During this flight, no manoeuvre should be attempted unless recovery can be completed above 3,000 feet agl.

Airframe Considerations

In recovering from attitudes close to the vertical, some reverse airflow over the flight controls is inevitable. In an aerobatic aircraft, these control systems should have physical stops, built into the mechanism or linkage, that limit control surface travel. If such stops are not present, you should not attempt any aerobatic figure that involves pitching up to, or through, the vertical attitude.

In aircraft with proper stops fitted, slow to moderate movement of the control against the stop will not cause damage. Damage may be caused, however, in the event of very rapid and powerful movement of the control surface from one extreme to the other. In any situation where you believe this eventuality is imminent, hold the control firmly against one extreme of its travel until the risk has passed.

In some aircraft with large control surfaces, trying to hold the controls fixed and central, under significant reverse flow conditions, is unlikely to be successful. In such situations, the best procedure is to place the control firmly against one stop and hold it there until forward airflow is restored.

Flight Manoeuvre

Ground References

In view of the high recovery height (above 3,000 feet), specific ground references are not required during the recovery actions. It is important, however, that general geographic orientation is restored after each recovery and before the next manoeuvre. Any large, unique, feature can be used for this purpose. But do not choose a town or village unless there are none other like it in the vicinity. The sun is always a good reference, when you can see it.

Loss of Control Situations

Overwhelmingly, the situations wherein loss of control occurs, other than those already covered in the PPL syllabus, are those where the airspeed is low and the nose attitude is high. Control can be lost for one of two reasons: the airflow over the control surfaces becomes too slow or is reversed; the pilot becomes spatially disorientated and is unable to make correct control inputs.

In either case, action must be taken immediately that will lead to recovery of control.

Control Recovery Technique

If the aircraft is slow, stopped or about to go backwards, the primary 3-axis flight controls do not work in the normal sense. Once control is lost in this manner, moving the flight controls is likely to make things worse rather than better. Similarly, if the pilot is disorientated he will be unable to judge the result of his moving the controls, and so should refrain from doing so.

In either case, strong engine and propeller forces will come to dominate the aircraft at very low airspeeds.

It follows that the best recovery action to take after losing control is to:

• close the throttle

- release the control column

- relax your legs and just rest on the rudder

- wait.

Closing the throttle will minimize all engine/propeller effects. The only things now working on the aircraft are gravity and the plane's own momentum.

If you still have forward speed when you release the control column, the flying controls will all simply trail in the airflow. They are no longer able to exert any force on the aircraft other than from their trim settings. All aircraft have static longitudinal and directional stability.

When the controls are left alone, gravity will ensure that the aircraft transitions into a descent with the nose leading. Once this happens, airspeed will increase and the flying controls will once again be capable of normal operation.

What happens between the loss of control and re-establishing a gliding dive depends on the initial conditions at the point when recovery action is taken. Depending on speed and attitude when the controls are released, the aircraft may just nose down while maintaining forward speed. It may become almost stationary and flop into a nose-down attitude. It may even slide backwards a small distance before changing ends and diving forwards once stability has reasserted itself.

As the nose is falling, monitor the attitude, to see if you can understand what is happening. As the glide starts and speed increases, monitor indicated airspeed. Once the ASI is showing something around normal climb speed, take control once again and pull the nose to the horizon.

To complete the recovery, re-apply climb power, set the wings level, ball central and nose in the normal climbing attitude.

Inadvertent Tail Slides

A serious inadvertent tail slide is a very rare beast. All aircraft are very unstable under reverse airflow. They want to go forwards, and this is a strong desire. To continue to slide backwards for any length of time, the aircraft must be truly vertical and very finely balanced. Compare it to balancing a pencil on its point on your finger tip.

In the overwhelming majority of instances of loss of control, such conditions will not apply. In many instances a short period of reverse flow may prevail before the aircraft pitches down to travel forwards. In such cases, the elevator will follow the local airflow.

If the aircraft falls wheels down (Diagram 6-1), the elevator will be pushed to the fully up position.

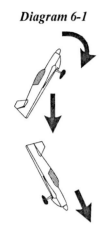

Diagram 6-1

Falling Wheels Down

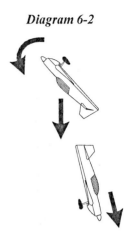

Diagram 6-2

Falling Canopy Down

In the cockpit, the stick will travel at moderate speed, but gently to the rear stop.

If the aircraft falls canopy down (Diagram 6-2), the opposite will occur. The stick will move fully forward during the period of reverse flow. In either case, after the aircraft changes ends the stick will return to the centre.

If you believe that you are in the very rare situation of a perfectly balanced vertical and about to slide backwards, simply place the control column into any corner (full elevator and aileron displacement) and apply full rudder. Keep power applied while the nose is high to counteract gravity.

Hold the controls firmly against the stops until the aircraft changes ends and goes forwards once again. As the nose comes down, close the throttle. Then quickly release all the controls so that they return to the centre. You do not have to put them into the centre; you may not do so accurately under stress. Just let them go once you are moving forward and they will have no adverse effect.

Inadvertent Autorotation

In order for autorotation to occur, the aircraft must sustain a high angle of attack for some time, while inertia is overcome, and the aircraft must have a significant amount of asymmetry in yaw. If the pilot closes the throttle and releases the controls early in the loss-of-control process, it is most unlikely that a high alpha will be sustained. The aircraft might slide backwards a short way and it will have an instantaneous angle of attack of 90° as it changes ends to go forward.

But this alpha will not be sustained as long as the pilot has his hands off the elevator control. The worst thing to do is to try to recover the pitch attitude with major elevator deflections when unsure of the direction of the airflow and of the direction the aircraft's momentum is taking it. To do so is most unlikely to resolve matters for the better. It is more likley to lead to an inadvertent spin.

The recovery procedure given above will always result in the aircraft transitioning to a gliding dive. This may be quite steep, even vertical, but that is not a problem. Once normal climb speed is reached, up elevator can always be applied to effect a recovery.

Under some circumstances, however, for example if some part of the recovery action is delayed, or if control was lost during some high-rotational figure, the aircraft may continue to rotate as it glides down. This is particularly probable if the botched figure involved prolonged application of full rudder, as in a stall turn. With the controls all released, this rotation must be self-sustaining, that is: autorotation. All that then needs to be done is to apply rudder to oppose the yaw that is taking place and the rotation will stop.

At this stage, if you are not sure which rudder to push, look at the turn needle (if there is one). If it shows a left turn, apply right rudder and vice versa. Take no notice of the slip ball as this is probably not working if you are under negative G. If you have no turn needle, apply rudder where it looks as though you might most need it, and wait a second or two. If the rotation stops, fine. If it speeds up, change feet and apply the other rudder. Then the rotation will stop.

During this process avoid the temptation to apply elevator, especially in the normal panic direction of fully back. This will probably make things worse, not better. Only when the rotation has stopped and the speed is above normal climb speed should you attempt to use the elevator.

Flight Exercise

A useful exercise is when the instructor pilot puts the aircraft into an un-sustainable, nose-high, low-speed situation. He then asks the student to recover. Recovery is deemed complete when the aircraft is in a sustainable climb, power on, wings level and in balance.

Typical loss of control attitudes at first could be:

* a 60° climbing attitude, Diagram 6-3, or

* a 45° inverted climbing attitude reached in a loop, Diagram 6-4.

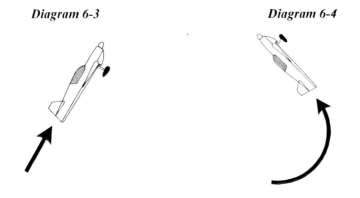

Diagram 6-3   *Diagram 6-4*

More advanced recovery situations might include:

- a failed vertical roll, Diagram 6-5, or
- an over-rotated stall turn, Diagram 6-6.

Diagram 6-5   *Diagram 6-6*

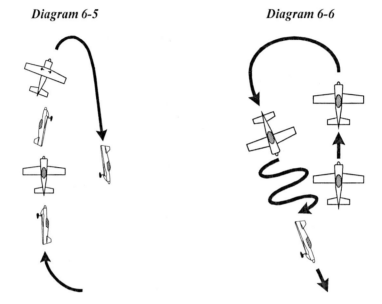

The latter will normally result in an autorotation after the throttle is closed, due to residual yaw from the turn and pitch-up caused by the gyroscopic effect of the rapid yaw rate. This is an accelerated positive spin in the direction of the rudder used for the stall turn. Application of opposite rudder will stop the spin.

Advanced Training Techniques

During mild tail slide recoveries, it is very informative for both pilots to use the light touch of one finger to monitor the movement of the elevator during the reversal. This not only shows the direction of the reversal (wheels down or canopy down) but also serves well to show how the elevator control returns smartly to the centre once forward flight is reestablished. This is a very good exercise for building confidence in the recovery action and in showing the benefit of not trying to force an impossible recovery using ineffective elevator inputs.

In later training, with more advanced students and specialist aircraft, the same loss of control and recovery procedure can be practised during quite complex auto-rotational or gyroscopic figures. Certainly this technique should be used to prove emergency recovery procedures before any such figure is flown at competition or display heights.

CHAPTER 7

Stalling

Stalling of a wing starts to occur when the angle of attack of some part of it exceeds a critical amount, typically 16° or so.

A wing is designed in such a way that the angle of attack is not necessarily constant at every part of it. So different types have markedly different stalling characteristics.

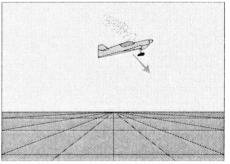

In normal training aircraft, many design features may be incorporated to give relatively graceful degradation of handling qualities as the stall progressively develops over the wing.

Modern specialist aerobatic aircraft generally have straight, symmetrical wing sections that are designed to stall thoroughly and suddenly. What follows in this section is sufficiently general to apply to both basic aerobatic training aircraft and to the specialized aerobatic types.

Stalling Won't Kill You ...

... hitting the ground may.

Modern ab-initio flying training is oriented toward stall avoidance, not toward stalling as a valid flight regime. Pilots are primarily taught to recognize the situations where a stall is approaching and to take recovery action before the stall actually takes place. Spinning is taught only as an elective option, and the only time a flying instructor has to demonstrate spin recovery is on an instructor's flight examination.

Consequently, most private pilots have very little experience of the fully developed stall and do not understand how to fly the aircraft through and beyond the stall.

Aerobatic pilots must be aware of the stalling and spinning characteristics of their aircraft. Ideally, they should actually enjoy exploiting these edges of the flight envelope.

Angle, not Speed

A wing does not stall at low speed. It stalls at a high angle of attack. It just happens that most pilots and most instructors associate high angles of attack with low speed.

It is possible, however, to have a critical angle of attack at relatively high speeds. Stalling is not just a low-speed phenomenon. It is also possible to have virtually no airspeed and zero angle of attack and still fly safely without stalling. In this case, you will be flying on a 'ballistic' trajectory.

Ignoring the variability caused by flap and power settings, the wing always stalls at the same angle. Because elevator position and angle of attack are very closely interdependent during forward flight, the aircraft also always stalls at the same elevator control position.

Read the last sentence again; it may well be news to you!

Up to the stall, angle of attack can effectively be measured by elevator displacement from its neutral point. Whether you stall conventionally, straight and level, in a gliding turn or at the top of a loop, the stall will always occur with the same elevator position. Of course the **feel** of the elevator varies in all these positions, both because of aerodynamic forces and because of different trim settings, but the stick/yoke position will always be the same.

Demonstration Exercise 1

Start with plenty of height. and then try the following.

◆   Fly straight and level, close the throttle.

◆   Continue flying level as speed reduces, by progressively moving the elevator control aft.

◆   Ignore lights, bells, whistles or any other artificial stall warning device.

◆   As the aircraft stalls, note the indicated airspeed (1g stall speed) and stop further elevator movement. Note how the airflow breakdown buffets the airframe, the nose drops, maybe a wing drops, whatever.

◆   Note the stick/yoke position.

◆   Recover by moving the control column centrally forward a small amount, then add power and fly away.

- Repeat the exercise in a gliding turn and note that the stick position at the stall is the same.

The elevator should have come close to the aft stop, but will not necessarily have reached it, in either of the above cases.

Demonstration Exercise 2

This exercise will rapidly familiarize you with the aircraft's stalling characteristics and show that the stall can easily be initiated at higher than the basic 1g stalling speed.

- Fly straight and level with some power applied at 10 knots above the 1g stall speed noted above.

- Briskly apply back elevator until heavy airframe buffet (stall) occurs; not necessarily fully back, just as far as in the first exercise.

- The right wing is likely to drop a little at the stall (gyroscopic effect - Lycoming engine) so be ready to add a little left rudder to hold the bank angle within acceptable limits.

- Release the back pressure immediately after the stall and note that the buffeting stops.

- Maintain 10 knots above the 1g stall speed, and repeat the elevator movement (accelerated stall and recovery).

- Set 15 knots above 1g stall speed and repeat the exercise.

A maximum of 2g will be recorded as long as the initiation speed does not exceed the 1g speed by more than 40%. At 1g stall speed plus 70%, the normal acceleration recorded will not exceed 3g.

This exercise will only work well if the elevator is applied briskly and with some commitment. Slow application will result in a climb and loss of speed before the stall occurs.

Diagram 7-1 shows how stalling erect with right rudder applied, or inadvertent yaw to the right, will cause roll to the right. This must be corrected with left rudder.

Diagram 7-1

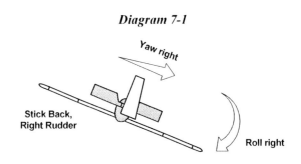

Flying Beyond the Stall

When the wing stalls, it is not the end of the world. Nor is it the end of flying. Fully stalled the wing still develops lift, albeit very inefficiently because it also generates considerable drag. But if the wing is stalled, and kept stalled, the aircraft does not just plummet out of the sky like a dead parrot.

Diagram 7-2

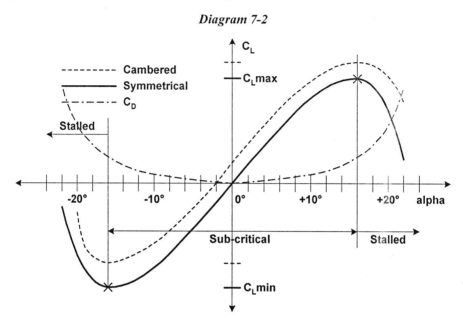

Diagram 7-2 shows the typical relationship between Angle of Attack (alpha) and coefficient of lift (C_L) for both symmetrical and cambered aerofoils. It shows that there are still significant amounts of lift available after the stall. It also shows how the drag coefficient increases dramatically after the stall.

Controlled flight is possible beyond the stall. The aircraft must descend, because lift will inevitably be less than weight, but bank angle and, consequently, direction can be maintained or changed by careful use of the rudder.

I have flown in this way in a great many light aircraft, from a Piper Warrior to a Pitts Special, and have found none in which it could not be done. The exercise is particularly testing, however, in aircraft with absolutely no mainplane dihedral.

Demonstration Exercise 3

Start off by flying straight and level at a safe height (minimum 4,000 feet).

♦   Close the throttle and gradually approach the stall maintaining level flight.

- Move the elevator aft only slowly, particularly at the critical point. If you actually pitch up or down just prior to stalling, gyroscopic effects from the propeller will make it hard to keep accurate balance.

- When the aircraft stalls, hold any wing drop with top rudder (the rudder on the up-going side) and bring the elevator control fully aft with the ailerons central. Under no circumstances apply aileron.

- Use rudder alone to maintain wings level as the aircraft descends. When making corrections, it is very important to keep the movements small and to take the rudder off again as soon as the aircraft responds.

- If control is lost, release the elevator control, which will move forward on its own to clear the stall. Use rudder to oppose any residual rotation. As speed increases to normal climb speed, ease out of the dive and level the wings with aileron.

- Providing the bank angle is under control, recover at no lower than 2,500 feet by releasing the back pressure and adding power. Remember to balance the power with rudder (right rudder with a Lycoming engine).

- Transition to normal climb configuration.

For want of a better term, I call this exercise 'parachuting'.

Once proficient in maintaining wings level during the descent, controlled turns can be initiated. Use the rudder to set perhaps 20° or 30° of bank in the required direction. Hold the bank angle as the aircraft turns. Keep full back stick and neutral aileron.

During the recovery, try to maintain a constant attitude as the elevator is moved slowly forward and power applied.

'Parachuting' is a great exercise for educating the feet. It is especially useful in a tail wheel trainer as it is a simple demonstration of instability, similar to that which will be experienced during the landing roll-out.

If a pilot can safely 'parachute' and turn during a controlled descent losing 2,000 feet, then he is well prepared to cope with ground-looping tendencies on landing.

Stalling in a Loop

Another valuable exercise that aids understanding of your aircraft under extreme conditions is to investigate stalling during a loop. Learn how the aircraft behaves in these different situations and store the information away against the time when you might need it unexpectedly.

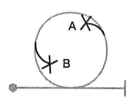

Diagram 7-3

Diagram 7-3 shows two good places to practice stalling during a loop. They are also the places where this event is most likely to occur during early looping practice.

Stall at Point A by pulling the elevator control back past the critical point. Airspeed will be relatively low. As the wing stalls the aircraft will probably buffet and roll gently to the right. Release the back-pressure on the elevator control to un-stall the wing. Use aileron to roll to wings level, upright. The throttle need not be closed unless rotation continues after the elevator control is released.

Stalling at Point B will require more effort on the elevator control to reach the critical position, because airspeed will already be higher than in the first case. As the stall occurs, the aircraft will buffet heavily and is likely to flick roll rapidly to the right. Immediately close the throttle and release the control column to un-stall the wing. Continue the roll using aileron until the aircraft is once again wings level and upright. Then add power and climb away.

The aircraft is most likely to flick right (Lycoming engine) in both these situations even though the aircraft may have been carefully balanced just prior to adding the back stick for the stall. The rapid pitch-up just prior to stalling will generate a gyroscopic fore from the propeller that will yaw the aircraft to the right, just at the critical time. This is also the reason why left rudder is advised during Demonstration Exercise 2 above.

Inverted Stalling

Provided that the aircraft used is cleared for inverted spinning, all the exercise described above can be carried out under negative G conditions.

Inverted Wing Drop

In an aircraft with a symmetrical wing section, stalling characteristics during inverted flight will be similar to those in upright flight. With an asymmetric wing section or, particularly, in an aircraft with wash-out in the wing section, the inverted stall is likely to be markedly different from the upright one. Usually this difference means more volatile, with more dynamic wing-drop tendencies.

Diagram 7-4 shows how stalling inverted with left rudder applied, or inadvertent yaw to the left, will cause roll to the right. This must be corrected with right rudder.

Rudder Corrections

If the aircraft rolls right during an upright stall, the left wing points more toward the sky. Yaw and roll movements are in the same direction.

Diagram 7-4

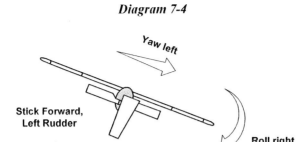

If the nose yaws right, the right wing drops and the aircraft rolls right. You then, quite naturally, apply left rudder to arrest the wing drop and to reset wings level. The key thing to remember is that it is the sky-side rudder or 'top rudder' that you use for this recovery.

The same rule applies inverted. You apply top rudder to arrest a wing drop.

The mental difficulty sometimes arises because you are then using, say, right rudder to stop a roll to the right. Don't be misled by the roll motion. Look at which wing is pointing more to the sky and use rudder that side.

This is because roll and yaw are in opposite direction in an inverted stall. If you yaw right at the inverted stall, the right wing will still stall and drop toward the ground. But you will see this from the cockpit as a roll to the left. The left wing will be pointing skyward and you use left rudder to stop the wing-drop.

To imagine this, stand with your legs a bit apart and bend forward at the waist until your upper body is parallel to the ground. Look behind you and then 'roll' your body to the left. See your right shoulder point at the ground, your left to the ceiling. Then imagine applying left rudder to straighten you up.

These are the corrections needed during inverted 'parachuting'.

Stalling in an Outside Loop

Diagram 7-5 shows the same positions for stalling in an outside loop started from inverted.

Diagram 7-5

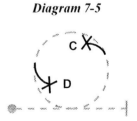

At Point C, push hard forward until the wing stalls. Gyroscopic effect will make the aircraft yaw left (Lycoming engine), and thus roll right.

Release the forward pressure and apply right rudder to stop any continuing roll.

At Point D, the stall will be sharp and the aircraft will quickly start a flick with left yaw and right roll components. Immediately reduce power and relax the push to un-stall the wing. If necessary use right rudder to stop the flick. Use left aileron to roll to wings level inverted, then push to level flight, more gently than before to avoid a second stall. Lastly roll upright.

If you briefly stall inadvertently during a push-out, **never pull** to regain level flight. You will lose a lot more height and gain an awful lot of speed. Reduce power, stop the flick, roll to level inverted and continue pushing to get level. Then half roll upright (Diagram 7-6).

Diagram 7-6

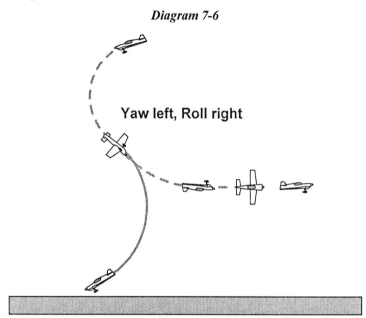

Yaw left, Roll right

Flying in Competition or Display

In normal competition flying, you only stall prior to an intentional spin manoeuvre. This will be described fully in the chapters on competition spinning.

Falling Leaf (Diagram 7-7)

Although I have not now seen it flown for many years, an interesting display figure derived from the stalling exercises described above is the Falling Leaf. To be effective, this figure needs to be flown in an aircraft with a low wing loading. Vintage biplanes like the Tiger Moth and Stampe are good for it. A CAP-10B looks quite graceful. Anything with a higher wing loading, including modern biplanes and monoplanes all oscillate too quickly and lose height much too fast.

Diagram 7-7 – Falling Leaf

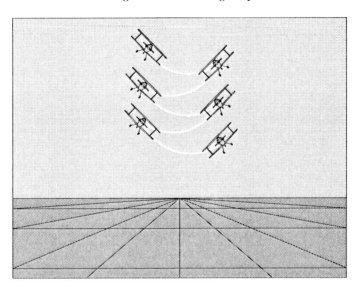

The figure is basically the same as the parachuting exercise described above. Once stalled and descending, alternating rudder applications can cause an oscillating flight path, with bank angles of perhaps 45° in each direction, very reminiscent of a large leaf falling from a tree.

The main drawback with the figure is the enormous energy loss. Height is lost without any balancing gain in speed. It can be a very nice start to a low-level sequence in a big old biplane, as long as you have enough height to begin with. After recovering from the falling leaf, further height must be lost diving for speed to start the rest of the sequence.

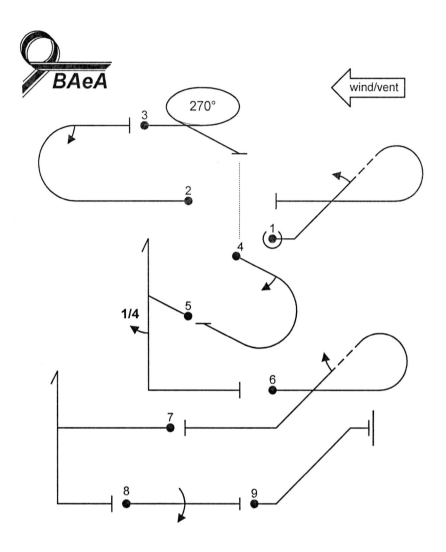

British Aerobatic Association (BAeA), Fenland Trophy, 1992
Standard Unknown Sequence

CHAPTER 8

Spinning

All aerobatic books cover this subject. Yet reading a number of such chapters, one after the other, does not necessarily lead to great clarity of thought. For example, former European Champion Neil Williams, in his book *Aerobatics* says:

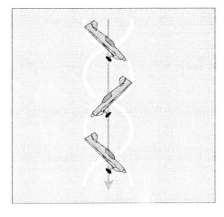

> *"Recovery is initiated with half a turn left to go to the desired exit heading, and consists of full rudder to oppose the yaw, pause, then stick smartly forward, as far as is necessary to stop the rotation."*

Williams is actually giving a technique for the Stampe, but some closely allied version of this is generally given under the heading of the 'standard spin recovery' in many other books and flight manuals. Another former European Aerobatic Champion, Eric Müller, on the other hand says:

> *"I will not leave any grey areas such as are found in some manuals, where for example you may be told that the correct recovery method is to 'give opposite rudder, then pause, then start moving the stick forward'. This kind of thing leaves an area that I would describe as not just grey but dark grey!"*

Müller also adds: *"But try to tackle an experienced pilot on his spin theories and recovery techniques, and he will react almost as though you had challenged his manhood!"*.

I will try to avoid this behaviour pattern. And if pressed to support another author's views, I will lean toward Müller as I feel I learned more of direct use from him in my early days than from any other.

Spin Theory

Although there is evidently much difference of opinion about recovery techniques, all experts agree about the theory of spinning. All aerobatic pilots should understand at least the basic principles of this theory, so I will describe them here. Later, I will also give my views on spin recovery.

Rotation and Autorotation

First understand the difference between rotation and autorotation.

♦   Rotation will happen when you make a control input and it will continue until you take that input away. Then it will stop.

♦   Autorotation, once started, is self-sustaining. A positive anti-rotation technique must be used to stop it.

There are two principal rotational motions in a spin, yaw and roll. The pitching element of a spin is relatively unimportant from the point of view of understanding autorotation.

In Chapter 7 on stalling Diagram 7-2 showed how lift decreases and drag increases after the wing exceeds the critical angle of attack – the stalled condition. In the real world, however, when an aircraft stalls it almost always has an element of asymmetry in yaw. Therefore the detailed conditions of the left wing are different from those of the right wing.

This means that the two wings, which still create lift, generate different amounts of lift. So an uncommanded roll starts.

As the uncommanded roll develops, the down-going wing has a relative airflow from more of a downward direction. In other words, its angle of attack increases. For converse reasons the up-going wing experiences a decrease of alpha. Diagram 8-1 shows this asymmetric condition on the alpha/lift/drag graph.

The horizontal axis shows increasing positive alpha, the vertical axis both lift (solid line) and drag (dashed line). The asymmetry is shown by the down-going wing having black squares and the up-going wing white ones.

Consider how this affects an aircraft in an upright spin to the right, Diagram 8-2.

Because the down-going wing has less lift, the aircraft continues to roll right even though this is uncommanded. Because the same wing also creates more drag, the

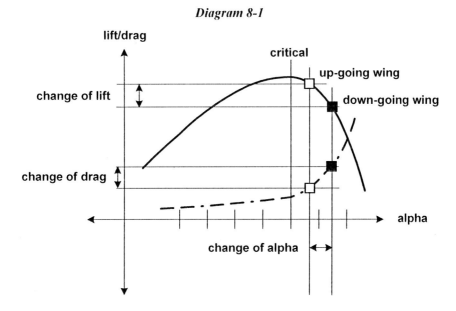

Diagram 8-1

lift/drag
critical
up-going wing
change of lift
down-going wing
change of drag
alpha
change of alpha

yaw asymmetry that initially caused the roll is perpetuated. In true autorotation, the pro-spin forces are sufficient to ensure that the rotation continues, even if the controls are subsequently centralized.

Some modern aircraft, often used for ab-initio PPL training, are designed such that true autorotation is unlikely to occur. Their elevator authority is reduced so that very high alpha cannot be achieved. The wing section is different across the span so that the angle of attack of the outboard parts, including the ailerons, is less than the inboard section. Thus only the inboard part of the wing stalls and autorotation forces are very small.

Diagram 8-2

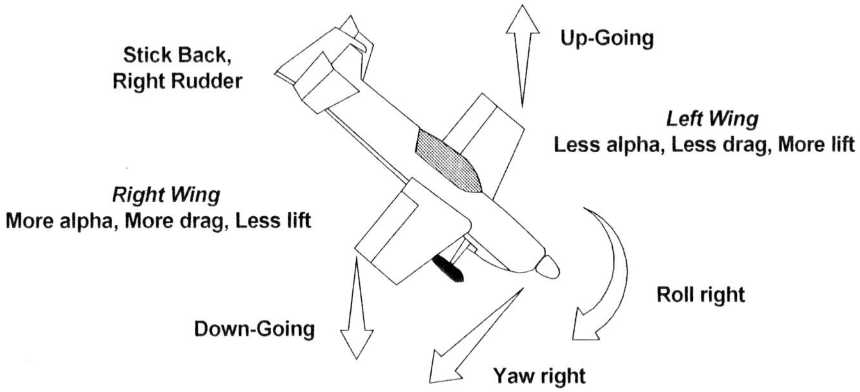

Stick Back,
Right Rudder
Up-Going
Left Wing
Less alpha, Less drag, More lift
Right Wing
More alpha, More drag, Less lift
Roll right
Down-Going
Yaw right

If spinning is approved in these aircraft, full pro-spin control must usually be retained for the spin to continue. In all specialist aerobatic trainers, however, the wing has no wash-out and a full-span stall is the norm.

Other Forces Involved

As the spin develops further, the pro-spin forces are gradually matched by anti-spin forces. Otherwise the aircraft would continue to accelerate and never stabilize. These anti-spin forces come mostly from the fixed aircraft keel surfaces.

Because the propeller continues to turn, even though the throttle may be closed, it generates gyroscopic forces because of the yaw and pitch present. The most noticeable of these is caused by the yaw. With a modern Lycoming-engined aircraft, the propeller turns clockwise as seen from the cockpit.

In this case, spinning to the right causes the nose to go more steeply down. In a spin to the left, the nose rises, flattening the spin, Diagram 8-3.

Diagram 8-3

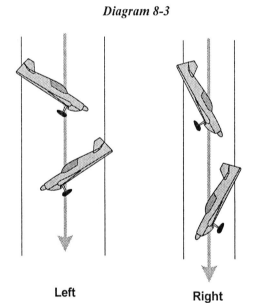

Left   **Right**

When the spin is flatter, and to the left, the aircraft mass distribution is over a wide area on either side of the spin axis. In the steep spin, the mass is more closely concentrated toward the axis. In the same way that skaters increase their rate of rotation by drawing their arms closer to their bodies, so the steeper spin turns faster than the flatter one.

For the technically inclined this phenomenon is called the 'Law of Conservation of Angular Momentum' and will be mentioned several times later as the angular momentum effect.

As the aircraft is yawing rapidly, the wings and fuselage also act like gyroscopes. They turn slower than the propeller, but have much more mass and are longer. These extra gyroscopes change quite noticeably the characteristics of the spin between different aircraft types.

In summary, an aircraft with a relatively light wing and heavy fuselage will spin more nose down; one with a relatively heavy wing and light fuselage will spin flatter. These generalizations all refer to upright, not inverted, spins.

Aircraft that spin relatively flat for these reasons, such as the Slingsby T67, have to transition through a more nose-down spin during the recovery process. They also, therefore tend to demonstrate an increase of the rate of rotation during the recovery, because of the angular momentum effect.

Effect of Elevator in the Spin

Even during a fully developed spin, the elevator controls the angle of attack of both left and right wings together. From the fully aft position, moving the elevator forward will reduce the alpha of both wings, even though they have different values due to the yaw present. Moving the elevator forward a small amount will thus have no initial effect to oppose the autorotational forces.

Diagram 8-4

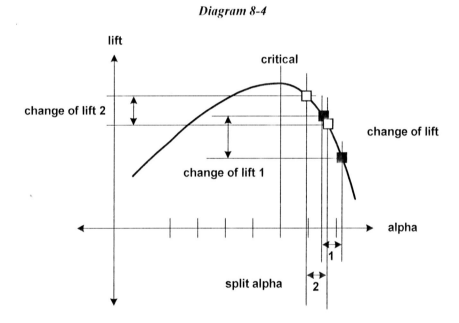

Diagram 8-4 shows the effect of unloading the elevator during the spin while maintaining the pro-spin rudder (the rudder that was used to start the spin).

The conditions change from Case 1 (black squares) to Case 2 (white squares). In both cases the split in alpha between the up-going and down-going wings is about the same. The change of lift between the two sides of the aircraft reduces slightly, but in both cases the pro-spin rolling force is still apparent.

The overall reduced alpha in Case 2, however, results in a more nose-down attitude and an increase in the rate of rotation due to the angular momentum effect.

Diagram 8-5 Different elevator/rudder configurations

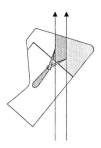 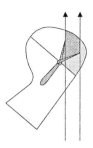 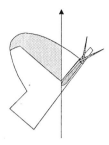

A second effect of the elevator during a spin is to change the amount of the rudder exposed to the effective relative airflow. Depending on the configuration of the empennage, forward and aft elevator can have different effects in this respect.

Diagram 8-5 shows a number of different elevator/rudder configurations, together with the relative airflow typical of an upright spin.

In each case the light grey area shows the rudder area surface available to produce effective anti-spin yaw with the stick forward. The dark grey area in the two left hand pictures show the increase in rudder effective area with the elevator still in the aft position.

Both left and right pictures have a good-sized light area. The centre picture shows that, with the stick forward, the amount of rudder available is low, but that this area at least doubles with the elevator in the aft position.

Apply this principle to the aircraft you fly and see what the respective areas might be.

Effect of Aileron in the Spin

Earlier I described why some aircraft are difficult to spin properly because of the wing design. In a large-span aircraft with wash-out along the wing, it is likely that the outboard portion of the wing will remain un-stalled even though the inboard section is above critical alpha.

In this situation the aircraft might be capable of being held in the spin with full pro-spin rudder and aft elevator. The ailerons, however, are likely to be in a reasonably normal airflow and could work in the usual way. In this case, aileron against the spin direction will decrease the pro-spin forces, perhaps enough to stop the autorotation.

Diagram 8-6 shows how applying left aileron in a right spin can provide a restorative roll force when only the inboard section of the wing is stalled.

Diagram 8-6

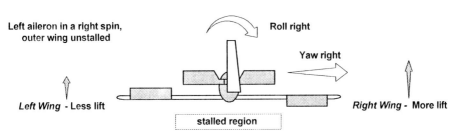

In specialist aerobatic aircraft this is not the case. The airflow over the ailerons will be disrupted, so the effect of aileron in these types needs further consideration.

Diagram 8-7 shows the same situation, but in an aircraft where the whole wing is in the stalled condition. Now the left aileron input causes a further roll force to the right. The right wing also generates more drag and so the pro-spin yawing force also increases. These combined effects will greatly increase the pro-spin forces and increase the rate of rotation.

The last picture in this series, Diagram 8-8, shows the effect of right (in-spin) aileron on a right spin. Now the effect of the aileron is to increase lift and reduce drag on the down-going side of the aeroplane.

These effects are anti-spin and assist with recovery.

Diagram 8-7

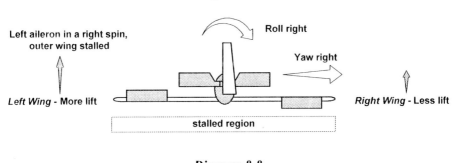

Diagram 8-8

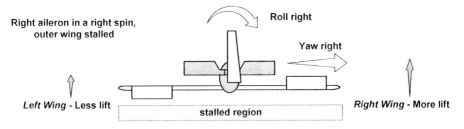

Effect of Rudder in the Spin

The rudder has the most critical effect in a developed spin. Rudder in the opposite direction to that of the autorotation yaw always provides an anti-spin force.

The strength of this force depends on two things: the amount of rudder exposed to the relative airflow and the strength of the relative airflow.

Effect of Power in the Spin

Adding power during a spin will have the following effects:

- increase in torque

- increase in p-factor

- increase in gyroscopic precession affecting yaw and pitch

- increase in propeller wash airflow

- reduction of angle of attack in propwash-affected areas.

Table 8-1 shows which of these effects are pro- and anti- for an upright spin. You can see from it that some power-related effects will make the spin worse and some will make it better. How they affect any aircraft type overall will depend on the relative magnitude of the different factors.

Table 8-1 Effects for an Upright Spin

Effect	Left Spin	Right Spin
Torque	Pro	Anti
P-factor	Pro	Anti
Gyro – Yaw	Anti	Pro
Gyro – Pitch	Pro	Pro
Propwash – empennage	Anti	Anti
Reduced alpha	Anti	Anti

I imagine that in days long gone by, when rotary engines were common, gyroscopic effects would dominate if power were added during a spin. As these effects are largely pro-spin, recovery would be most assured with the throttle closed.

In modern aircraft the only significant rotating mass in the power plant is the propeller. Gyroscopic forces are relatively small, except in the most powerful aircraft with the biggest propellers. The effects of prop-wash, however, are very significant and in all cases make the elevator and rudder controls more effective.

Diagram 8-9 shows the improved airflow over a rudder with power applied during a spin. The direction of the relative airflow has changed because of the slipstream from straight ahead.

The airflow speed is also increased. The result is rudder and elevator with greatly increased effectiveness.

The angle of attack of the wing will also be reduced in the propwash area, slightly reducing the pro-spin forces.

Diagram 8-9

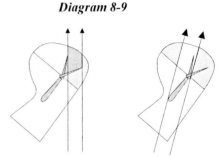

In all the modern aircraft I have flown during the years I have been active in aerobatics, the improved rudder effectiveness with added power has always overtaken the detrimental gyroscopic effects in a conventional spin.

Spin Recovery

To recover from a spin the aircraft's asymmetry in yaw must be removed. This will bring both wings to the same angle of attack and must be done primarily by applying opposite rudder. Recovery can be assisted by in-spin aileron where the wing is not built with wash-out. For any particular aircraft type, there are variables that determine the effectiveness of the rudder. These include the angle of the elevator and the speed/mass of the airflow over it.

In a modern conventional light aerobatic aircraft, therefore, the best control positions for upright spin recovery are:

- opposite rudder
- in-spin aileron
- aft elevator.

Control positions markedly different from these, with pro-spin rudder still applied, will invariably make matters worse. The conventional spin will be modified in some way.

In the event of an inadvertent spin, the most important recovery action is to apply rudder immediately to oppose the yaw. It is then important that the pilot should not make things worse while the rudder does its job. One way to ensure that the correct aileron and elevator positions are approximated is to let go of the stick/yoke altogether. The elevator and aileron control surfaces will then trail in the local airflow in an aft/in-spin position. This is the same as the technique already recommended in Chapter 6 on Recovering Lost Control.

The amount of time it takes for the rudder to overcome the yaw momentum that has built up varies between aircraft types and also depends on the rate of yaw that has developed. During the first two turns, when the spin is not fully established, recovery will probably be quicker than in the case of an established multi-turn spin.

Especially in large-span aircraft, such as the Slingsby T67 and the Zlin 326 series, yaw momentum can be high and the spin attitude can be relatively flat. In these cases, the nose will drop gradually and the rate of roll rotation will increase as the yaw decreases. This may give the impression of things getting worse before they get better, but this is to be expected and can easily be explained.

In aircraft with short span, such as a Pitts S1, the spin attitude will normally be steeper and there is less momentum established. In such machines, recovery will be quicker and there may be no appreciable steepening or acceleration, especially when recovering from a spin to the right.

Standard Spin Recovery

Over the years, a 'standard' spin recovery has developed which is widely taught and is effective. For aircraft which are cleared for intentional spinning, the flight manual or Pilot's Operating Handbook should give the manufacturer's recommended recovery action. For example, the Pitts S-2A Airplane flight manual states:

> *"For spin recovery put ailerons neutral, apply full opposite rudder briskly and then apply nose down elevator. Use power off for all spin recoveries."*

However, it then goes on to say, four paragraphs later:

> *"For flat spins use aileron with the spin for recovery."*

The first quotation above is a good example of the 'standard' spin recovery, but unfortunately leaves two questions unanswered: it does not specify when the nose down elevator should be applied, nor does it say how much should be applied.

The recommendation to use in-spin aileron for recovery from a flat spin accords with the analysis given above which shows that in-spin aileron is anti-spin and helps with the recovery. This is not recommended for normal spins, however, probably because normal spin recovery is much quicker and does not need the extra help.

The unanswered question of *"How far forward?"* is an unfortunate omission, because moving the control column too far forward too quickly can lead to a dangerous situation. In recovering from an upright spin, going to full opposite rudder and almost immediately to full forward stick will cause the aircraft to transition from an upright spin to an inverted one.

The Pitts rudder is very powerful and can change the yaw direction very quickly. The full forward stick can effectively stall both wings inverted. The resultant inverted spin retains the same roll direction as the upright one and the change over is sustained by the aircraft's roll momentum. Furthermore, the ease of transition from upright to inverted spin is enhanced after 1½ turns (see "Relative Wind Effect" on page 184).

Recovery from this inadvertent inverted spin is actually quite easy, but recognition of the situation can be beyond the inexperienced pilot. It is probable that this 'change-over' spin has cost the lives of a number of Pitts pilots over the years, and the condition is certainly achievable in a wide range of aircraft. For this reason, if no other, it is essential that spin training be undertaken dual and with an instructor very experienced on type.

Conclusion

Spinning is now a phenomenon that is well understood, and is not, of itself, dangerous. A great deal of intentional spinning is safely performed each year around the world in a large variety of aircraft types, both for training and competition/display purposes. Failure to recover from a spin, however, remains a life-threatening situation.

Anyone contemplating any form of aerobatic flying must undertake comprehensive spin training, with an aerobatic instructor with considerable type-specific experience, at an early stage in his aerobatic education. Emergency and planned spin recovery technique should always be taught in a type-specific manner.

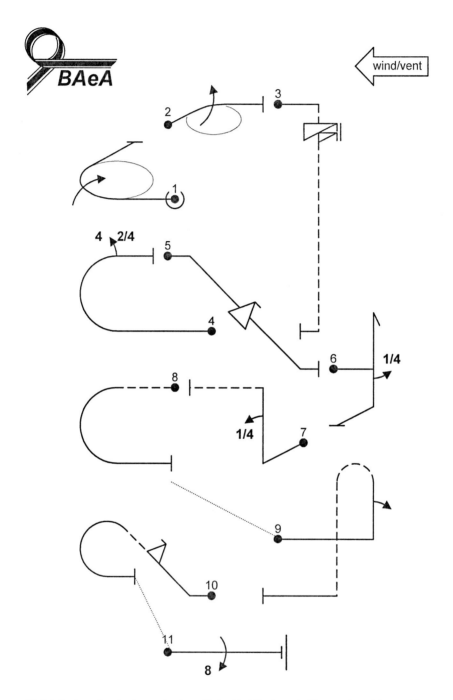

British Aerobatic Association (BAeA), National Championships, 1985
Intermediate Unknown Sequence, Cranfield

CHAPTER 9

Rolling

The names given to different types of roll have developed over a long time, and this has regrettably led to some misunderstandings. For example, many people talk of a 'Slow Roll' and mean a particular type of manoeuvre, but the actual meaning of 'slow' is not really defined.

Alternatively, pilots talk about 'Aileron Rolls' and imagine in their minds one particular type of rotation, which may be at odds with another's definition of this figure. There is therefore a need to be rather more analytical and precise in defining the different ways an aeroplane might be rolled, and for what purpose.

Diagram 9-1 shows in diagrammatic form how the various types of roll should be classified and how they differ, one from another. The names in italics, on shaded backgrounds, give the nomenclature; the other text entries show how the classification is broken down.

The first order differentiation is between aileron rolls and rudder rolls. The term 'rudder rolls' is not in general use for the very reason that they were invented first. Before aileron technology had developed to the stage where those controls had sufficient authority to completely roll the aeroplane, rolling was achieved by aggressive use of the rudder at high angles of attack, stalling one wing and thus creating a large left/right lift differential. This naturally was called rolling.

Once ailerons could also enable a full roll, a new term was needed to differentiate these new rolls from the old ones. Hence 'Aileron Roll', and please note that this really means nothing other than that the rudder is not the principal cause of the rolling motion. Rudder rolls are more generally called Flick or Snap Rolls in modern English or American, *Déclenchements* in French which is very nicely descriptive. Because the roll rates generally achieved with aileron alone are less than those possible with one wing stalled, rolls performed primarily by aileron inputs were also called 'slow' rolls. This term, however, has very little meaning nowadays as modern aircraft have ailerons that can produce a wide variety of roll rates. Only in glider aerobatic competitions is the roll rate to be used ever specified, and in this case the term 'super-slow roll' is used to define a roll that takes at least 10 seconds for a full 360°.

Diagram 9-1

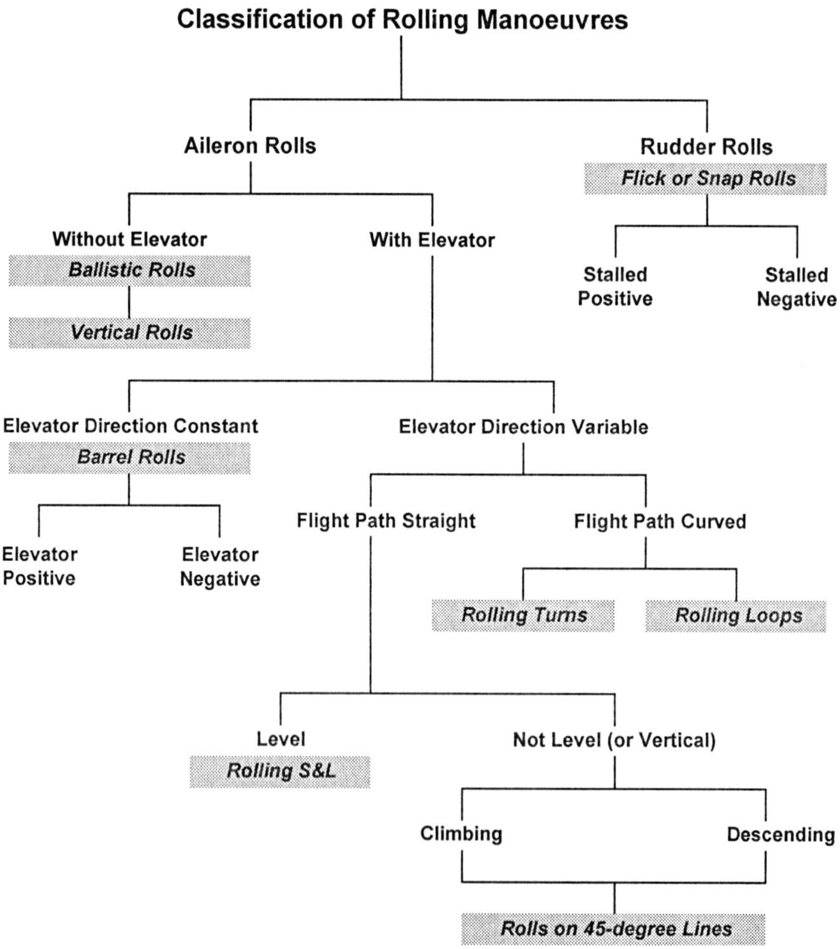

Classification of Rolling Manoeuvres

Aileron Rolls

Rudder Rolls
Flick or Snap Rolls

Without Elevator
Ballistic Rolls

Vertical Rolls

With Elevator

Stalled Positive   **Stalled Negative**

Elevator Direction Constant
Barrel Rolls

Elevator Direction Variable

Elevator Positive   **Elevator Negative**

Flight Path Straight   **Flight Path Curved**

Rolling Turns   *Rolling Loops*

Level
Rolling S&L

Not Level (or Vertical)

Climbing   **Descending**

Rolls on 45-degree Lines

Keeping 'aileron roll' to its original, broad sense allows us to use better descriptive terms for the great variety of rolling forms flyable in modern aircraft. To understand how to define and fly these myriad possibilities, I will now differentiate between the different rolling types primarily by describing what is done with the elevator control while rolling takes place. This is really the only thing left once the primary use of rudder and aileron has already been taken up.

The simplest further differentiation, then, is to consider an aileron roll in which the elevator does absolutely nothing. This means, also, that the trimmer must be doing nothing to cause the elevator to do any work. It also means that the wing has no angle of attack and therefore generates no lift.

During such rolls, the aircraft will fly in a straight line but its flight path, if not vertical, will curve down towards the ground in a quasi-ballistic path, rather like a thrown stone, but still with some thrust to prevent the curve being truly parabolic.

In all aileron rolls other than those now defined as 'ballistic' or 'vertical', the elevator is going to be working and most of the time the angle of attack is going to be other than zero. If the sense of the elevator is constant, in other words if the elevator is always backwards, or always forwards, then the flight path will be 'barreled', rather than straight. We will have flown a barrel roll of some description.

If we vary the sense, that is the direction, of the elevator control while we are rolling, then we will sometimes have a positive angle of attack and sometimes a negative one.

This can produce a bewildering variety of different appearances. So differentiating between different types of roll in this group is best done by considering the flight path desired by the pilot. Examples are rolling straight and level, rolling while turning and rolling while looping. All of these are possible, though with increasing complexity of co-ordination, and have their place in the aerobatic repertoire, though the latter are definitely not 'basic' in any sense.

This deconstruction of rolling terminology and classification is rather un-exciting, but it is crucial to being able to understand exactly what is happening during rolling manoeuvres, and therefore how to fly them.

By introducing new terms, such as 'ballistic roll', and avoiding ill-defined older terms, I hope to avoid both ambiguity and imprecision, both in my writing and your flying.

Yak-55M, RA-01333. The author flew it from Russia to UK in 1993 and flew the same type in AWACs in 1995 and 1997.   *Peter March*

The author in CAP G202, F-WWMX with Nick Wakefield in F-GYRO behind. A 2000 publicity shot for Securicor Security Services Ltd.   *Ed Hicks*

CHAPTER 10

Ballistic Rolls

The Ballistic Roll has two important applications in aerobatic training.

The first of these is to demonstrate the purest form of roll that requires only very simple elevator and aileron inputs to perform. It is the easiest way to introduce a novice to the feel of rolling through a complete revolution.

The ballistic roll is also a vital tool for determining a key control position that is critical for performing a whole range of more complex manoeuvres. This is the position of the stick/yoke required to produce both maximum aileron deflection and zero angle of attack: the 'Neutral Point'.

Airmanship

As full aileron will be applied, entry speed must be less than manoeuvre speed (V_A). If the aircraft does not have an inverted fuel system, momentary loss of thrust may occur if the elevator is moved too far forward.

The Flight Manoeuvre

The form of a ballistic roll is a curving flight path, initially climbing, then descending, on a constant heading, while the aeroplane rolls axially through 360°. In relatively fast, high-powered aircraft, more than one complete roll will be possible.

Before you read this description of how to fly the figure, take a moment to re-read the section on "The Elevator and Elevator Trimming" on page 37.

Ground References

Upon completing the area clearance checks, it is sensible to arrange for the aircraft to be pointing directly towards some prominent landmark in the middle distance. This will enable the pilot to confirm that the heading has not changed when the figure is complete.

This starting position, before pulling up, is shown in Diagram 10-1. It assumes you are in the left-hand seat of a side-by-side cockpit.

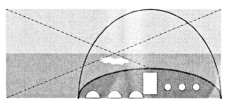

Diagram 10-1

Technique

Start the figure by setting the entry speed. Use the flight manual speed for an 'Aileron Roll' if there is one, if not use normal cruise speed or just a little over. In a low-powered aeroplane, apply full throttle if this can be done without over-speeding the engine. Raise the nose above the horizon (Diagram 10-2, left picture). The angle of climb will typically be 30° in a basic aerobatic aircraft, but could be as much as 60° in a high-powered aircraft.

The climb attitude should be set briskly, to minimize height gain at this stage, but not violently. With practice, any climb angle may be set that permits you to roll without ending with an uncomfortably steep dive angle at the completion of the rotation. The best way to determine the actual pitch angle is to look at a wing tip and the horizon while pulling up.

Once the required attitude is reached, move the elevator control forward until the angle of attack is close to zero. Use a small amount of forward pressure to overcome the effect of any positive elevator trim. The G-meter should read 0.5g or a bit less. Then apply full aileron in the required direction.

In basic aircraft, it is sensible to use engine torque to assist the roll until some experience is gained. So if you fly behind a Lycoming engine, you should roll to the left. In a Yak, Stampe, Tiger Moth or Chipmunk, it is most probable (but not inevitable – some have been modified) that the engine turns in the opposite direction, so you will find a roll to the right easier.

As you rapidly apply the aileron, it is crucial to take care over what you simultaneously do with the elevator. Indeed this is the most important part of the exercise. Ideally, you should find the 'neutral point' referred to above. This means moving the elevator just a bit further forward than it was after you stopped pulling up but before you started rolling. In this position, the wing's angle of attack is zero, so it produces no lift. Then there will be no heading change nor any adverse yaw.

You should do nothing with the rudder, but feel for the balance of the aircraft by feeling the sideways motion of your torso.

Note that in an aircraft without an inverted fuel system, the engine may stop running properly at close to zero alpha, and will certainly cough and splutter if you reach negative angles. This should not be of major concern; normal service will be resumed as soon as the roll is complete.

Look directly ahead as the aircraft rolls. You will see the nose dropping slowly straight down through the horizon. This is exactly what is required, so just keep the aileron input maintained and the elevator in the neutral point. At the fully inverted point, the nose should be on or still above the horizon.

The right hand picture of Diagram 10-2 shows the inverted position. Note whether you are still pointing directly at the landmark you chose as a heading reference.

Diagram 10-2

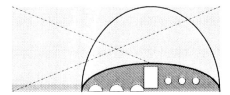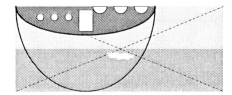

As the wings eventually come level at the end of 360° of roll, put the ailerons quickly to neutral, but do not pull back on the elevator yet. If you apply an angle of attack while you are still rolling, you will generate a heading change, and more out-of-balance forces because of increased adverse yaw.

Once you have fully stopped the roll, then you can ease gently out of the dive by releasing the slight forward stick pressure and adding a little back pressure.

During the recovery, look forward and check that you are still pointing towards the landmark you picked as a heading reference before pulling up. If you have a fixed-pitch propeller, monitor engine rpm during the pull-out and make throttle adjustments if necessary to avoid over-speeding.

In many high-performance aeroplanes, you can stop rolling very quickly, just by releasing the stick completely. In this way you can assess the roll damping and aileron inertia effects by seeing how quickly the roll stops and whether it overshoots a little in the process.

Error Analysis

If the nose is below the horizon after 180° of roll, then you are going to finish the roll in a dive that is steeper than was your initial climb. This is not a great concern, but the situation will be made worse if you apply any back elevator while inverted. So if you appear to be arcing towards the ground too quickly, maintain the slight forward pressure on the elevator control and re-check that you have full aileron applied.

If you finished the figure with a nose-down attitude steeper than the initial climb, and you rolled with maximum aileron all the time, the initial climb angle was not steep enough or the entry speed was too low. Next time start with a greater pitch up and a little more speed.

If the elevator position is at 'neutral point' during the roll, then your body will stay balanced in the centre of the seat.

If the elevator is not far enough forward, the aircraft will barrel positive and the out-of-balance force will move your torso to the same side of the fuselage as the direction of the roll. If the elevator is too far forward, the out-of-balance force will move your torso to the opposite side of the fuselage.

If the roll has been influenced by an inadvertent elevator input, it will be slightly 'barrelled' and the heading will change throughout. Even if you have barrelled the roll, you should be back on the original heading at the finish as long as the small elevator input was constant.

Think back to what you saw at the inverted stage. If you were rolling left and saw the landmark ahead slightly to your left, it means you were still applying some aft elevator during the roll. Diagram 10-3 shows this slight error as seen from the cockpit.

Diagram 10-3

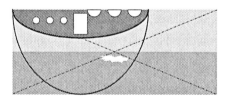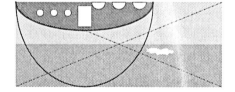

On Heading	**Aft Elevator Error**

Further Development

Once you are comfortable with the figure, explore it further to continue to educate both your hand and your bottom. While rolling with full aileron, make small forward and aft elevator movements a centimetre or so each way. Feel the change in the out-of-balance forces through your seat (Diagram 10-4). Learn precisely where the elevator neutral point is. This will help greatly in performing many more advanced figures.

Diagram 10-4

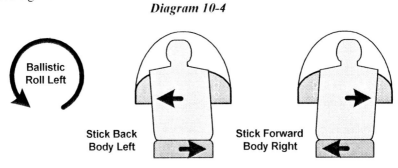

Ballistic Roll Left

Stick Back
Body Left

Stick Forward
Body Right

If you fly with a control column, not a yoke, you will probably find that at full aileron deflection the stick and your hand are resting in the inside of your thigh. Once you can find the neutral point consistently, note the exact spot on your leg where the stick touches it. You will be able to detect very small differences in stick position using this area, which is very sensitive to touch. Use this extra sense to become more consistent in all your rolling figures.

In a higher performance aircraft, you will find that with practice you can use more speed, a steeper initial climb and perform two, three or more complete rolls before stopping the figure. Repeat the figure, again paying particular attention to the elevator position while rolling, to ensure a constant heading throughout.

Flying in Competition

Aerobatic Catalogue

The ballistic roll as drawn and described above is not defined in the Aerobatic Catalogue and does not occur in Aresti-based competition flying.

Vertical Roll Affinity

Extending the ballistic trajectory to its extremes, however, produces a vertical line, either up or down. A vertical roll is in fact a ballistic roll, in that the angle of attack is zero throughout the roll. One of the key points of vertical rolling is maintaining zero alpha during the roll. This means putting the aileron control rapidly to full deflection while simultaneously putting the elevator control into the neutral point.

The exercise described in the section above on Further Development has great value in helping to determine the control column position for vertical rolling. It is one of the first things to do in preparing to fly vertical rolls in training and is also an excellent exercise to gain familiarity before performing vertical rolls in a new aircraft type.

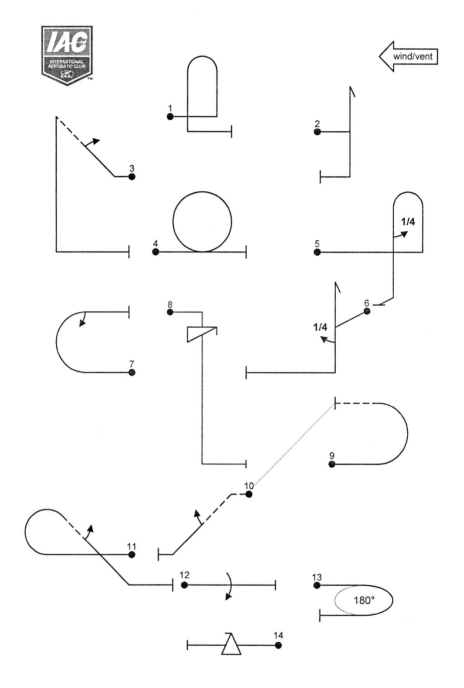

International Aerobatic Club (IAC), 1989
Intermediate Known Sequence

Steep Turns

Steep turns are some of the very first exercises to be completed in any aerobatic course.

They mark the extreme of the PPL handling syllabus, yet represent one of the most basic ways in which to extend any pilot's personal flight envelope.

In this chapter the steep turn will be treated as an aerobatic figure with a

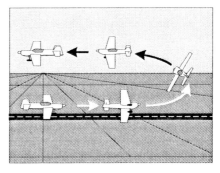

definition somewhat at variance with that taught for the PPL. This will provide an early instance of goal-setting in terms of aerial geometry, and will also introduce some new hand-and-foot co-ordination techniques.

The Flight Manoeuvre

Aerobatic Turns – A Definition

An aerobatic steep turn requires a constant bank angle of at least 60°, a constant turn rate and constant height. This definition implies that there must be no turn while the bank angle is being established, then the aircraft must turn at constant bank angle.

Lastly, the turn must stop, on heading, before the bank angle can be reduced to zero in level flight. This varies noticeably from regular PPL teaching wherein bank angle and turn rate increase together with the aircraft kept in balance. To fly the aerobatic definition, the aircraft must be deliberately flown out of balance while the bank is applied and then removed.

Ground References

For this figure you require a straight line ground reference. Fly the turns directly over the landmark so that you can monitor the aircraft's relative heading constantly.

Technique

Fly the aeroplane straight and level at cruise speed. Then roll on 60° of bank without changing heading. In order not to turn while the bank angle is applied, you must generate some fuselage lift by adding opposite rudder. You also need slightly to reduce the elevator back pressure to reduce wing lift. Diagram 11-1 shows an aircraft with a bank angle of 45° and shows the forces acting on it.

Diagram 11-1

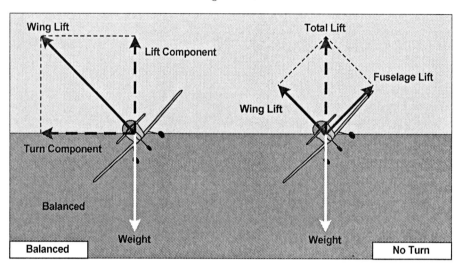

In the left picture, it is in a balanced turn. It is generating 1.7 times normal wing lift, which is resolved into a 1g lifting component (to stay level) and a 1g turning component. In the right hand picture, the aircraft is still flying straight and level as it passes through 45° of bank. The wings are generating 0.7g of lift and the fuselage is generating 0.7g of lift through the application of quite a lot of right rudder.

These two lift forces are combining to give 1g of lift vertically upwards. Depending on the aircraft type, some of the yaw needed to generate the fuselage lift will be provided by the adverse yaw caused by the aileron. The more adverse yaw a type has the less rudder will be needed initially to generate the fuselage lift.

Once you have set the bank angle, immediately apply back pressure to start the turn. At the same time remove the top rudder and apply a small amount of rudder with the turn to restore balance

Diagram 11-2 shows the aircraft at 60° of bank. The left picture shows the forces just before the turn starts. This needs 0.86g of fuselage lift and only 0.5g of wing lift to fly level.

The picture on the right shows the aircraft turning at 60° of bank. You apply enough back pressure to raise the wing lift from 0.5g to 2g. Simultaneously release the top rudder and apply a small amount of bottom rudder to balance the turn.

Diagram 11-2

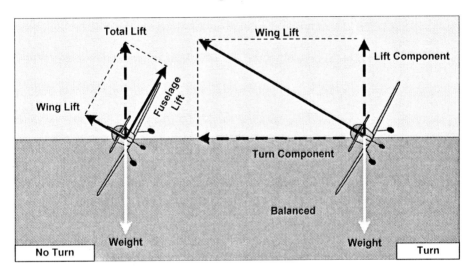

Make the change of elevator and rudder as quick and as smooth as you can. You can be sure the rudder is correct if your body is centred in the seat. Look over your shoulder into the turn and down toward the line feature.

Maintain all the control pressures until the fuselage becomes aligned with the heading for the end of the turn.

Now keep the bank at 60°, but immediately reverse the control inputs made on starting the turn. Relax the elevator back pressure to 0.5g and add top rudder to hold the height.

The aircraft will now fly straight and level. Smartly apply aileron to start the roll out. As you do so, you will initially need to increase the top rudder to account for the adverse yaw generated. As the wings come level, centre both the aileron and rudder controls

While turning, look primarily well into the turn, keeping a good look-out for other traffic while monitoring the progress of the turn in relation to the line feature. Spare only an occasional glance over the nose to re-check the attitude.

Diagram 11-3 shows the view ahead from a side-by-side trainer and from a tandem biplane, turning both left and right. Notice the improved symmetry in pictures C and D, and that the horizon is, in this case, parallel to one of the cabane struts that run from the fuselage longerons to the top wing.

Diagram 11-3

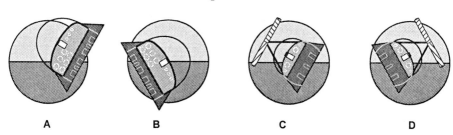

| A | B | C | D |

Error Analysis

The first likely error is to start turning while the bank angle is being applied, especially in aircraft that roll slowly. The key thing is to apply lots of aileron and at the same time let the stick forward a little. Using opposite rudder to help keep straight is also tricky at the start, because it goes against earlier training. The main thing is to be accurate, rather than energetic. It is not a race.

As you stop the roll and start the turn, you make quite noticeable elevator and rudder changes at the same time. It is crucial that as you apply the elevator quite smartly, you do not change the bank angle. This is seldom a problem in an aircraft with a control yoke, as you can use both hands to ensure you pull straight. In an aircraft with a stick, however, ergonomic problems can often arise when rapid movements are needed.

Diagram 11-4 shows the downward view inside the cockpit in an aeroplane with a stick. In the left picture, the dark stick tops shows how the stick should be moved to apply left aileron and simultaneously release back pressure.

Diagram 11-4

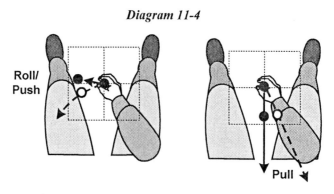

Roll/
Push

Pull

There is, however, a natural tendency for the right arm to move in more of a curve, shown as a dashed arrow, which adds back pressure at just the wrong time. Then when the elevator is applied more emphatically, the right arm has a tendency to pull in the direction of its elbow, not straight back towards the navel. The right picture shows how pulling in this direction will reduce the bank angle in a steep turn to the left. In both pictures, the white stick top shows the position that can easily be reached because of these simple ergonomic problems.

The elevator problem can have greater unwanted effects in a turn to the right, as it results in an increased bank angle. If the bank increases to 80° or more, height will be lost as a spiral dive starts. Recovery then has to be initiated by removing the bank and then raising the nose, thus stopping the turn exercise.

Take great care, in practising steep turns to the right, that you learn to pull straight back towards your navel, not towards your elbow.

Most pilots quickly learn to assess the point when the correct heading has been reached and recovery to level is appropriate. At this stage, however, the novice will forget to stop the turn and then remove the bank as two separate actions. The final error is usually to forget to apply extra top rudder to keep balance during the roll out.

Further Development

Stop/Start Turns

A good developmental exercise for improving all the co-ordination and timing skills is the Start/Stop turn. To do this, begin a steep turn as described above. After perhaps 90° of turn say out loud *"Stop-two-three-Start"*. On the first 'command', release the back pressure so the elevator is just forward of trimmed position and apply top rudder to maintain straight and level. Do NOT change the bank angle! On the word *"Start"*, re-apply the back stick and bottom rudder and go sharply back into the steep turn.

Repeat the Stop/Start process two or three times and then do *"Stop-two-Wings Level"* to finish. During the stop/starts, concentrate on being precise and consistent, not too aggressive. After becoming familiar with this trick, you will not in future have a problem separating *"Stop"* from *"Wings Level"*.

Fast-Rolling Aircraft

Modern trainers such as the Pitts S2 or CAP-10C have moderately high roll rates, around 270° per second. They also have some adverse yaw characteristics which are noticeable when applying aileron quickly.

In the quarter-of-a-second or so that it takes to establish the steep bank angle, the adverse yaw is enough to ensure that the aircraft stays straight initially. So rolling in to the turn will require little if any opposite (top) rudder. In these aircraft, make sure you do not over-do the top rudder as you roll on the bank. In any aeroplane that rolls faster than these, opposite rudder will not be needed at all. Just roll quickly to 60°, stop rolling, then apply the back pressure and a little bottom rudder.

Flying in Competition

Steep turns are flown in competition sequences from Basic/Beginners up to Intermediate. In this latter category, where aircraft are expected to have inverted fuel and oil systems, inverted turns are common, but these are dealt with in a later chapter. Diagram 11-5 shows some sample depictions from the Aerobatic Catalogue, Family 2. The fourth picture, the 90° turn is shown with a dashed line, indicating inverted flight.

Family 2 of the Catalogue also includes rolling turns, which are dealt with in "Inward Rolling Turns" on page 311.

Diagram 11-5

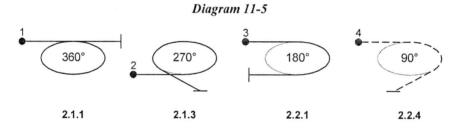

| 2.1.1 | 2.1.3 | 2.2.1 | 2.2.4 |

Varying the Radius of Turn

In a balanced 60° turn the radius is fixed and depends on the airspeed. At 70°, the radius is smaller, but it is still fixed by the airspeed. At a given airspeed, the largest radius balanced turn you can fly, and still comply with the definition of 'steep', is 60°. It is quite likely, in a contest flight, that you might want to fly a bigger radius to counter a nasty cross wind, but not be marked down for infringing the constant bank angle (minimum 60°), constant turn rate judging criteria.

You can do this, or you can fly a tighter radius than normal, by flying the turn out of balance.

Diagram 11-6 shows the plan view of three steep turns flown in still air. They are all started from the same spot at the same speed, and all have a bank angle of 60°. All meet all the judging criteria for a perfect competition turn. Balance is not included as a criterion, as it cannot be evaluated from the ground. The effect of being out of balance, when viewed externally, is just the same as the effect of a strong wind.

Diagram 11-6

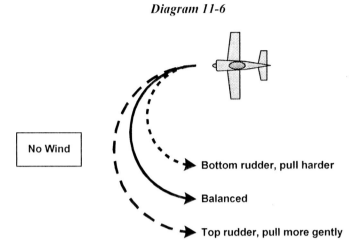

For the more technically minded, Diagram 11-7 shows the forces acting on two identical aircraft during balanced and unbalanced turns. The aircraft on the left is balanced (no fuselage lift). The aircraft on the right has a more complex situation. An imbalance has been caused by applying top rudder. The back pressure has been reduced to generate less wing lift.

The two forms of lift are combined to form a Total Lift vector. This is then resolved vertically (against gravity) and horizontally to determine the turn component. Compare the two pictures. Both have a vertical lift component equal to the weight, so fly level.

The unbalanced aircraft is generating about 1.35g of wing lift (as opposed to 2g when balanced) and about 0.35g of fuselage lift. Total lift is about 1.4g at about 45° to the vertical.

Diagram 11-7

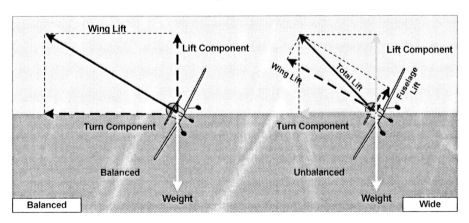

The unbalanced aircraft flies level in the turn, but the turn component is only about 60% of that in a balanced turn, giving a slower turn rate and therefore a larger radius. You can draw for yourself a similar picture showing fuselage lift in the opposite direction, increased winglift to compensate and a much larger turn component to give a tighter radius.

One result of the imbalance is increased drag and therefore more power required to sustain the figure. This technique can be readily exploited in an aircraft with plenty of surplus thrust.

The amount of imbalance sustainable in low-powered aircraft, might be quite small, and can only be determined by experimentation.

Sight-Line Issues

In a prolonged turn, the judges will see you from a variety of angles. At times it will be easy for them to assess your bank angle, at times hard. The problem points are when you are flying parallel to the judging line.

At the furthest point your bank angle will appear quite shallow, even if it is actually 60°. At the closest point the bank angle looks steeper than it really is (Diagram 11-8).

It will thus pay dividends if you increase the bank angle when you are furthest from the judges. It is less important to reduce the bank when close, as few judges get excited if you appear a bit steep, while they get to take a lot of points off if they think you are very shallow!

Diagram 11-8

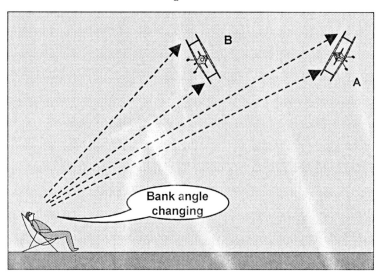

Energy Matters

If a turn is started from low speed it may be possible to accelerate as you turn. This is a good way of building energy, but not as good as accelerating with wings level. Delay the start of a turn, if it starts into wind, to build energy.

If you have a low-powered aircraft that will not accelerate during a turn, and if the next figure requires more entry speed than you will have after the turn is finished, then you have a problem to solve. You need to gain speed without the judges noticing. You can do this while turning, if you descend while tracking toward or away from the judging line.

Do not descend when parallel to this line. If the turn finishes on the B-axis, let the nose down slightly for the last 45° of the turn and then a little more once you have stopped. You may then have enough speed for, say, a level roll without your modifications being noticed. In any event, the K for a turn is small, so it is better to lose points for descending in the turn than to mess up the subsequent higher-K figure.

If a turn is started at high speed, for example after a stall turn, then you are likely to slow down during the turn because of high induced drag. So don't put such a combination in a Free Programme! To conserve energy in a high-speed turn, take a bigger radius if you can, so that you are not pulling so hard.

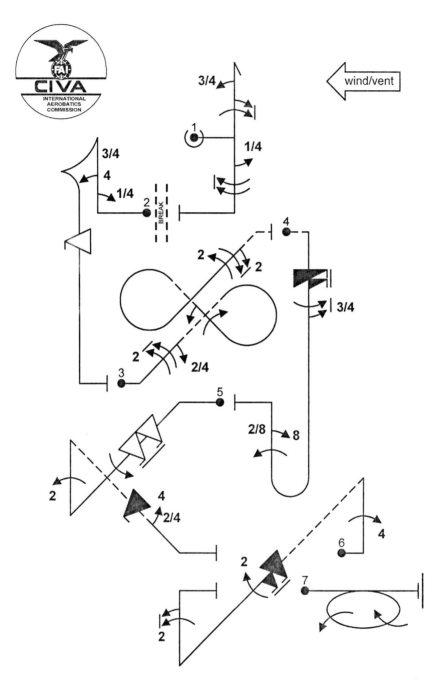

World Aerobatic Championships, 2000
Free Programme, Tom Cassells, UK

CHAPTER 12

45° Lines

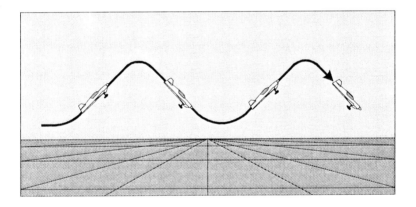

This chapter could equally be called 'Advanced Climbing and Descending'. The use of 45° as the defining attitude is arbitrary, but it is elegant, as it comes mid-way between level and vertical. Additionally, the 45° attitude is specified in many figures used in competition flying, wherein other round numbers, 30° or 60° are not used.

This section describes a training exercise that has a number of important objectives. These are to:

- determine rudder-neutral speed

- demonstrate gyroscopic yaw resulting from pitch changes

- fly close to V_{NE} and below V_{S1}

- accustom the student to looking sideways

- maintain balance using the seat of the pants.

Any aircraft authorized for aerobatic training is capable of flying 45° lines. In low-performance aircraft, however, the amount of time available on such a line will be limited, especially on a climbing line.

All the lessons can be learned flying 30° attitudes up and down. This may initially be more suitable for low powered aircraft, as it will allow more time for instructor patter and student comprehension. Once the pilot can fly consistently on 30° lines, 45° attitudes will become easily surmountable.

The Flight Manoeuvre

Fly a straight line, with the aircraft at all times in balance. Make progress by a series of climbing and descending lines. At the top and bottom of each line fly a smooth 90° looping segment to start the next line. Measure the climbing and descending lines by aircraft attitude, not flight path.

Ground References

Fly for several minutes in a straight line. Choose a major landmark in the far distance straight ahead as an aiming point. You will need a good horizon to the left, which is where you will look for the vast majority of the exercise. You might also try to arrange a good long-distance landmark below the horizon off the left wing tip.

Technique

Start straight and level at the maximum level speed for the aircraft. With a fixed-pitch propeller, this means at maximum continuous rpm. With a constant speed propeller, use climb power settings. Typically for a Lycoming engine this would be 2,500 rpm and full throttle above 3,000 feet.

Head towards the landmark. Take your feet off the rudders completely and notice that the slip ball goes out to the left (Lycoming engine). Confirm that your body is leaning slightly to the left also, following the motion of the slip ball. Keep your feet off the rudder for the first exercise. Look to the left wing tip and the horizon beyond.

Pull up smoothly but firmly to a climbing attitude of 45°. Check the wings remain level. As you pull up, gyroscopic precession will induce a yawing force. This will push both the slip ball and your body a little further to the left. Diagram 12-1 shows the view toward the left horizon in a 45° climbing attitude. If your aeroplane is fitted with a wing tip sighting device, the attitude will be somewhat easier to fix accurately. The gyroscopic force will dissipate as the pitch stops.

Established in the 45° climbing attitude, the aircraft will continue to slow down. The left out-of-balance will disappear as the engine and rudder trim effects come

Diagram 12-1

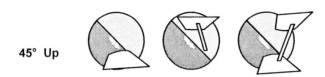

45° Up

into equilibrium. At a certain speed, the aircraft will be perfectly balanced. This is rudder neutral speed for this power and setting.

As the aircraft climbs and slows further it will start to yaw to the left (Lycoming engine). Do not correct this the first time you try the exercise, so that you determine the extent of the yaw that can occur. You must move the elevator progressively backwards to increase the angle of attack and maintain the 45° attitude. As the aircraft yaws left it will also try to roll in that direction as a result of the secondary effect of the rudder.

You must use right aileron to counter this tendency. Eventually, the torque effect from the engine will also try to roll the aircraft to the left and you must use more aileron to keep the wings level. As the aircraft approaches the critical angle of attack you will perceive the usual artificial and/or airframe warnings of an imminent stall.

Diagram 12-2

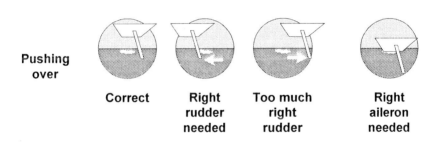

Pushing over

| **Correct** | **Right rudder needed** | **Too much right rudder** | **Right aileron needed** |

Just before the stall occurs, move the elevator control smoothly forward to the zero G, neutral point. The angle of attack will go to zero and engine P-factor will disappear, but now an induced gyroscopic force will start and that also will try to turn the aircraft to the left.

The extent of the gyroscopic force will depend on the relative weight of the propeller (metal propellers are usually heavier than equivalent wooden ones) and the engine rpm. If the aircraft has no inverted fuel system, maintain just a little positive G to keep the engine running properly: perhaps +¼g or thereabouts.

As you push and float gently over the top of the figure, the aircraft will continue to yaw left and will still need right aileron to keep the wings level (Diagram 12-2). Keep looking to the left and keep making the nose go down until you reach the 45° diving attitude (Diagram 12-3). As you stop on this attitude, the gyroscopic effect

Diagram 12-3

**45°
Down**

will disappear and the aircraft will start to accelerate rapidly downhill. Keep looking left to maintain the attitude. As rudder neutral speed is passed the aircraft will stop turning left and start to go out of balance in the other direction.

As the aircraft accelerates you will need to hold more forward stick pressure to prevent the aircraft coming out of the dive uncommanded, due to the effect of the elevator trim. Check airspeed and engine rpm to ensure the respective maxima are not exceeded. The aircraft will now be out of balance once again (the slip ball and your body to the left). Ease out of the dive and then back up into the 45° climbing attitude and start again.

By flying this exercise without any rudder inputs, you will learn the particular characteristics of each new aircraft type you fly: the respective rudder neutral speeds, the magnitude of the gyroscopic and torque effects. Repeat the exercise using the rudder to maintain balance. Learn to use your body, as you look outside, not the slip ball to monitor balance.

Develop the habit of looking out toward the wing tip nearly all the time, with just occasional scans for lookout. Avoid the temptation to stare straight ahead, especially on the climbing lines, as the visual feedback will give much less information than looking sideways. Once per cycle, you can re-check your heading by looking at the landmark ahead, but the primary reference for keeping straight at all times should be the landmark off the wing tip. You can see this all the time.

Error Analysis

Attitude Errors

The principal attitude error is not to achieve and maintain the target pitch attitudes. On the climbing line, keep moving the elevator control slowly backwards or the natural trim effect will be for the nose to gradually drop below the target position. Most pilots initially have trouble setting 45° nose down, because they are unfamiliar with this steep diving attitude. You must select this attitude confidently and briskly. If you delay in achieving it, speed will increase too much too soon and pushing down will require more negative G.

While descending, the natural effect of elevator trim is to raise the nose once the trimmed speed has been passed. Maintain increasing forward stick position to hold the 45° down line against the trimmer, being careful not to exceed maximum dive speed.

A secondary attitude problem is failure to keep the wings level at all times. This stems from two sources.

You must pull and push the elevator control centrally back and forward. There is a natural tendency to add inadvertent aileron inputs when pulling and pushing, due to the angle between the pilot's arm to the aircraft centre line. Usually novices add right aileron when pulling and left aileron when

Diagram 12-4

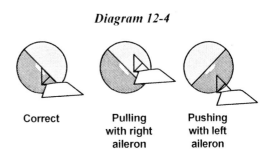

Correct   Pulling with right aileron   Pushing with left aileron

pushing. Diagram 12-4 shows the results of these errors pictorially.

The second source of bank errors is the torque effect from the engine at low speed. Correction is natural, but uncommanded roll rates can be quite high in aircraft with powerful engines and short wings (eg Pitts biplanes).

Direction Errors

Direction errors come from inability to keep the aircraft in balance. Practice will make things better. Avoid the temptation of looking often at the slip ball. This will cause you to lose precise control of the pitch attitude as you look away from the wing tip.

Learn to judge balance and make rudder corrections using the feel from your torso and seat. Your body works just like a slip ball.

Further Development

An excellent advanced development of this exercise is to add half rolls on the climbing and descending lines. It is described fully in "Half Rolls on 45° Lines" on page 165.

Flying in Competition

Diagram 12-5

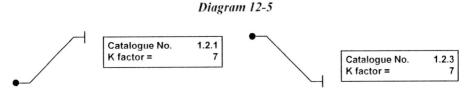

| Catalogue No. | 1.2.1 |
| K factor = | 7 |

| Catalogue No. | 1.2.3 |
| K factor = | 7 |

Forty five degree lines have many applications in contest aerobatic figures. The un-embellished (vanilla) lines are also flown as simple figures in Sportsman/Standard category sequences, where they can help with speed and energy management in order to minimize the advantages of high-performance aircraft (Diagram 12-5).

The judging criteria do not require that the two looping radii are the same, but they must be internally consistent. The attitude during the climbing/descending segment must be exactly 45° from vertical. The horizontal lines flown at the beginning and end must be on a horizontal flight path.

Very few judges are concentrating much on the radii. Radius changes are unlikely to be spotted. They will concentrate on the 45° attitude, and on the level flight paths. The transition from level to inclined should be made briskly with sharp but precise movements of the elevator.

Notice that when pulling up to a 45° at high speed, the attitude change is likely to be of the order of 40°. This is because the angle of attack at high speed is relatively low, perhaps about 5°. During the low speed level segments, however, angle of attack will be high, perhaps around 15°. Thus the extent of the pitch change when levelling off from a climb is only around 30°.

When starting the downward 45° line, the pitch change will be about 55° to 60°. That is from 10° to 15° nose up to 45° nose down. When coming level at the bottom, the attitude change is about 50°, from 45° down to plus 5° alpha. Failure to understand these different pitch change magnitudes often leads to shallow 45° down lines, and excessive sink after levelling off in the climbing figure.

Energy Matters

The 45° climbing line can be started at surprisingly low speed. In Sportsman Free sequences it is always a useful figure to put before a spin entry as it converts any surplus speed to height. Slowing down in level flight for a spin entry is throwing away energy for no good purpose.

The 45° down line usually precedes a high entry speed figure in Standard/ Sportsman sequences. The amount of height lost for a given exit speed can be minimized by accelerating level before pushing down. The down line is then shorter, but the next figure will be started higher than if speed were reduced before going down. Pushing down to 45° from cruise speed, however, generally requires about -2.5g to -3g (negative) and will cause engine problems in aircraft without inverted fuel systems.

CHAPTER 13

Wingovers

Along with steep turns, Wingovers are some of the very first exercises to be completed in any aerobatic course. They take over from where the PPL handling syllabus stops, in terms of increased climb, descent and bank angles. Only occasionally is a wingover flown as an end in itself, for example in entry-level glider aerobatic competitions.

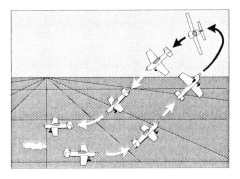

The most common use of the wingover is as an exercise to teach spatial orientation, control co-ordination and angle-of-attack management. If flown properly, it forces you to concentrate your field of view away from the straight ahead direction.

Airmanship

Lookout during unusual attitudes. Control co-ordination. Understanding the wing lift vector and monitoring angle of attack.

The Wing Lift Vector

The wing lift vector, which I shall just call the lift vector in this chapter, is the instantaneous representation of the second-by-second function of the wing/ elevator system in producing lift.

During the exercises described in this chapter, try to develop the ability to imagine the direction and effect of the lift vector at all times.

Diagram 13-1

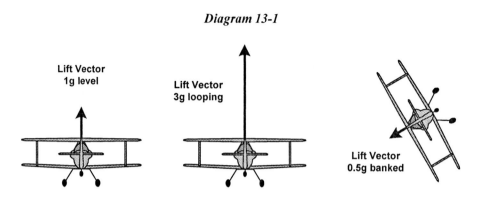

Diagram 13-1 shows three rear-view images of the same biplane, but with different lift vectors.

The left picture represents straight and level. The middle picture shows the aircraft at the start of a loop with 3g applied. The increase in lift generated is shown by the increased length of the arrow. The right picture shows the aircraft banked at 120° and pulling 0.5g. This is typical of the configuration that might be achieved at the apex of a steep wingover.

Note that lift is always generated at right angles to the axis of the wings. This effectively means that the nose will always travel in the direction of the lift vector when elevator is applied. Conversely, to see where the aircraft will go when you apply up elevator, you must look directly up, out of the top of the canopy, even if that means looking towards the ground!

It is also important to remember the relationship between airspeed, angle of attack and lift generating capacity. The wing can always generate lift as long as it has forward speed, however slow it might be going. The amount of lift that can be generated is proportional to the square of the airspeed.

The minimum speed at which it can generate 1g of lift is what is conventionally called the 'stalling speed'. Because of the speed-squared function, at twice this speed the aircraft can generate 4g of lift.

At 70% of the stalling speed, say 42 knots for an aircraft with a 60 knot stalling speed, the wing can still generate 0.5g of lift before stalling.

When flying any figure during which the speed is varying greatly, such as a wingover or a loop, learn to appreciate where your lift vector is pointing, and what its maximum length can be without stalling.

Remember that stick position is a direct measure of angle of attack, whereas stick force is just an indication of how far the current state is from the trimmed state.

The Flight Manoeuvre

The figure has five basic segments consisting of:

- a pull up from level flight
- a climbing section
- a turn which starts climbing and ends descending
- a descending section
- the recovery to level flight.

The angles of climb and descent, the bank angle during the turn and the overall change of heading are all unspecified. You can set a wide range of target values for each of these parameters. Initially, climbing and descending at 30° may be enough, with 60° of bank at the apex and a heading change of only 45°. Conversely, the climb and descent may be as steep as 60°, the bank angle 120° and the change of heading a full 180°.

The targets set will depend both on the pilot's experience level and the aircraft's capabilities. The important thing is to make sure a reachable target is set and that an objective post-figure assessment is made to determine the accuracy of the figure flown.

Ground References

The ground reference for this figure is a point feature. Choose something that is not too big, but can be easily identified – a characteristic farm complex, for example, or a motorway bridge, or a small lake. The point you pick is going to be your aiming point for the descent phase of the figure. The idea is a bit like making a ground attack strafing run against your chosen target.

The accuracy with which you can place this object in your windscreen during the dive is the measure of success.

The target should be at least 45° to left or right and perhaps three kilometers away if you are flying at about 3,000 feet. Later, you can choose points at 90° (off the wing tip) or behind the wing. Ultimately you could find a target almost hidden by the tail-plane for a 180° reversal.

Technique

Throughout the figure, keep your attention overwhelmingly on the ground target reference. Use as little time as possible to check the various flight parameters and to keep a more general lookout. Entry speed can be normal cruise speed, or faster, depending on the size of the planned figure. The greater the planned heading change, the longer the climbing-turning-descending phase is going to last and the more height is going to be gained and lost. The entry speed would have to be correspondingly greater.

After checking it is clear ahead and above, look at the target and then pull the nose up into the desired climbing attitude. Apply full power as permitted without over speeding the engine. As the aircraft slows you will need more angle of attack (stick back) to maintain the climb and some right rudder (Lycoming engine) to maintain balance.

Once steady in the climb, smoothly roll on the required bank angle, and keep the turn coordinated. Keep looking at the target.

During the turn, speed will continue to decay. You can allow the nose to start dropping as you progress towards the apex. At the highest point you should have completed half the turn. During this low speed part of the figure you must remember lift vector and maximum available lift. You must not stall during the turn, so you must not pull the elevator control back to the stalling position. Do not try to hold the nose up, you want it to go down for the descending segment.

Even if the indicated airspeed falls below the conventional 1g 'stalling speed', you need not stall as long as you keep your demand for lift proportionally less than 1g. This just means releasing back pressure on the elevator control and letting the nose gently go down.

Once past the apex, speed will increase and you can concentrate on finishing the turn on the target heading. Aim to reach wings level again, directly on target and with the descent angle approximately the same as the previous climb angle. As you approach the start height, begin a smooth recovery to level flight. Reduce power as necessary to avoid engine overspeed.

Error Analysis

The only criterion I have defined for this figure is the heading during the descent and exit. If you are not on this heading at the end, you must try to work out why. The most likely reason for being off-heading is that you lost sight of the ground feature at a critical moment during the turning phase. So keep looking at the target while you are turning.

Turning depends on having a bank angle and using the elevator. If you have undershot the target heading, then next time use more bank angle and a little more back-pressure. Remember, though, the stalling position for the elevator control and be sure not to pull through it.

Even if you achieve the target heading, the figure is not error-free unless you also were in balance the entire time. While you are looking out, try to maintain balance by keeping your body centred on your seat. Your body works in just the same way as the slip ball.

Further Development

In a basic aerobatic training aircraft, with a typical roll rate of 180° per second or less, and with relatively little vertical penetration, most pilots will be content with wingovers that have 90° of bank at the apex and heading changes of 90° to 120°. In aircraft with higher roll rates, typically 240° per second or more, a more dynamic wingover can safely be flown.

In this figure, the technique more closely resembles a military ground attack profile and places particular emphasis on the placing of the lift vector during the turning phase.

In all cases, this more exaggerated technique requires bank angles in excess of 90° and high turn rates. Diagram 13-2 shows five snapshot views during a high performance wingover.

Diagram 13-2

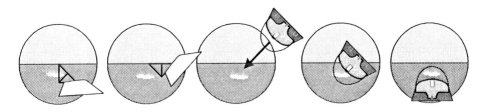

The first two pictures show the target lake just behind the wing tip during level flight and then during a 45°climb. The middle picture shows how to roll the aircraft so that the lift vector is pointing at the target. In this case the bank angle is 135°. This bank angle should be achieved as quickly as possible, using a large aileron deflection, and without very much turn.

Once established at this bank angle, all that is needed to acquire the target is back pressure on the elevator until the position shown in the fourth picture is flown. Stay aware always of your elevator control position and thus of your angle of attack. Do not stall the wing by bringing the elevator too far back.

Notice the nose is now below the horizon. The aircraft has changed from climbing to descending. Once the target is directly ahead, in the windscreen remove all back pressure on the elevator so that the lift vector shrinks to nothing. Roll the aircraft back to wings level as quickly as possible, using rudder in the same direction as the aileron to maintain balance.

Flying in Competition

The only competition application of the wingover is in some
lower category glider sequences
(Diagram 13-3). In this case the
bank angle at the apex is pre-
scribed as being 90°. The figure
is used to produce a full 180°
heading change, a turn-around
figure.

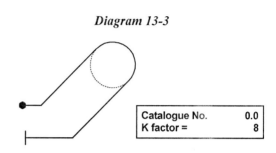

Diagram 13-3

Catalogue No.	0.0
K factor =	8

The direction of the turn is not specified and, in gliders, the direction of rotation of the engine is not a consideration!

Practice so you can fly the figure with equal grace and precision to both left and right. On the day, choose the direction based on any cross wind component to or from the judging line. This probably means turning into the cross wind component to maintain position. Sometimes, though, it may mean turning with a tail wind component so as to increase the distance travelled on the B-axis.

CHAPTER 14

Barrel Rolls

Gentle Misconceptions

The Barrel Roll is every new aerobatic pilot's idea of a simple, gentle figure. Something you could do with Mum in the other seat on a quiet Sunday after church and before lunch. Yet it is subject to more misconceptions than probably any other manoeuvre, and has led to the demise of a number of display pilots, both the highly experienced and the less so.

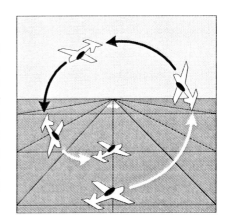

Many books have left the story only half told. This one should fill any such gaps.

Airmanship

During this figure, the aircraft should not approach closely to any edge of the speed-loading (V-g) envelope. In aircraft with fixed-pitch propellers, the entry and exit speeds may require care in engine handling to prevent over-speeding. Looking out towards the direction of roll, not straight ahead, is important to maintain area clearance.

The Flight Manoeuvre

During the barrel roll, the aircraft is both pitching and rolling at the same time. There is no universal definition, however, of the flight path to be followed nor of the quantitative relationship between the amounts of elevator and aileron controls to be applied. A loop with some aileron applied will lead to a crooked loop, but this will have all the attributes of a barrel roll. Similarly, a ballistic roll with some elevator input will give a 'barrelled' roll, which not surprisingly also has the attributes of a barrel roll.

In concept, the figure is a roll with constant application of elevator in one sense, usually aft (nose up). Bear in mind for further development, however, that the figure can be flown under negative G throughout, with the elevator always deflected in the forward sense (nose down). Height and heading at the conclusion of the figure should be the same as at the start. The aircraft should be in balance throughout.

Angle-Off

During the figure, the aircraft will roll through 360°. It will climb to be inverted at the highest point, before descending while coming upright again. At the inverted position it will be significantly off heading from the start, but it will finish upright and back on heading.

This difference in heading from upright to inverted will be referred to as the 'Angle-Off' for the figure. Its value is variable, typically 60° or 90°, and (should be) under the pilot's control. In training, it should be agreed between instructor and student before starting the figure.

Ground References

Because of the pitch input, the vanishing point of the roll axis is on the horizon but displaced to one side in the direction of the coming roll. This central reference point will be on a relative bearing of half the angle-off from directly ahead. In the heading picutre, the reference point is indicated by a lake close to the horizon.

What the Pilot Sees

Diagram 14-1 shows what the aircraft's occupants see, looking left toward the off-centre axis. It can be misinterpreted to show that the aircraft is at its highest at Point 2. This is incorrect, as we will see shortly, and this illustration must be taken solely for what it represents – *what you see from the cockpit looking generally forward and into the roll.*

Diagram 14-1

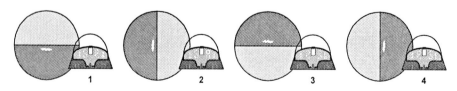

At Point 1 the aeroplane is flying straight and level at the entry speed given in the flight manual. It may have been necessary to dive to achieve this speed. While gaining the entry speed, it is important to also achieve a heading that places the primary landmark at half of the angle-off to the side in the rolling direction.

Some short time later the aeroplane will be at a 90° bank angle and climbing, Point 2. Note that the landmark is still displaced to the pilots's left by half the angle-off and this angle is also a measure of the nose above the horizon.

As it continues rolling, the aeroplane will gradually reach the inverted position. Because positive G is being maintained, the nose is now coming down through the horizon, Point 3. When the wings come to the second knife-edge position, the nose will be as low as its going to get, Point 4.

Finally the aircraft will arrive back again at Point 1.

To understand this description more fully, look at the figure from another viewpoint.

What Others might See

Diagram 14-2

To see the figure from another viewpoint imagine you
are watching from outside,
behind the aircraft and
looking directly along the
start heading. To follow this,
look at Diagram 14-2, which
has the same key positions
marked with the same
numbers.

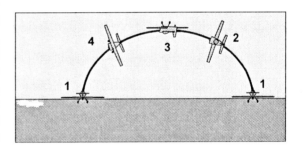

As the figure starts, the aeroplane will climb and bank towards Point 2. In knife edge the first time, it is higher than at the start. From Point 2 to Point 3 the nose is still above the horizon and the aircraft climbing. Point 3 is actually the highest point, where, by laws of energy exchange, the airspeed will also be slowest.

Look at Diagram 14-1 again carefully, and be sure you understand why Point 3 is the highest position, it is crucial to performing a good symmetrical roll.

Rolling and pulling gently from Point 3 to Point 4 the aircraft starts to descend so that its height at Point 4 is the same as at Point 2. Finally it returns to Point 1, straight and level on the original heading, but displaced laterally. The drawing at Diagram 14-2 is what led Eric Müller, in his book *Flight Unlimited*, to call the figure 'a tunnel roll' as opposed to a barrel roll. Diagram 14-3 shows this same left barrel roll seen from directly above.

You will see that, at the end of the roll, the aeroplane is back on the original heading but that its track is now displaced distinctly to one side. It is now running parallel to, not in line with, the original flight path. In this case the angle-off, at Position 3, is 70°. The aircraft is headed directly toward the lake in Positions 2 and 4. The 'tunnel' projection is shown in the upper part.

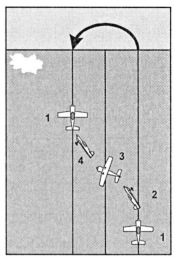

Diagram 14-3

Different Viewpoints

To resolve the two descriptions, and see why they are both correct, look at Diagram 14-4. This is the top view of the aeroplane's sinuous track as it completes three barrel rolls in a row. Each time it is inverted it has an angle-off of 90°.

Seen by someone watching along the original heading, white arrow A, there are three of Müller's tunnel entrances. But seen by someone looking along arrow B, at 45° to the original heading (half the angle-off), the picture is greatly different. Now the aeroplane appears to fly a helical flight path, from left-to-right at the bottom and right-to-left at the top. Now it might just look like a barrel.

Diagram 14-4

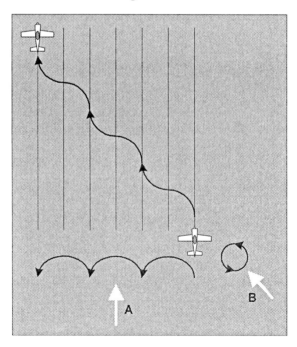

Different Angles

In the figures illustrating the barrel roll, I have shown the aircraft with varying amounts of heading change when inverted. The angle-off is infinitely variable at the pilot's discretion. It is controlled by the amount of elevator back pressure applied during the period when the wings are close to the knife-edge position. Because it is here that pulling gives the greatest amount of turn.

A certain amount back pressure might give a 60° angle-off, less might give 30°. It follows therefore that zero back pressure would give a roll with no heading change at all: as described in "Ballistic Rolls" on page 99.

It is important to decide what approximate angle-off you are aiming at before starting the roll. This gives a criterion against which to determine your accuracy during post-figure analysis.

Technique

At Point 1, the aircraft is fast and the ailerons at their most effective. Use only partial deflection to have a chance of keeping a constant roll rate throughout. At this time stick forces are at their highest and a lot of effort is needed on the elevator to generate the required pitch rate. Start with a 2g to 3g pull and apply just enough aileron to set a roll rate you can maintain.

Monitor the bank angle carefully, but look primarily toward the visual reference point on the horizon at half the angle-off. By the time the bank angle has reached 90°, you must have pitched enough to be pointing directly toward the landmark, with the nose half the angle-off above the horizon. In other words, if the angle-off is 60°, at Point 2 you must be 30° nose high and have changed the heading by 30°.

Speed is now reducing quite quickly. The ailerons are becoming less effective and the stick forces lighter. The roll rate should stay constant, but the pitch rate must reduce. From Point 2 to Point 3, increase the aileron input to maintain roll rate, and at the same time greatly reduce the back pressure so that the aircraft 'floats' over the top at perhaps 0.5g and a low pitch rate.

From Point 2 to Point 3 the climb angle has been reducing, seen from inside the cockpit by the nose descending toward the horizon.

It is absolutely essential that the wings are level in the inverted position (180° of roll) by the time the nose actually cuts down through the horizon. With less than this amount of roll the figure is bound to lose height overall and exit speed will be much higher.

As we descend from Point 3, through Point 4 back to Point 1 again, the speed will be increasing. So now the aileron input must be reduced and the back pressure once more increased to get a symmetrical roll. Add enough back pressure to ensure that the aircraft is once again pointing directly at the landmark at Point 4, and returns to its original heading on completion of the roll. Remember to reduce the aileron deflection once you have left the inverted position, so that there is time available to make the required heading changes and the roll rate remains constant.

Throughout, rudder should be used to keep the aircraft balanced. Because adverse yaw is proportional to angle of attack, the rudder input needed is generally highest when the back pressure is highest, and least when you float at lower angle-of-attack over the top.

Error Analysis

The first likely error is not to pull enough at the beginning, so that the nose does not get high enough above the horizon.

Remember that in a roll with 60° angle-off, the nose must be 30° above the horizon after 90° of roll. In other words, the nose must be the same distance above the distant landmark as it was beside it initially (Diagram 14-5, Picture 2 shows an error here). As you climb and roll, watch the nose and the landmark and use enough back pressure to make sure that these two references stay the same distance apart.

The second likely mistake is to achieve less than 180° of roll by the time you get to the highest point, as shown in Picture 3. This is a critical error as it means you will finish low and fast. The view from behind is shown in Diagram 14-6. Not achieving this 'gate' attitude has resulted in a number of fatal air show accidents. So be aware and fly high.

The cause of the error is to maintain too much back pressure, so that the rate of pitch does not reduce as the aileron effectiveness reduces. It is essential to slow the pitch rate by moving the control column further forward and to increase the aileron deflection to take account of the lower speed at the highest point. Having made this correction, the view will now be as in Picture 3a (Diagram 14-5).

Fight the temptation to pull back on the stick if things seem not to be going right; that is exactly the opposite of the proper correction.

Diagram 14-5

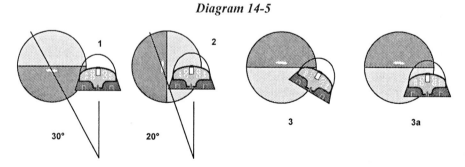

If the key inverted position is achieved correctly, then the chance of a major error thereafter is much reduced. The main point here is not to rush to a conclusion. The second half should take just as long as the first. Slowly apply more back pressure as you descend so that the landmark is directly ahead after 270° of roll and the nose 30° below the horizon (60° angle-off).

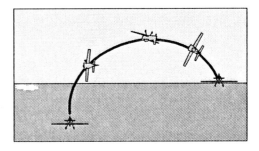

Diagram 14-6

Balance errors are not really significant from a geometrical point of view. One of the aims for this figure, however, is to develop roll/rudder co-ordination, so balance is important for this reason and also to maintain comfort.

With a right-turning engine, both p-factor and slipstream effect will help maintain balance by countering adverse yaw when barrel-rolling to the left. Accordingly, the left rudder inputs required to maintain balance will be fairly small. Rolling right, however, these effects will be anti-balance and so the right rudder inputs required to keep both your body and the slip-ball centred will be significantly more than when going left.

Further Development

During training, set precise goals for the angle-off and strive to meet them. Aim eventually to be able to fly the figure to a 90° heading change, rolling either left or right.

When you can fly the symmetrical roll consistently, vary the exercise to illustrate further aspects of the geometry. For example, from the inverted position, maintain full aileron deflection and move the elevator control even further forward to the zero G position (neutral point). Complete the figure with half a ballistic roll and the heading should not change further.

Note that the roll finishes at a higher altitude than it started, slower and a bit nose down.

This 'push and roll' recovery is always the safest route if orientation is lost when inverted, so this is a good technique to have in your repertoire. One day it may save considerable embarrassment.

Outside Barrel Rolls

Outside barrel rolls can be a great deal of fun, with relatively low negative G, once the pilot is proficient at climbing, descending and turning in prolonged inverted flight.

This is an excellent advanced training exercise, both for developing roll/rudder co-ordination and spatial orientation under negative G loading. Diagram 14-7 shows a familiar pattern, but this time with the aircraft performing an outside barrel roll to the left.

Diagram 14-7

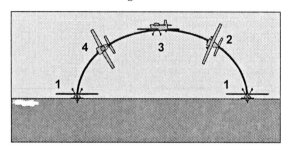

Diagram 14-8 shows the pilot's-eye views during this same roll. Notice that while rolling left, the pilot's field of view is to his right, toward the landmark. Right rudder will be needed to maintain balance while rolling left. Point 3 is again the highest, this time the aircraft floating canopy up while still maintaining about minus 0.5g. A gentle hump-backed bridge!

Always keep the angle between straight ahead and the line of sight to the landmark constant, at half the angle-off.

Diagram 14-8

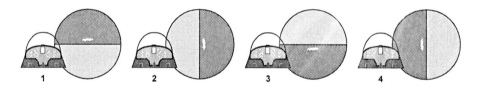

Hesitation Barrel Rolls

If you want a different, but interesting, challenge, try a 4-point barrel roll. You will need more speed than normal at the beginning. At the first and third points, you will be climbing or descending in knife edge and you must unload the back pressure to stay briefly on heading. The middle stop will be straight and level inverted and a very good illustration of the achieved angle-off. Forget eight points; it's too messy.

Flying in Competition and Displays

The barrel roll is not included in the Aerobatic Catalogue and is not used in Aresti style competition sequences. This is because of the lack of an agreed definition of the geometry.

It is often used in display and Freestyle sequences. In its basic form, the barrel roll's flexibility of rate and angle can be exploited to make different wind corrections without spoiling the flow of figures.

It can be flown with a flick roll placed at the highest point, just as a flick is added to a loop to make an avalanche or Porteous Loop. Fractions of barrel rolls can be combined with parts of other figures to form a wide range of graceful shapes to assist with changing axes or to set up an entry position for a more complex or dynamic manoeuvre. Some combination figures that are part loop, part barrel roll, are described in "Clovers" on page 137.

Diagram 14-9 shows a simple barrel roll as it may be flown as part of a display sequence. The figure has an angle-off of 70°.

Diagram 14-9

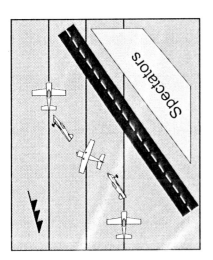 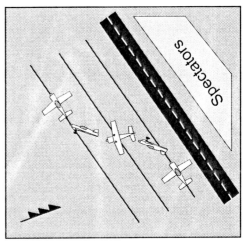

In the left picture, the wind is more or less straight down the display axis. The roll starts and finishes flying towards the crowd line at an angle of 35°. At the apex, the flight path is 35° away from the crowd. The centre of the barrel, the sight line from the cockpit to the landmark, is parallel to the display axis, shown typically as a runway.

In the right picture, the wind is on-crowd. Now the roll starts parallel to the crowd line and separation is maintained or even increased. Note that the 'tramlines' showing the roll axis are now closer together, because of the cross wind component.

In *Flight Unlimited,* Eric Müller describes how, in line abreast formation, the following aircraft can barrel roll from one wing tip to the other. He also uses this to support his nomenclature of tunnel roll, not a barrel roll. But it is possible to fly a barrel roll completely around the leader by adopting a different start position.

I have seen Nigel Lamb do this in an Extra 300 around a pair of mirror formation Pitts S-2As, and very impressive it looks too.

The key to this formation manoeuvre is shown in Diagram 14-10.

The white aircraft rolls around the black one, which flies straight and level, parallel to the crowd line. The white aircraft starts directly below the black and on a different heading equal to half the angle-off. Inverted, he is higher than the leader; when the white plane is in climbing and descending knife edge, the two aircraft have the same heading.

Diagram 14-10

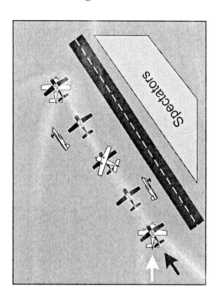

CHAPTER 15

Clovers

Imagine four looping circles in the sky, the angles between them 90°. The aircraft flows gracefully from one circle into the next on a windless day, trailing a lazy trail of smoke into an intricate pattern as it goes.

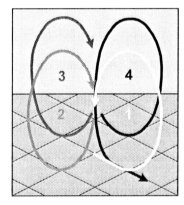

A Clover starts with the white loop (1) In the descending half, the aircraft subtly changes heading through 90°. Each successive loop has been drawn in a darker shade of grey than the last, with the last (4) being completely black.

It takes a lot longer to fly than to describe, but is a wonderful exercise for improving co-ordination and spatial orientation. It is much easier to comprehend when broken into four quarters. The key is understanding how to make a 90° heading change in a half loop, and in fact this has already been described ("Barrel Rolls" on page 127).

Airmanship

Maintain lookout at all times, but especially look up before pulling up. Monitor airspeed and engine rpm closely in descending flight to ensure you do not exceed limits. Fly the aircraft with grace and precision.

The Flight Manoeuvre – Quarter Clover

The quarter clover is a combination of half a loop and half a barrel roll. Like the half Cuban eight, it can be flown in either of two ways: rolling in the climbing

Diagram 15-1

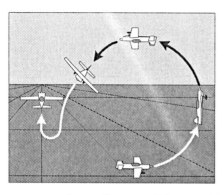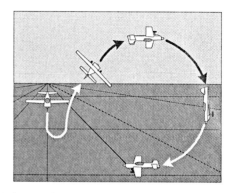

part or the descending part. Diagram 15-1 shows (the left picture), a quarter clover rolling down and, on the right, one rolling up.

Quarter Clover Down

The left hand picture of Diagram 15-2 shows the plan view, looking down, of an aircraft flying a quarter clover with the roll going down. The grey area at the top of the drawing shows the profile of the figure looking horizontally.

To fly this figure, choose a heading at 90° to a prominent line feature, shown in Diagram 15-2 as a railway line. Point 1 in the figure shows the aircraft before crossing the line feature. Once past the line, directly below Point 3 in the diagram, fly a normal half-loop to the inverted position. Point 2 shows the aircraft in the

Diagram 15-2

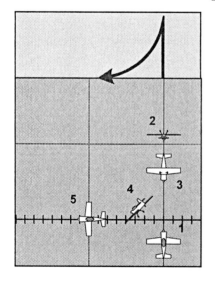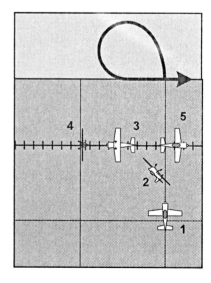

vertically-climbing part of the half-loop. As the nose starts to come below the horizon start rolling at the normal rate for a barrel roll. Put your head right back as far as it will go and look through the top of the canopy for the railway line.

Continue on the downward path as for the second half of a normal barrel roll, blending the aileron and elevator inputs smoothly together to finish above, or at least parallel to, the railway line. At Point 4 the aircraft is 45° nose down and half way through the 90° heading change, still rolling left. At Point 5 the figure is complete.

Quarter Clover Up

The right hand picture of Diagram 15-2 shows the plan view of an aircraft flying a quarter clover with the roll on the upward part.

To fly this figure, start on the same heading as before. Start the figure just before flying overhead the railway line, but be sure to be looking directly at the line feature off the wing tip toward the horizon. Fly the first half of a barrel roll, aiming for a 90° angle off. This means a 45° climb at Point 2 in the figure, where the bank angle is 90°. Keep watching the distant point along the line feature and use a lot of back pressure when the wings are vertical to ensure that the 90° heading change is achieved.

As you relax the back pressure and increase the ailerons at the top of the figure, tilt your head back to confirm you are directly above, and parallel to, the railway line. As the wings come level inverted, centralize the aileron control and continue to float into the second half of a normal loop.

Watch the railway line all the way down and use ailerons to maintain the correct heading as you increase the pull.

Half and Half

This is a further extension of the half-barrel roll idea, and is a useful final exercise in this series of figures. It is not, however, a clover leaf but more of an extreme wing-over. It fits well here because it follows on from the two figures just described.

The task is to fly a complete barrel roll, but to change the direction of roll at the highest point. Achieve a 90° angle-off and you will perform a very neat, graceful and satisfying turn-around figure. Diagram 15-3 shows the now familiar plan view of the figure and should need relatively little explanation.

Diagram 15-3

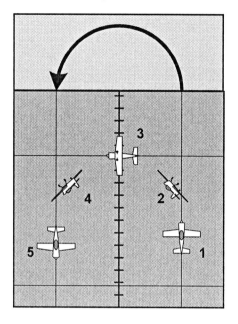

To fly the geometry shown, complete a half barrel roll left, changing heading by 90°. As you float through the inverted position at the highest point, reverse the ailerons, changing rudder at the same time to maintain balance. Continue the downward half barrel roll to the right.

Note from Diagram 15-3 that this is best flown initially parallel to, and then across, the line feature. When inverted, keep your head well back to maintain eye contact with the railway.

Flying in Competition

Like the plain barrel roll, none of these figures is included in the Aerobatic Catalogue, at least for powered aircraft.

The two quarter clover figures, rolling up or down, are used in Glider aerobatic sequences, in the UK, America and possibly elsewhere, in the Sports(man) and Intermediate categories (Diagram 15-4).

In the UK, two non-Aresti categories of contest are held. These are called Apprentices and Masters. They are flown by pilots qualified in the Intermediate and Advanced categories respectively. These sequences sometimes use various clover combinations.

Diagram 15-4

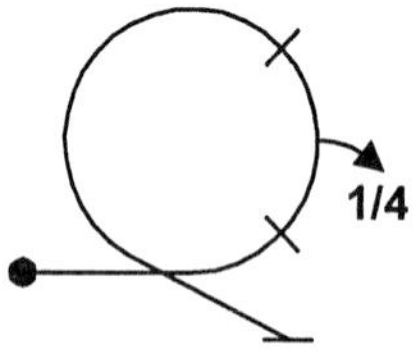

| Catalogue No. | 0.1 |
| K factor = | 16 |

CHAPTER 16

Loops

The Loop is one of the most fundamental aerobatic figures. No aeroplane, nor any pilot for that matter, can claim to be 'aerobatic' lest he can perform this basic shape.

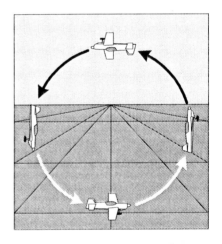

Looping is equally a fundamental part of many other figures that form part of the aerobatic repertoire. Ignoring figures that also involve rolling or turning, there are still many different types of looping figures created by inserting straight sections between the pitching segments.

These might be called 'hesitation' loops, but are generally referred to by the modified shape overall: P-loops, square loops, diamond loops, octagonal loops and so on.

Pilots must understand not just how to fly a loop accurately, but also the forces acting on the aircraft during the loop and how the likely errors are generated.

The Flight Manoeuvre

The basic requirement of a loop is 360° of pitch, with no rolling or yawing. A secondary aim is keeping the aircraft in balance. Even though you achieve both the above aims, there are still many types of loops you can fly.

The type chosen depends on the purpose of the loop or, at least, the purpose of the flight during which the loop is undertaken.

Variations on the theme might include:

- in a contest – a perfectly round loop, as seen from the ground
- in an air show – a loop started from ground level, where you want to live to tell the tale
- on a pleasure flight – a loop with minimum G forces all the way round.

Each of these cases requires a different technique, yet all meet the basic requirement. For the purpose of teaching this figure, however, I will use the round loop as the aim.

Ground References

The most important visual reference is a line feature. The best orientation is to fly directly over the feature and in line with it. Secondary considerations are twofold:

- to find a line feature that is into the wind of the day
- to find a point feature close to the horizon at right angles to the line.

Technique

Each aircraft's flight manual will include an entry speed for a loop. This will generally be a median figure about 2.5 times the basic 1g stalling speed. This is the speed to use during early aerobatic training. Later, you might choose lower or higher speeds to achieve different goals. While achieving this entry speed, reduce the throttle if necessary to avoid overspeed on a fixed pitch propeller.

From a starting position directly over the line feature, look toward the horizon beyond the wing tip and briskly start the pull-up. The aim initially should be to achieve between 3g and 4g for at least the first 45° of pitch.

Do not be tempted to spend time monitoring the G-meter. Look at the horizon beyond the wing tip. This is the point that will show you any initial error. As the speed is now decreasing fast, you can apply full power even with a fixed pitch prop. Diagram 16-1 shows the view to the left from a typical low-wing trainer at the start of the loop. The numbers below the pictures show the pitch angle.

Diagram 16-1

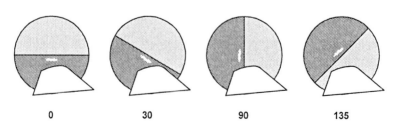

| 0 | 30 | 90 | 135 |

Diagram 16-2

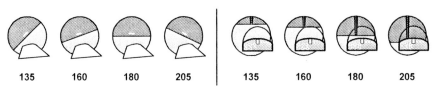

| 135 | 160 | 180 | 205 | 135 | 160 | 180 | 205 |

Notice how the wing tip is describing a circle around the horizon just above the lake in the distance. Do not look ahead over the nose during this phase, for all you will see is featureless sky, which will give no feedback about attitude.

Beyond 135° of pitch, you might start to gain good information from looking ahead, but your sight line must also be up at 45° above the nose in order once again to see the horizon.

Diagram 16-2 shows the wing tip and windscreen views of the loop from 45° before the apex until 25° thereafter. The windscreen pictures show the ease with which you can assess wings level as the nose passes down through the horizon. By looking up at the windscreen top rail, you can also pick up the line feature at an early stage. The wing tip picture also gives this information, but interpretation takes more practice.

Notice that the wing is still describing the same circular path about the horizon above the lake. Diagram 16-3 shows the last 135° of the loop. Again the wing tip and windscreen views are shown. Either can be used effectively with practice.

The pictures in the diagrams above show what you will see at the different stages. They do not show the rate of pitch, nor do they convey the feel of the stick forces, nor the extent of the G-loading on the airframe. Consider these now.

Diagram 16-3

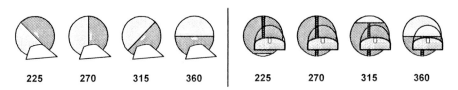

| 225 | 270 | 315 | 360 | 225 | 270 | 315 | 360 |

Pitch Rate

Remember the aim for the moment is to fly a loop that looks perfectly round to a ground observer. Diagram 16-4 shows a circular shape split into four segments. In the first picture, numbers show the average speed of the aircraft for each of the segments. The middle picture shows the time taken for each segment. The last picture shows the average pitch rate (in degrees per second) needed to complete 90° of loop in the time available.

These pictures say nothing about the G being pulled at any stage (because you should be looking outside, not at the G-meter). Nor do they say anything about stick force (because the differences are not easy to estimate accurately). While looking at the wing tip, however, you can quite accurately assess the pitch rate. Similarly, looking over the nose you can also estimate the rate at which cloudy stuff, or green stuff, is whizzing past.

At the top of this loop the pitch rate over the top must be exactly half of what it is at the beginning and at the end. You must start the pull-up smoothly but firmly to set a high pitch rate early on. You reduce this to about ¾ of its value as you go through the vertical.

Over the top, the rate of rotation (of the wing tip against the horizon) must be about half what it was at the start. The down-side is quicker than the up-side as both thrust and gravity are combining to bring you downhill fast.

This illustration, of course has just talked about speed. Not airspeed, indicated or true. Nor groundspeed, which is actually zero in the vertical bits and negative at the top! The speed, of course, that matters is your speed relative to the ground observer.

The illustration above is in fact worked on the assumption there is no wind at all. If you are flying for basic training or fun, at altitude, you can fly as though there was no wind as you will have no worthwhile spectators.

So much for the visual cues and the necessary variation of pitch rate. While flying the figure and looking outside to assess all this visual feedback, you can also use your sense of touch to monitor the elevator control inputs and stick forces.

Diagram 16-4

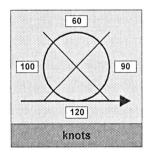 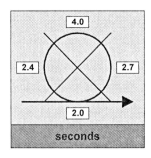 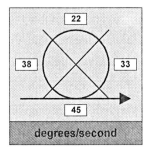

knots · seconds · degrees/second

Stick Feel

Diagram 16-5 uses descriptive words to explain what the loop should feel like as it progresses if you are to achieve the round shape. Start quickly to establish the fast pitch rate that is required at the beginning.

Maintain a steady pressure until you reach the vertical, then you can start to relax the elevator force a little. For about 90° of the loop across the top, you need to reduce the back pressure considerably so that the aircraft floats lightly through the low pitch-rate portion. Then squeeze more back pressure down through the vertical and keep accelerating the pitch rate until you can suddenly release the control force completely at the stop.

Now a word about balance. At the beginning and at the end you will be fast. Usually this will be above rudder-neutral speed. So with a right-turning Lycoming engine you will need a little left rudder before you start to pull and after you finish.

As you start to pitch up, there will be an added gyroscopic force making the aircraft yaw right, so a little more left rudder may have to be added.

Through the vertical up segment, the speed is rapidly decreasing, the pitch rate is slowly decreasing and the angle of attack is slowly decreasing. The

Diagram 16-5

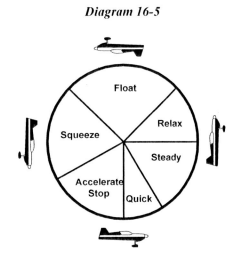

need for left rudder will go away as the aircraft passes through a rudder-neutral configuration. As you float over the top of the loop, pitch rate, alpha and gyroscopic effect will all be low, but slipstream effect will magnify. Some right rudder will be needed through the apex to keep the aircraft balanced.

On the descent, the need for right rudder will go away, the neutral phase will again be passed. Toward the end, the initial conditions will again prevail and some left rudder will be required.

On completion of the loop, the height should be the same as on entry. The airspeed will most likely be different. This will depend on the energy balance during the figure. In most cases, the energy lost through increased drag in the high speed, high pitch-rate periods will exceed that gained by burning fuel to produce thrust. As a result, exit speed will be lower than entry speed. Only in an aircraft with a very high power/weight ratio could you expect to gain energy during a loop.

G-Forces

The G-force during the loop should vary a lot. It will be at a maximum at the beginning and the end. At the top of the loop, during the 'floating' segment it will be small, a little less than the 1g of normal straight and level. The maximum G you use during the figure will depend on aircraft type and entry speed. In typical training aircraft this will be between 3g and 4g.

Even if the aircraft is stressed for more, using more G at an early stage will be counter-productive. Firstly you will cause a lot of un-necessary induced drag and the energy balance will suffer. Secondly, you will tire quickly during the flight and perhaps not get the best training value from your efforts. Don't regularly pull any harder than you actually need to for completion of the figure. To do so is to start learning a bad habit.

To gain the satisfaction of a round loop you must reach your peak G value quickly during the initial pull-up. The elevator movement to achieve this should be quick but controlled. Do not overstress the aircraft by pulling too far. Move just precisely the right distance, but quickly.

In the descending half of the loop, the G-force will increase gradually and progressively so that the maximum is reached again just as the aeroplane reaches level flight. The elevator control must then be returned quickly and precisely to the centre.

Error Analysis

Big Problems

There are two gross mishandling errors which you must avoid. One is stopping looping altogether while still upside down; the second is pulling too far back on the elevator and stalling the wing. Remember the primary method for keeping a round loop is to correctly modulate and monitor the pitch rate. Keep this always under review and it will not become zero. However …

Stopped Loop

If you stop looping in an inverted nose-high attitude airspeed will rapidly decrease. The most likely first result of this is that the aircraft will start to roll left (Lycoming engine) in reaction to engine torque which is no longer being countered by aileron effects. In the early stages of training, this un-commanded roll is likely to be very disorientating. The elevator position under this condition is likely to be close to neutral and angle of attack will be low. Stalling will not happen if the elevator control is kept close to the neutral point, but the nose will drop because of gravity and the bank angle will be unpredictable.

The best recovery from this unusual loss of control is to reduce power and to keep the elevator and aileron controls central (you can even let go to achieve this) until the aircraft is again descending and gaining speed. Once the airspeed has increased to approximately 1.5 times the level 1g stall speed, roll to upright and recover to level using elevator. Do not over-react and pull too far back as a secondary stall during the recovery is easy to perform. Do not add power until you are sure that airframe and engine speed limits will not be exceeded.

Stalling in the Loop

Stalling during the loop occurs when the pilot stops thinking about elevator position and instead relies on the feel of the elevator.

It is very easy to be fooled into keeping constant stick force as you go through the vertical up phase. This results in the elevator control coming inadvertently further and further back until the onset of buffet and stall. Equally, it is easy to be over-eager in re-applying elevator on the downward half before the speed has increased enough. In this phase stick forces are still low and rearward movement easy.

In either case, relax the back pressure as soon as you feel any buffet and continue the loop with more attention to the elevator position. If you do not react quickly enough, a severe stall may occur accompanied by uncommanded roll. The immediate action must be to release the elevator back pressure to ensure a sub-critical angle of attack before making any other control inputs. Then recover by rolling to wings level and pitching to level flight. Reduce power as necessary so that you do not exceed any limitations.

Geometric Problems

Roundness

Though you might strive to fly a round loop, you will never know whether you achieved it from what you see inside the aircraft. Only someone watching from outside can judge this. All you can do in this respect is the real-time monitoring of pitch rate. If you come close to the ideal you will be flying a good, safe loop.

Crooked Loops

Apart from its roundness, the key feature of the loop is that the fuselage should remain in the same vertical plane throughout. In other words, the heading at the top should be the reciprocal of that at the bottom. Additionally, the wings should remain level at all times and the aircraft should not be yawed in the vertical. Any of these errors will produce a loop that could be called crooked.

The primary cause of all geometric errors in crooked loops is erroneous aileron input. Being out of balance, making small rudder errors, will not significantly affect the geometry. In fact you can fly a straight loop without your feet on the pedals at all – there will just be some sideslip at various places but the wings can always be kept level with aileron. So the golden rule of looping is to pull straight, with no aileron.

Diagram 16-6 shows how such errors can arise. The solid arrow shows the direction the elevator should move. Dotted Arrow 1 shows the most common error: pulling toward the elbow. Arrow 2 shows the other ergonomic possibility: rotating about the elbow as you pull. The first applies erroneous right aileron, the other left. You can spot these errors and correct them if you are looking at the wing tip when you start to pull.

Diagram 16-7 shows the view to the left side at the start of the loop. It then shows the aircraft after 30° of pitch. Pulling towards the elbow will add right aileron and the left wing will rise. In this case, it will obscure the lake just below the horizon. The opposite error will cause the left wing to drop a little, and the wing tip will move too far away from the lake.

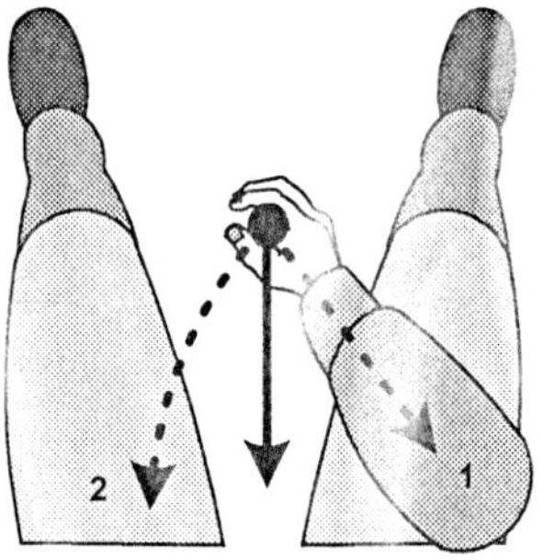

Diagram 16-8 shows the same view as seen from the rear seat of a biplane fitted with a diamond-shaped sighting device.

Diagram 16-6

In both these cases, you can detect and correct even small errors of bank angle during the pull-up. Keep watching the wing tip/horizon, and keep making small aileron correction until you are past the vertical. Keep this central aileron position as you unload the elevator through the top of the loop and you will stay straight. At the apex of the loop you can confirm wings level against the horizon over the nose if you wish, or you can keep looking to the side.

Diagram 16-7

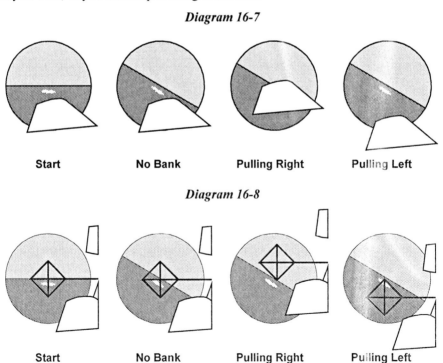

| Start | No Bank | Pulling Right | Pulling Left |

Diagram 16-8

| Start | No Bank | Pulling Right | Pulling Left |

During the descent, you can still keep straight by looking at the wing tip, or at a line feature directly below you if there is one. As you re-apply back pressure through vertical down, there is a strong possibility of pulling crooked again. Remember to use aileron as the primary control to keep the loop straight. Use the rudder only to correct balance errors, not geometric ones.

Further Development

A very valuable advanced looping exercise is to determine the minimum looping speed for your aircraft. This will almost certainly be slower than the recommended entry speed. You must be able to complete the 360° movement and maintain three-axis control all the time. The indicated airspeed at the top can be very low, because the angle of attack needed during the float is minimal, but the aircraft must not just stop and flop.

Start at normal entry speed and fly successive loops at slower entry speeds. Typically reduce the entry speed by 5mph/knots once you are comfortable with the current speed. Notice that the time taken to complete the loop gets shorter as the entry speed diminishes.

During the pull-up for a normal loop, there is a band of possible pitch-rates that will get you round. As entry speed reduces, so does the width of this band. At minimum speed there is just one precise pulling technique that will get to the apex without stalling or falling out. This is what you must learn.

Bear in mind the increased likelihood, one might even say the inevitability of either stalling during the loop or of stopping and flopping during this type of practice. Always have sufficient height above your planned minimum height to effect a recovery. Once mastered, this type of loop will give great satisfaction because of the amount of 'feel' you have developed for the aircraft in order to perform it cleanly.

Outside loops, hesitation loops and loops with rolls in them will be treated in later chapters.

Granny Loops

Diagram 16-9

A Granny Loop (Diagram 16-9) is not round, but it has a valid purpose. If you are flying a passenger who has never flown be-fore, and they want to see what a loop is like, this is the one to do. The purpose is to keep the G-forces to a minimum overall.

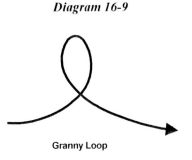

Granny Loop

Start faster than normal, perhaps 20 or 30 knots/mph faster than the recommended loop entry speed.

Pull up carefully, keeping to 2.5g. Let the loop take some time. As you climb and speed decreases, try to keep 2.5g. Keep bringing the stick back, and increasing the pitch rate, as you slow down. Over the top, pitch as quickly as you can without actually stalling. Keep the elevator forward of the stalling position, but only just so. You probably will not be able to maintain 2.5g, but 1.5g to 2g should be possible.

As you descend, reduce power to keep the acceleration low. Increase to 2.5g but no more. As the speed increases, gradually let the elevator control further forward so that the G does not increase further.

Low Level Display Loop

Flying a round loop during a display would require a hard pull very close to the ground at the finish. Any loss of thrust during the climbing half could get you to the top without enough height to recover in the half loop down.

Diagram 16-10

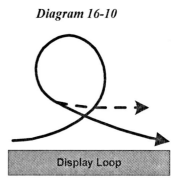

The aim of a low-level display loop (Diagram 16-10) is to start and finish close to the ground, but to be pulling only a small amount of G as the ground is approached at the end of the down line.

As in the Granny loop, start with a surplus of speed. Fly the up going half so as to maximize height gain while maintaining full control at the apex. Float the apex as in a round loop.

From perhaps 30°s nose down keep increasing the pitch rate and G so that if you continued you would finish quite a lot higher than you started. When there is perhaps only 10° or 20° of pitch remaining, then reduce the G-force so that a gentle descent is made down to low level.

Flying in Competition

Loops of all sorts are flown in competition.

Diagram 16-11

The basic vanilla loop shown in Diagram 16-11 occurs in most Primary/Beginners and Sports-man/Standard category sequences. Getting a perfect score is very difficult indeed because of the variation in technique needed in different wind conditions.

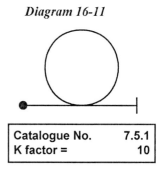

Catalogue No.	7.5.1
K factor =	10

Main Axis Wind Correction

Diagram 16-12 shows three now familiar pictures, this time with a 20 knot head wind for the loop. The vertically climbing and descending segments are not much altered by the wind.

The differences between the bottom and top segments are now much reduced, as the speed differentials are all compressed. The pull-up can be a little less severe; the pitch rate at the top is more than three quarters of what it was at the bottom. Notice, also, that the pitch rate at the end is very much like the average for the down-going segment, so there is need not to rush at the end. This figure is generally easier to fly than the previous one, because the pitch-rate differences are smaller and thus less prone to misjudgment. Now consider the opposite case.

Diagram 16-12

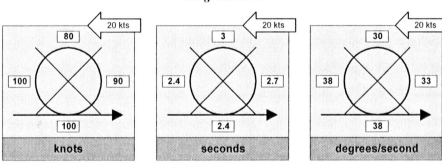

Diagram 16-13 shows the same loop started in the same 20 knot wind, but in the opposite direction. The observer-speed differentials are now very great, even though the indicated airspeeds are the same as the last two times. This time the pull-up and finish must be really very sharp. The percentage reduction at the quarter point is greater than even the first time, and the pitch rate over the top is very slow indeed. Indeed it is quite likely that this very slow pitch rate will mean that the centrifugal force is less than gravity and you will actually be under negative G, perhaps close to -1g.

Diagram 16-13

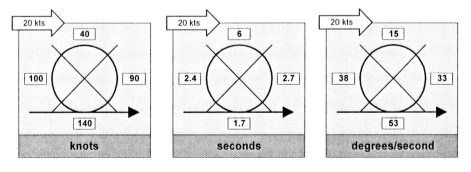

151

Failure to make the wind-correction for these two opposite conditions will result in figures that look quite different from the ground. If the still-air loop is flown perfectly, and then repeated in the other wind conditions, the result, from the ground, will look like Diagram 16-14.

It is easy to correct the problem illustrated in the middle picture, as you can easily increase the pitch rate by 'floating' a little less. Be sure to remember to pull a little less sharply on entry and, especially, at the end. It is quite easy to lose marks for pinching the last bit of pull-out into a strong head wind.

Diagram 16-14

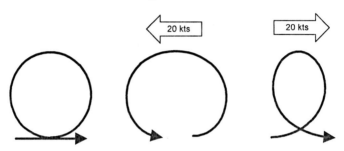

Correcting for a loop started down wind is more difficult. If possible have a higher entry speed than normal. Initially pull harder. If you normally loop at a maximum of 4g, then you will need 5g here. Make sure you know your aircraft's limits and stay within them. Keep the loop tight for a little longer than normal, but beware of a high-speed stall if you get the stick too far back.

Floating over the top may actually have to be almost straight and level inverted to make the necessary headway back into wind. This is where an aircraft without an inverted fuel system will be at a severe disadvantage because of the likelihood of the engine losing power. Toward the end of the downward half, remember that you must accelerate the pitch rate very quickly to reach the new, increased maximum G just before coming level.

If ever you are designing a Free sequence, be sure to start your loop into wind.

Loop Size

A key point to remember is that the difficulty in flying a round loop stems from the observer-speed differences at the top and bottom. Anything that helps minimize this speed differential will bring the required technique closer to a constant pitch-rate and thus easier to perform.

One way to achieve this in competition is to keep each loop as small as you can. Big, lazy loops mean big speed differentials, and hard decisions over pitch-rate variation. They also give the judges a lot of time to measure the errors.

CHAPTER 17

Straight and Level Rolls

The Straight and Level Roll is a complex co-ordination exercise requiring continuously variable aileron, elevator and rudder control inputs. This figure is often called the 'slow roll', but as I explained in an earlier chapter, the description

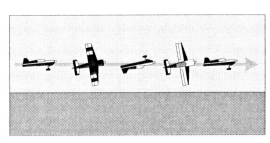

was originally coined to distinguish the slower aileron roll from the faster rudder, or flick, roll.

The key point of this exercise is to learn to roll the aircraft through 360° while flying straight and level. The rate of roll can be whatever you choose, subject to the aircraft's capabilities and limitations and subject also to your ability to maintain the required co-ordination.

The Flight Manoeuvre

The concept of this figure is simplicity itself: to roll through 360° at a constant rate while maintaining straight and level flight.

Flying the figure accurately is actually very complex. Here is another description that perhaps goes some way to explaining the difficulty: to roll the aircraft through 360° at a constant rate while changing wing and fuselage lift forces so that their vector sum is a constant, vertically (upward) directed, 1g.

Wing and Fuselage Lift

The principles of wing lift are well covered in the PPL aerodynamics syllabus. So is the idea of using the rudder to maintain balance during turns, changes of power and so on. This may well be the first time, however, you have heard the term 'fuselage lift'.

Any reasonably sleek object, if forced through the air with an angle of attack will generate lift. During normal straight and level flight the wing and fuselage both generate lift and the two are complementary. They add together. And together they produce induced drag which varies as the angle of attack varies. In "Local Gravity Vector" on page 27, I showed diagrams wherein the rudder provided a lateral force to balance or unbalance the aircraft. This lateral force is, in fact, fuselage lift.

What you should now consider is an aircraft flying straight and level with a bank angle of 90° (Diagram 17-1). The wings and tail plane of this aircraft are shown deliberately in light grey so that you can concentrate on the action of the fuselage. In the right picture, the rudder is working in just the same way as a conventional elevator. It is generating a downforce to keep the fuselage at an angle of attack of 10°.

Diagram 17-1

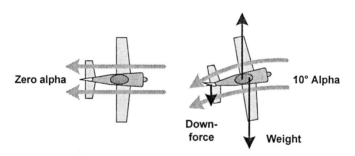

The fuselage is acting now like a very inefficient wing. It is inefficient because its shape is not optimized for lift and because it has a very low aspect ratio. The result of this inefficiency is much increased drag compared with a wing generating the same amount of lift.

Like wing lift, the amount of fuselage lift that can be generated by a particular aircraft is dependent on airspeed and angle of attack. The angle of attack that can be sustained itself depends on the rudder authority of the particular type.

Despite these dependencies, most specialist aerobatic aircraft can generate 1g of fuselage lift and thereby maintain level flight at 90° of bank, so-called knife-edge flight. This ability, however, is subject to a number of caveats. Though the fuselage might be able to generate this much lift at high speed, if the drag generated exceeds the available thrust, then the aircraft will slow down.

As speed decreases, fuselage alpha must be increased by greater rudder deflection. This in turn will generate more drag and so on. Inevitably a limit condition will be reached where the rudder runs out of effectiveness and fuselage lift can no longer sustain level flight.

This requirement for fuselage lift and the related limit on rudder effectiveness will determine the minimum speed at which a true straight and level roll can be flown in any particular type of aircraft.

Lift Forces at Various Bank Angles

The lift forces required at the cardinal points of the roll are easy to understand. Diagram 17-2 shows a biplane rolling to the left. In the second picture it has 1g of fuselage lift from application of right rudder. The aeroplane is grossly unbalanced, the pilot is lying heavily on his left side. In the third picture, 1g of lift is being generated by the wings with the elevator well forward, creating a negative angle of attack. The pilot feels this as -1g and is hanging upside down in the straps. In the fourth picture fuselage lift is again the order of the day, this time generated by left rudder with the pilot lying on his right side. Notice that when the bank angle is 90° or 270°, the wings generate no lift at all. If they did, then the aircraft would turn, contradicting the 'straight' part of the aim of the exercise.

Diagram 17-2

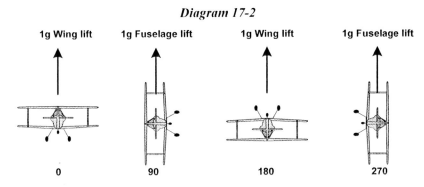

At intervening points, the situation is a bit more involved (Diagram 17-3).

Diagram 17-3

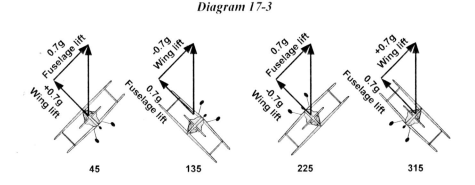

Now both sorts of lift must be generated at the same time, each providing about 70% of 1g so that their sum just counteracts gravity

Visual References

When rolling straight and level, the primary visual reference is the horizon directly ahead of the aeroplane. Diagram 17-4 shows an aircraft with a symmetrical wing which has no angle of incidence relative to the fuselage. The fuselage datum is shown as a dashed line, while the pilot's line of sight to the horizon is shown as a black arrow.

In the left picture the aircraft is upright, with an angle of attack of 5°; on the right it is inverted with the same, but negative alpha. When upright, the pilot's line of sight to the horizon is just above the engine cowling and converges with the aircraft's datum line by 5°. When inverted the sight line diverges from the datum by 5°.

Diagram 17-4

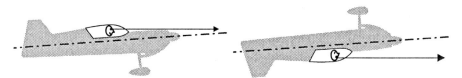

Diagram 17-5 shows the two pilot views from these upright and inverted positions. As the aeroplane has rolled, the engine cowling has moved round an imaginary circle which represents the conical field of view in front of the pilot.

The cone angle, and hence the apparent diameter of the circle, is the sum of the positive and negative angles of attack needed to fly straight and level, upright and inverted, at the chosen airspeed. At a lower speed, the circle would be larger, at a higher speed, smaller.

The late Eric Müller, in *Flight Unlimited*, called this the 'sacred circle', which seems to me a sound term, as long as you realize that the position of the centre is not fixed in relation to the horizon, but is dependent on airspeed.

Diagram 17-6 shows the derivation of a sacred circle for a typical biplane. The top wing and the fuel cap have more or less changed places.

Diagram 17-5

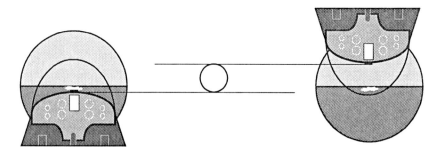

Diagram 17-6

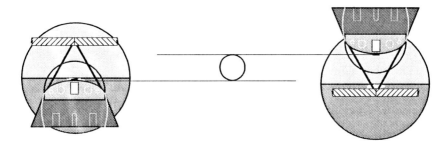

Technique

Entry Speeds

Before starting you must decide on an entry speed. The aircraft flight manual will probably quote a figure for a 'Slow Roll' which is a good starting point. Generally something faster than this figure, but less than manoeuvre speed (V_A) if you are going to use full aileron deflection, will make things a bit easier.

In older or under-powered aircraft, this speed may be greater than you can achieve in level flight, in which case a dive will be necessary. In such aircraft full throttle should also be used to overcome the extra drag you are going to create. In modern, specialist aircraft rolling can be performed from level flight at cruise power settings.

Each aircraft type has its own minimum speed for this figure, which is determined largely by rudder authority and fuselage aerodynamics. Remember, it is necessary at each knife-edge point to generate 1g of fuselage lift and there is a speed below which you cannot do this.

Below this speed, one of two things will happen as you get to the first knife-edge bank angle. Either you will just run out of rudder and the aeroplane will sink, or the drag induced will be so large (rather akin to the fuselage 'stalling') that descent will again be inevitable.

In modern aircraft with good fuselage lift/drag properties, the minimum straight and level rolling speed will probably be defined by a different failure mode whereby a negative flick roll starts just before the inverted position. The reason for this will be covered later.

For the rest of this description I will assume you are rolling with left aileron. When you roll right, much the same will apply, but the rudder inputs will naturally be reversed. When I say 'off heading left' or 'right' I mean this as you would see it from outside the aircraft looking in the original flight direction and standing upright.

The First 90°

To truly roll straight and level, you should not raise the nose before making any aileron input. So don't. If you just cannot roll the aircraft level without such initial 'cheating', then you need a higher entry speed.

Start with left aileron and simultaneously start the nose going upwards with a small amount of back stick. Strictly speaking, this elevator is also 'cheating' but it is much more acceptable because you have at least made the effort to start with aileron. The other principal geometric consideration at this stage is maintaining heading, while, in aerodynamic terms, you will also have to think about adverse yaw.

For the first 20° or 30° of roll, you can keep lifting the nose with back stick but you must not use so much that you get a significant heading change as the bank increases. At this stage, some mild adverse yaw is actually helpful as it allows you to use elevator to lift the nose without turning left.

If your aircraft generates a lot of adverse yaw, such as a Zlin 326 or a glider, then you will also need to apply a little bottom (left) rudder, but not so much that you counter all the yaw. Leave a little of the adverse effect to help you stay straight while using the 'cheating' elevator.

Beyond 30° of roll you must stop cheating with back stick and start to unload the wings, or you will start to pull off-heading to the left. By 45° of roll you must also be generating 0.7g of fuselage lift, so you will have to start increasing the top (right) rudder. As you progress towards 90° of bank the elevator must be moved steadily forward until the position is reached where the wings have zero angle of attack.

This will probably feel like a gentle push, as you were almost certainly trimmed for level upright before starting and you must now counteract the trimmed elevator system. At the 90° point you must have no wing lift at all and 1g of fuselage lift.

The Second 90°

As you leave knife-edge towards inverted you must continue moving the stick forward so that you once again generate some wing lift, albeit in the opposite direction. As wing lift increases, the need for fuselage lift decreases, so you might expect less right rudder to be required. Actually, you will need to apply more. Why? Because of the return of adverse yaw – possibly with a vengeance.

Most aircraft have non-symmetrical ailerons. Many have ailerons designed to minimize adverse yaw (Friese ailerons etc), but these modifications are only effective when rolling at positive angles of attack. When rolling with the stick forward, the effect of these 'improvements' is to make adverse yaw worse than it would have been with 'simple' ailerons. Because of this, rudder inputs become much more important when the stick is forward than when it is back.

If you fly a factory Pitts built after 1980, or a modern specialist aerobatic mono-plane, then you probably have a wing with symmetrical ailerons. You will have the same amount of adverse yaw inverted as upright.

Regardless of the type of ailerons, it is almost certain that the amount of right rudder you need to use during this roll is going to be greatest as you reach 180° of roll. So as you go from 90° to 180°, keep smoothly moving the stick forward so that you reach the top of the sacred circle when inverted. And keep progressively adding more and more right rudder in order to keep straight. If you do not keep adding right rudder, you will generate a noticeable heading error to the right of your initial track (as seen from outside).

You will see this error manifested by the movement of your initial aiming point to YOUR right, but it looks off heading to the right from outside and behind.

The Third 90°

As you leave the wings level, inverted attitude you should maintain forward stick pressure to keep the nose up for the next 20° or 30°. After this, the forward stick will begin to turn you to the left so you must gradually reduce it. Remember, however, that at the second knife-edge position you must have zero wing lift and this means still holding a small amount of forward pressure to counteract the trimming system.

 As the elevator controls move towards neutral point the wing lift will decrease and so will the adverse yaw being experienced. So once you are 30° past inverted you can gently release the right rudder and gradually feed in left rudder so that you reach second knife-edge generating 1g of fuselage lift again, this time with the left rudder.

As you pass through 225° of roll (45° after inverted) you will be changing from right rudder to left rudder. For the last 180° you have been using right rudder when rolling left. So the secondary effect of the rudder, which is roll, has been working against your aileron input and slowing the roll rate. You might not have noticed this but it has been happening.

As you change feet the secondary effect direction will also change and it is likely that the roll rate will increase. You should therefore make a corresponding reduction in aileron deflection to maintain a steady roll rate.

The Last 90°

From the second knife-edge attitude to wings level, maintain the roll rate with aileron while you gradually come off the left rudder and bring the elevator control back towards its starting point.

If you have a low-powered aircraft and have lost speed during the roll (because of the excess drag produced by the fuselage lift as well as the aileron deflection) you should finish with the nose higher than you started. If your aircraft is more powerful and retains its speed during the roll, the finish attitude must be the same as at the start.

When you reach wings level at the end of the roll, you should be on heading and you should not need to carry a lot of residual left rudder. If you finish out of balance in this way, you can improve your technique by following the error analysis in the next few paragraphs.

Summary

Diagram 17-7 shows a summary of elevator and rudder inputs during a level roll to the left.

Diagram 17-7

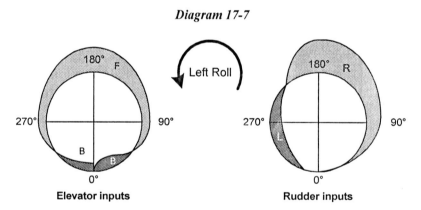

Elevator inputs | Rudder inputs

The thickness of the shaded bands, measured radially, indicates the magnitude of the control inputs. The elevator diagram assumes you are entering the roll from a trimmed condition and that the aircraft loses a little airspeed during the roll. Hence the need for a little aft stick at the end of the roll: to fly level at reduced speed.

Note that if some forward elevator input is maintained through the 270° position, then there should be no need for a large left rudder input at the end of the roll. The forward stick is needed at both 90° and 270° positions to ensure zero wing lift despite the initially positive trim state.

Error Analysis

Height and Heading Errors

Height and heading errors can be caused by incorrect use of the elevator or the rudder. Of these two controls, however, the elevator is much more powerful as it controls wing lift. The rudder, which controls fuselage lift is much less effective. For this reason, it is axiomatic that the largest rolling errors are caused by incorrect elevator inputs. So I will deal with these first.

The three most common errors, in order of occurrence during the roll are:

- insufficient up elevator (back stick) during the first 20° to 30° of roll

- insufficient down elevator (forward stick) at the inverted point

- failure to maintain enough forward stick from inverted to the second knife-edge position.

The first two errors will result in a roll on a descending flight path. Correct them by visualizing the sacred circle and by making sure that the nose of the aircraft follows it.

The third error results in 'dishing out' which is a combination of height loss and heading change to the right (remember to reverse this comment if you are rolling with right aileron). If you find yourself applying a large left rudder input toward the end of the roll, in order to maintain heading, then you are trying to correct an elevator error with a rudder input. It is better not to make the elevator error to begin with. Therefore concentrate on maintaining forward stick from inverted to the second knife-edge position.

If you do not have an inverted fuel system, and you still want to roll straight and level, then you are going to have to live with the fact that you will be gliding for most of the figure. As you will thus have little or no thrust to overcome the extra drag, you must have ample entry speed to ensure controllability throughout the figure. You will also have problems finding the true sacred circle because you cannot fly level inverted at constant speed.

However, see what you can achieve. Once you succeed in developing the correct elevator inputs, the amount of rudder you regularly use (misuse!) will reduce.

Inexpert pilots make two common rudder errors:

- not increasing right rudder from the first knife-edge position to inverted as the adverse yaw changes direction

- excessive use of left rudder from the second knife-edge position onwards.

You will notice the first error because your distant aiming point will move to your right as you approach inverted. Just add more right rudder. If you have no more right rudder to add you need to increase your entry speed.

The amount of left rudder you actually need at the second knife-edge point is less than you might think. At the first knife-edge position, your right rudder had to produce 1g of fuselage lift while also countering the slipstream effect of propwash yaw. At this second knife-edge position, the slipstream is aiding the left rudder. Again, if you run out of rudder but otherwise have good geometry, you need to have a faster entry speed. You may also still be using the left rudder to counteract sloppy elevator technique, so keep that stick forward in the third quarter of the roll.

Roll-Rate Errors

The aim is to maintain a constant roll rate throughout. As you add more right rudder during the second quarter of the roll, add left aileron also. As you change feet during the third quarter, remember to reduce the aileron input so that the roll does not speed up.

If you are rolling at a very low airspeed and the roll rate suddenly increases just before you reach inverted, then you have probably discovered the delights of the inadvertent negative flick roll. You need then quickly to centre both stick and rudder to restore normal flight.

This flick roll starts because you have a combination of a large right rudder input with a lot of forward stick. Both these inputs are required to maintain height and heading when rolling and their magnitudes increase with reducing airspeed. This phenomenon characterizes the minimum level rolling speed in, for example, a two-seat Pitts, which is roughly 80 mph IAS.

Further Development

Rolling technique can be developed and improved by practising at different airspeeds and with different roll rates.

The principal difference when rolling at different airspeeds concerns the size of the sacred circle. At high speed, the angles of attack, both upright and inverted are reduced. The diameter of the sacred circle is also reduced. At lower speeds the opposite is true. Lower airspeed also implies lower roll rate.

The main concern when rolling very slowly is whether your aircraft is able to sustain close to 1g of fuselage lift for a longer time. In all aircraft, fuselage lift carries a penalty of excessive drag.

In high-powered machines, this is not a problem, as there is sufficient thrust available to maintain speed despite the extra drag. These aircraft can fly on fuselage lift alone for extended periods (subject to maintaining oil pressure in the engine) and can thus be rolled at very slow roll rates.

Less powerful machines will be retarded dramatically by the extra drag induced from knife-edge flight. They will rapidly slow to a speed at which level knife-edge can no longer be sustained. This problem defines not only the minimum airspeed for level rolling but also the minimum roll rate.

The straight and level roll is also further developed into the different families of hesitation rolls, with 2, 4 or 8 stops in every 360°. Indeed, many other numbers of stops can be tried; 3, 6 and 16 being obvious examples. I will, however, devote another chapter to these figures.

Flying in Competition

Straight and level rolls are added to a host of basic figures from the Aerobatic Catalogue to make a very large variety of compound figures. They do not simply occur on simple straight lines.

Diagram 17-8 shows three exam-   *Diagram 17-8*
ples. In all cases, however, the
technique described above is
appropriate. On level lines, rolls
may be of just 180°, or indeed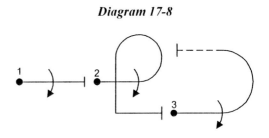
540° or 720°. In each case, once
again, the technique does not
vary, just the duration and the
number of repetitions.

Some rolls are started from inverted flight. In such cases, you must remember the reversal of adverse yaw when forward stick is applied and initially apply the rudder on the side nearest the ground when starting to roll.

I stated earlier that in some aircraft you could ignore the adverse yaw when starting to roll from upright, as a little of it is helpful in keeping straight as you start to raise the nose. That is so, but you cannot ignore adverse yaw when inverted. It is usually much worse than when upright, because of design features such as Friese ailerons. And you are not now trying to lift the nose, just to hold it. If you have symmetrical ailerons, you should really be countering adverse yaw both upright and inverted every time you start a roll.

Many rolls are also flown in competition on straight lines that climb or descend at 45°. In these cases, the technique is slightly different, because the start and end conditions require different elevator positions. They also demand that the pilot looks in different places to see the horizon and other key visual features. Rolling on these lines is covered in "Half Rolls on 45° Lines" on page 165.

Energy Matters

During a level roll, by definition height does not change. Energy may change, however, as the aircraft can slow down or, in some cases, accelerate during the roll. In either case, the only additional matter for the pilot to bear in mind is whether he will have enough speed for the next planned figure.

In low-performance aircraft the exit speed will be noticeably less than at entry, and subsequent upward looping figures might prove impossible. In contest flying it may be necessary to give some points away by descending during a roll in order to maintain speed to make the next loop possible.

In high-performance machines the opposite may be true and power may have to be reduced during the roll to avoid being too fast for the next figure – above flick-roll limit speed for example. In practice, this is as much of a problem as having not enough speed!

CHAPTER **18**

Half Rolls on 45° Lines

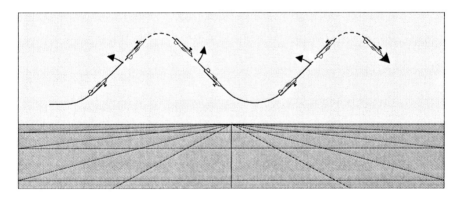

This chapter describes a valuable flight exercise that consolidates your ability to perform half rolls on climbing and descending lines. These Half Rolls form a key part of the technique for horizontal eights and half-eights. The continuous exercise is useful as it allows numerous repetitions of the half roll technique without changing heading and without the stress of long looping segments. It is especially useful during transit flight to or from a practice area.

Low-powered, slow rolling aircraft may be incapable of sustaining a 45° climb for long enough to make a half roll with visible lines on either side. In such aircraft, this exercise can be flown with 30° lines. It remains intense and powerful, even in this less extreme form.

The Flight Manoeuvre

Fly a straight line, with the aircraft at all times in balance. Make progress by a series of climbing and descending lines. Divide each 45° line into three segments: a line, a half roll and a further plain line of equal length to the first.

165

Of the two plain line segments, one will be upright and the other inverted. At the top and bottom of each line fly a smooth 90° looping segment to start the next line. Measure the climbing and descending lines by aircraft attitude, not flight path.

In a low-powered aircraft with a slow roll rate, you will lose a fair amount of height in each cycle of this exercise. Take care to re-establish a safe altitude after one or two cycles.

Ground References

You will fly for several minutes in a straight line. Choose a major landmark in the far distance straight ahead as an aiming point. You will need a good horizon to the left, which is where you will look for part of the exercise. It will help if there is a good long-distance landmark just below the horizon off the left wing tip.

Technique

Climbing Half Roll

Fly your aircraft upright at cruising speed directly toward your major landmark. Dive to attain an entry speed of perhaps 20 knots faster than normal looping speed. Remember to retard the throttle with a fixed-pitch propeller so that you do not exceed redline rpm. With a right-turning engine, you will need some left rudder pressure to maintain balance as you exceed rudder-neutral speed.

Look at the left wing tip, or left sighting device, and establish a 45° climbing line (Diagram 18-1). You will need a little more left rudder during the pull-up to counter the gyroscopic effect. Count *"One-Two"* and then start an aileron roll to the left. Look at the sky above the nose. Use a little back stick for the first 20 ° or 30° of roll to prevent the nose from dropping toward the horizon.

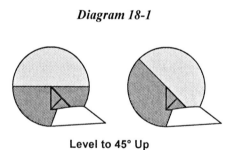

Diagram 18-1

Level to 45° Up

As you approach the 90° point add some right rudder pressure to initiate fuselage lift which will sustain your climb during knife-edge. By the time you reach the 90° point, you must have moved the elevator forward to the 'neutral-point' position in order to have no wing lift in knife-edge. Remember that this neutral point actually feels like you are pushing forward a bit because of the effect of the elevator trim.

Keep rolling towards inverted, slightly increasing the forward stick and also increasing the right rudder as the negative angle of attack increases, bringing with it some reversed adverse yaw.

Look further up, through the upper part of the windscreen or canopy, such that you are looking up at 45° above the aircraft longitudinal axis. Here you will see the horizon and the major landmark ahead of you (Diagram 18-2). Stop rolling sharply as the wings become parallel to the horizon, and release the right rudder.

Diagram 18-2

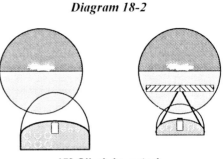

45° Climb Inverted

In this inverted climbing 45° attitude, P-factor is reversed while slipstream effect is normal. It is likely that they will cancel each other out and that no rudder will be needed to maintain balance. You will know if you are in balance because your body will simply hang in the centre of the seat.

At this point the aircraft will be slowing down quite noticeably and the fuel flow will be interrupted if you do not have an inverted fuel system. You should try to hold this climbing attitude perfectly still while you count *"One-Two-Three"* at the same pace as before. Then you can start the upper 90° looping segment.

Upper Looping Segment

During this segment the airspeed will be low. As you start to lower the nose by bringing the stick back the reverse P-factor will disappear and some right rudder will be needed to counter the remaining slipstream effect. Try to have close to zero G as the nose slowly comes down through the horizon.

Diagram 18-3

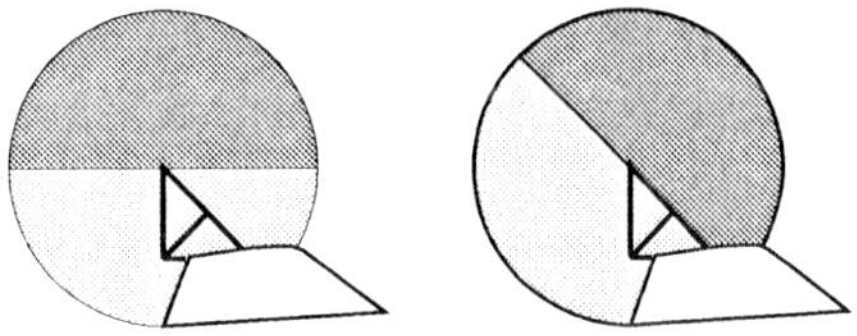

Level Inverted to 45° Down

Now look at the left wing/sighting device again so that you can accurately establish the 45° inverted down line (Diagram 18-3).

Descending Half Roll

When you reach the correct attitude, make a firm check forward with the stick to take the weight of the aircraft inverted and make sure that the attitude stays at 45°. Count *"One-Two-Three"* again and then start a second half aileron roll to the left. Use full aileron deflection to roll as fast as you can.

Keep some forward pressure on the control column, however, to ensure that you still have elevator 'neutral point' at the 90° position. Also, apply some right rudder as you start to roll. With the initial negative angle of attack, reverse adverse yaw will occur as you deflect the aileron.

As you approach the knife-edge roll angle, release the right rudder and apply a small amount of left rudder. Once again look up at 45° to the aircraft axis, dead ahead, and you will see the horizon rotating. Stop rolling when you reach wings level in the 45° descent.

It will be easy to see wings level if you are looking up at 45° to the longitudinal axis (Diagram 18-4). If you look directly over the nose, however, it will be more difficult to determine the exact roll angle for stopping.

Hold this descending attitude while you count *"One-Two"* again.

During this count you will have to maintain increasing forward stick pressure as the trimmer tries to bring the aircraft toward level flight. You must resist this tendency and stay on the 45° down.

You will also need a small amount of left rudder, as by now you will be above rudder-neutral speed in the dive. You will have to throttle back in a fixed-pitch machine to avoid engine overspeed.

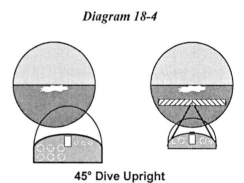

Diagram 18-4

45° Dive Upright

Lower Looping Segment

After the last two-count you can start the lower looping segment and bring the aircraft once again to the climbing 45° attitude. Look to the left wing tip again and raise the nose smoothly with a small amount of back pressure.

Add an additional bit of left rudder as the pitching action will generate some right-yaw due to gyroscopic precession.

Error Analysis

During the initial pull to 45° climbing upright, be sure to pull straight so that the wings remain level. You can check this easily if you have a wing-mounted sight that is correctly adjusted.

Without such a sighting device, be sure to check by looking both sides during the pull and use small aileron inputs to maintain a symmetrical view to both left and right.

Climbing Half Roll

At the end of the climbing half roll, be sure to look forward and up at 45° to the longitudinal axis, so you can see the horizon and your major landmark. When you stop rolling, you can make small rudder correction to eliminate any residual heading error by reference to the landmark.

The most likely heading error will be a result of insufficient right rudder during the part of the roll when you have the stick forward. You can fix this by adding some right rudder after you have stopped rolling (left Diagram 18-5).

Diagram 18-5

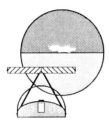
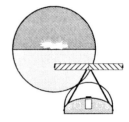

Left heading error,	**Right heading error,**
use right rudder to correct	**use left rudder to correct**

Alternatively, you may have had some residual back stick at the knife-edge position during the half roll. This will pull you off heading the other way. You will then need left rudder to correct the heading while inverted (right Diagram 18-5).

At the end of the climbing half roll, you must have just the right amount of forward stick to maintain the inverted climbing 45° line (Diagram 18-6). You can judge this by looking at the horizon ahead and gauging its distance from the top of the windscreen or the top wing (biplanes only) to the horizon. Of course, you can also check this angle by looking at the wing tip/sighting device, but then you will not be able to check the heading at the same time.

Many experienced competition aerobatic pilots attach a small piece of sticky tape inside the canopy at the position that coincides with their sight line while looking at 45° up from the aircraft's longitudinal axis. When climbing inverted at 45°, or when descending upright, this piece of tape will appear to be directly on the horizon ahead.

Diagram 18-6

Put tape here
45°

Horizon

Diagram 18-7 shows how this tape can be used to make small pitch attitude adjustments during a climbing inverted 45° line, while still maintaining heading towards a major landmark.

Diagram 18-7

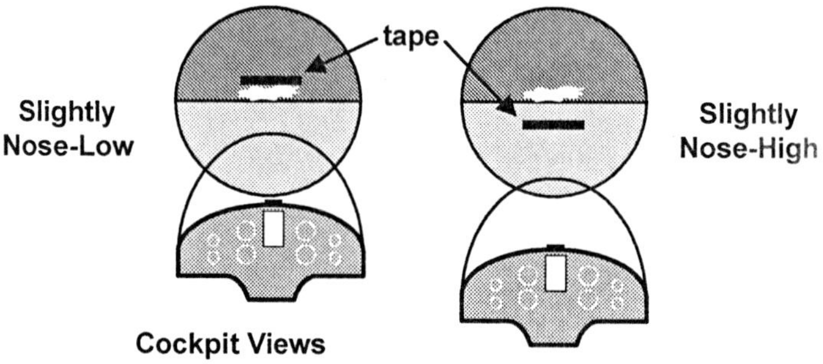

Cockpit Views

Caution: Torque Roll hazard

After the climbing half roll, and especially if the subsequent attitude is made steeper than 45°, the aircraft will rapidly lose airspeed. In an aircraft with an inverted fuel system the engine will continue to produce thrust and torque. At very low speed, the torque may be pronounced and may cause uncommanded roll (to the left in the case of a right-turning engine such as the Lycoming O-series).

If this occurs, simply release your forward pressure on the control column and allow the nose to drop below the horizon. Speed will then increase and you can roll to upright using the engine torque to help you.

Setting the Down Line

The next error is to do with setting and maintaining the 45° down line. This can only be done consistently and accurately by looking at the wing tip horizon. Having a well-aligned sighting device is a great advantage (Diagram 18-8).

It is impossible to set an accurate 45° down line while looking out of the front of the aircraft. You must now properly maintain this line up to the point of starting the half roll. It is easy to under-estimate the amount of forward stick pressure needed to hold the correct 45° attitude at relatively low speed. As a result, the nose drops ever steeper until the roll is started. This results in increased speed and additional height loss.

Descending Half Roll

The most common, and the biggest, error during the descending half roll results in a significant change of heading. This is to the right when rolling left and vice versa. The problem is concerned with the elevator. It means that you have not held enough

Diagram 18-8

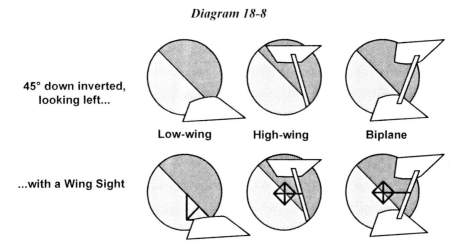

45° down inverted,
looking left...

Low-wing   High-wing   Biplane

...with a Wing Sight

forward pressure during the roll to achieve zero angle of attack at the knife-edge point.

When you start this descending half roll, you should use full aileron deflection **and maintain forward stick pressure** to the extent necessary to maintain heading in knife-edge (Diagram 18-9).

You will still need some forward stick pressure after completing the half roll as the speed will almost certainly now be higher than that for which you have trimmed. As a result, the nose will rise, making the 45° line shallow, before you start the lower looping segment.

Diagram 18-9

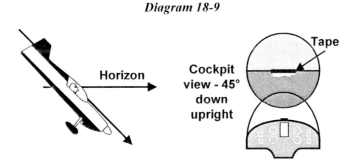

Horizon

Cockpit view - 45° down upright

Tape

Further Development

In relatively high-performance, fast-rolling aircraft, such as the Pitts Special series or better, the amount of time taken to perform the half rolls at full aileron deflection is quite small. Consequently, the amount of attitude or flight path change during the half roll, due to gravity, will be small. In these aircraft the aileron can be applied very quickly and need be held at full throw for only a short time to complete the 180° of roll.

In these aircraft you can exercise sufficient elevator control during the roll by simply maintaining zero angle of attack throughout. Chapter 10 on Ballistic Rolls described how to find the stick position which combines full aileron with zero elevator. Moving the stick quickly and accurately to the neutral point position with full aileron will facilitate accurate half rolls with very small, if any, heading or pitch attitude errors. The accompanying rudder pressures need only be very small.

In Intermediate level or higher competition, the simple half roll can be replaced by increasingly-complex roll elements. Initially this might be by including a hesitation at the knife-edge point (2-of-4 half rolls), or by making 4-of-8 or even 1½ rotations. The aileron rolls may be replaced by half flick rolls or even 1½ flick rolls.

When making a hesitation in knife-edge, be sure to look directly at the horizon and major landmark directly ahead of the aeroplane. This entails looking at 45° away from the nose in the direction of the lower wing-tip. This will enable you to maintain an accurate heading (by having zero elevator) while keeping the wings at 90° to the horizon.

Energy Matters

Energy is lost most dramatically when airspeed is significantly higher than maximum level speed. In this exercise, little time is spent at the highest speeds as the next climb is started immediately. Energy can be better preserved, once experience has been gained, by making the lines either side of the descending roll shorter. The maximum speed will then be less.

Reducing power on the descending lines will give more time for any given increase in speed, but will actually result in more energy loss over a series of figures because of the lower fuel burn.

CHAPTER 19

Half Cuban Eights

A Cuban Eight is a horizontal figure-of-eight incorporating half rolls on the internal lines so that all the looping segments are flown under positive G.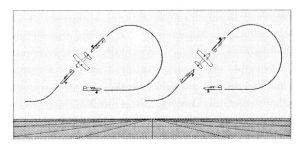

The Looping segments can be flown such that the half rolls are on descending or climbing lines. For simplicity, just half of either type of 'eight' can be flown to produce a smooth, graceful turn-around figure.

It is a requirement in competition flying that the internal lines and rolls are performed with a 45° climbing or descending attitude.

In low-powered, slow rolling aircraft it may be difficult to sustain this climbing angle long enough to complete the half roll, and you will run the risk of excessive speed on such a steep descending line. In these aircraft, at least until you have gained more experience, you would be wise to aim for 30° climbing and descending lines. The technique will not alter significantly in any other respect.

The Flight Manoeuvre

The plain half-Cuban (at least in current Anglo-American civilian terminology) consists of a 5/8th loop followed by a half roll to upright on a descending 45° line and then a 1/8th loop to horizontal flight. This is illustrated on the left hand side of the title diagram.

The Reverse Half Cuban, using this parlance, has the half roll on a climbing 45° line after an initial 1/8th loop. The figure is completed by a 5/8th pull back to horizontal flight in the opposite direction, as illustrated on the right of the title diagram.

It is, again, a competition requirement that all the looping segments in these figures appear, from the ground, to have an equal and constant radius. In other, less regimented, forms of aerobatic flight such regimented ideas can give way to other ideals. As in the case of the simple loop, different shapes can be flown for different situations.

There are versions of the half-Cubans that directly equate to the Granny Loop and the Display Loop described earlier. No one form of such a figure is 'right' or 'wrong', 'better' or 'worse' than any other. To be a complete pilot you must learn to change styles with changing circumstance.

In the Technique section below, I will describe fully all the inputs and pictures that go to make up the perfect competition figure. Some of these you can then modify slightly in order to fly the other versions.

Ground References

In all cases, it is really useful to fly these figures above a line feature, so that you have a good heading reference when the aircraft is pointing towards the ground (Diagram 19-1).

For the half-Cuban, rolling on the descending line, it is also very useful if you can arrange to be flying directly away from a distant landmark when you start the figure. Similarly, for the reverse half-Cuban, it helps to have a distant landmark dead ahead when entering the figure.

These conditions can be met with a line feature and just one distant landmark, as with the railway line and lake shown above. You can change the entry direction to suit the figure to be flown.

Diagram 19-1

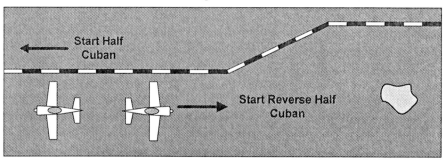

Technique

Half Cuban

Start as for a normal loop; everything is going to be the same until you are approaching the $5/8^{th}$ point (Diagram 19-2).

Use the wing tips or your sighting device to make sure you pull straight at the beginning. Remember that as you 'float' over the top of the loop you will need rudder to counteract the slipstream effect – right rudder in a Pitts or CAP, left rudder in a Yak or Chipmunk.

Diagram 19-2

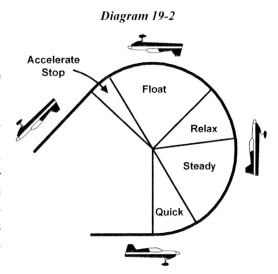

When starting the float, you can look up straight ahead to see the 'lake' or up and to your right to see the 'railway line'. Either of these will help you to check direction. The correct amount of rudder will keep you on heading and also keep your body centred on the seat.

Once the nose is below the horizon, look quickly toward the wing tip/sight and monitor the pitch attitude closely. From 25° to 45° nose down, accelerate the pitch rate so you can emphasize the stop on 45° down. Make the stop with a quick, deft forward stick movement to take the weight of the aeroplane inverted.

Count to three and then make the half roll as described in the previous chapter. Remember that you are rolling from a negative angle of attack. Keep some forward pressure so that your heading does not change in knife-edge.

Use 'bottom' rudder (the one nearest the ground – opposite to the roll direction) when you briskly apply full aileron. Look to the 'railway line' as you roll to monitor heading. Change to a little 'top' rudder just before knife-edge and remember you will need to retain some of this after the half roll is complete, because of finishing above rudder-neutral speed.

If you have a fixed-pitch propeller, remember to throttle back to maintain correct engine rpm.

As you stop the roll, look up at your canopy tape and see the 'lake' and the horizon in front of you – heading, wings level and pitch attitude can be confirmed together. Count to two and then make a brisk pull to level flight.

Reverse Half Cuban

This figure starts in level flight with a brisk pull-up to a wings level, 45° climbing line. In a low-powered aircraft you will have to start the figure at an airspeed considerably faster than for a normal loop. With increasing power/weight ratio and increasing roll rate comes the ability to start this figure from lower speeds.

High performance aircraft can draw long 45° lines and with this extra time comes the added problem of being able to place the half roll in the centre of the line. Despite the extra line length, the ratio of time spent before and after remains much the same. The trick with higher performance is just to count slower.

After holding the up line for a count of *"One-Two"*, start the half roll as described in the previous chapter.

When you stop rolling, remember to look up and forward to see the horizon and your landmark. Use your canopy tape to check pitch attitude, the horizon to check wings level and your landmark to check heading.

Count *"One-Two-Three"* and then you can start the 5/8th loop to level flight.

Diagram 19-3

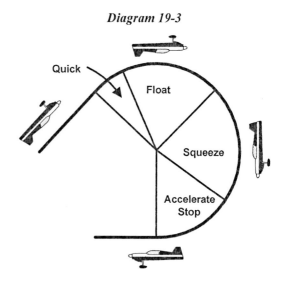

Diagram 19-3 again shows the 'stick feel' diagram for this long looping segment.

During the descent you can look towards the line feature and use aileron as necessary as you pull so that you stay on heading. In other words, expect to pull a little crooked, usually toward your right elbow, and make aileron correction so that you actually pull straight.

Error Analysis

Half Cuban

Throughout the first 5/8th loop, the errors and their correction are just as in a normal loop. Thereafter, some other problems normally arise.

Errors during the descending half roll have been covered in the previous chapter. Remember, though, that if you get a big heading error during the half roll, it is almost certainly due to incorrect elevator position. Do not try to correct this by a big rudder input as the roll finishes. Repeat the figure and this time keep the elevator control far enough forward to prevent dishing-out.

The last small point is to remember that the two radii in this figure should be the same. The radius of the final pull to level flight is therefore important. You should therefore compare your exit speed with your entry speed for the figure.

If the exit speed is higher, then the final pull to level should be proportionately higher G than the maximum achieved at the start of the long pull. Thus, if you start the 5/8th loop at 4g, you may need 4½ g or 5g (if permitted) on exit.

It is common to see less experienced pilots spoil an otherwise nice half Cuban by a slack final pull, which not only spoils the geometry but also loses an extra 100 feet or so of precious altitude.

Reverse Half Cuban

The most significant, and potentially most dangerous, error in the reverse half Cuban is to have a climbing inverted attitude, after the half roll, that is too steep. Rapid speed-loss results which can lead to loss of control by torque-rolling or stalling inverted.

The most significant step you can take toward preventing this problem is to make sure you look forward and upward at the end of the half roll and locate the horizon correctly with reference to the canopy or other clear vision panels in the roof of the plane. The canopy-mounted sticky-tape solution described in the previous chapter is really helpful in this respect,

... but you must remember to look at it.

Above all, avoid the temptation to simply stare straight ahead through the windscreen after the roll. All you will see is sky/cloud from which you can determine no attitude information. Just put your head back a bit, look up, and you will see exactly what you need to know. As in most aerobatic figures, the road to success starts with knowing where to look, and what to look for.

As you start the downward looping segment, keep looking upwards, but now also to the appropriate side, so that you get earliest possible visual contact with your line feature. If you pulled up with the 'railway line' on your left, you should now look up by your right shoulder to see it again.

When pulling down toward the ground, use small aileron position changes to make sure you remain parallel to the line feature.

Further Development

Full Cuban Eights

Not surprisingly, if you fly two consecutive half-Cubans, without pausing for level flight between the two, you will fly a full Cuban eight. But there are a couple of points to be aware of.

Firstly, if you lose height flying a single half-Cuban, rolling on the down line, then you will probably lose twice as much height in a full eight. Be sure to take this into consideration before you start the figure.

Secondly, if your reverse half Cuban finishes at a lower speed than you had for its entry, then the second half-eight might just be impossible without falling out of the top. So be sure to make the downward looping 5/8th large enough to give sufficient entry speed to continue safely.

Changing Heading Intentionally

In "Clovers" on page 137, I described how to combine a half-loop with a half-barrel roll to give an intentional 90° heading change in a graceful, flowing figure. Something similar can be done with the half Cuban eights.

You can start the half-Cuban with half a barrel roll up, with a 90° heading change, instead of a straight pull (left half of Diagram 19-4). Thus the descending 45° line and half roll will be on an axis at right angles to the entry.

Similarly, a half barrel roll down can replace the last half-loop down in a reverse half-Cuban, so that the heading change is incorporated into the down line (right half of Diagram 19-4).

Diagram 19-4

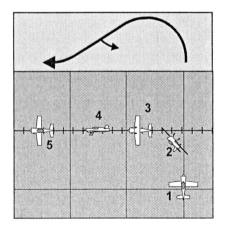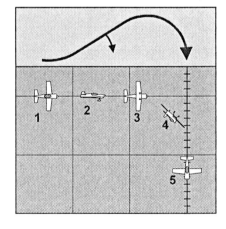

Diagram 19-5

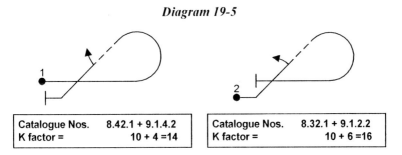

Catalogue Nos.	8.42.1 + 9.1.4.2
K factor =	10 + 4 =14

Catalogue Nos.	8.32.1 + 9.1.2.2
K factor =	10 + 6 =16

Flying in Competition

"Main Axis Wind Correction" on page 151 gave a broad analysis of the problems to be solved in flying looping shapes that appear round, to a ground-based observer, with either head or tail wind components. The same considerations apply to the long looping segments of half Cuban eights. Additionally, you should bear the following in mind.

When a reverse half Cuban is flown starting into wind, the ground speed at the apex of the figure will be even slower than the airspeed, which we know can be very slow indeed. In this situation, it may be necessary to fly almost level inverted for some time to produce a radius that can be sustained through to level the opposite way.

If the speed here is so low that -1g cannot be sustained without stalling, it will be impossible to make the shape appear round.

In such conditions, you should perhaps increase the entry speed a little but you should definitely reduce the time spent drawing lines either side of the roll. In other words, count quicker. This will enable you to have more speed into wind at the apex.

This problem is illustrated in Diagram 19-6. The flight paths labelled A and B show the result of applying the same technique and timing. What may be a perfect shape performed down wind will look really distorted into wind. The diagram marked C

Diagram 19-6

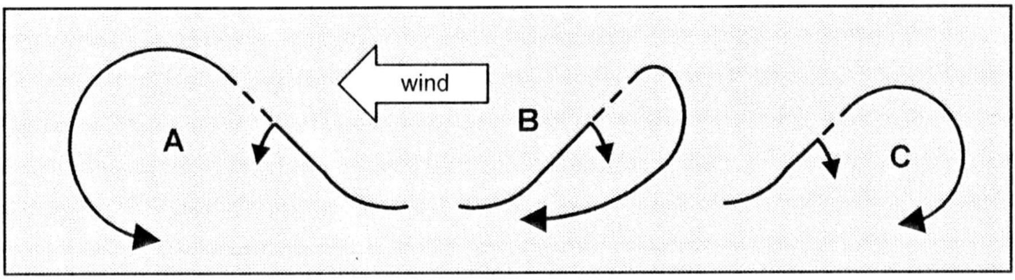

shows what might be achieved with shorter lines either side of the climbing half roll, more speed at the apex and modified pitch-feel through the looping phase.

The competition judging criteria state definitively that 45° lines are judged on the aircraft attitude, not its flight path. Theoretically, therefore, these climbing and descending lines should be flown the same regardless of wind strength and direction. Such is the nature of human perception, however, that 45° lines flown with a strong tail wind appear to get shallower as the aeroplane's speed decreases. This illusion is made more pronounced when the judge is looking obliquely toward the down wind edge of the box rather than straight ahead across the B-axis.

It is usually the case that, when flying a down wind climbing 45° line, you get a better grade if you start a little steep and end a little steeper still. At very low speed at the down wind end, you will probably find that in fact a 55° to 60° attitude is necessary to avoid this optical illusion and to score well.

Energy Matters

There is potential for losing more energy than is necessary by flying the down-line of a half Cuban for longer than you really need to. This results in excessive speed which is always accompanied by lots of drag.

You can limit speed gain by power reduction, but this just results in lost height. Remember always to try to burn as much petrol as you can (respecting engine limitations) to combat energy loss.

The best solution in a low-powered aeroplane is to draw balanced, but very short, lines either side of the half roll. By working faster, you can conserve energy without having to sacrifice accuracy.

Better Aerobatics

Part Three

Sportsman / Standard Figures

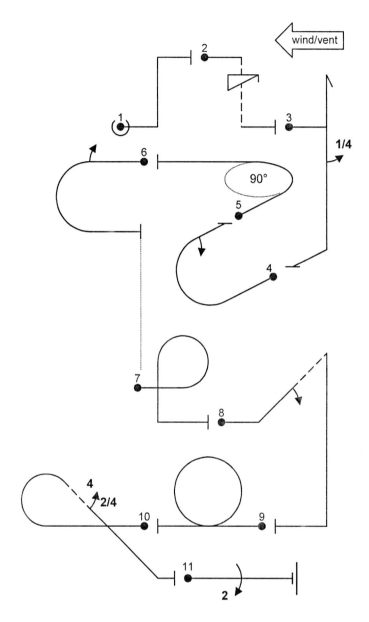

wind/vent

2

1

3

1/4

6

90°

5

4

7

8

9

10

4
2/4

11

2

International Aerobatic Club (IAC)
Sportsman Known Compulsory Sequence 2001

CHAPTER 20

Competition Spins

There was a time, after I left University to join the Royal Air Force, when I thought spins not to be real aerobatic figures.

I considered that they represented a loss of control, rather than being controlled finely throughout. I was wrong, of course, as is usually the case at such a young age. But my misconception was, I am sure, at least in part due to the way spins had been described and taught.

The spin in an aerobatic competition sequence is, indeed, a finely controlled figure throughout. A lot of finesse is required to achieve a good result that conforms precisely to the judging criteria.

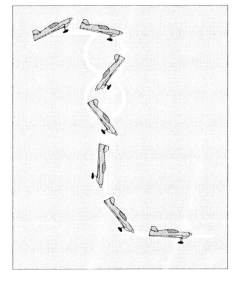

A great deal of practice is necessary to gain the confidence and feel to be comfortable with, and fully understand, the figure and how it develops. Once mastered, this figure is of enormous importance in removing those artificial limitations that are always placed around a student's own personal flight envelope during both initial and continuation training.

The Flight Manoeuvre

All competition spins begin with a stall in level flight. Those judging from the ground have to see the stall, which they recognize from the nose dropping towards the ground from a nose-high, wings level attitude. At the same time as, or immediately after, the nose drops a wing must also drop and autorotation must start. The autorotation must clearly continue at a constant rate until it stops suddenly with the aircraft on the correct recovery heading with the wings level. At this point, the pitch attitude is not important as it will vary between different aircraft types. The aircraft must then quickly adopt a vertical down attitude.

While flying vertically down, after recovering from the spin, optional aileron or flick roll elements may be added, after which the rest of the figure must be flown. This may consist of a simple recovery to level flight, or something more complex.

Diagram 20-1

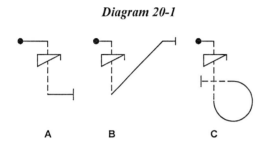

A   B   C

In competitions, spins are employed as rotational elements superimposed on basic shapes that specify the overall figure to be flown. In Diagram 20-1, a one-turn upright spin is followed by a simple recovery (A), a climbing 45° line (B) and a ¾ loop (C); all valid figures.

Ground References

Apart from a good horizon, the only ground feature needed for spin practice is a line feature directly below, or just to one side of, the aircraft.

Technique

Close the throttle; fly straight and level as the aircraft slows. Maintain direction and balance. Keep increasing the angle of attack to stay level. This means you keep moving the elevator control backwards. Don't stop pulling before the stall, or the aircraft will lose height. Keep increasing the back stick and raising the nose until the stall occurs.

When the wing stalls the nose will drop. As this happens apply full rudder in the direction you want to spin. 'Full rudder' means just that, and you cannot make this input too quickly! After you have put the rudder in, you can bring the stick fully aft. You are now spinning.

The spinning attitude varies significantly between aircraft types, but there are also differences between right and left spins in the same aircraft.

The differences between types are largely a function of the aircraft mass and its distribution. In particular, the relationship between wing mass and fuselage mass is important, as are the fuselage length and wing span. Generally, the heavier and longer the wings, the flatter the aircraft will spin. In an aircraft with a right turning engine, a spin to the left will be flatter, due to propeller gyroscopic forces, while a spin to the right will be steeper.

If your aircraft spins in a flattish attitude, you will probably find that the pitch attitude and the rate of rotation oscillate slightly once the spin develops. These changes of attitude and turn rate will lose points in a contest.

One way to make the spin more steady is to unload some of the back stick after about half a turn. If you unload before this point, the spin may not develop properly, but moving the stick forward a short distance, after half a turn, will usually stabilize the rate and attitude. The amount of forward stick movement will vary between aircraft types, and can only be properly determined by trial and error.

To monitor heading you must locate your line feature as early as possible and then track it by rotating your head in the opposite direction to the spin. It will disappear and reappear, behind the aircraft structure sporadically.

The instant to initiate recovery will vary between types. For aircraft with relatively small, light wings (for example a Pitts), this is 90° of rotation before the exit heading. For aircraft with longer, heavier wings (for example a Slingsby T67), it is about 150° early.

Initiate recovery by applying full anti-spin rudder. In other words, change feet as briskly as you like. Then move the stick forward and the spin will stop. How far forward you have to reach will depend on the aircraft type, and on the exact amount of rotation of the spin. Therefore I cannot generalize here about the amount, but the correct amount of forward stick will stop the spin.

As the spin stops, look at the ground below and then at the wing tip to check heading and vertical attitude respectively. Centralize the rudder and then make small adjustments to heading and attitude with ailerons, rudder and elevator.

You are now ready to start the next roll element or to recover from the vertical down line and continue the rest of the figure.

Error Analysis

Entry Errors

Many pilots fail to maintain height prior to the entry. They are reluctant to get the nose high enough as the stall gets really close. The aircraft is then descending ('sinking') before the yaw, not to mention travelling further than necessary through the box. Once sink has started, especially in an aircraft with some dihedral and a forward centre of gravity, it will be difficult to get a quick wing drop and a clean entry to the spin.

This problem is often seen in the Pitts S-2B when flown solo, for example. To avoid this situation, get the nose higher earlier and keep bringing the stick positively backwards. Climbing a little is not a major error, in fact it is difficult to spot at typical entry heights, and this technique also ensures you get into the spin before too much box is used up.

Most specialist aerobatic aircraft have a lot of elevator authority and will stall without the stick fully aft. Avoid the temptation to pull fully aft at the stall before you apply the pro-spin rudder. If the judges see the nose go up, you may get a zero for a 'flicked' entry. When the stall occurs, apply the rudder and **then** bring the stick fully back after the wing has dropped.

Because of its rigging, or even because your technique is a bit coarse, your aircraft may have a tendency always to drop one particular wing at the stall. You may want to spin in the other direction. If this is the case, use just a small amount of rudder pressure in the desired direction while you are still slowing down for the stall. Be sure not to use so much that your heading changes, but enough to ensure the spin starts in the direction you want. A better solution is to re-rig the aircraft so that it stalls straight, or to develop a finer feel for aircraft balance just before the stall!

Relative Wind Effect

Competition spins are usually one, 1¼ or 1½ turns. When the spin starts, the aircraft does not just suddenly stop in mid-air and fall vertically. It falls towards the ground on a curved trajectory which will only become vertical after many more turns than will be performed in a contest sequence.

Diagram 20-2

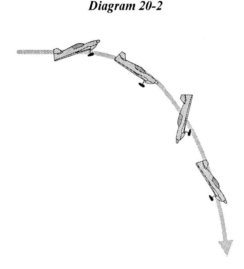

The implication of this is that when you stop your competition spin the aircraft will still have a component of travel in its original direction. The direction of this relative airflow depends on the extent of the rotation performed.

This curving trajectory is illustrated in Diagram 20-2 as it might appear in still air. If the spin is started into a strong head wind, the descent will **appear** more vertical, but the relative wind will still be as shown.

If the spin is started down wind (definitely not recommended for competition sequences) the true

Diagram 20-3

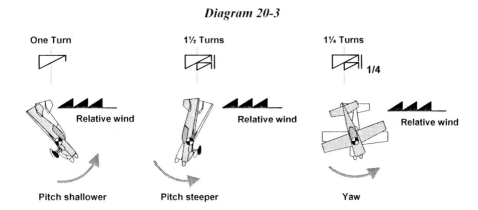

aerodynamic situation will be the same but the appearance of sideways travel will be even more pronounced.

Diagram 20-3 illustrates the result of these relative wind effects on the recovery attitudes of competition spins of different amounts of rotation. In each case, the aircraft was flying from left to right before the spin, and the grey aeroplane shows the likely post-recovery attitude.

After one turn the relative airflow is from above the aircraft. This means the aircraft stops spinning in a shallow attitude and needs a lot of forward stick to become vertical down. The opposite is true after 1½ turns. Now much less forward stick is required to become vertical as the spin stops.

The 1¼ turn spin presents a yaw attitude problem on recovery, not a pitch one. Immediately after recovery has been made, a re-application of rudder on what was the pro-spin side is needed to bring the wings level.

The amount of forward stick needed will be somewhere between the two previous positions. The yaw error apparent after a 1¼ spin is greater if the preceding spin is flatter. So the worst case in a Lycoming-engined aircraft will be after 1¼ to the left. The re-applied pro-spin rudder may have to be maintained throughout the vertical down line after the spin, only being removed during the recovery to level flight.

If you are called upon to perform a 1¾ turn spin, there will, again, be a yaw effect at the finish due to the relative wind. But it will be less pronounced than previously, because the flight path will be more vertical after the prolonged spin. Also, the rudder used to stop the spin is also the one used to make the wings level. So a good recovery attitude can be attained simply by slightly delaying the centralizing of the rudders after recovery.

After a two-turn spin, the flight path is even closer to vertical and so the relative wind effect will be less than for one-turn. But you can still expect to need more forward stick at the recovery than in the 1½ turn case.

The Change-Over Spin

Diagram 20-4

Now that you understand the effect of the relative wind on the recovery attitude, you are in a position to understand the change-over spin (Diagram 20-4).

You can then learn how to avoid this life-threatening situation. Later you can also learn how to perform it safely and eventually to teach it as either an emergency situation or as a bit of fun. The difference is purely in the mind and on the altimeter.

To stop a one-turn spin and be vertical down takes a lot of forward stick. In many aircraft this will be full forward stick.

Recovering from one-turn spins will make you very conversant with the idea of full opposite rudder and then full forward stick. In fact you may have been taught something very like that as the 'standard spin recovery' during early training. Now consider what will happen if you apply this technique, with full force, in an aircraft with good elevator authority and after 1½ turns to the left.

After you change feet and push the stick fully forward, the relative wind effect will help you rapidly develop a high negative angle of attack. Keep the stick forward and you will have a very dynamic inverted stall.

The full right rudder will initiate an inverted spin with right yaw and left roll. In fact, the left-rolling momentum developed during the upright spin to the left will help carry you through into the right-foot inverted spin with hardly a slowing of the roll component.

If you are not familiar with this situation, you will become very stressed, very quickly. You have taken the standard spin recovery action, albeit a bit aggressively, but the spin has not stopped. In fact it has become more violent and is still in the same apparent direction as before. Because of the stress, you may not notice that you are now negative and that the yaw has actually reversed, because the roll component dominates your visual field.

The emergency recovery from this spin is quite simple. It is the same as the emergency recovery described earlier in the book. You let go of the stick and change feet again, so that you re-apply left rudder.

The inverted spin will stop very quickly once you do this. Avoid this situation by reviewing the recovery action before starting the spin, and reminding yourself of the differences caused by the relative wind effect.

When moving the stick forward to stop the upright spin, don't just slam it forward without thinking; move it forward progressively while you actually observe its effect. Don't get excessively negative on the down line as the spin stops.

Further Development

The effect of power on spin recovery is seldom addressed in text books. Authors are reluctant to advocate or describe techniques which are counter to the 'standard' recovery taught in early training, even though they may use such methods themselves. But a competition spin is a very different philosophical concept from the inadvertent loss of control which can bring about the need for a standard 'power off/hands off' safety recovery.

A competition spin is a precisely controlled manoeuvre which is repeated over and over again, with ever finer degrees of precision. Experienced pilots progressing through to the higher categories of competition need to develop better under-standing and to learn more advanced techniques if they are to be successful.

Modern aerobatic specialist aircraft have relatively large rudder and elevator controls that give great authority. All competition spins can be stopped with the throttle closed. If power is added during a spin, several things happen.

The torque and propeller-induced gyroscopic forces will increase and may be pro-spin or anti-spin. So adding power may be detrimental or beneficial from this respect. The airflow over the empennage will increase, and in every case this will give greater rudder and elevator authority. This extra authority is always beneficial. In my experience, the benefit gained from the increased airflow is more than the deficit that may occur from the torque and gyroscopic effects.

The overall result of this is that, once you have mastered all the recoveries with power off, you can continue to learn to make even better stops by judicious use of power during the recovery.

Of the situations described earlier in this chapter, the one that most benefits from the use of power is the recovery after 1¼ turns. Adding power just before starting the recovery will give greater elevator authority. This increased authority can enable the spin to be stopped with rudder neutral or, in some cases, even with the pro-spin rudder still applied. It is therefore possible to counter the yawing effect of the relative wind before it becomes apparent from the ground, and to stop the 1¼ perfectly wings level every time.

Flying in Competition

Flying the same sequence on different days or at different locations leads to the need to be able to spin with equal accuracy in either direction. This is obviously true for 1¼ spins, where cross-box wind correction may be involved, but is also important for the one and 1½ turn spins because of the position of the line feature below you. Take a look at Diagram 20-5, which shows a plan view of an aircraft in a box parallel to a paved runway.

The left hand picture shows aircraft A just prior to spin entry. In the right hand picture, the pilot of aircraft B will have a very good view of the runway, the prime feature for orientation, while the pilot of aircraft C will be desperately trying to set his eye upon the box markers and to imagine a line feature between them. Clearly, pilot B has a better chance of finishing the spin on heading.

If the spin is meant to be just one turn, pilot B will be spinning right, while pilot C is spinning left. If the spin is meant to be 1½ turns, the opposite directions are true: B to the left and C to the right.

Diagram 20-5

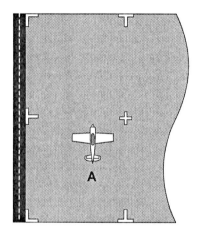
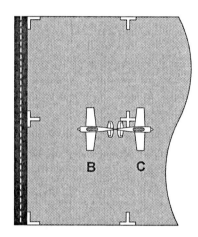

The lesson here? Always choose the spin direction that will give you the best view of the line feature during the recovery phase. For a one turn or two turn spin, go initially away from the line feature. For 1¼, go towards the line feature.

If you have to do 1¼, plan ideally to go toward the feature at the finish. Only recover with your back to the runway if the cross wind is really strong and you have no other choice in planning the cross-box correction.

Energy Matters

The spin is, fairly obviously, an energy loser because it involves descending (during the spin) without gaining speed. Thus, potential energy is lost without any commensurate increase in kinetic energy. Once the spin has stopped, a conventional energy swap occurs.

The overall loss of energy can be minimized by having power full on as soon as recovery has been made. Flying the vertical down line after the spin with the throttle closed is simply a way of maximizing energy loss. In sequence design, always take care to structure the spin entry so that energy is not needlessly discarded. Diagram 20-6 shows two examples from the Sportsman category.

Diagram 20-6

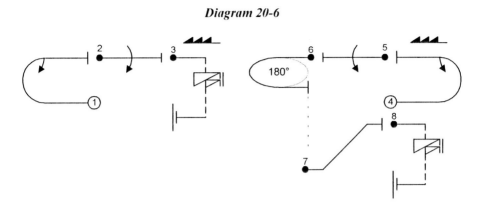

In the left-hand example, speed has to be gained at the end of the Immelmann (1), maintained through the roll (2) and then suddenly lost for the spin entry (3). This loss of speed in level flight is very bad energy management.

In the right-hand example, the speed gained through the roll and turn (5) and (6) can be converted into height during the 45° climb (7) so that the spin is entered from minimum speed. Even in the lowest powered competition aircraft, the difference between the two spin entry heights will be at least 400 feet.

The Spin Entry from a Climbing Line

Entering the spin immediately after a climbing figure is an example of excellent energy planning, but increases the workload and work rate during the transition from one figure to the next. During this transition, the judging criteria change from attitude to flight path. Very precise control is required to make a good spin entry every time.

Study Diagram 20-7. At relatively high speed before the pull-up the angle of attack is low; in this case 3°. During the climb the attitude must be precisely 45°, so the change of attitude during the pitch up is 42°.

For consistency, always fly the transition from climb to spin the same way. Make any delay for head wind correction before the climb is started. Do not try to extend the period of level flight immediately before the spin; its judgement is very difficult and the spin entry technique will have to vary also.

Diagram 20-7

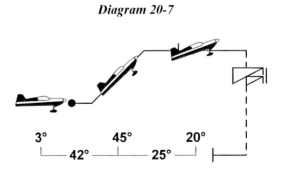

Continue the climb at exactly 45° attitude until you reach normal power-off spin entry speed or even a few knots slower. The power will give you control and prevent stalling.

Make a quick attitude change of only 25°, so that your flight path becomes level but you remain at an attitude of 20° or so nose-up. The speed should not change significantly. If it does, start next time 5 knots slower. Count *"One-two"* to draw a level line and then close the throttle, keeping the high nose attitude. As the thrust dies away, the aircraft will 'sag' and stall.

Apply full rudder as soon as the thrust has gone and the spin will start. Spin entry will be precise as long as the nose is high enough to keep the speed from increasing.

Use a very similar technique when the climb preceding the spin is a vertical one. Just start the attitude change about 10 knots faster to make the required radius to level flight. In this case the attitude change will be about 70°.

Make sure you do not push to a level attitude, or your speed will increase and the aircraft will 'sink', resulting in a forced spin entry.

CHAPTER 21

Stall Turns

As this figure is defined below, the name 'Stall Turn' is very misleading. Laymen interpret the term 'stall' as meaning the engine stops (like in a car). This does not happen! Pilots rightly interpret 'stall' as meaning an over-critical angle of attack, yet this is the complete opposite of what we are actually trying to achieve.

The American term 'Hammerhead' is rather more descriptive in that it describes the rapid yaw rotation that we see at the top of the figure.

At the end of this chapter I will suggest a possible derivation of the term 'Stalled Turn' which I believe has been 'morphed' over time into 'Stall Turn'. Bear with me now while I describe the modern inter-pretation

Airmanship

Extreme engine/propeller effects and handling at zero airspeed.

The Flight Manoeuvre

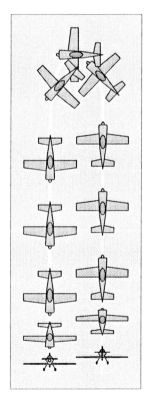

From straight and level upright flight, loop the aircraft into a vertical climbing attitude. Do not be concerned that in a strong wind your flight path will not be vertical. It really is the attitude that matters.

Maintain the vertical attitude as the aircraft slows. Counteract slipstream effect and, later, torque reaction. At the top of this zoom climb there will be an instant, and only an instant, when the centre of gravity stops rising and starts to descend. Around this instant you must superimpose the amount of time it will take to yaw through 180° using full rudder deflection. So, some short time before the aircraft stops climbing you initiate a yaw turn, in the direction that is aided by the slipstream effect that, up to now, you have been countering.

While the aeroplane is turning, you must counteract torque reaction, which tries to roll the aircraft in the same direction as the turn, and also the gyroscopic effect which tries to pitch the nose 'up' in the direction normally associated with rearward elevator control movement.

Depending on the aileron effectiveness, you may have to reduce power to reduce engine torque in order to maintain roll control.

Stop the yaw turn after 180°, whereupon the gyroscopic effect will go away. Re-apply power and descend vertically as speed increases to normal climb speed. Then loop to straight and level in the reciprocal direction from the entry.

Even this brief description betrays the complexity of this figure.

There are many ways in which a stall turn can go wrong. Remember, you are intentionally flying the aircraft vertically upwards to a virtual stop. With ever-decreasing airspeed, engine effects are set to dominate the aircraft as aerodynamic controls become less effective.

Be sure to review fully "Recovering Lost Control" on page 67 before you attempt to fly stall turns in your aeroplane solo.

Ground References

You should practice stall turns directly over a line feature. You can fly along or 90° across this line. It doesn't matter which, although your choice might be influenced by the wind of the day. It will be easier to maintain good position if you minimize the cross wind component.

It is also very useful to have a prominent distant landmark that you can view directly off the wing tip, toward the horizon.

Technique

Throughout this section I will describe control inputs for a right-turning engine. If you fly behind a Gipsy Major or a Russian radial you will have to swap left for right as you read.

Getting Vertical

Your aeroplane flight manual will probably recommend an entry speed for the stall turn. With practice, you might find you can perform a satisfactory figure from less than this speed, but initially you should regard this recommended figure as a minimum.

You can enter from a higher speed, up to V_{NE} of course, and you will be able to spend more time examining the detail of the subsequent vertical line. The bad news about higher speed is that you will have to give away more height in attaining it, so such a technique is less efficient. But with enough height the extra speed can make life easier in the short term.

If you have followed my earlier advice you will be trimmed on entry for at least the recommended entry speed. At this speed, you will probably be carrying some left rudder to remain in balance, as this is almost certainly above rudder neutral speed. So, from level at this high speed, look to the horizon on your left wing tip, start looping and add a little more left rudder to counter the gyroscopic effect of pulling.

To get to the vertical reasonably quickly, you will probably need 4g initially. Just be aware of stick position as you pull to make sure you do not get into pre-stall buffet as this will destroy a lot of energy.

After the initial sharp onset of the G keep the pitch rate steady until you are about 60° nose up (Diagram 21-1). Then increase the pitch rate until you are vertical and stop the looping segment by quickly releasing the back pressure.

Diagram 21-1

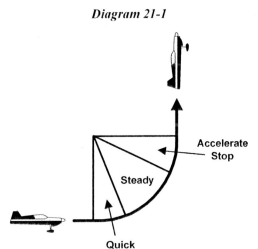

At the same time, release the left rudder pressure as the gyro will now stop and you will probably be flying slower than rudder neutral speed.

Remember the trim setting now. If you have no elevator stick force, the trimmer is still providing 'down force' to produce lift.

What you actually want now, to fly vertically upwards, is no lift. So as you stop looping add a small amount of forward stick pressure to overcome the trimmer, otherwise you will continue to pitch past the vertical.

What IS Vertical?

Review the section on "Zero Lift Axis" on page 33. It is this axis that must be vertical.

During the looping segment you have been looking toward one or both wing tips to make sure you pulled straight and reached vertical with the wings level. You will now see a picture like one of the illustrations in Diagram 21-2. In the left-hand picture, the aircraft has no sighting device, but it has been possible to set the vertical by reference to the pitot tube extending forward from the leading edge. This is analogous to the Yak 52 which has just such a pitot tube.

Flying The Vertical Line

You have set the vertical attitude by stopping the quarter loop and adding some forward stick pressure. Now you have to maintain the vertical as the aeroplane slows down. Keep monitoring pitch attitude and maintain vertical with small changes to the forward stick pressure.

Diagram 21-3 shows the result of insufficient forward stick pressure: each image shows the aircraft 'on its back' by 5°. As the aeroplane slows down, slipstream effect will now become the dominant factor in yaw and you will have to counteract it to keep the wings level.

Diagram 21-4 shows how the picture might change as the aircraft slows down. Compare the three images with the previous figure. In picture A the left wing is a bit high (remember it as a Yak) while in the other two the left wing is a bit low. The sight frames make it very easy to detect the yawing movement. In cases B and C, it is necessary to add right rudder to maintain the vertical, and this is what you must expect in the default aeroplane with its right-turning engine.

As the airspeed continues to reduce, you will need to gradually increase the right rudder pressure. If your aeroplane has a relatively large engine and short wings, like a Pitts Special, you will also notice the effect of engine torque as the speed gets very slow. The aircraft will start to roll to the left and you will see the Wing and the Earth move as shown in the left of Diagram 21-5.

You will need to apply right aileron to counteract the torque. If you add too much right aileron, the relative movement will, of course, be the other way. Study the diagram so that you can work out quickly which movement is which, as this correction must be applied delicately but automatically if you are to stay on heading

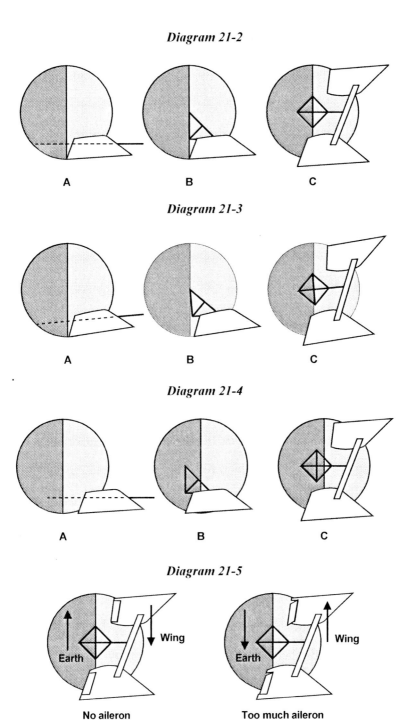

Diagram 21-2

A   B   C

Diagram 21-3

A   B   C

Diagram 21-4

A   B   C

Diagram 21-5

No aileron   Too much aileron

As you reach the top of the vertical line, you will therefore be holding some forward stick pressure, some right rudder and maybe some right aileron. You now have to determine the right moment to apply left rudder to start the yaw turn. This is another major challenge.

When to Turn

In a book such as this, which is not specific to one type of aircraft, I cannot define precisely the indications that show the ideal instant for the application of rudder to start the turn. But here are some general principles.

The time it takes to yaw through 180° depends primarily on the rudder authority and the yaw inertia of the aircraft. You can do nothing, in terms of technique, about the inertia. Rudder authority is an amalgam of rudder size, deflection and airflow. Which of these is under your control? Not the size of the rudder.

Certainly the deflection, so it is a good plan to use full rudder. And remember you were using some right rudder on the up line so you have plenty of left rudder available. Now, what about airflow? With a fuel-injected engine, or a pressure carburettor, the engine will still work well under zero G conditions, as in the vertical. Maintaining full throttle will give good airflow.

If your fuel system cuts off at zero G, then you have two options: stay slightly positive so the carburettor still works, or accept that airflow is going to be lost and fly your aeroplane like a glider. More of the glider technique later.

Let's assume for the moment that you have an engine that keeps running.

The combination of full throttle and full rudder deflection will give the best available yaw rate. If it takes two to three seconds to complete the turn, then you need to start turning one to 1½ seconds before upward motion ceases. This means at a true forward speed of about 20 to 30 knots. Because of lag in the Air Speed Indicator (ASI), the Indicated Air Speed (IAS) at this point is probably 35 to 45 knots, but this is below the useful range of most instruments. So IAS is not very often a really good guide to initiating the yaw turn.

One exception to this is found in Russian aircraft, where the ASI works reliably down to about 60 kph (33 knots). Applying rudder at 58 kph IAS in the Yak-55M always gave me good results.

In western aircraft, however, the ASI is not a good guide to determine the point of application of rudder. So, what other clues are there when the ideal time comes after the ASI ceases to function reliably? Surprisingly, the 'feel' of the aircraft can be an excellent guide. This 'feel' is a combination of engine/canopy noise, slipstream vibration and control feed-back. With practice, you can learn to determine this repeatably.

196

There are a number of ways to speed up this process. The first is to fly on days with a well-broken cloud base at a convenient height. If you fly your vertical line so that you climb above the base, beside a cloud, you can actually watch the cloud 'go down' as you go up (Diagram 21-6). As the cloud 'slows down' you will see a very clear indication of your actual air speed that suffers from no instrument lag!

A second or so before the clouds stop moving is the time to put in the rudder. You can then associate this visual cue with the 'feel' of the aircraft as this point approaches.

Diagram 21-6

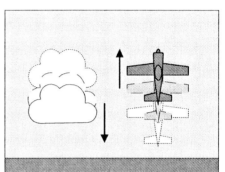

Another way to achieve the same thing is to be watched from the ground by an experienced pilot with whom you are in radio contact. He can then tell you when to kick.

For this to work well, you have to fly relatively low, so that you are easily seen, certainly no more than 3,000 feet at the highest point. Also, there really needs to be some high cloud against which the observer can measure your speed. It is difficult to make this determination against a perfectly blue sky.

For those flying high performance biplanes, there is yet another way. This is because torque effect comes into play before the ideal rudder time.

Diagram 21-7

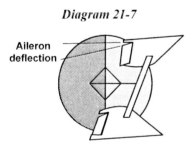

Aileron deflection

You have to apply a noticeable amount of right aileron to maintain 'heading' before the turn starts. Because you can look at both the horizon and the top wing in the same field of view, and as long as you make a good aileron input to correct the torque effect, you can determine the point of rudder application by looking at the aileron deflection at the trailing edge (Diagram 21-7).

During the Turn

To recap, you have pulled accurately to the vertical, flown a good vertical line until the airspeed is very low, and have then applied full left rudder to start the yaw turn. What next?

To maintain a good rate of turn, keep full throttle if your engine is one that keeps going! Also keep full rudder. This should go without saying, but you can easily relieve the rudder input without realizing it. While you are turning, torque will still be working to roll you left. You will need to add more right aileron to counter this, perhaps using full aileron deflection.

The rapid yaw will also cause the propeller to generate a gyroscopic force due to precession that will tend to pitch the aircraft nose-up (it is always nose-up if you are turning with the engine, as described here, regardless of whether your motor rotates right or left). So you will need to counter this effect with forward stick.

The big question concerning both aileron and elevator control inputs during the turn is *"How much?"*

Look again at the wing tip picture just before starting the turn (Diagram 21-8). Notice that this time you have pulled up with the wing tip pointing towards a good landmark: a power station. When you start the turn, keep looking at the power station. As the nose of the aircraft comes into view, you can use your peripheral vision to monitor the roll angle. The three pictures in Diagram 21-10 show zero, 5° and 10° of bank respectively.

You can see this error easily. In pictures B and C, the pilot has not correctly countered torque. These views show you how much aileron to use during the turn, or whether you have to reduce power once you have reached full right aileron. All show you have the right amount of forward stick to counter the gyroscopic force. What happens if you don't achieve this?

If your elevator input is insufficient to correct for the gyroscopic precession, you will lose sight of the power station behind the engine (Diagram 21-9).

Diagram 21-8

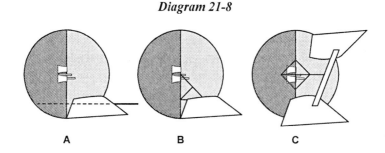

A   B   C

Diagram 21-9

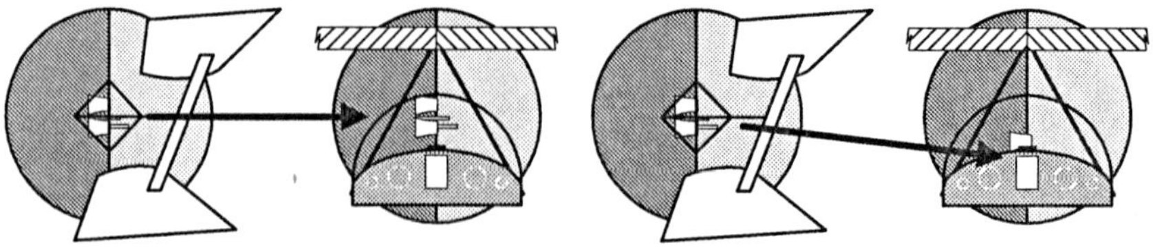

Correct forward stick   Not enough forward stick

As you track the power station from the wing tip toward the nose, add forward stick to make sure it stays in view. If you use too much, this too will be obvious as the power station passes too high through the windscreen.

As the turn continues from 90° to 180°, keep watching the power station. It should track towards the right wing tip, so that you finish in a mirror-image reflection of the start point (Diagram 21-11).

When you approach the end of the turn, remember torque is still working against you, trying to roll the aircraft to the left. Make sure you keep enough right aileron, and do not reduce it as you stop, or torque will win! (Diagram 21-12).

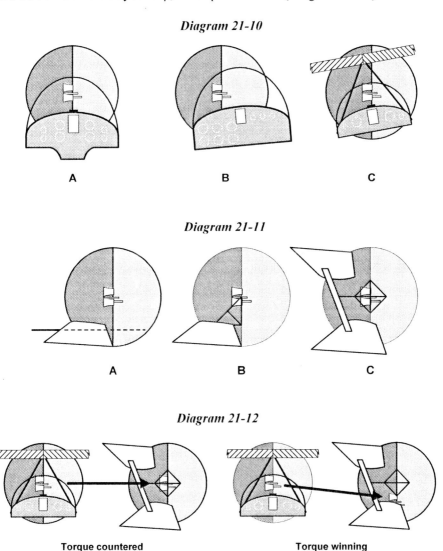

Diagram 21-10

A   B   C

Diagram 21-11

A   B   C

Diagram 21-12

Torque countered   Torque winning

Stop the turn by making a big change from full left rudder to full right rudder. Then quickly centralize your feet. Press hard with the right foot, then release it immediately the turn stops. At the same time, remove the forward stick.

The gyroscopic force will disappear as soon as the yaw stops. Bring the elevator control back to the position where it has only slight forward pressure, as on the up line. The torque will not suddenly go away, however, so maintain enough right aileron to stay on heading until the aircraft gains more forward speed.

Flying the Vertical Line Down.

Try to sit still and do nothing for a while, as the aircraft accelerates. Leave it alone while you check the attitude and heading. The time spent vertically down will vary depending on aircraft performance and desired exit speed. But don't rush unnecessarily. Enjoy the moment.

Coming Level

Diagram 21-13

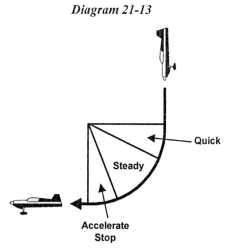

Start the pull to level flight with a quick aft movement of the elevator control. Use this to establish a comfortable steady rate of pitch.

During the last 30° of the looping segment, accelerate the pitch rate and then stop with a quick release of back pressure (Diagram 21-13).

This precise technique will clearly mark the point when you leave the vertical line and when you attain level flight.

Error Analysis

I have dealt with some small errors and their corrections during the technique section so that I can deal here with major errors and their prevention. Remember, this manoeuvre is probably the first in which you intentionally fly the aircraft in a vertical attitude up to the point where all airspeed is gone. The risk of losing control at the apex of the figure is quite large, so you must understand what might go wrong and how to avoid such traps.

Inadvertent Spins

If control is lost, risks will be highest if there is a large angle of attack sustained for some time. Maintaining a true vertical up line is important. If the aircraft is allowed to get noticeably onto its back (negative up) when it is about to stop climbing, you will be tempted to put in more and more forward stick.

Despite your best efforts, and especially if you are also late in applying left rudder to start the turn, the aircraft may fall with a high negative alpha (Diagram 21-14).

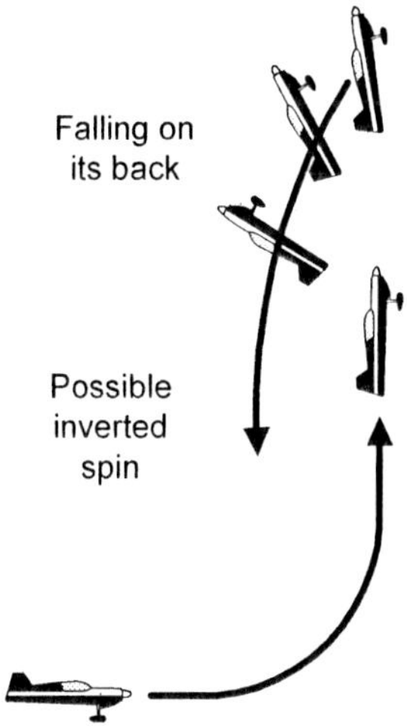

Continuing with left rudder and forward right stick under these conditions will almost certainly result in an inverted spin. To avoid this, release the stick so that the negative angle of attack during the fall will be only transitory. Reduce power and centralize the rudder once the nose starts to drop toward the ground.

Similarly, if the aircraft is too positive on the up line (on its front), and you are late with the rudder for the turn, the aircraft can fall with a high positive alpha. With the stick held back and rudder applied, a positive spin is likely.

To avoid this, again release the stick so that any high angle of attack is only transitory. Reduce power and centralize the rudder once the nose starts dropping towards the ground.

If you are correctly vertical (zero angle of attack) and a bit late with applying the rudder for the turn, the aircraft will slide back a little before turning but should still pivot in yaw with little angle of attack in the process.

Under such conditions, loss of control and spinning is impossible. You can only spin inadvertently if you sustain a high angle of attack for some time during the yaw.

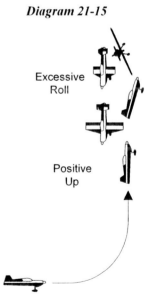

Diagram 21-14

Falling on its back

Possible inverted spin

Diagram 21-15

Excessive Roll

Positive Up

Excessive Roll

Rolling during the turn is caused primarily, but not exclusively, by torque (Diagram 21-15). While the aircraft is turning, the left and right wings have different airspeeds. As long as the angle of attack remains zero, neither will generate lift. However, if the angle of attack is positive the outer wing will generate more lift than the inner one.

This will result in a rolling couple that adds to the problem caused by torque. In this situation, just about every aeroplane type I can think of will have insufficient aileron control to counter the combined effects.

It follows that one way of countering excessive roll is to apply more forward stick, to make sure you have absolutely no alpha during the turn. You may also have to reduce power for the torque.

Ruddering Early

The problems associated with falling on your back, or front, and of high torque, are all associated with very low speed. You might be tempted, therefore, to rudder early in order to avoid such problems. This will not, however, result in a good figure. This is primarily because all aircraft are designed to be, more or less, directionally stable. This means that if a sudden yaw occurs, the aircraft tries to return to the no-yaw state.

Diagram 21-16

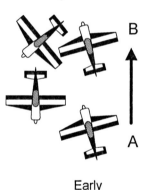

Early
Rudder

This stability is conferred by the vertical keel surface aft of the centre of gravity, which is mostly the vertical fin area.

The faster you are flying, the more this stability is apparent. If you rudder early for the turn, there will still be a lot of directional stability and this will work against your rudder input until the aircraft slows down further.

Thus the yaw turn will start on rudder application but will then slow or stop almost immediately, despite full rudder being maintained.

Only when forward speed decreases sufficiently for stability to reduce will the turn continue at a better rate (Diagram 21-16), where the aircraft travels from A to B with a fixed 15° of yaw before starting to turn again.

Further Development

Sliding in the Vertical Up

This is an advanced technique which is very useful in two situations:

- aircraft with a forward centre of gravity, and

- turning against the engine.

Forward Centre of Gravity

The directional stability problem, described above under the heading of ruddering early, is exacerbated in aircraft with a forward centre of gravity. You will find this condition most often in a two-seat aircraft when flying solo from the front seat. This is the norm in both the Yak-52 and the DHC Chipmunk. You may know of other examples. As these two aircraft have left-turning engines, turning with the engine is with right rudder. To best overcome the directional stability you need to fly so as to increase the rudder effectiveness at the start of the turn. Do this by sliding in the vertical. In other words by using crossed controls during the pull-up.

You know from the simple loop that if you pull up with some right aileron you will reach the vertical with the right wing low. This attitude error should normally be corrected at an early stage by removing the right aileron input. However, the attitude can be put right by adding left rudder whilst still pulling with right aileron. This results in a slide to the right (Diagram 21-17).

Diagram 21-17

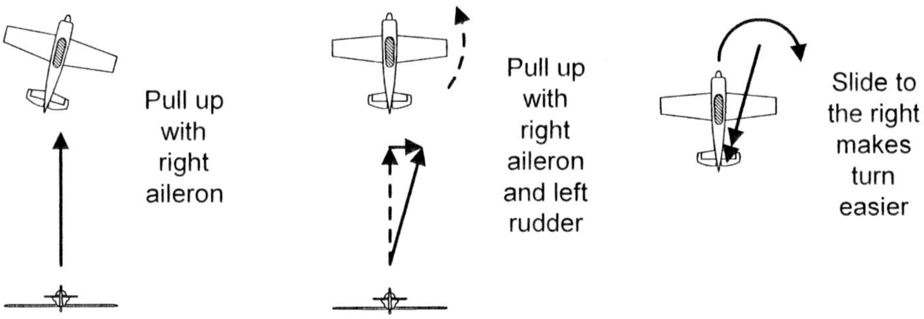

Pull up with right aileron

Pull up with right aileron and left rudder

Slide to the right makes turn easier

In other words, you will reach the vertical with a component of relative airflow from the right. As you slow down you will then continue to add more left rudder to counter the slipstream effect. Thus when the time comes to use right rudder to turn right, you will have a lot of control deflection available and the turn will be more rapid.

This technique brings with it a penalty: lost energy. The slide will generate a lot of drag, and the extent of the vertical line will be reduced accordingly. So you can understand why the technique is more easily recommended for a 360 hp Yak-52 than for a 145 hp Chipmunk!

Against the Engine

The technique illustrated above also works for a stall turn against the engine. As described it would suit any aircraft with a right-tuning engine, such as a Pitts or a CAP 10. There is a difference, however, between this and the forward centre of gravity condition.

During the pull up, the slide is caused in the same manner, using right aileron against left rudder.

Once the vertical is reached, though, maintaining the correct attitude will require gradual release of the left rudder in order to counter slipstream effect, so that the advantage gained will be lost if the up line is long. So it is best to enter from a reduced level speed so that the up line is relatively short. Plenty of right rudder will then remain available for the turn once the speed has been lost.

Once the turn has been initiated, reduce power to minimize the slipstream effect which works against the turn. Keep the elevator control a little aft, as yawing in this direction will cause pitch forward. Expect still to require a little right aileron against the torque, though this is again reduced when power is brought back.

When turning against the engine, the rate of yaw will be relatively low: initially, because rudder movement is less, and then because rudder authority is reduced when power is reduced. Once 90° of yaw has been achieved, try adding power again to re-establish a good flow over the rudder and get a sharper finish to the turn.

Flying in Competition

Diagram 21-18

Of all the basic shapes in the Sportsman's repertoire, this is the most complex from the viewpoint of pure technique. It has a correspondingly high difficulty co-efficient, or K-factor (Diagram 21-18).

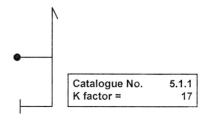

Catalogue No.	5.1.1
K factor =	17

In some sequences the stall turn is flown in such a position, on the main axis, that the judges can see only the side view of the aircraft. In this situation, you need pay no heed to wind direction. Just make sure you fly an accurate vertical attitude up and down, and that you do not roll or pitch in the turn.

Fly consistent radii during the two looping portions. It does not matter that your flight path, in a strong wind, will not be vertical. Nor does it matter if you finish at a height different from whence you started.

In other sequences, however, the judges will be able to see the plan form of your aircraft when you make the turn. Now the wind strength and direction can be very significant. This is because you can lose points for making a 'bridge' during the turn; that is moving laterally more than half a wing span.

Diagram 21-19 shows how this applies to different turn geometries. In cases A to C, no penalty should be applied, but C will certainly not please an over-critical judge (is there any other kind?). Case D is the theoretical limit for the lowest downgrade (0.5 pt), but would probably be treated more harshly by most judges because of the general trend to subjectivity.

Diagram 21-19

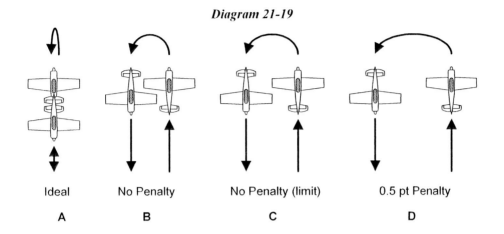

Ideal	No Penalty	No Penalty (limit)	0.5 pt Penalty
A	**B**	**C**	**D**

The difficulty for the competition pilot is that the four different geometries shown may reflect different skill levels, or they may just show the effect of wind on four identical examples of good technique.

In other words, the difference between A and D may be because pilot D ruddered very early or may be because D was flown with a strong wind from the right. The judge is not expected to understand the cause of the 'bad' geometry, just to downgrade for it. The judge should make no allowance for the effect of the wind on the figure, just downgrade what he sees.

In fact, the ideal pivot, case A as shown, is very rarely achieved in practice. The overlap case, B, is probably a good illustration of very good technique on a wind-less day. But the point is that B can be made to look like D, or even like A, by the actual wind on the day.

Consider the case in Diagram 21-20. A stall turn on the B-axis set between steep turns. This is, obviously, a simplified sequence, but it illustrates the point very well for Sportsman-level pilots. You can easily imagine it comes in the middle of a programme.

If the actual wind on the day of this flight was calm, then it would not matter in which direction the two steep turns were made, as long as they were not both the same (for then figure 3 would end down wind!).

Diagram 21-20

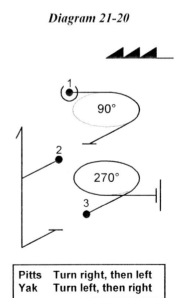

Pitts	Turn right, then left
Yak	Turn left, then right

On a day with a strong actual wind from the right, the experienced competition pilot would perform the turns as listed in the box. In both cases a stall turn **with** the engine would have the nose into the wind during the yaw turn, minimizing or eliminating the risk of 'bridging'.

At Intermediate and Advanced levels, stall turns are often associated with ¼ or ¾ vertical rolls. A simple example might be a stall turn with ¼ rolls up and down. If you start this into wind, you should do the ¼ roll up to the same side that you will turn **with** the engine. Roll left if you stall turn left. If you do the same figure started down wind you should roll right prior to turning left.

In some extreme circumstances, it may be necessary to do the stall turn against the engine. Diagram 21-21 shows an example of this from the 2001 UK National Championships.

Diagram 21-21

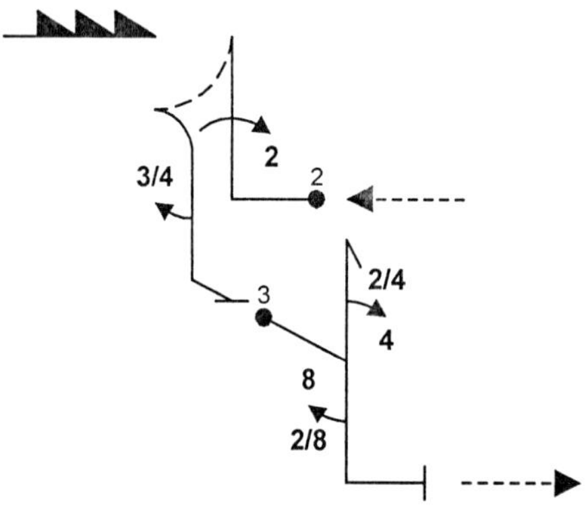

It was the second unknown sequence on a very windy day. The wind was not only from the judges' left but also had a strong on-judge component.

The line between the tail-slide and the stall turn was the only line giving a chance to fly into this cross wind and there were eight or nine more figures to come after that.

It was inevitable that this line would have to be flown away from the judging line and that after the two vertical quarter rolls the judges would be looking at the belly of the aeroplane. In order to avoid a major downgrade for 'bridging' the stall turn, it had to be done with right rudder. Easy for the Sukhoi pilots, but rather more of a test for those of us flying CAP-232s.

As it happened, I was able to stall-turn my CAP against the engine and still score 79% for the figure. A pleasing result after a lot of practice and some very careful planning on the day.

Energy Matters

There is not a lot to be said here. One point is the usual exhortation not to use more speed than necessary for the entry or the exit. Remember, any time spent flying faster than maximum straight and level speed results in a big loss of energy. The other concerns throttle management.

Don't spend time on the down line with the throttle closed if by opening it you can produce thrust. You really only have the luxury of throwing energy away like this if you have a very high performance aircraft. And then only to prevent you gaining too much height during a sequence.

When practising individual figures, always try to conserve energy as much as possible. You will get more done in a shorter time and save yourself both time and money in the longer term. Burn petrol whenever you can, to add energy to your aeroplane.

Terminology

As I said at the beginning of the chapter, 'stall turn' is almost certainly a corruption of 'stalled turn'. So what is a stalled turn? Well, try this.

Set your aeroplane on a steep climbing line, maybe 45° or 60° nose up. Hold the attitude and pretty soon you will be approaching the stall. When you get pre-stall buffet, add full rudder **with** the slipstream effect (left rudder with an American engine). Immediately the left wing will drop at the onset of an incipient spin. Complete half a turn of the incipient spin, then centralize the rudder and unload the back stick.

You will probably end pointing vertically down and can then recover back to level flight in the reverse direction from entry. This technique would have worked very well in very early aircraft, and can still be fun today.

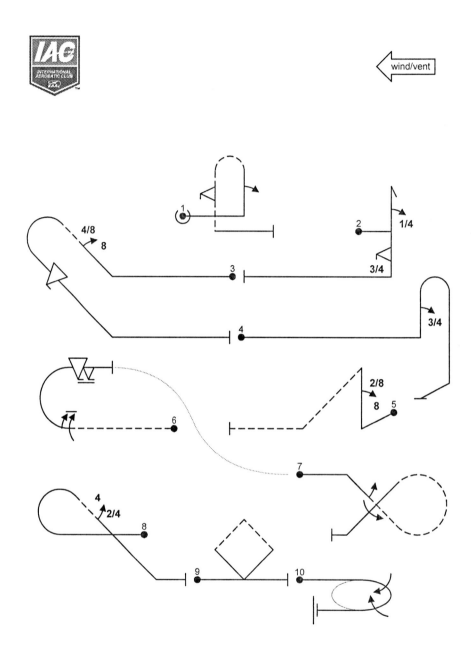

wind/vent

International Aerobatic Club (IAC), 1999
Championship of the Americas, Advanced Unknown

CHAPTER **22**

Hesitation Rolls

Hesitation Rolls are a natural extension of your aileron rolling repertoire. I use the term 'aileron' here as a distinction from 'rudder' rolls.

Most people will think of hesitation rolls as being exclusive to rolls performed on a particular linear flight path, such as level, vertical, 45° up or down.

In this chapter I will deal with level and 45° lines, but exclude vertical hesitations as there is a distinct difference with those: namely gravity is in line with the longitu-

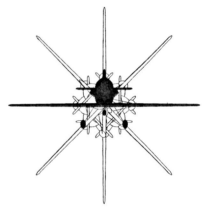

dinal axis and can effectively be ignored. "Hesitation Barrel Rolls" on page 134 touched on putting hesitations there.

The current Catalogue includes sections for 2-point, 4-point and 8-point rolls. I believe the earlier Aresti Dictionary included 3-point and 6-point as well, but these were dropped by the FAI in its 1987 publication.

Also excluded are hesitation flick rolls. I'm not sure if anyone else has even considered these as an option, and they are certainly not coded in any catalogue of aerobatic figures. Half flicks are, of course, part of the advanced pilot's repertoire, so it is feasible to conceive of a 2-point flick roll. Naturally, one of these halves would have to be initiated from upright and one from inverted, but this is no cause for inhibition, just lots of practice.

Carrying this idea further, I did once fly with a Russian pilot, Sergei Tatevosov, who did a good illustration of a quarter flick from level upright. But I'm not sure even he was up to starting the next quarter from knife-edge, let alone two more to make a full 4-point flick. And as for an eighth flick – when you have perfected that you can write your own book!

Anyway, back to rolling with aileron.

The Flight Manoeuvre

The first aim is to complete a straight and level roll, as described in a previous chapter, but with the ability to stop the roll and hold a precise attitude at various stages of the 360°. Secondly, I will describe the differences that apply when doing much the same thing on a 45° line, up or down.

One aspect of hesitation rolls that has bred a number of rules-of-thumb over the years is the question *"How long is a hesitation?"* The answer really depends not only on the type of aircraft you are flying, but also, and more importantly, on the reason you have for doing this figure in the first place.

The old adage most frequently quoted goes along the lines of *"Hold each hesitation for as long as the roll element that got you there"*. But this has its shortcomings. After all, some old aeroplanes roll really slowly, like they talk in Wyoming (no offence …), and have poor fuselage lift characteristics. Not only would holding a knife-edge point for that time be difficult, but it would probably cause a very large energy loss due to the high lift-drag ratio of the fuselage.

At the other end of the spectrum are modern carbon-winged aircraft that can roll at over 400° a second. Holding knife-edge for so short a time would render it rather meaningless, for an outside observer or even for the pilot's own benefit.

There are two overwhelming reasons for flying aerobatics. To improve your skill for your own satisfaction, and to show others (within or without the aircraft) what you can do. The answer to how long the hesitation should be is the same in both cases. **Long enough for it to be appreciated.**

If it is for your own appreciation as pilot, hold it for long enough to determine whether the attitude is just right or, if not, what might be wrong with it. If it is for the appreciation of others, be they passengers with you, an audience or line of judges below you, hold it for long enough for **them** to make the determination. And remember, some, if not all, of them are slower-thinking than you. You are the pilot; they are the audience. If you do it well, don't rush it. Take your time and enjoy the moment.

Ground References

Ground references are surprisingly important. Not so much directly below you but in the middle to far distance straight ahead. Especially useful for rolling level can be a 'ground' feature just above the horizon directly ahead, like a small puffy cloud. This is fine in England, where there is nearly always some cloud around. But if you fly where there is permanent wall-to-wall blue sky, get used to using distant points that are just below, not above, the horizon. Oh! And do tell me where this mythical place is.

Technique

As a general rule, you will not be able to do a good hesitation roll until you can perform the equivalent continuous roll consistently and with reasonable accuracy. The exception is the 2-point roll, on the condition that you have an engine that runs happily inverted.

In this case, it is sometimes useful, when learning the full roll, to break it down into its two component halves. The pause at the inverted stage can be used to analyse what may have gone wrong during the first half, and thereby distinguish errors in that part from those in the second. The inverted stop also gives you an opportunity to think about what comes next. That is, to keep forward stick pressure and use 'bottom' rudder when you start the half roll from inverted.

2-point Roll

So, if you are doing a 2-point roll, fly just as for a full roll for the first 180°. Then stop by quickly centring the ailerons and getting both feet off the rudder. This last bit is important. Most inexperienced pilots carry inadvertent rudder when stopping inverted because their concentration is elsewhere. Level inverted, especially at relatively low speed and high angle of attack needs surprisingly little rudder to maintain balance. One reason is that p-factor and slipstream effect, which normally work in the same direction, now work against each other. P-factor reverses with angle of attack; slipstream effect does not.

When you leave inverted for the second half roll, remember initially to re-apply 'bottom' rudder, to counteract the reversed adverse yaw, and to keep enough forward pressure to keep you on heading through the second knife-edge position. Use only the minimum amount of 'top' rudder as you pass through the 270° point.

4-point Roll

Now we have to consider stopping and flying, albeit only briefly, in knife-edge (Diagram 22-1).

Diagram 22-1

Earlier in the book I said that the key to accurate rolling is the elevator. I cannot emphasize that strongly enough. The reason is that the elevator controls wing lift, while the rudder controls fuselage lift. The former is much more efficient. In many situations you will find yourself using rudder to fix a problem you caused just a short while before with an erroneous elevator input. This is very inefficient. It is much better to get the elevator input right in the first place.

When you stop at the 90° point you will need an adequate fuselage angle of attack to sustain 1g of fuselage lift for a short while. This means the nose will have to be above the horizon by a fair amount. Make sure you get this nose-high attitude before you get more than 30° of bank. In that way you can use elevator to raise the nose, which is very efficient. After 30° of bank, however, the elevator will have a big effect on your heading so you must release the back pressure quickly and take over gradually with top rudder.

It is important from a drag viewpoint to use the smallest amount of rudder in knife-edge that will serve the purpose of sustaining the fuselage alpha for the short stop. Don't rely on the rudder to **lift** the nose, just to **sustain** it once you have lifted it with elevator. Make sure your initial elevator input is enough to get the nose up there where you need it to be.

When you re-apply aileron to recommence the roll, you may be tempted to release some of the top rudder. This would be a mistake. Not because the nose will drop particularly, but because you will end up with a heading error by the time you are inverted. This is because the adverse yaw from the ailerons is now changing direction as you move the stick further forward for the level inverted attitude. So as you roll from 90° to inverted, keep adding more 'top' rudder. You will then maintain heading as well as keep the nose up. When you stop rolling inverted, the adverse yaw will suddenly disappear, so you can just as quickly centre the rudder.

As you start to roll from inverted, the adverse yaw will re-appear, so you will have to re-apply the rudder you just had a moment before. This is now 'bottom' rudder. You must also keep forward stick pressure so that you have zero wing lift at the 270° mark. If you lose heading between inverted and the second knife-edge position, it is almost certainly because you have relaxed the forward stick pressure too much. Keep it on.

When you stop after 270° of roll the nose should still be high enough that you have a fuselage alpha to generate 1g of fuselage lift. At this point you will need a little 'top' rudder to sustain this nose attitude. If you find at this point that the nose is too low, it will be because you did not keep enough forward stick pressure as you left inverted. Don't try to lift it back up with a large 'top' rudder input. You will just add a lot of drag and cause the aircraft to 'sink'. Get the elevator right next time and you will only have to use the minimum 'top' rudder that your aircraft type demands.

As you leave the second knife-edge position all you should need to do is to slowly release the top rudder and finish rolling with all the controls centred. If your aircraft is one which loses a lot of airspeed during the roll, then you will have to finish with the nose a little higher than where it started.

8-point Roll

All the points I made above for the 4-point apply to the 8-point. Now you have the added complication of stopping at the 45° points. On these stops you will have to resolve fuselage lift and wing lift components to create 1g vertically. Once again, the key control is the elevator because of its efficiency.

Concentrate on making the nose track up and down accurately using mainly elevator with rudder used as sparingly as possible.

Error Analysis

As I have described in the Technique section, try first and foremost to correct errors you see by making a change in your elevator handling. If you are sure the error you see is caused by rudder only, then change your rudder technique.

One major error you will detect, and which is in fact a rudder problem, is that you will tend to overshoot the desired roll angle when you make stops in the second half of the roll. During a 4-point roll this means the second knife-edge stop, and in the 8-point roll it relates to all three intermediate positions. You probably won't overshoot so much during the first half of the 360°.

The cause here is that each time you stop you will be adding 'top' rudder, even if only a little, and that this is rudder on the same side as the ailerons you are using for the roll.

During the first half of the roll, 'top' rudder was always on the opposite side to the direction of roll. So, in the second half you are adding pro-roll rudder, and maybe just a little too much of it, just as you centralize the aileron.

The result is an overshoot in roll. The answer is that, for these later stops, you must not simply centre the aileron control but actually over-centre it slightly so that you hold a tiny bit of opposite aileron to counter the pro-roll rudder.

A very good exercise to help you master this rather sophisticated technique is to start upright and roll continuously through 270°. You must then stop the roll with a little anti-roll aileron held in opposition to a little 'top' rudder.

You must also have the elevator control in just the right position, the 'neutral point' so that you have zero wing alpha and therefore no elevator-induced heading error. Hold this point for a *"One-two"* count before returning to wings level. Practice this over and over.

Further Development

Hesitations on 45° Lines

Diagram 22-2

The key thing here is where you look. At each hesitation you need to look at a location that confirms both your bank angle and your heading. The only place to do this is at the horizon directly in front of you. That means looking half way between the nose and one wing tip, **not** straight over the nose.

Of secondary importance is that, if you are in competition, you are being judged on attitude, not on flight path. So the fuselage longitudinal axis must always look as though it is at 45° to the horizon.

Avoid the normal change of attitude between upright and inverted, which is particularly obvious in aircraft with asymmetrical wing-section and an angle of incidence between wing and fuselage. In practice, this means that the 'sacred circle' for rolls on 45° lines is smaller than for level rolls.

Diagram 22-2 shows a descending 4-point roll, assuming still air conditions. The attitude is always 45° exactly, which means that the flight path is closer to 50° from horizontal. This looks, more or less, like a built-in head wind. With an actual head or tail wind, the flight path will be further changed, even though the 45° attitude is flown very precisely.

3-point and 6-point Rolls

Even though they are no longer in the competition catalogue, these are good exercises for developing technique and, particularly, roll orientation. The latter because the stop attitudes avoid the relatively easy cardinal points. Technique is generally as detailed above, so there is not much more to say from that respect.

From the orientation viewpoint, stopping a 3-point roll at the correct place always seems to cause mental confusion.

On paper, these points are easy to work out. In the air, and because of their being less familiar, pilots lose track – especially when the roll is flown from inverted to inverted.

Diagram 22-3

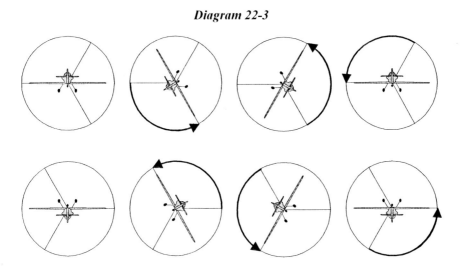

Use the following rule-of-thumb to help you (Diagram 22-3): when you do a 3-point from upright, each stop is 30° **negative** from knife-edge. When you start from inverted, each stop is 30° **positive** from knife.

The Pitts aircraft seem to be especially optimized for flying 6-point rolls! They have a full range of 60° bank indicators built into the cabane strut system that sites in front of the pilot's face between the nose cowling and the top wing. Rolling left, just put the following parallel to the horizon:

Right strut, left strut, top wing; right strut, left strut, top wing. (Diagram 22-4).

Diagram 22-4

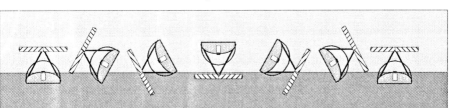

Flying in Competition

There are two issues to raise here. Both concern holding the points.

You must hold them long enough for them to be seen. If you are convinced the attitude is perfect, you might even consider holding it a bit longer than necessary, just to prove a point. You must at all costs avoid the risk that a judge or two will blink and miss the stop altogether, especially if you are toward the back of the box in a small biplane. So don't rush. Take your time.

The last point here concerns an optical illusion that is apparent when you are holding knife-edge and being watched from the ground. The judges are looking up at an angle. This angle might be quite large, especially if you are relatively high and not very far away. The consequence is that a true 90° bank angle often looks as though the aircraft is in fact tilted away.

In Diagram 22-5, if the aircraft had just rolled 90° to its left, would appear as an under-rotation. To give a better impression, it would be necessary to actually over-roll by 10° or so, so that the judge sees more of the top of the aircraft. It will then give the impression of being truly at 90° of bank. The actual angle of bank does not matter.

It is what the judge *thinks he sees* that will determine your grade for the roll. Try it. It works!

Diagram 22-5

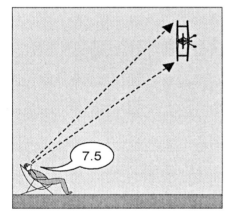 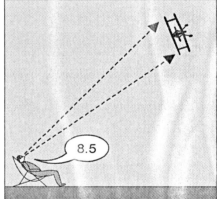

CHAPTER **23**

Hesitation Loops

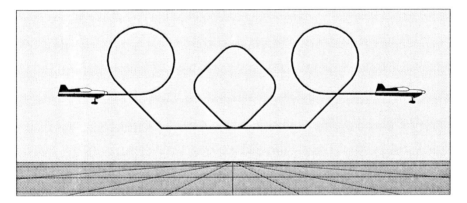

Just as you can stop during a roll, you can stop during a loop and fly constant attitude for a short while. How long you can stop for, and in which attitudes, will depend on aircraft performance.

Simple hesitation loops with a single stop, without sustained inverted flight, are interesting developments from the basic loop and require a re-think of speed and radius. More advanced figures have four or eight stops and require sustained inverted capabilities.

The Flight Manoeuvre

Consider first simple hesitation loops with a single, down-going straight segment. The examples, shown in Diagram 23-1, are used quite regularly in Sportsman level competition. The heavy line shows how the loops should appear to an observer, while the smaller shapes show how the figures are represented in the Catalogue.

Diagram 23-1

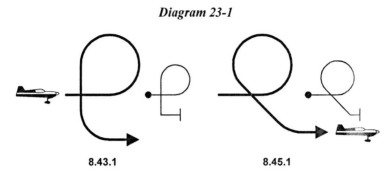

8.43.1   8.45.1

The principal difference is that the catalogue depicts any looping segment of less than 180° as an angle rather than a curve. Hence the bottom corners are shown as sharp angles whereas they can only in the real world be flown as curves. The numbers shown are the respective catalogue numbers for the two shapes, which are both from Family 8.

Ground References

For practice, these figures should be flown over a terrestrial line feature. An added bonus is having an obvious landmark just below the horizon off the wing tip, which will give a heading reference throughout the climbing part of the figures when the ground below is out of sight.

Technique

Looping technique was described fully in Chapter 16, which dealt at length with a simple loop. All the matters discussed there are equally applicable here, especially with respect to pulling straight with no aileron input. I should emphasize again here that most major errors in looping manoeuvres are caused by inadvertent aileron application associated with backward stick movement.

The insertion of a straight descending line at a pre-determined angle (usually vertical or 45° down) requires only that the normal loop is stopped at a very precise attitude. This attitude can only be judged accurately by looking at the horizon, by the wing tip, as you approach the set attitude.

It is therefore necessary to look to the side as soon as the nose is below the horizon at the apex of the figure, and to keep looking there until one of the pictures shown in Diagram 23-2 is seen. These are shown looking to the left wing of a low-wing monoplane with a wing sight.

Diagram 23-2

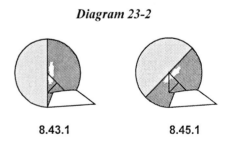

8.43.1   8.45.1

Diagram 23-3

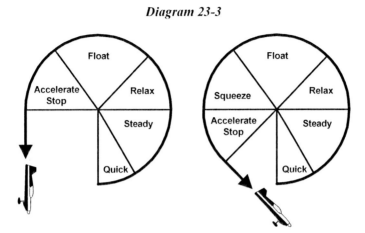

As in the normal loop, you must have a pitch-rate or stick feel plan for the looping phase so that the shape is round and the start and finish are clearly defined. Plans for these two figures are shown in Diagram 23-3. Notice that they start the same, and that the last portion of the loop is always characterized by an accelerating pitch rate prior to the stop. By making the stop in this way, you will always have a definite attitude which you can assess for its proximity to the ideal.

For both shapes the speed during the last pull to level flight will be high. Expect to reach the highest G here for the figure, just as you come level, because at high speed, higher G is always required to maintain a constant looping radius.

This last segment must have its own pitch-rate plan, even if it is just for 45° of pitch (Diagram 23-4). Remember also, that the nose attitude at the finish will have to be a bit lower than at the start, again because of the higher airspeed.

Error Analysis

Heading errors stem primarily from inadvertent aileron inputs. These can be avoided as described for the plain loop.

Diagram 23-4

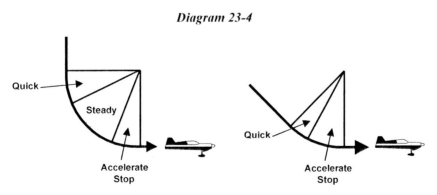

Attitude errors will occur on the straight line portion, not only in the initial setting of the line but also during it. Setting the down line can only be done accurately using a wing sight or in response to critique from a ground observer. If you are not in competition, then you can make your own judgement from inside the aircraft.

If you set the vertical correctly, angle of attack should be zero and maintaining this condition should be relatively easy. If you are trimmed for other than zero G, however, the stick force required to maintain zero alpha will increase as speed increases. The stick force for the 45° down condition will change regardless of trim state. In particular, if your exit speed is greater than your trimmed speed, then the down line will become more shallow as you speed up, unless you take care to increase forward stick pressure.

Further Development

Square, Diamond and Octagonal Loops

Diagram 23-5 is a selection of more regular hesitation loops. They all include the requirement for sustained inverted flight and so are restricted to Intermediate and higher categories. In the catalogue they are, again, shown with angular corners although they can only be flown with rounded corners. High speed corners have to be flown with high G levels, low with low.

Once again, accuracy of angle is predicated upon looking at the wing tip and the horizon. The time spent on each line will vary with aircraft performance, but can be thought of in terms of ratio rather than absolute value.

Diagram 23-5

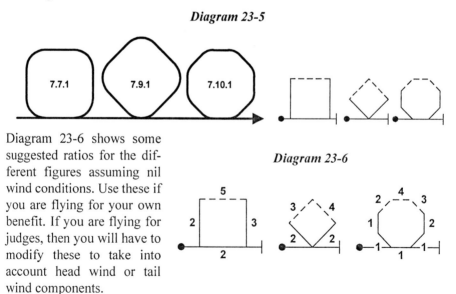

Diagram 23-6 shows some suggested ratios for the different figures assuming nil wind conditions. Use these if you are flying for your own benefit. If you are flying for judges, then you will have to modify these to take into account head wind or tail wind components.

Diagram 23-6

Flying in Competition

Loop Size

The overall size of the hesitation loop will be a combination of two parts: the size of the basic loop and the length of the straight line. To make these figures noticeably distinct from the normal 360° loop, and to enable you to accurately assess the attitude during the line phase, the line length needs to be maximized. But there are also reasons why you want to limit the exit speed. Firstly, you must not exceed V_{NE}. Secondly, you are aware that the higher the speed (above maximum straight and level) and the more time spent there, the more energy you will dissipate.

The key, then, to a successful figure is to minimize the speed at the start of the line phase, and this can only be done by making a small loop with a slow apical speed. In other words, these figures are best started from minimum looping speed.

Flight manuals for aerobatic aircraft usually prescribe a single loop entry speed. In fact, of course, you can enter loops from a range of speeds. Maximum loop entry speed is, of course V_{NE}. The recommended speed in the flight manual will be less than this, but will be more than minimum looping speed in order to provide a margin for sub-optimal technique.

From entry speeds higher than the minimum, you can fly a number of different loop geometries. The actual size of the loop will depend on how hard you pull. Of course, if you pull too hard you will stall at some stage and if you pull too softly you will not be able to fly over the apex properly. The higher the entry speed, the greater will be the difference between a minimum radius loop and a maximum radius one.

At minimum loop entry speed these radii become one. In other words, there is no flexibility of loop size. You can just get round, always on the cusp between stalling and being below effective control speed at the top. This concept of reducing looping envelope is illustrated in Diagram 23-7.

Diagram 23-7

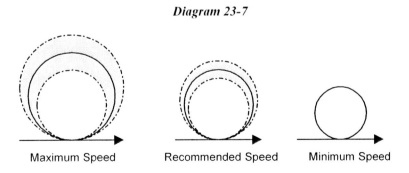

Maximum Speed   Recommended Speed   Minimum Speed

If you look at the three flight paths, it is clear that the airspeed as you hit vertical down will be least in the case of the smallest loop, the one that starts at minimum looping speed. Starting the vertical down line at the lowest practical speed allows a greater line length before you have to start to pull level.

Look at Diagram 23-8, which show flight paths for a hesitation 'P' loop with a vertical down line Both shapes comply precisely with the judging criteria. They have all corners of equal radius and they have a vertical section from A to B. Both finish at the same height.

Diagram 23-8

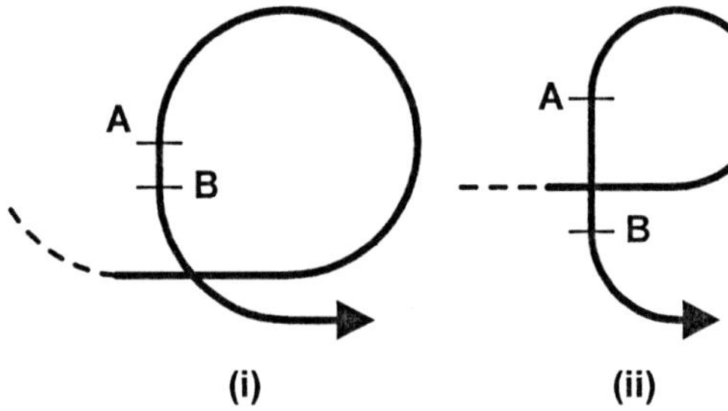

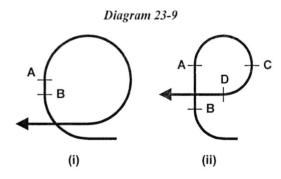

The difference is that the shape marked (ii) has a slower entry speed and thus allows a longer down line.

This right-hand shape looks much more like the Catalogue drawing for the figure and may well get a better grade, even though it should not.

Now imagine that a vertical roll had to be placed centrally on the down line. This would be much better in case (ii) because the time available flying vertically down is greater. It might even be possible to place a flick roll here, because the initial entry speed has been kept down. Trying to place a flick roll in case (i) might well result in exceeding maximum flick speed.

Climbing Straight Line Segments

Diagram 23-9 shows two similar situations, but this time flown in the opposite direction. Shape (ii) is, again, probably going to get a better grade from an average judge, even though both fulfil the criteria exactly.

Shape (ii) is, however, rather more difficult to fly accurately because of the need to be very close to the stall margin during the last 90° of the loop from C to D.

Diagram 23-9

Another big risk factor with shape (ii) is the precise airspeed at Point A. Being just a little bit slow here, particularly with a wind from the right would render the required round shape impossible to achieve. Diagram 23-10 shows the likely result of holding the up line a little too long.

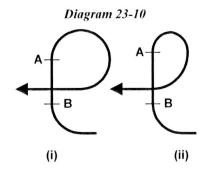

Diagram 23-10

(i)   (ii)

The total height gain is about the same, but the initial loop radius is too small and cannot be sustained without stalling on the down line. As a consequence the radius increases noticeably as speed increases and the looping shape is very poor.

If you now superimpose a wind on to these two shapes, the looping radii will change again. With a strong wind from the left, the poor technique may just be excused, but with a wind from the right it will become even more dreadful.

Energy Matters

Diagram 23-11 shows two 'P' loops flown with identical geometry. The difference is that one is flown with power applied continuously, while the other has the power reduced at A. The end result is that the aircraft with the throttle closed loses energy overall. However, it does gain time on the down line because it is flying slower.

If the pilot has to insert a ¼ roll, for example, on the down line or, even more appropriately a ¾ flick, then it might be a better strategy to close the throttle at A or even a short while before.

Here is a classic case of having to sacrifice energy in order to generate time to complete a manoeuvre.

Knowing that the 'P' loop should be started from minimum loop speed can help greatly in making good sequence design that is optimized for energy conservation.

Diagram 23-11

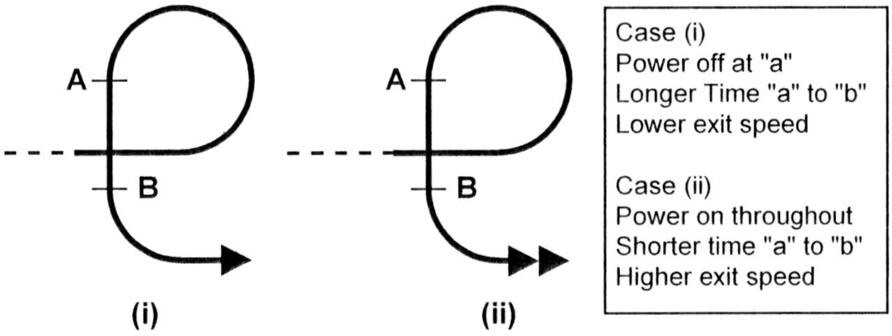

(i)   (ii)

Case (i)
Power off at "a"
Longer Time "a" to "b"
Lower exit speed

Case (ii)
Power on throughout
Shorter time "a" to "b"
Higher exit speed

This is especially so if your aircraft can reach minimum looping speed in level flight, as in a Pitts S-2A or CAP-10B.

Here are two possible ways of turning round in mid-sequence and setting up for the 'P' loop (Diagram 23-12). In case (ii) the designer has made best use of energy by always turning excess speed into height.

Diagram 23-12

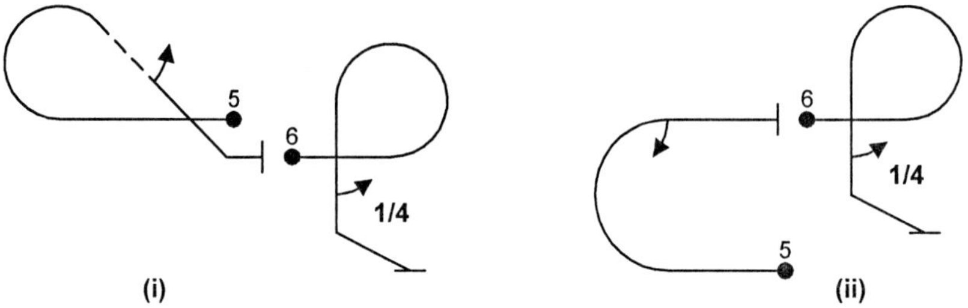

(i)   (ii)

CHAPTER 24

Half Loop / Half Roll

In American parlance this figure is named after the German pilot Immelmann, though the veracity of such an etymology is lost in time.

In the Royal Air Force it used to be called a 'roll off the top' (of a loop), although it should really be a 'half roll …'.

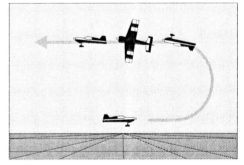

Whatever you call it, this is a neat way of converting excess speed to height while changing heading 180°.

It is, however, an easy figure to mess up. In all sorts of different ways. Yet, with a little understanding, it can get suddenly much easier, much less risky and thus much more satisfying.

The Flight Manoeuvre

From high speed upright, level flight, perform a half positive loop. At the highest point, perform a level half aileron roll. Once again wings level and upright, fly off at low speed in the opposite direction. Simple, huh? Well, yes, but beware …

Ground References

As in all looping figures, you will spend a lot of your time looking at the wing tip. It helps, therefore, to have a distant landmark just below the horizon at 90° to your initial flight direction. It is also good during practise to have a straight line feature below you, although you will see this only during and immediately before the roll.

Technique

The 180° looping segment has to be planned carefully. Many flight manuals will give a higher entry speed for this figure than for a plain 360° loop, but just starting faster is not really the solution.

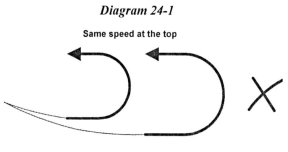

Diagram 24-1

Same speed at the top

Faster start, bigger loop

The important thing, looking ahead into the second half of the figure, is that you arrive at the top of the half-loop with enough airspeed to accomplish the roll and then fly away level. In a regular loop, the airspeed at the apex may well be less than that at which you can either roll easily or fly level without stalling.

The first key point, then, is to fly the looping shape so as to have a higher apical speed than normal. This may require starting the loop from higher than normal looping speed. An extra 10 knots should be sufficient. But it also means flying the loop so as to minimize the height gain and thus have the best chance of flying away at the end. It is quite easy to start the loop faster than normal, but if you then just fly a bigger loop than normal you will end up at the top with the same, too-low, speed (Diagram 24-1).

The solution is to start a little faster, sure, but to make the loop tighter than normal, especially for the 45° either side of vertical. You will then gain less height overall, but you will retain more airspeed for the rolling phase (Diagram 24-2).

Start with a shallow dive to gain speed. Do not exceed maximum engine rpm.

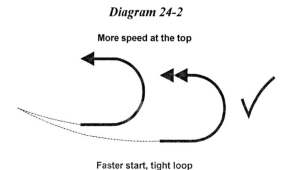

Diagram 24-2

More speed at the top

Faster start, tight loop

Maintain precise balance as you accelerate. This will require a little left rudder with a right-turning propeller. Look at the wing tip and bring the aircraft briefly to level flight. Start the loop briskly, using perhaps 4.5g initially, and maintain a good pitch rate through the vertical.

As ever, look at the wing tip and use small aileron corrections to make sure you are pulling straight. If you do not have a wing sight, make sure you look at least twice at each wing tip before you reach vertical. This is the best way to make sure you correct any inadvertent aileron inputs at the beginning of the loop. Make sure you have full throttle once engine speed is not a problem.

Diagram 24-3 is a 'stick-feel' diagram for the half loop. Notice that the 'steady' pull period is much longer than for the normal loop. This keeps the half-loop small when you would normally begin to ease off the back pressure.

Diagram 24-3

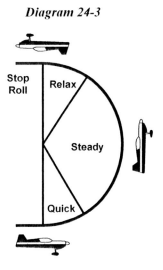

Start the 'relax' segment with only 30° of the half-loop remaining. This will improve the roundness of the figure but now you will lose no more speed before you start the half roll. You are now almost certainly below normal climb speed.

When you ease off the back pressure, there is enough thrust to keep the aircraft's speed as you gently come to level inverted. In fact for the last few degrees, you will probably be gaining speed before the looping segment is actually finished.

Now look ahead. You will see the nose of the aircraft and the horizon that began behind you. As you look from the wing tip to the nose, you should also pick up an axial heading reference. This may be the line feature below you or something prominent just below the horizon. The nose and the horizon should be coming slowly together as you reach the apex of the loop.

As soon as you see the normal level, inverted attitude with respect to the horizon move the stick briskly forward to stop any further pitch and immediately apply full aileron in the direction of roll. This will normally be to the left with a Lycoming engine.

To stop the loop, you will have moved the stick far enough forward to have a small negative angle of attack. This means that when you rapidly apply full aileron you will generate some adverse yaw. Counteract this by a small application of bottom rudder, in the opposite direction to the aileron. That is, right rudder if you are rolling left.

As you approach 90° of bank, ensure that the elevator is put to the neutral point while maintaining full aileron. Any wing lift at this point will cause a heading change. This means easing the control column back slightly from the position at the start of the roll. You should also now change feet to apply a small amount of top (left) rudder through the knife-edge position.

Continue the roll, but make sure it doesn't speed up because of the left rudder.

Remove the left rudder and then stop the roll as the wings come level. Bring the control column back to give a relatively high positive angle of attack to fly away at low speed with the nose high. Re-apply right rudder to maintain balance in this new configuration.

Error Analysis

Pulling Crooked

During a rapid pull, a little inadvertent aileron will give quite a noticeable heading change. You must pull straight toward your navel in order not to 'drag a wing' while looping.

The only way to be certain of pulling straight is to look at the wing tip sight, or at both wing tips alternately, while pulling and to make small aileron inputs to maintain symmetry until you reach the inverted position.

Stalling in the Half Loop

As I showed in "Loop Size" on page 221, a high entry speed leads to a looping envelope with maximum and minimum radii.

To arrive at the apex with the highest airspeed, you must aim to fly the inside edge of the envelope. This means being close to critical alpha throughout most of the pulling phase (Diagram 24-4). It is therefore quite easy to be just that little bit too enthusiastic with the elevator control and get into pre-stall buffet and then into the stall proper.

From experience, the most likely attitude for this is about 30° past the vertical, when speed is rapidly decreasing and stick forces are reducing accordingly. The immediate solution, should buffet occur, is of course to slightly reduce the back pressure so that the wing once again produces more lift and less drag. If the stall is

Diagram 24-4

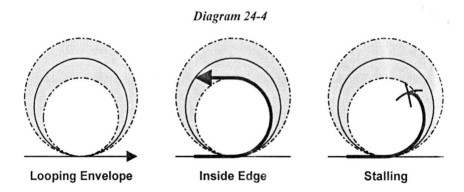

| Looping Envelope | Inside Edge | Stalling |

a deep one, however, energy loss will be high and some roll will almost certainly be induced.

In this instance, abandon the planned figure. Move the elevator forward to the 'zero G' neutral position and roll the aircraft upright in the same direction that it wants to go through engine torque.

Heading Change while Rolling

Diagram 24-5

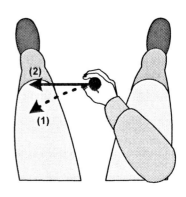

The principal cause of unwanted heading change during the half roll is incorrect elevator input. Remember the Ballistic Roll (Chapter 10) and the definition of neutral elevator.

During the half roll there will be a knife-edge point where wing lift must be zero. If you inadvertently apply some back stick when you apply the aileron for the roll, you will turn in the opposite direction to the roll (Diagram 24-5). In other words, if you roll left with some parasitic back stick you will end up off-heading to the right.

When you apply full left aileron, be careful not to apply any back stick because of the ergonomics of cockpit layout (1). Stretch out with your arm so that you apply aileron while finding the neutral elevator position (2).

Yaw/Balance Errors

During the half roll, good footwork is essential. Bad footwork can cause heading errors but is more likely to result in excess drag combined with 'sinking' instead of flying off cleanly. In the worst case, misuse of the rudder can result in an incipient spin occurring, just at the end of the rolling phase.

The main rudder error is to apply rudder in the same direction as aileron at the start of the half roll. Remember that adverse yaw changes direction when the angle of attack is negative. When you move the elevator control forward to stop the half loop, you set up a negative angle of attack. It is thus really important to use 'bottom' rudder initially to maintain balance. While the half roll is taking place, you need to make three rudder movements, in phase with the bank angle, as shown in Diagram 24-6.

During the first third of the half roll to the left, apply a small amount of right (bottom) rudder. Follow this with left (top) rudder during the second 60° of roll. For the last third of the half roll be sure to remove the rudder so that you have no

Diagram 24-6   Rudder inputs

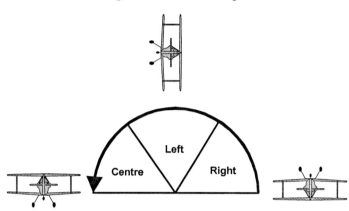

significant rudder input as the weight of the aircraft comes to be carried on the wings just before you fly away.

Remember, as soon as the roll stops, you will need stick back to maintain a high angle of attack to fly off at low speed. This will require right rudder, once again, after the roll has stopped. If you are still carrying left rudder at the time that you apply the back stick, the least that can happen will be that the roll goes beyond 180° and you finish left wing low. The worst is that you enter an upright spin to the left because you are slow, have a too-high angle of attack and have left rudder adding to the engine forces (P-factor and slipstream effect) yawing the aircraft to the left.

Further Development

Rolling Early

Diagram 24-7

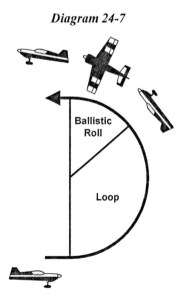

Here is an example of a technique which might be considered an error or a solution to a problem. It depends rather on your definitions.

In some low-powered aircraft with poor ailerons, you may find it impossible to get to the top of a half-loop with enough speed to complete a level half roll, with its attendant need for 1g of fuselage lift in the knife-edge attitude.

One option in such an aircraft is to start rolling earlier, while the aircraft still has a rising flight path, with the aim of completing the half roll by the time the aircraft comes to level flight (Diagram 24-7). This can work well as long as drag is kept to a minimum consistent with full aileron application. This is effectively a ballistic half roll; the aircraft is rolling under zero G.

As the roll is started, it is important to put the elevator control into the neutral position so that no wing lift is generated and hence no induced drag. As long as the angle of attack remains zero, there will be no adverse yaw and thus no need for rudder to counter it. There will likewise be no P-factor. There will be some slipstream effect and this must be countered by a little right rudder throughout the roll.

Diagram 24-8

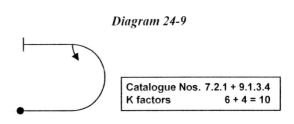

Left rudder by mistake!

Once more, it is very important if rolling in this way to avoid any kind of left rudder input with the left aileron application. This will result in the nose staying too high. A large left rudder input will lead to fuselage 'stall' and huge amounts of drag, followed by a sinking trajectory (Diagram 24-8).

From the earliest stage of flight training, all pilots are taught to apply aileron and rudder to the same side to enter a balanced turn. There are numerous examples in aerobatic flight when making these two inputs together, automatically, will cause problems. Learning to overcome this early indoctrination usually takes some time. So don't be disheartened if your early attempts at 'rolling off the top' are a long way from perfect

Flying in Competition

There are three really important judging criteria for this figure in competition: the looping segment must appear to be of constant radius; the roll must start as soon as the loop has been completed,

Diagram 24-9

| Catalogue Nos. 7.2.1 + 9.1.3.4 |
| K factors   6 + 4 = 10 |

with no straight line in between; the half roll must be on a straight and level flight path (Diagram 24-9).

Diagram 24-10 shows the same flight geometry in three different wind conditions. In A there is no wind and the half-loop is nicely round. The point where the pitching stops is directly above that where it started. In B and C there is wind as shown by the triple arrows, with consequent distortion of the circular flight path as observed from the ground. The actual changes in loop radius are difficult for a judge to discern and quantify. But it is very easy for the judge to see that end points of the loop (the top corners of the grey segments) are not directly above the start points.

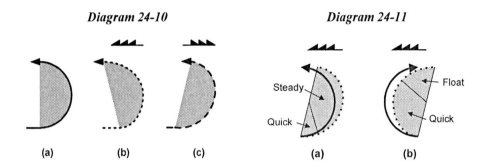

Diagram 24-10   *Diagram 24-11*

(a)   (b)   (c)   (a)   (b)

To make a compensation for these wind variations, and present an apparently round shape, you must modify the looping profile so that the end points are directly above the start points. If you achieve this, the judge is very unlikely to determine any internal changes of the radius.

To make the adjustment, you must mentally swap over the two 'bad' shapes. You must fly an intentionally 'pinched' loop when starting with a head wind, or fly an exaggerated 'float' when starting with a tail wind. These two situations are shown in Diagram 24-11, where the shaded segments show how the loop feels from inside the aircraft, while the solid lines show the resulting 'good' shape.

If you are putting figures such as this in your Free programme design, then be aware that the wind correction is much easier to achieve, and more energy efficient, if you start the Immelmann into wind and have wind assistance when at low speed at the top of the loop. Making the wind correction the other way round requires a higher entry speed and very high initial and sustained g-level which create a great deal of induced drag.

At the completion of the half loop you must ensure that the judge sees no straight line before the roll starts. To do this you must have in your mind no separation between the two elements. You must think *"Stop-Roll"* as one entity, where 'stop' is the deft forward stick movement to show the end of the loop and 'roll' is the application of full aileron. If these are not one action in thought, they will not appear as one action in the judges' perception.

Assuming all the other problems discussed above have been overcome, the remaining common error in higher performance aircraft is not finishing the half roll with the nose high enough to sustain level flight at the reduced airspeed. When you practice, study the vertical speed indicator (VSI), or altimeter if there is no VSI, carefully for several seconds to make sure you remain level. As the aircraft accelerates, you will be able to lower the nose slightly.

If you find you are unable to fly level without stalling at the end of the half roll, you have two options. The first is to start a little faster and make the half loop even smaller than before in your attempt to get more airspeed for the roll. The second, and this may be necessary in low-powered aircraft, is to partially adopt the 'roll early' technique described above.

You should, of course, be downgraded for starting the roll before completing the 180° of looping, but this downgrade may be less than for stalling or sinking badly at the end of the roll. Often, those in low-powered aircraft have to work out the lesser of two evils and fly for the better score rather than for perfection!

Energy Matters

During the half loop you must be close to the stall margin. You will therefore induce quite a lot of drag. If you try to save energy by pulling more gently, it is very likely that the radius at the top will be too small, or that you will complete the half loop with insufficient speed for a good half roll.

Similarly, trying to gain as much height as possible during the half loop will usually result in a poor figure.

So there really is no strategy that will give a good figure and also conserve energy during the process. Your energy management thinking with regard to this figure must really concern the pre-entry and post-roll conditions. In other words, learn to fly the Immelmann from as low a speed as possible in your aircraft type. Then try not to waste more height, during a dive or during a preceding figure, than is necessary to achieve this minimum speed.

At the completion of the figure, you will be in a low-speed level configuration with full power applied. This is an energy-building state and you should aim to spend as much time as you can in this situation before starting another figure.

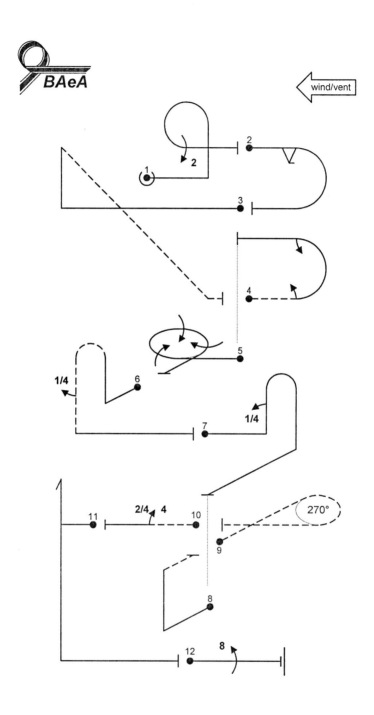

British Aerobatic Association, 2000
National Championships, Intermediate Unknown Sequence

CHAPTER 25

Half Roll / Half Loop

Here we have the opposite of the Immelmann described in the previous chapter. It is sometimes called a 'Split-S', sometimes a 'half roll-and-pull-through' which is rather more explanatory. I suspect the 'Split-S' name derives from the figure being half of a 'Vertical S' which has been split in two, but it really is not of great importance 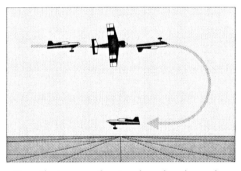 how these terms come about. It just matters that we understand each other when we discuss our pastime.

This is one of the figures which, when I am judging a low category contest, causes me the most frustration. This is because so many pilots approach the figure in the wrong state of mind and therefore with the wrong entry parameters. Poor execution of the figure results in an unnecessarily large height loss and has been the cause of many height penalty marks in Sportsman level contests, especially when the figure appears near the end of the sequence.

The key thing in many pilot's heads, as they set the aircraft up for the figure, is concern about the high exit speed.

This is apparent because they close the throttle and try to slow down in level flight before starting the roll. They obviously believe that if they enter the figure really slowly they will exit the figure relatively slowly. This is just not the case. Airspeed on exit is largely governed by height loss and by drag induced during the half loop downwards. The way to keep exit speed down is to sustain high alpha all round the half loop.

The simplest way to do this **and** keep the shape reasonably round is to have a relatively high entry speed. This also makes the half roll much easier, especially in low powered aircraft with a slow roll rate.

Diagram 25-1

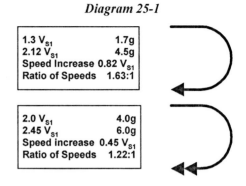

1.3 V_{S1}	1.7g
2.12 V_{S1}	4.5g
Speed Increase 0.82 V_{S1}	
Ratio of Speeds 1.63:1	

2.0 V_{S1}	4.0g
2.45 V_{S1}	6.0g
Speed increase 0.45 V_{S1}	
Ratio of Speeds 1.22:1	

Here are some figures to support my argument (Diagram 25-1). This part of the analysis is generic, in that the figures are true regardless of aircraft type. In the first case we have a relatively low entry speed: just $1.3V_{S1}$. The most G you can pull at this speed without stalling is just 1.7g. This is a relatively lightly loaded condition and the aircraft will accelerate quite quickly as it starts to descend. At the end of the loop you are likely to have 4.5g on the clock and to be travelling at $2.12V_{S1}$. The speed has increased by $0.82V_{S1}$ and the ratio of exit and entry speeds is 1.63:1.

In the second case, entry at $2.0V_{S1}$ means you can immediately pull almost 4g and the aircraft will be heavily loaded throughout the half loop. The drag induced will prevent rapid speed build-up and you are quite likely to finish the loop at 6g and $2.45V_{S1}$.

In this case the speed increase is barely half of that in the first case, while the ratio of exit and entry speeds is just 1.22:1. The fact that the entry and exit speeds are much closer in the second case means that it is much more likely that the half loop will appear round.

The last part of this analysis is arguable, because it does depend on aircraft type characteristics. It concerns how much height is lost in the figure. Speed gain does not directly relate to height loss, because the drag profiles during the two half-loops are not the same. However, in many typical aircraft you will find that the height loss in the second case is actually less than in the first. In other words, by slowing down before the roll you have ensured more height loss and a slower exit speed. Just the opposite of what is desired.

The soundness of this analysis was demonstrated very forcefully one day a few years ago when I was flying as safety pilot in the front seat of a Pitts S2A during a Standard level competition flight in the UK.

We were flying 2-up for insurance reasons. It was a known sequence, but the back-seat competing pilot was new to this location. An Immelmann was to be followed immediately by a Split-S. The Immelmann finished a bit off-heading however, and the pilot was not sure by how much. He therefore, quite sensibly, decided to take a break before restarting on the correct heading with the Split-S. So he flew three wing rocks, almost a complete 360° level turn and then three more wing rocks to signal the restart. During the whole of this time, however, he had been so concerned about his positioning that he somehow forgot to reduce power.

We thus were set up for the Split-S figure at close to maximum level speed of about 140 mph. Normally I would recommend 120 mph, but I knew that 140 mph was safe as long as the loop was kept small, if not quite what was expected. So as not to distract the pilot any more I said nothing. The half roll came, followed immediately by a sharp pull of about 5.5g. This quickly increased to 6g and we reached the bottom of the loop at about 155 mph. Height loss was no more than 500 feet and the figure scored quite well because it just had to be fairly round; the entry and exit speeds being so close.

This discussion has come at the beginning of the chapter, not at the end under Energy Considerations because the first part of any 'technique' section should always be consideration of entry speed.

Airmanship

Lookout, high-G looping, grey-out, engine handling, high speed flight. Of all the figures so far described, this is the one during which you are most likely to reach the maximum permitted G for your aircraft.

If you fly one of the semi-aerobatic types where this limit is less than 6g, I recommend you do not fly the figure solo until you have been trained and authorized to do so by an aerobatic instructor with considerable experience on that type.

The Flight Manoeuvre

Following on from my comments above, I should recommend an entry speed for this figure of $2V_{S1}$, twice the 1g stall speed with power off. This is actually the speed I want you to have at the start of the half-loop. So if your aircraft is one that will lose speed during a half roll in level flight, then you might actually start a little faster than this. From this level entry, fly the first half of a straight and level roll as described in Chapter 17 on page 153.

Then make a positive half loop downwards staying on, or regaining, the original flight axis. At the end of the figure fly away at high speed in the reverse direction from the start.

Ground References

Try to be directly over a straight line feature when you practice this figure. A bonus is to have a prominent landmark just below the horizon, or a small cloud feature just above the horizon, at the start.

Technique

Diagram 25-2

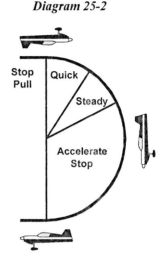

During the half roll, keep looking ahead so that you are sure to maintain heading. Use normal straight and level roll technique.

As you reach 180° of roll, centralize both aileron and rudder and immediately make a quick backward stick movement so that you break the horizontal line and start pitching down. This quick movement should make just 10° or 15° of nose down attitude change.

While doing this look up through the top of the canopy and visually locate the line feature on the ground below you. This will help you to keep on heading during the half loop.

If there is no such feature, look at the wing sight during the half loop and use small aileron corrections to make sure you pull straight.

After the initial stick movement you should rapidly reach 3g. As the loop develops, keep gradually increasing the pitch rate as the speed slowly increases.

Try to reach peak G just as you come to the new level attitude and then release the back pressure quickly so that you return again to the 1g condition. The stick 'feel' diagram for this is shown in Diagram 25-2.

Error Analysis

If you are off-heading after the half roll, then recap "Height and Heading Errors" on page 161. The most likely cause is not having enough 'top' rudder just before you stop rolling, when the adverse yaw has reversed. Do not be tempted to let the nose drop during the half roll; the aircraft must not descend before the wings are level in inverted flight.

Diagram 25-3

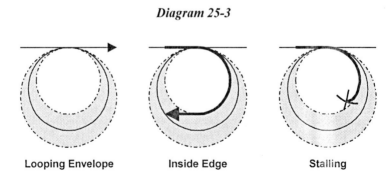

Looping Envelope   Inside Edge   Stalling

Throughout the pull down, you should be close to the stall margin. If you make a larger loop than necessary, you will have excess speed at the end and may also lose a lot more height than you need.

Diagram 25-3 shows the downward looping envelope and where you are most likely to overstep the stall boundary if you are too energetic with your back stick. If you do create a high-speed stall here, don't worry about it, just ease off the back pressure a little and complete the figure.

Diagram 25-4

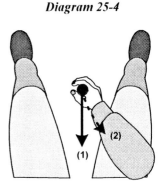

Finding the 'edge' here once or twice will be good experience in training, and will give you a better feel for just how hard you can pull in this particular aircraft type.

If you lose heading during the half loop, it will most likely be off to the right. Once again you have fallen prey to the ergonomics of your right hand operating a central control column (Diagram 25-4). Look at the line feature or the wing tip, and make sure you pull towards your navel (1), not your elbow (2)!

Further Development

If you have more than the minimum performance aircraft, you might like to try adding a hesitation or three into the half roll. In other words, do half of a 4-point or 8-point roll before the half loop (Diagram 25-5).

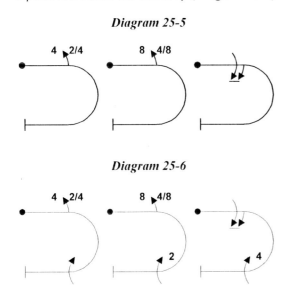

Diagram 25-5

Diagram 25-6

Alternatively, you could practice more low-speed rolling technique by making 1½ rolls level before going down.

For even more fun, try starting a level roll of some sort as soon as you finish the looping segment. These kinds of additions are often made in competition sequences and give you a lot more to think about (Diagram 25-6).

Now you will be rolling at quite a high speed, so the centre of the sacred circle will be a little lower than normal and you should benefit from a quicker roll rate. Be sure to keep your hand/foot coordination of the highest quality. Do not stop using your feet just because the directional errors in a high speed roll are less. Keep the rhythm, just decrease the magnitude of the rudder inputs compared to lower speed rolls.

Flying in Competition

The Split-S has an exactly analogous set of problems in competition to those of the Immelmann. A lot of my discussion in the preamble to this chapter will help with the dominant problem of getting the round shape of the loop distorted. Be especially aware if you find you are starting a Split-S into wind with low airspeed. Don't start. Accelerate more in level flight.

Get the optimum speed before the half roll. You won't travel far in the process. The stronger the head wind the more this is true.

Diagram 25-7 and Diagram 25-8 are very similar to those for the Immelmann, but upside down and with a few more words. I'm sure you can appreciate their wisdom by now, without me having to comment on them at length.

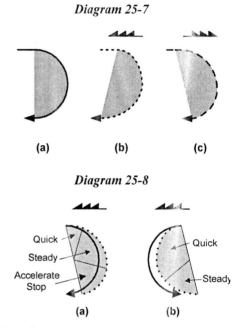

Diagram 25-7

(a)   (b)   (c)

Diagram 25-8

Quick
Steady
Accelerate
Stop

Quick
Steady

(a)   (b)

Energy Matters

Because it finishes with a high speed exit, most probably faster than maximum level speed, and because it requires looping at high angles of attack, the Split-S is always something of an energy consumer. The gain in speed never really justifies the loss of height. So, like the roll off the top, it is what you do before and after that matter most in terms of energy management.

If you are in low speed flight before the Split-S, maximize the time spent accelerating before you start the figure. Always try to get up to the optimum entry speed before you start the half roll.

At the end of the figure, especially if you are indeed flying faster than you can maintain in level flight, start a climbing manoeuvre without delay. Do not spend time decelerating in level flight while you analyse what just went right or wrong.

CHAPTER **26**

Humpty Bumps

The Humpty Bump (I'm sorry, I don't know why its called this, it's a silly name, has no real meaning, but that's what everybody calls it), or just 'Humpty' for short, is another type of hesitation loop. It was excluded from the earlier chapter on hesitation loops because the technique and profile are somewhat different from the others.

The difference here is that, during the small half loop at the apex, we are not trying to fly the same radius that we have when we pull up for the figure or when we pull out at the end.

The radius at the top will always be smaller, than the two at the bottom, and this gives us the opportunity to learn how to control the aircraft precisely in pitch at very low speed and at less than 1g.

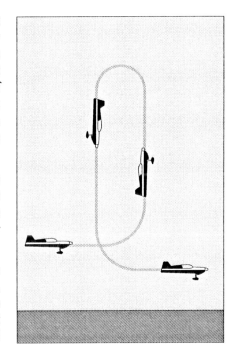

The Humpty is introduced in Sportsman or Standard level competition sequences and forms a principal part of most sequences at the higher levels. The two vertical lines can be embellished with a variety of aileron and flick rolls in order to increase the complexity as aircraft performance increases.

But this apparent difficulty should not deter newcomers from trying the 'vanilla' humpty, that is the basic figure unadorned by added rolls. This is a simpler figure

241

than the stall turn, with less risk of losing control at the apex. It is the ideal platform for learning more about ultra-low speed handling, balance and elevator management.

The Flight Manoeuvre

The concept of the Humpty is simple. From a high speed level entry, pull to the vertical and fly a stable, precise vertical line. At a suitably low speed, make a small half loop of constant radius that gets the aircraft to the vertical down attitude at the same height that the up line was broken. Then fly a stable, precise vertical down line for a few seconds. Finally pull to level in a constant radius quarter loop that is the same size as the entry curve.

The humpty, like the loop, should involve no change of heading and the aircraft should be perfectly balanced throughout.

Ground References

As usual, a line feature below and a horizon landmark off the wing tip form the ideal set of visual references.

Technique

The entry speed for the Humpty should be perhaps 20 knots faster than for a plain stall turn. This will enable you to fly the vertical line up for about the same time as for the stall turn and still have enough residual airspeed for the small half loop. Remember that at this high speed you will need a small amount of left rudder to maintain balance when level and that you will need to increase this a little as you start to pull up because of the gyroscopic forces that will be induced by the pitching motion.

Diagram 26-1

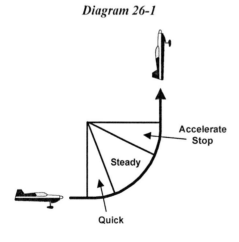

The 90° pull to vertical should be just the same as for the stall turn. The pitch 'feel' diagram for this is reproduced in Diagram 26-1. As ever, you must pull straight and the best way to check this is to look at the wing tip.

The amount of time you spend in the vertical is not crucial. It should be long enough to become stable and for you to assess its accuracy. I would usually recommend you count out loud, *"Check, one, two, three, pull"*. Of course a lot depends on how fast you count, and this will vary from type to type. If you sneak a quick glimpse at the ASI, you should be looking for a speed that is about 1.2 times V_{S1}, but I cannot be too pedantic about that. You will just have to experiment a bit to find out what suits you and your aeroplane. If you wait too long, you will lose too much speed and the half loop will be impossible.

While the plane climbs you will need to maintain the vertical using very small pitch and yaw inputs. Keep looking at the wing tip horizon to see what is happening. To remind yourself of how these inputs work, look again at the stall turn chapter. You should not get so slow at this stage that you notice any tendency to torque roll. You must start the apical half loop before you get that slow.

The half loop at the top is the key to the Humpty. Like many such looping segments, it is best to break it down in your mind into three sub-segments (Diagram 26-2).

Diagram 26-2

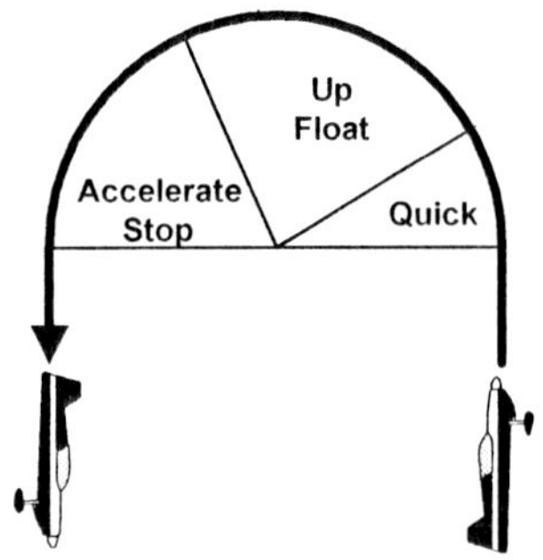

As always, it is important to show exactly when the line is 'broken' and the loop starts. So the first arc is a quick 'pop' just as at the beginning of the pull up. This should change the pitch attitude by about 15° to 20°, no more.

The next section should carry you up and into a 'floating' curve to establish the new radius. Be careful not to pitch from vertical to horizontal in one harsh pull. The stick force is quite low at this speed; apply some delicacy to match the feel of the machine. While floating, you can look up through the top of the canopy to see the horizon and the nose come together.

You will, soon enough, be at the apex with the fuselage horizontal. Thrust and gravity will now work together to take you quickly back toward earth, so be sure to work a little quicker for the third section.

As soon as the nose is below the horizon, look to your wing tip again and start to accelerate the pitch rate. Keep increasing the pitch rate and try to get to the new vertical attitude as quickly as you can without stalling. You want to be close to the stall margin just as you reach vertical down. Then release the back pressure in one quick movement to stop precisely vertical.

During a lot of the small half loop your speed will be very low, but you will not stall because you will be under less than 1g loading. At the end you will probably be at about 1.5 times V_{S1}, and can just reach perhaps 2g at this final stage.

During this low-speed loop, there will be a full range of engine forces and these will affect the aeroplane's balance. You must use your feet precisely to keep everything straight and in order. You will probably have needed a little right rudder during the later stages of the vertical up line because of the slipstream effect.

Diagram 26-3

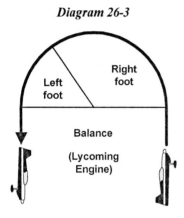

The initial 'pop' at the start of the half loop is very short and effects are negligible because of this duration. Once you start to float, angle of attack will be small so P-factor will be small. Gyroscopic forces will be also small because the pitch rate is slow.

These two work to cancel each other out anyway in this configuration. Slipstream effect will remain, however, so you should keep that little bit of right rudder until you reach the apex.

As you accelerate the pitch rate towards the vertical down, however, gyroscopic effects, which need left rudder, will increase quickly. Depending on aircraft type, the gyro can quickly become greater than the sum of slipstream and P-factor that require right rudder. So expect to need a little left rudder just before vertical down if you pull quickly and have a small aircraft and a big propeller. This is really quite pronounced, for example, in a Pitts with a 2-bladed metal propeller. These rudder inputs are illustrated in Diagram 26-3.

Diagram 26-4

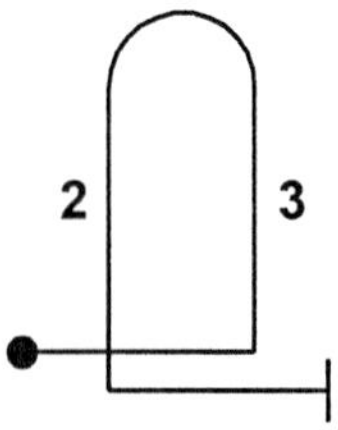

If you counted to three on the up line, count at the same speed to two on the way down. This will give roughly the same distance on both vertical legs (Diagram 26-4).

You count for less time on the down line because gravity and thrust are working together; on the way up they work against each other and it takes more time for the same distance. Then carry out a regular pull to level just as after the stall turn. Once again, the pitch feel diagram is in Diagram 26-5.

Diagram 26-5

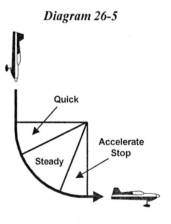

Error Analysis

Any errors that occur during the pull up, or on the vertical up line, are the same as for the stall turn, so I will not repeat them here.

The next opportunity for major error is leaving it too late before starting the half loop. It is not possible to give a definite answer to the question of *"When should I start the loop"*, so inevitably all pilots learning this figure will occasionally leave it too late. This is no bad thing.

You have to learn about getting too slow, and how to recover, in order to have the confidence to approach the figure at relatively low level. If you always err on the safe side, and start the half loop too soon, you are not learning to get the most out of your aeroplane, nor are you really understanding the real delight of the Humpty.

Diagram 26-6

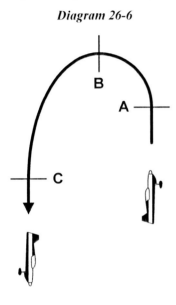

The key to satisfaction here is to learn to stay with the vertical line as long as you can, and to make the half loop as small as you can.

You must therefore be prepared for the loss of control that is likely to happen on the occasions when you leave it too late. See "Recovering Lost Control" on page 67.

I have already mentioned rudder inputs during the half loop. It is possible if you are very slow, and have an aircraft with a lot of torque and short wings, that the engine will cause a roll reaction at this low speed. This can easily be countered by aileron, but you must realize that at this low speed it may take quite a large control input to be effective.

The most common mistake of geometry for the Humpty is failure to keep a constant radius as the aeroplane speeds up after the apex of the figure. This is sometimes called 'closing late', and is illustrated in Diagram 26-6. It is usually caused by simple laziness, perhaps caution, by not increasing the pitch rate quickly enough once the nose is below the horizon.

Diagram 26-7

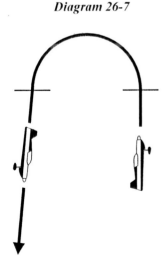

The consequences are not dire, especially if the figure is to be flown without any added rolls, but do have speed and energy implications.

By losing excess height between B and C, the whole figure is going to lose more height than necessary. Also, the airspeed at C will be higher than if a good shape is made. This in turn greatly increases the potential height loss if you have to roll on the down line, and leads to higher risk of flicking above limiting speed if you plan to execute a flick roll on the down line.

Another common error is stopping the loop a little early and being 'negative' on the down line (Diagram 26-7). This is caused by being too anxious, wanting to get the loop over with quicker than it should, or by simply looking over the nose and thinking you can accurately judge the vertical attitude from that picture. You cannot. The only sure way of setting an accurate down line is to look at the wing tip, preferably with a sight frame attached. The vertical error shown in the diagram is quite obvious, but is only 5°.

Further Development

The Pull, Push, Pull Humpty Bump

This is strictly a different figure, and really is only for aircraft with inverted fuel and oil systems, but is included here because of the similarities to what has already been described in this chapter.

As you will see from Diagram 26-8, the geometric difference is that the small half loop is done by pushing instead of pulling. So what are the differences in technique?

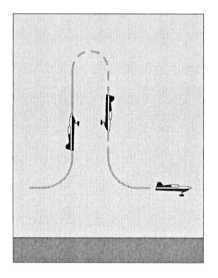

Diagram 26-8

The pitch feel diagram is the same as for the positive half loop:

> *Quick, Up/Float, Accelerate/Stop.*

You must just push instead of pull. The rudder situation, however, is somewhat different.

When you push, especially if you create a high pitch rate, you generate gyroscopic force from the propeller. The direction, not surprisingly, is opposite to that induced when you pull. So now the gyroscopic force adds to the slipstream effect and there is a great tendency to yaw.

In the Lycoming-powered aircraft this will be yaw to the left and must be countered with right rudder. The slipstream effect is effectively constant as the speed is low throughout the half loop. The magnitude of the gyroscopic effect is proportional to pitch rate, so this varies with the pitch feel diagram.

The result of all this is that you have to use right rudder constantly, with the greatest input just before you reach vertical down (Diagram 26-9).

It is now even more important to make sure you do not push too hard all the way round the half loop. You must have the 'Up/Float' section and during this phase the pitch rate must not be too quick. If it is, you are likely to run out of right rudder completely and the aircraft will continue to yaw left.

Diagram 26-9

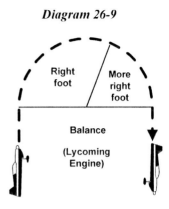

So, if you find you are running out of right rudder during the pushed Humpty, just ease off the forward stick a bit as you float over the top.

Flying in Competition

The technique described above is valid whether your Humpty is just for fun or in earnest in competition. The factor that I have not allowed for so far in this chapter, however, is wind. By definition, the speed during the top half loop is small and so wind can make quite a lot of difference. Before you start the figure, you must consider whether the top section is going to be wind assisted or into a strong head wind.

Into wind at the top, you must start to pull, or push, at a higher speed than you could get away with down wind. Add one knot for every knot of head wind, as a rough guide, up to a maximum of about 20 knots.

If the wind is more than 20 knots, increase the float time as well. You do not really need to compensate so much for a tail wind at the top, but if it is strong, greater than 15 knots, then float a little less. Be very careful if you are tempted to reduce the pull speed.

Energy Matters

There is not a lot you can do about energy management in a Humpty. The most important thing is to get to vertical down at as slow a speed as you can. Avoid closing late as described above. Don't close the throttle on the way down, your energy at the exit will be less than with power on. On the other hand, don't prolong the down line for longer than is necessary. If you do, your exit speed will be very high and you will lose energy through excess drag.

The author in CAP 232, F-GYRO over Northern Spain at the World Air Games in 2001. *Robin D. W. Norton*

Same credits as above, but this one is for the modellers who seldom get a picture of the underneath. *Robin D. W. Norton*

Better Aerobatics

Part Four

Intermediate Figures

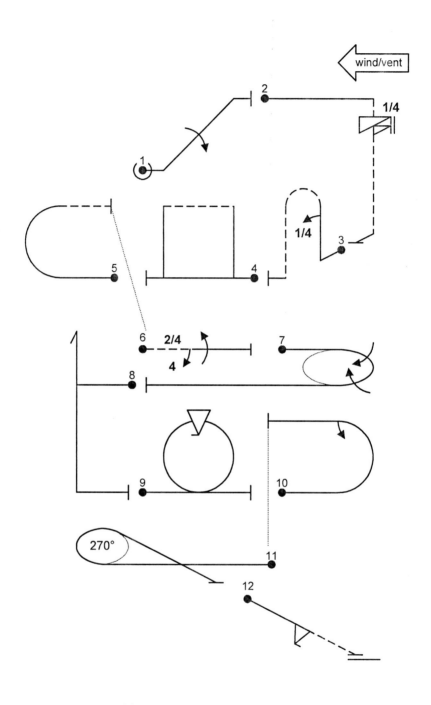

wind/vent

British Aerobatic Association (BAeA)
Intermediate Known Compulsory Sequence 2003

CHAPTER 27

Inverted Flight and Turns

If you have an aeroplane with inverted fuel and oil, then you are certainly going to want to fly upside down. At first you will find it quite disorientating. You will find it very hard to work out what does what, which way is North, what 'up' and 'down' now mean and so on. The point is that your brain really has no experience to work with when you first try flying upside down.

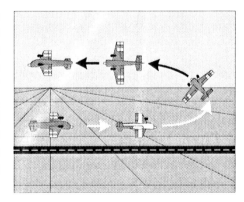

During your daily life, your brain is constantly filling in background knowledge for you without you even thinking about it. Your brain has been doing this for years and in that time it has built up its own, very comprehensive, 'model' of how the world works. This includes answers to such 'obvious' questions as left and right, up and down, North and South. Once you turn yourself upside-down, however, all these years of background conditioning are useless.

Your brain has to avoid 'obvious' reactions and has to work things out all over again from scratch. And it matters not how many hours of upright flying you have in the bank. Your first time inverted will give you immense difficulties.

I have demonstrated this on numerous occasions while flying with experienced airline pilots who, nevertheless, have not spent any previous time inverted.

We head West, say, and half roll to inverted. We confirm we are still heading West. I let them fly straight and level inverted for half a minute, then ask them to turn onto North through 270°. A long, thinking hard, pause then always occurs, followed by a short curse and, usually, a right aileron input which, of course, is the wrong way.

It takes a lot of dedicated practice to become familiar with the inverted world, so that aileron and rudder inputs come naturally. Once your brain has built its inverted 'model' you can revert to it at will. You can adjust headings while pushing outside loops, maintain balance or slide to defeat a cross wind. All without a great deal of planning or preparation.

When you can do all this, you have truly become, like me, an aerobatic anorak!

Airmanship

A key piece of knowledge here is the working of your fuel system when inverted. In some aircraft all the fuel is available all the time. This is usually achieved by having a single big aerobatic tank with a flop tube inside. Such is the case in factory-built two-seat Pitts Specials for example.

Other installations have a smaller, subsidiary tank with the fuel change over mechanism in it. In such cases, there will be a limit on the time you can spend inverted before you have to get upright again to recharge the small tank. Be sure you know the inverted fuel system time limit for your aeroplane, because running out of fuel inverted is just a little more stressful than doing so upright.

The Flight Manoeuvre

The task initially is simply to fly straight and level inverted. Once comfortable with this, the next exercise is to complete level inverted steep turns with up to 60° of bank, stopping accurately on heading by reference to visual ground features.

Ground References

Have a straight line feature on the ground nearby. Use it in a number of ways as described below.

Technique

If you are going to spend a moderate amount of time upside down, then you should plan to make your life no more difficult than it need be. So a good plan is to trim the aircraft for zero G before you start the inverted exercises. This will reduce by a small amount the need for forward stick pressure inverted. I do not recommend re-trimming once level inverted (for -1g) because this will make things too easy, you will forget you've done it and then when you next roll upright you will have a big surprise when the aircraft bunts towards the ground. The recommended technique for zero G trimming is in "The Elevator and Elevator Trimming" on page 37.

Straight and Level Inverted

Having trimmed to neutral, fly upright at normal cruise speed directly above the line feature. Note the altitude. Roll the aircraft to wings level inverted using the technique described earlier for the first half of a straight and level roll. After you stop the roll, maintain some forward stick pressure to keep the attitude level and relax your legs so that you have no rudder input at all. Slipstream effect and P-factor will oppose each other in this attitude and you will find that the aeroplane keeps balance quite well with your feet off. It's better to be like this than to be applying rudder without thinking about it, which will certainly happen when you first start this exercise.

Check the altimeter, or the VSI if you have one, and make any small pitch adjustments necessary to remain level. Check that the wings are still level. Once you are steady, check the oil pressure, as this is the first chance you have had to make sure that your inverted oil system is actually working. In Lycoming powered aircraft with the Christen oil system, the inverted oil pressure is usually 5 to 10 psi lower than when upright. If your oil pressure is zero, don't panic. Don't pull the stick back!!! Just roll upright as in the second half of a level roll.

Diagram 27-1 shows the straight and level inverted attitude in a single seat biplane and a side-by-side monoplane.

Diagram 27-1

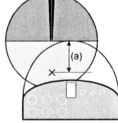

In the biplane it is easy to note the exact pitch attitude by reference to the top wing and the horizon. In the monoplane, however, you have to estimate distance (a) and remember it, unless, as in the case illustrated, the top of the windscreen frame happens to be convenient.

While flying straight and inverted, make small pitch changes, climbing or descending, and then return to level by selecting the correct picture. Before you get too much blood in your head, roll back up the right way again and take a few moments to re-orientate yourself before rolling inverted again.

Inverted Turns

Don't start the inverted turning exercise until you are comfortable in the straight and level inverted exercise and able to keep steady in that configuration.

This time, set yourself up parallel and to one side of the line feature. Let's say it is a main road on your left, about 300 yards away. Roll to level inverted as before and get settled in the inverted attitude. Look up and notice that the line feature is now above your right shoulder. In other words, it is now apparently on the other side. The task now is to turn towards the line feature.

Note that the road is on your right and that you will need right rudder to balance the turn. Then move the stick **AWAY** from the road, set a bank angle about 30° and **PUSH** slightly to start the turn. Remember the bold words **AWAY** and **PUSH**.

Make sure the nose does not drop. To monitor balance while looking out at the road, use rudder to keep your body centred in the seat. You don't need an inverted slip ball. If you have one, looking at it will distract you from the road and from the horizon. Look at these two things and keep in balance by using your body as a stationary pendulum.

When you judge that you are pointing directly at the road, roll back to wings level inverted. Do this by moving the stick to the 'ground' side of the aeroplane, and use **opposite** rudder to balance the roll-out. It is quite usual for newcomers to mistake the direction of rolling out and go the wrong way. You then end up wings level and upright having started inverted. If this happens, just try again, remember which aileron you use to roll into the turn. Use the opposite aileron to roll out to inverted.

Do this in both directions with 30° of bank, until you are familiar with the start and finish. Always start from the same place and always finish with the same picture of the line feature. Diagram 27-2 shows such a turn, rolling left into the turn, this time with 60° of bank, and rolling right to stop the turn.

These images are based on the view from a single seat Pitts. See how useful the top wing and the cabane triangle are for setting and holding a steady 60° bank angle.

Once you are comfortable with the turn through 90°, start again and this time try for 180° (Diagram 27-3). Stop turning when you are again parallel to the line feature.

Diagram 27-2 60° Bank

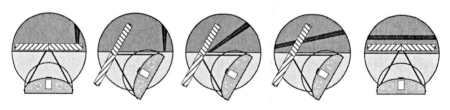

Diagram 27-3 180° Turn

Error Analysis

Straight and Level Inverted

The most common basic error in straight and level inverted, in aircraft with a control column, is the inability to keep the wings level. At the beginning, every new pilot tends to roll to the left a bit as soon as they try to fly straight. The reason for this is simple cockpit ergonomics.

To fly level inverted you have to push against the trim to stay level. When you first start to push, you inadvertently add left aileron because you push from your right elbow towards your hand.

You can see how this happens in Diagram 27-4, which also shows the resulting forward view in, say, a CAP-10. When you push, you have to extend your arm forward, directly away from your navel.

Diagram 27-4

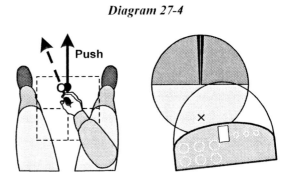

If you came from the planet Zorg, and had the usual central arm protruding from your sternum, this would be simple. But as you are probably an earthling, like myself, then it has to feel a bit as though you are pushing with the back of your hand, and you have to flex your wrist a bit.

After a while this will become natural, but at the beginning it will feel a little strange. If, of course, you fly with your left hand on the stick because you have only a single central throttle in a side-by-side cockpit, then you will probably find the reverse error occurs. But as I teach in tandem seat aircraft the problem is always a right-handed one.

Another common error is not exactly staying level, but climbing or descending a bit. The error is equally common in either direction, but tends to reduce once you have the knack of keeping the wings level. You can then concentrate on the pitch reference picture and settle down more easily to level.

There are some aircraft where, looking forward, you have very little fixed reference other than the nose cowling. In a Pitts, you have the top wing and the cabane triangle. In the CAP-10 and a Sukhoi you have the windscreen frame. But in monoplanes with a bubble canopy, Extra 200 or CAP-232 for example, you have nothing but the nose cowl. In such aircraft it is quite usual to fix a bit of sticky tape on the inside of the canopy straight ahead to use as a pitch reference against the horizon in level flight.

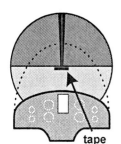

Diagram 27-5

tape

I have illustrated this in Diagram 27-5, with the nose slightly high (low speed) so that you can see the tape against the sky. Bits of tape like this are not particularly attractive, but they are very effective, once you are used to placing them slightly differently at different speeds. They are not 'cheating', they are just like another instrument. Nobody accuses you of cheating in an Instrument Rating test because you use an artificial horizon!

The last matter of concern with flying level inverted is balance. When you start flying upside down, you are not sure exactly how you will cope with your legs and feet.

Some aircraft have leather straps to stop your legs 'falling' off the pedals towards your chin. The very advanced CAP single seaters have special shoes and bindings that attach your feet to the pedals as on a racing bicycle. But none of these luxuries is actually a necessity.

You will soon learn how to keep a slight tension in your legs to keep your heels on the 'floor' and apply little bits of rudder with your toes. But to begin with, you will have a tendency to brace both feet firmly against the pedals. This will inevitably result in a bit more pressure on one side than the other and a consequent uncommanded rudder input.

So try to relax and positively keep your toes off the pedals. Just keep your heels on the floor to begin with and try to make no rudder input at all. Sit still and relax and feel where your body is 'hanging' in relation to the seat.

Diagram 27-6

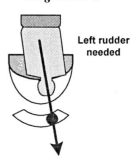

Left rudder
needed

You will probably find, if your feet are 'off', that you are pretty well centred. If necessary, add just a little rudder pressure whenever you are manoeuvring inverted with the aim of keeping your body centred in the seat. This will soon become natural too. In Diagram 27-6, the pilot's left shoulder is leaning against the cockpit wall. Left rudder will put him back in the middle. The ball is on the pilot's left, even though it is on your right as you look at the page.

Inverted Turns

As with upright turns, the principal problem with inverted turns is maintaining a constant bank angle. Only practice will really make this easier, but understanding the ergonomic tendency to push with left aileron will help speed up the process. As the bank angle varies, along comes the attendant problem of avoiding climbing and descending.

If the bank angle becomes shallow, you will tend to climb during the turn. This is relatively safe as long as you do not allow the airspeed to drop too much. Solve this problem by adding a little more bank.

More dangerous is any tendency to steepen the bank angle and then start descending. If this happens, you must reduce the bank angle and push harder to put the nose back on the horizon. At all times,

resist the temptation to pull the stick back

if things start to go wrong.

Now, what about stopping on heading? When you first learn to fly, you are taught to stop on heading by gradually rolling out in a coordinated manner and with reference to a distant landmark. During early instrument flying, you do much the same thing with reference to a gyroscopic instrument, the Direction Indicator.

Inverted, if you have a directional gyro, it may well topple, and in any case, you cannot see the horizon in the direction of turn because it is hidden by the aircraft's nose.

Diagram 27-7

 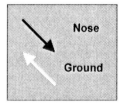

Look at Diagram 27-7. This is your view out of the front in an inverted turn, having rolled 45° to the left from wings level inverted.

The nose is moving in the direction of the black arrow, while the ground is being revealed in the direction of the white arrow. You will not see any distant landmark until it suddenly appears directly ahead. Then if you roll out in a coordinated fashion you will overshoot the required heading significantly. Looking ahead is therefore of no use if we want to roll out accurately on heading.

Diagram 27-8

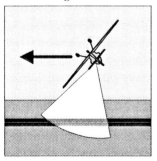

Diagram 27-8 shows the same inverted turn as before, but from behind the aeroplane. The white segment shows the pilots field of view down toward the ground. In other words, looking over his right shoulder.

The pilot can easily see the road which is almost directly below. So, the key to stopping inverted turns on heading is to work with line features that are close to the aircraft, not with point features that are distant.

Diagram 27-9

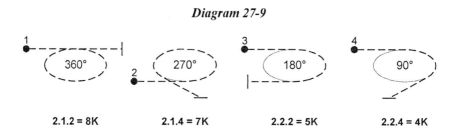

| 2.1.2 = 8K | 2.1.4 = 7K | 2.2.2 = 5K | 2.2.4 = 4K |

Flying in Competition

Plain inverted turns often appear in Intermediate sequences, where they are used to build energy, disorientate the pilot and/or to help with cross wind correction. Building energy and correcting for the wind are pilot-beneficial reasons, so these occur in Free programmes too (Diagram 27-9). The disorientation motive is there for the designer of Unknowns!

Because of the difficulty of orientation, you must apply a lot of thought to any inverted turn in a sequence. In particular, you must plan to fly the figure so that you have a definite picture in your head of what you will see when you approach the point to stop the turn. In other words, you must plan to finish in an orientation and a direction where you are sure you can see a line feature below you – usually a runway at the contest airfield. If you can see no such feature at the point where you should stop and fly level, you will have uncertainty in your orientation and this is always a bad thing.

As with upright competition turns, the bank angle must be at least 60°. The bank angle must be rolled on and off quickly with no heading change. All the turning must be done at the constant bank angle. In most aeroplanes the adverse yaw is increased (compared with the upright case) as you roll in to the inverted turn. A little bottom rudder is therefore usually needed just to keep the heading straight as the bank is rolled on.

Diagram 27-10

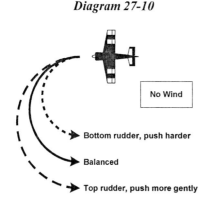

While actually turning, you may vary the balance of the aircraft to change the radius, just as in an upright turn. Remember, if you add top rudder to unbalance the turn you must push a little more softly and the radius will increase. If you add a little extra bottom rudder and push a little harder than usual, the turn radius will be reduced (Diagram 27-10).

Other competition issues, such as judges' sight-line illusions, and energy matters, are the same as those described earlier for upright turns.

CHAPTER 28

Pushing Out, Pushing Up

This chapter is not dedicated to a particular aerobatic figure, but to bits of outside looping technique that are applicable to a host of figures that you will want to try once you start to get comfortable with inverted flight.

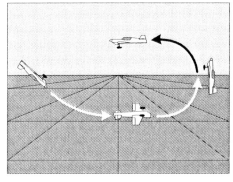

I have to assume from here on that you have an engine with inverted fuel and oil systems, otherwise you should not be trying this sort of thing unless you are in a dedicated aerobatic glider!

Taking the first steps in outside looping is always a major milestone in a pilot's flying education. It is rather like your first trip to the dentist when you were a child; a bit un-nerving. There is bound to be a little trepidation, as with the first time you fire a gun or walk in the rainforest at night. As in all these cases, I can give you assurance that everything will be alright, once you have just given it a try. But you must not lack commitment, especially when you start a push in a descending configuration. Hesitancy or dithering will make things worse. Once you have decided you want to learn how to push some negative G, do it with conviction or not at all.

Diagram 28-1 is a short training sequence of figures that all contain a segment of outside loop. Once you have tried out the various individual segment techniques described below, you could bring a little structure to your practice by

Diagram 28-1

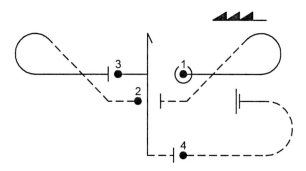

flying this mini sequence, or a similar one of your own design. I will deal with each of these four segments in the order they appear in the diagram.

The Flight Manoeuvre

Pushing to Level through 45°

Look at figure 1 of the sequence in Diagram 28-1. The shape is very much like a half Cuban eight, but without the half roll on the descending 45° line. You start by flying a 5/8ths positive loop until you set the 45° down inverted attitude. Then pause to draw a straight line for a short while, maintaining the inverted descent. Then you push through 45° of outside loop until the aircraft is straight and level, but still inverted.

Pushing Up through 45°

Next push again through 45° of loop, until you are on a steady inverted 45° climbing line. Hold this line for a short while as speed decreases, then complete a 5/8ths positive loop back to upright flight, just as in the last part of a half-reverse Cuban eight. Beware of pulling too hard as your G tolerance will be reduced after the prolonged inverted flying.

Pushing Out from Vertical Down

From level upright flight, fly a normal stall turn up to the point of starting the vertical down line. As you are about to reach normal climb speed, start a quarter outside loop continuing to push until you reach level inverted flight.

Half Outside Loop Upwards

From level inverted, at relatively high speed, start an outside loop. Continue to push through the vertical until you come level, upright at low speed in the reciprocal direction. Fly off level and accelerate to cruise speed.

Ground References

It is a good idea to fly all these figures directly over a straight line feature. Secondary assistance, of great value, can be had from a distant landmark off the wing tip at 90° to the direction of flight.

Technique

Pushing to Level through 45°

You will arrive at the 45° down inverted attitude from a positive 5/8 loop (Diagram 28-2). You should set the 45° attitude by reference to your wing tip, preferably with a sight frame.

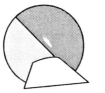

Diagram 28-2

45 Down inverted

Make sure your check forward with the stick is positive, and that you hold enough forward pressure to maintain the 45° attitude. Imagine that you are taking the weight of the aeroplane inverted with the forward stick. Make sure you take the full weight. Transfer your gaze to the line feature below, which you can see through the canopy above you.

Keep your feet relaxed on the rudders, not braced with a stiff knee. You need no significant rudder input at this stage, so make sure it is not being applied inadvertently. Count *"One, two, three, push"* and then move the elevator control centrally forward to bring the nose up to the horizon (Diagram 28-3).

Diagram 28-3

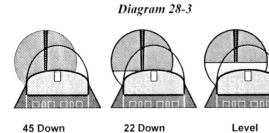

45 Down   **22 Down**   **Level**

Speed is increasing as you push, so expect the G-meter 'memory' needle to read minus 2.5g or minus 3g once you are level.

Maintain sufficient forward pressure to stay level, but otherwise try to remain as relaxed as you can. You should also maintain balance, while looking ahead, by using small rudder pressures to keep your body 'dangling' centrally in the seat.

When you are sure you are in balance, you can check this by a quick glance at the inverted slip ball, if you have one. If you don't have an inverted slip ball, just trust the feeling you get through your seat.

259

Pushing Up through 45°

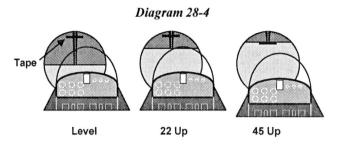

Diagram 28-4

Level   22 Up   45 Up

You should start level inverted at the same entry speed as you would normally use for a half-reverse Cuban eight. Looking straight ahead, push to start the 1/8 outside loop. Push straight ahead, using small aileron inputs as necessary to keep the horizon parallel to the aeroplane's lateral axis.

It is really invaluable for this figure to have a piece of sticky tape on the inside of your canopy in a spot you would normally call straight ahead and 45° up and effectively half way between the line straight ahead over the nose and the one vertically up through your head. You can see from Diagram 28-4 that the 45° nose up inverted attitude is easily fixed by reference to this piece of tape. Without this simple and cheap aid, you can only set this climbing attitude by reference to the wing tip, and you will lose valuable milliseconds of visual feedback as you turn your head to the side as you push.

Once you have set the line using the tape, you can more leisurely, turn your head to the side to check the view to the side. What you should see is illustrated in Diagram 28-5 (looking left).

Hold this steady climbing attitude for a count of *"One, two, pull"* and then start the 5/8 positive loop back to level flight. The precise technique for this positive segment is described in "Half Cuban Eights" on page 173.

Diagram 28-5

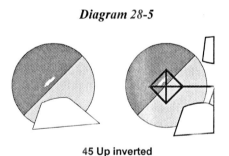

45 Up inverted

Pushing Out from Vertical Down

The first time you push out from the vertical down, you will need the confidence and conviction to do it firmly and without hesitation. Once you start this push **you must not change your mind!**

Never, ever, get part way round a push-out, then chicken out and change to a pull. The ensuing height loss and speed increase will invalidate all your safety planning before you started the figure. To be successful at outside looping on descending lines you must show determination and commitment. End of lecture, except to say that, once you master this type of figure your self-respect will grow disproportionately.

To keep speed and G-force to a minimum when you begin to practice this push, you must initially have a low entry speed in a vertical-down attitude. The best way to get to this start point is to fly a stall turn. The speed at which you start to push out of the vertical needs some thought.

If you are over-cautious and start your push at very low speed, conventional 'stall speed' or lower, then there are two things to bear in mind. Firstly the stick feel is going to be very light, so it will be easy to overcook the down elevator. Secondly, this stands a good chance of producing an inadvertent negative stall just when you are trying to prove how brave you are. You won't like the result.

If you wait too long, however, before committing to the push, your exit speed and G are going to be high, with disproportionate discomfort and the risk of overstress of the aircraft as well as the brain.

So, my recommendation is to study the Airspeed Indicator closely after the stall turn and to start pushing at the speed given in the flight manual for best angle of climb. For example, this would be about 80 mph in a Pitts Special. This will give a good margin over the inadvertent stall and also an excellent chance of completing the push to level at a reasonable speed without exceeding -3g.

Perform the stall turn over a line feature and parallel to it.

Diagram 28-6

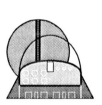 

Vertical down   **45 Down inverted**   **Level**

As you see the ASI needle reach the chosen speed, push firmly and centrally forward on the elevator control. Do nothing with your feet other than keep them on the pedals. It is certainly better to have no rudder input at this stage than a wrong one. Watch the line feature and use small aileron inputs to correct the heading if you see you are going off line (Diagram 28-6).

As speed continues to increase, make sure the pitch rate also increases to keep the radius going. Check the G-meter to keep within limits. When you first try this in any aircraft, you should aim not to exceed -3g in any case. Just as you begin to wonder how much more of this there is to withstand, the horizon will suddenly pop into view through the windscreen. Stop pushing when you have the level inverted attitude you know well from your level rolling experience. Check that the flight path is staying level, and then you are free to decide what to do next.

Half Outside Loop Upwards

This is the first half outside loop you should try; not the other one that starts upright, level and goes down. When things go wrong in the up going half loop you are, at least, going away from the ground and into the low stress part of the flight envelope. Low stress, that is, as far as the aircraft is concerned, so you are most unlikely to break it. But you can expect some interesting moments when you first try this half loop figure.

The entry speed for this manoeuvre should be listed in the aircraft flight manual. If it is, use it. If for some reason you do not have this figure available, you will probably be tempted to use the same speed as for a normal positive loop. You may just get away with this if your aeroplane has a symmetrical wing section. If, on the other hand, you have as asymmetrical wing, as in a CAP-10 or a Pitts S-1C, then you will be effectively flying a much less efficient aerofoil and you will need more speed than for the equivalent positive figure. So add perhaps 15 mph/knots or 30 kph to your normal looping speed (assuming this does not take you over V_{NE}).

You can get to this inverted entry position by using the first figure described above, or by simply half rolling from level upright. In the latter case, be sure not to climb during the half roll or you will lose speed and perhaps not be ideally placed for the outside half loop. Remember that this is probably much faster than you normally fly a level roll, so when you stop inverted, you should have a slightly lower nose attitude to maintain accurate level flight.

The first half of the outside loop will be the same as the push up through 45° described above. As you pass through the climbing inverted 45°, you will begin to lose sight of the horizon as it moves further up towards the top of the canopy. So at this stage you must transfer your attention to the wing tip if you are to be able to maintain a good impression of your attitude and heading.

Continue to push and use small aileron corrections to keep the wings level and thereby maintain heading. Avoid the temptation to try to make corrections using the rudder – the source of any error at this stage is almost certainly the ailerons. As the aircraft comes towards the vertical up, you should see a wing tip picture you recognise from the stall turn.

As in a normal loop, once you are some way through the vertical you should reduce the pitch rate in order to make a round shape. This will also help in avoiding a negative stall that may well occur as the stick force gets lighter and you move the control column inadvertently further forward as a result of the changing 'feel'. When you have just the last 45° of loop to go before level, you should be 'floating' round the curve with only a slow rate of pitch and very little stick force. At this stage you will need a little rudder to maintain heading against the slipstream effect. So press a little with your right foot or you will feel your body start to lean to the right as a result of the yaw.

Remember to stop the loop when you have the attitude for level flight at the now very low speed. If, when you set this attitude, you notice buffeting, wing-drop or any other stalling symptoms, just release a little of the back pressure and let the nose down a little until some more speed is gained. Check your heading now against your line feature.

Use of the Throttle

Some of these figures involve the aircraft pointing straight down towards the ground and you pushing forward on the control column. This is not a normal situation for other than the dedicated aerobatic pilot, which I assume you are trying to become (or already are).

Inevitably, when faced with this situation for the first or second time, you may think it a better and safer practice to push down and push out with the throttle closed. You may think it will help you make the loops smaller and keep the speed down. Unfortunately this is not the case.

What primarily happens when you close the throttle is that you greatly reduce the air flow over the empennage and thus reduce considerably the effectiveness of your elevator.

This will lead to a reduced pitch response, when compared to that which you are used to in positive looping. Consequently, you will most likely react by pushing harder against a control with less aerodynamic 'feel'. This is a very easy way to set up a high-speed negative stall just at a critical time when you were already a bit apprehensive about what you were attempting.

If you have a fixed-pitch propeller, you will most probably have to move the throttle in the later stages of the push out in order to keep within engine rpm limits. This is alright, as it will only be a small retardation of the lever, not a complete closure, and will probably occur late in the figure when you already have good speed and hence good aerodynamic resistance against pushing too far forward.

When pushing out from vertical down, or when starting an outside half loop down (see Further Development below), always start with the power well on. Towards the latter part of the figure, perhaps when you have 60° or 45° left to go before level, then it is quite safe to throttle back some more, as you now have plenty of speed in hand and this will reduce the overall stress level.

The very act of reducing power will, of course, cause an overall energy loss. This will only be of concern if you are flying a sequence, so take this into consideration as well. Remember you must always try to finish one figure with the correct entry speed for the next.

Error Analysis

As with normal, positive looping, the principal source of errors in outside loops is the aileron system. Especially that bit of the system that forms the seat-to-stick interface.

Diagram 28-7

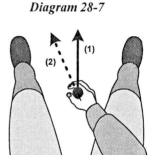

In other words, you cannot push straight. Just as when you started you could not pull straight. In effect, this means that you will almost certainly make an inadvertent application of left aileron when you start to push, because of the ergonomics of your elbow (Diagram 28-7). You must push in direction (1), not direction (2).

Some avoid this error by using two hands on the control column. Of course, success is not guaranteed this way, so they must still learn to make corrections based on the visual feedback system you initiate by not closing your eyes at the critical moment but by looking in the right direction. I don't think you should be using two hands on the stick unless you are not strong enough to move it with just the one, in which case you should either be looking for a different aeroplane or spending more time at the gym.

Here are some pictures that illustrate the problem of the ailerons when pushing (Diagram 28-8 and Diagram 28-9). All show the result of inadvertent left aileron.

So, as you start to push, think ...

"Ailerons, Ailerons, Ailerons".

You can draw for yourself the pictures you will see when making this error in the other exercises.

Diagram 28-8 Pushing out from 45° down

45 Down on heading	22 Down 7.5° off	Level 15° off

Diagram 28-9 Pushing to 45° up from level

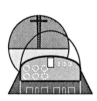

Level	22 Up, 4° off	45 Up, 8° off	45 Up inverted Left wing high

If you add aileron when pushing, inadvertently or otherwise, you will also generate some adverse yaw. You will probably feel the aircraft out of balance as your body leans to one side or the other (usually to the right). When you first start these pushing exercises you will not yet be fully 'converted to inverted' in your brain. When you feel the out of balance you may well react instinctively in the wrong way.

In other words, you might well add left rudder with the left aileron, as you would when upright, and this of course will now be wrong. Remember, adverse yaw is in the opposite direction when you have a negative angle of attack.

While learning to push straight, you should concentrate solely on the elevator and ailerons. To keep yourself from making inadvertent 'automatic' rudder inputs, it is best initially to take your feet off the rudders altogether and put them flat on the floor.

The first three of the four exercises in this chapter could be quite proficiently completed with your feet cut off at the ankle. Only right towards the end of the negative half loop up will you see a noticeable yaw error caused by engine effects, so at that stage you can get your feet back on and have a little right rudder. But the first few times you try any of these exercises, do so with your feet flat on the floor.

Before you start to push, think

"Feet off, Feet off".

Further Development

Half Outside Loop Down

Diagram 28-10

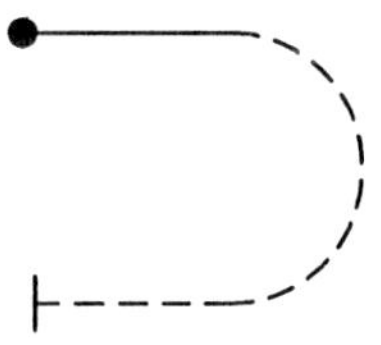

In most competition classifications, this is an Advanced figure, rather than an Intermediate one (Diagram 28-10). However, it fits rather neatly at the end of this chapter so I'll cover it here anyway.

The important consideration at the beginning is to have a fairly low entry speed. A good place to start would be about 1.2 times V_{S1}. When you start to push, the controls will be very light and you must take care not to stall negative by pushing too far forward.

Catalogue No.	7.1.3
K factor =	8

You will reach vertical down at a higher speed than you had when starting to push out from vertical after a stall turn, so the exit speed and G will be higher unless you take measures to prevent this. Apart from ensuring a low entry speed, the other, less obvious, way to keep the speed down is with induced drag. To exploit this, you must fly the whole looping segment at high alpha, close to the stall margin.

This technique is especially useful in a biplane, where the effective aspect ratio of the wing is usually low and where induced drag builds quickly with increasing alpha.

Probably the worst thing you can do if you think you are getting too fast is to ease off the push, or even think of reverting to a pull-out. Resist this temptation at all costs. Just grit your teeth and push a little harder. If you do feel a bit of a 'nibble' as you approach the inverted stall, you must ease off a little, but then only enough to avoid the imminent onset of the stall.

You should know, before you start, a good approximation of the likely height loss during this figure. The similarity to your familiar positive looping diameter will depend somewhat on the wing section and the negative G limit of your plane. For example, if you have a non-symmetrical wing section, you can probably add 30% to the loop diameter. Even with a symmetrical wing, the outside loop is likely to be somewhat bigger.

Most Pitts Specials have G limits of +6g and -3g. Most pilots looping a Pitts in the normal sense probably pull between +4 and +5 at the start and finish. So the -3g limit means a bigger radius and a higher exit speed. Only in specialist aircraft with symmetrical wings **and** symmetrical limits will you be able to approach inside and outside loops with the same radius from the same entry conditions.

CHAPTER **29**

Vertical Rolls

Arguably the greatest change in classic aerobatic flight over the last 30 years has been the increasing range and complexity of vertical rolling. This has been brought about by huge gains in aircraft performance.

As improvements have been made in aircraft power-to-weight ratios, longer and longer vertical lines have been possible between pulling up from V_{NE} and falling off at the top. To add further to what is possible, the introduction of carbon fibre composite wings, with their immense stiffness, has enabled designers to fit massive full-span ailerons. Today's top-level aircraft achieve roll rates in the 400° to 500° per second range.

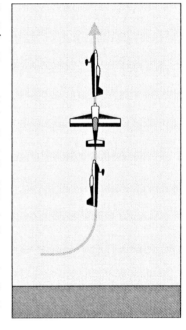

I can still clearly recall one of my own early experiences of vertical rolling in a machine capable of multiple rotations. In this case it was a Yak-55M.

It was a cold autumn evening with high pressure and a very low inversion layer below which visibility was quite poor. Above 1,200 feet, however, it was a brilliantly clear sunset. It was also, quite by chance, that special day in the lunar cycle when the full moon rises to be a few degrees above the horizon in the East just as the sun is at the same elevation in the West.

The top of the inversion was like a perfectly still ocean. You could dive at it at great speed and then pull up at the last minute with absolutely no danger of hitting anything. The subsequent vertical rolls, looking left with full right aileron, presented a succession of sun/moon/sun/moon images that will stay with me forever, especially as I have now been able to share this wonderful experience with others in high-performance two seaters.

I may one day regret making this forecast, but I do not expect the next 30 years to see very much more development in these directions in sport aircraft. Power-to-weight may increase a little more, but it is no use designing a sport aeroplane with a vertical penetration of 5,000 feet because no one will see it up there! Nor will any more increase in roll-rate serve much purpose, because of the consequent difficulty for the pilot to maintain his directional awareness while rolling. Rolling faster than is possible now might be more spectacular in an air show, but it will not help in competition. In fact these very high roll rates make it much harder to stop hesitations precisely on heading because of the degradation of visual perception as the world begins to blur.

Lastly, the cost of certifying new designs is effectively prohibitive, so that only small changes to existing designs are likely in factory production aircraft.

Most aerobatic pilots today are easily able to get access to an aircraft that can do vertical rolls of 90° or 180°. Many of these will move on to those capable of multiple vertical rolls, both to the left and right. So a sound grounding in the principles of the vertical roll is a modern day essential for any pilot with aerobatic aspirations towards other than the very basic Sportsman category figures. Even in such proud but lowly competition tradition, you will be called upon occasionally to do a quarter vertical roll while going down, so there is something to be learned here by everybody.

The Flight Manoeuvre

Preparation

Earlier in this book I described a training exercise called the Ballistic Roll (page 99). The main point of the exercise was to find the control position that corresponds to full aileron and zero angle of attack for the wing: the 'neutral point' of the elevator.

Remember that when the elevator is at this neutral point, the wings will generate no lift but that the control column will only 'feel' neutral if you have trimmed the elevator for zero G. If you are trimmed for 1g, straight and level, even at high speed, you will need some forward stick pressure to keep the elevator at the neutral point.

Before starting your first session of vertical rolls, it is a very good idea to recap and fly a few ballistic rolls so that you can consistently find the neutral point with full aileron deflection.

Vertical Penetration

For any given level entry speed there is a maximum height that can be reached in the vertical attitude before all speed is lost. The way to maximize this height gain is to minimize the drag induced during the pull, but you then will only just reach vertical as your speed reaches zero. To have a vertical line on which to place even a quarter roll you will have to pull a little harder and cause more drag. You will then be able to fly a vertical line of some length, but the maximum height you will reach overall will be less than if you had pulled more gently.

Diagram 29-1

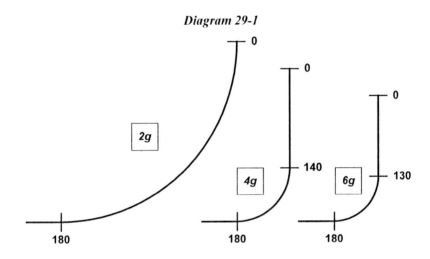

Diagram 29-1 is an illustration that should convey my point better than a heck of a lot of words. In each of the three profiles the aircraft has started a pull up at speed 180 mph. In a gentle pull, with a peak of 2g, it may be possible to create a large height gain before the speed drops to zero, but there will be no vertical line.

From the same start, a pull with a peak of 4g might get the aeroplane to the vertical at speed 140 mph and produce a usable vertical line. But a really hard pull peaking at 6g might well mean a small radius but so much induced drag that there is only speed 130 mph left by the time vertical is reached. From this point, the vertical penetration achieved before speed zero is less than in case 2.

All the figures used above are conjectural and chosen to illustrate the point of principle which remains true. It is most unlikely that your aeroplane flight manual will have data to give you the optimum vertical performance for any given entry speed, but you can try to measure it for yourself if you have a stop-watch.

For the same entry speed make a series of pulls to the vertical with different profiles. Each time, start the watch with your non-control hand as you set the vertical and again when you apply rudder for the stall turn at the top. The profile that has the longest vertical line in time will be the one that has the highest speed as you hit vertical.

Don't try to do this by noting the airspeed as you hit vertical because of the errors in the instrument and the rapidly moving needle. Trust the watch.

Rolling

The minimum amount of rotation to really count as a vertical roll is 90°. The maximum you can do is determined by a combination of your aeroplane's performance and your technique. Rolls can be continuous or interspersed with hesitations as with level rolls. Even a humble quarter vertical can be split into two eighths.

Once the rolling element is complete, you will hopefully still be vertical up, but now at much reduced speed. The vertical roll itself is not a complete figure. After it is stopped you have a number of choices, some of which are shown in Diagram 29-2. Each figure contains a vertical quarter roll.

Diagram 29-2

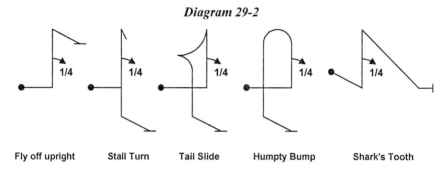

| Fly off upright | Stall Turn | Tail Slide | Humpty Bump | Shark's Tooth |

Ground References

The first task is to learn how to roll accurately in the vertical with no pitch or yaw to give the appearance of 'barrelling' or 'fish tailing'. For this the only visual cue needed is a very clear horizon.

The second task is to learn how to stop the roll at the right 'heading' and to know that you have done so. For this you may be able to make good use of a line feature below you together with a distant landmark toward the horizon.

Technique

Before pulling up, you must start level with enough speed to complete the planned figure. Use the flight manual speed for a stall turn as an absolute minimum. Add speed over this if you want to do more than a quarter on the way up. The information in manuals varies a lot. In the Pitts S2A manual, for example, they quote a range of speeds from 130 mph to 180 mph for entry to a stall turn. To do a good stall turn after a quarter roll up, with two aboard, needs at least 140 mph. You could then add an extra 10 mph for each additional quarter after the first. If you want to fly off level at the top of the line, then you must add an extra 20 mph or so on top of the Hammerhead speed.

With some practice, you will find a useful range of speeds for your aircraft. As your technique improves, both for the pull-up and for the roll itself, you will find that you are able to achieve more with less, so to speak.

Fly the pull-up itself just as if you were going vertical for a stall turn. During the pull-up, do not think ahead to the roll. Concentrate on pulling dead straight and setting a really accurate line, because the first rule of vertical rolls is:

Be Vertical!

When you reach the vertical, pause for a breath and then put the control column smartly to the full aileron, neutral elevator position. You can make this application full and firm because you will now be below Manoeuvre Speed (V_A). The roll will start. Getting the full aileron part is easy; hitting the elevator neutral point takes precise control. If you are just a little too far forward or back a noticeable error will result. So the second rule of vertical rolls is:

Put the Stick in the Right Place!

While it is rolling quickly in the vertical, the aeroplane possesses some of the characteristics of a spinning top. It will tend to stay upright despite gravity and slipstream effects until the airspeed and rate of rotation decay. This dynamic stability helps you to stay vertical. If you have established a true vertical you will be at zero angle of attack with the wings. There will therefore be no adverse yaw from the aileron input, unless your aircraft type exhibits a particularly large amount of asymmetrical aileron drag.

So, if you have a reasonably modern type of aircraft do **nothing** with your feet at this stage.

Keep your feet off the rudder when you start to roll. If you do not, you will make some input that changes the aircraft attitude from vertical and makes analysis of your elevator position much more difficult.

While rolling, watch the wing tip and see that it tracks around the horizon without going up or down. Stop the roll by centring the aileron control. If not trimmed for zero G, maintain forward elevator control pressure to keep zero alpha. Now you must apply rudder to counteract the slipstream effect, just as in a stall turn.

Downward Rolls

Rolling on the vertical down is easier in one respect than rolling on the way up: it is much easier to gauge precisely the extent of the rotation. In other respects, it is just as difficult.

You must be exactly vertical before you make the aileron application. You can **only** be certain about this attitude by looking at the wing tip where you can assess both pitch and yaw. You must maintain precisely zero angle of attack while rolling. You must resist the temptation to add rudder automatically when you apply the aileron, because, once again, there is no adverse yaw at zero alpha.

Error Analysis

'Not Vertical' Errors

Quarter Rolls

At the completion of the quarter roll, before you go on to complete the figure, you must make an assessment of your attitude with respect to the vertical. You should do this by looking at the wing tip. Some possible situations are shown in Diagram 29-3, assuming you are looking at the left side and have rolled to the left.

Diagram 29-3

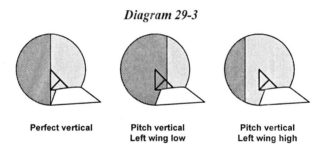

| Perfect vertical | Pitch vertical
Left wing low | Pitch vertical
Left wing high |

These cockpit views, at least the not-perfect ones, are representative of the aircraft attitudes shown in Diagram 29-4. In both cases you have made a good axial roll, but you have an error after 90° because the vertical attitude was wrong before the roll.

In the first case you were positive before the roll; in the second negative. Note that the meaning of 'positive' and 'negative' in this context is shown by the lower aeroplane of each pair in the diagram.

These are typical illustrations of breaking the first rule. The aircraft was not truly vertical before the roll started. The pilot was probably thinking too much about the coming roll and not enough about setting a really good vertical line.

Diagram 29-4

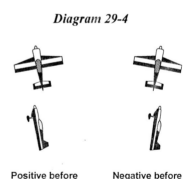

| Positive before
Left wing low | Negative before
Left wing high |

Diagram 29-5

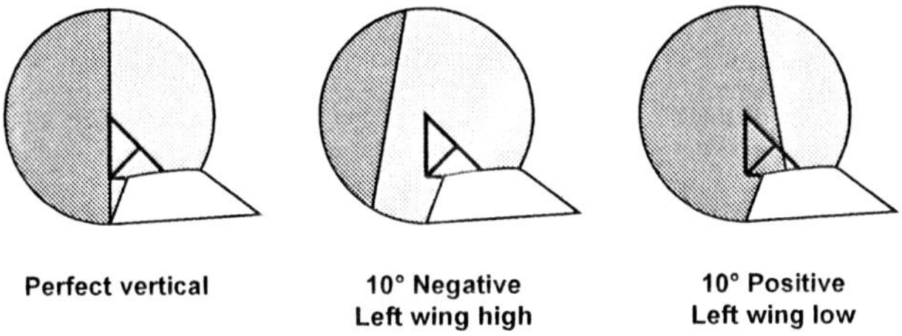

Perfect vertical	10° Negative Left wing high	10° Positive Left wing low

Diagram 29-6

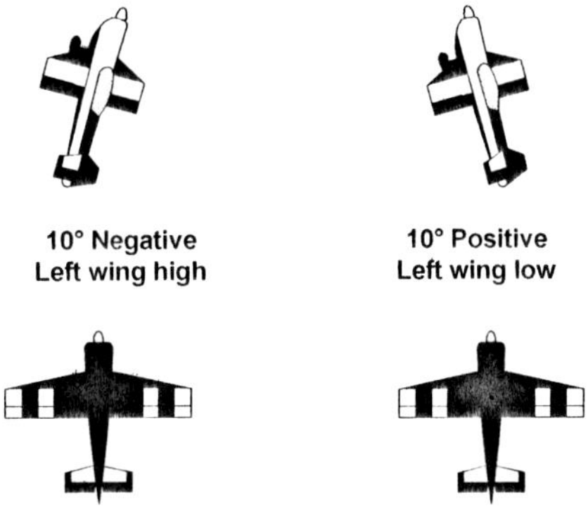

10° Negative Left wing high	10° Positive Left wing low

Diagram 29-5 is another set of cockpit views. The negative/high error will occur if you have the control column slightly aft of neutral point when you roll from a perfectly vertical start. The positive/low error is the opposite. You started vertical but added forward stick during the roll. These are the two results from breaking rule number two, not putting the stick in the right place.

The associated aircraft pictures are in Diagram 29-6.

If you break both rules, you will get a combination of these two errors. If you are not sure what is wrong, just make sure you fix rule 1 first, then work on rule 2.

Half Rolls

Assuming a half roll to the left as shown in Diagram 29-8, if you are positive before the roll the left wing will go down at the quarter point and then back up to the horizon after 180°. Now you will be on your back, negative. Likewise, if you start negative you will end up positive, with the left wing going high in the middle. These are the results of breaking Rule 1.

Diagram 29-7

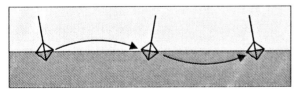

Rolling left, looking left, 360° roll

While you are looking at the horizon during this roll you will see the wing tip, or wing sight, go down then up, or up then down. If you did a full 360° vertical roll you would see both these cycles, as shown in Diagram 29-7 for a negative start.

Diagram 29-8

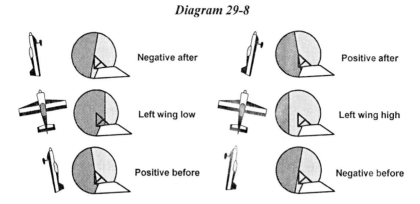

Negative after

Positive after

Left wing low

Left wing high

Positive before

Negative before

In this condition, you should see the wing tip start to rise as the roll starts. An early, deft forward stick movement may get you back on the correct track, but you must make this correction before you have rolled as much as 30° or it will not have the right effect.

There is a similar back-stick correction if you start positive and the wing goes down when you start to roll. Remember all these corrections relate to rolling left, looking left.

If you roll right, or look right, or both, you will have to work out the appropriate correction using similar logic to mine. This in itself will be a good exercise for you, but it is best to do it on paper on a rainy day, not in your head while airborne burning expensive gasoline.

If you are nicely vertical but then break Rule 2 during the half roll, you will actually fly a little half barrel roll (Diagram 29-9). If you have a little inadvertent back stick, this will be a positive barrel roll. With the stick a bit too far forward it will be a negative barrel roll.

Diagram 29-9

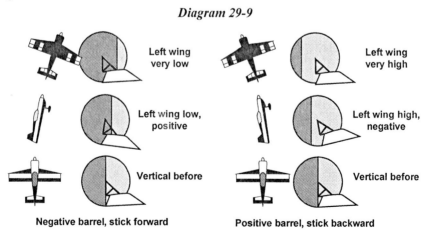

Left wing
very low

Left wing
very high

Left wing low,
positive

Left wing high,
negative

Vertical before

Vertical before

Negative barrel, stick forward

Positive barrel, stick backward

Downward Rolls

Here are some similar pictures that show the equivalent errors in the vertical down case (Diagram 29-10). Most inexperienced pilots find it very, very difficult to look to the side at the start of the vertical down. They simply cannot resist looking over the nose at the ground below.

Diagram 29-10

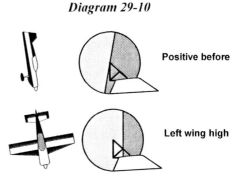

Positive before

Left wing high

Looking ahead prevents real consistent accuracy in setting the vertical down attitude. Learn to look sideways, it won't kill you!

Barrelled Roll Errors

Diagram 29-11 shows what happens in a barrelled vertical roll to the left. Now after half a roll the aircraft is roughly vertical in pitch but has one wing very low compared to the start position. Again, a small, deft elevator input right at the start, as soon as you see the wing go up or down, can save the day. But as before, this correction must be made really early if it is to be fully effective. It is much better to follow Rule 2 and put the elevator in the right place from the start.

Diagram 29-11

Vertical positive barrel roll left

Diagram 29-12

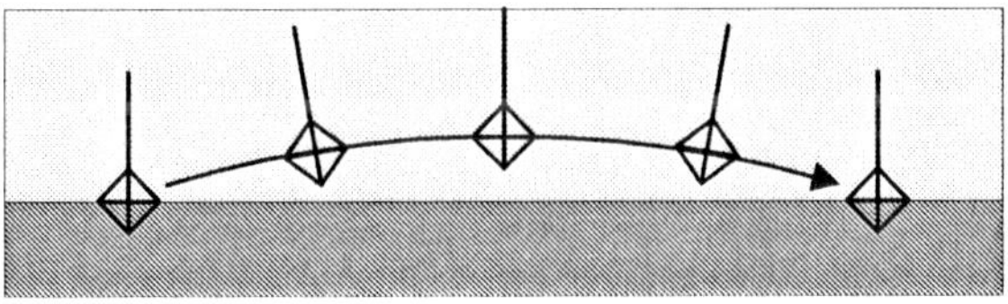

Rolling left, looking left, 360° roll

If you fly with this little barrel error uncorrected for a full 360° roll, you will get back to the perfect vertical with which you started. In the process the wing will have made only one gentle curve above or below the horizon. Diagram 29-12 shows a slight positive barrel (stick back) from the view of the wing sight.

Notice the difference between this wing sight picture and the earlier one when Rule 1 was violated. If you get a 'S' curve in 360° you have a Rule 1 problem, if you get a single curve in a full roll you have a Rule 2 problem.

Actually deciphering your own Rule 1 and Rule 2 errors in vertical rolls is a slow, difficult process. Especially if you combine elements of both errors in the same manoeuvre. It is much quicker to seek the help of an astute and knowledgeable ground observer. For expert professional help, you may have to pay a little money, but you will save this many times over on reduced fuel bills from extended, frustrating, lonely practice.

Downward Rolls

If you make a Rule 2 error on the down line, you will again perform a tight little barrel roll. You will see the nose make a circle on the ground, rather than simply rotating on a spot. With most students, the fault is to apply back stick with the aileron, especially when rolling right. When you do start vertical and find exactly the right stick position for zero alpha, your vertical rolls down will suddenly feel a whole bunch more balanced and comfortable.

Final Roll Position Errors – Stopping on Heading

In an ideal world you would always fly over a fully marked competition box and attached to the aeroplane would be a giant, weightless, drag-free rear-view mirror. Optically perfect, of course. While rolling in the vertical you would simply gaze into the mirror and watch the box axes revolve and stop precisely at the right moment (Diagram 29-13).

Diagram 29-13

The rear-view mirror!!

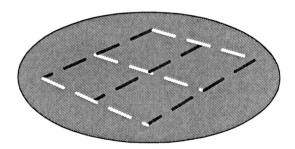

Dreams can come true, but this one has a lower probability than most.

So what are the alternatives?

If you are very flexible, you can turn and look behind you. Once the roll is established and tracking level round the horizon, turn further in your seat and try to see the ground rearwards past the horizontal stabilizer.

If you can continue the roll accurately in this contorted condition, and can see your line feature clearly, you have a good chance of stopping accurately. To get your head that far round requires a flexible spine and is helped greatly by having loose shoulder straps so that you can also turn your torso. Loose straps are fine in an upright seat, like a Pitts, but are really inconvenient in a reclined seat, like a Giles 202 or a Sukhoi 26. In these latter cases, loose shoulders mean a lot of upward body movement under negative G and while rapidly rolling. Neither of these is conducive to delicate manipulation of the controls. In aircraft like these, I always found it impossible to fly accurately without the shoulder straps very tight.

Diagram 29-14

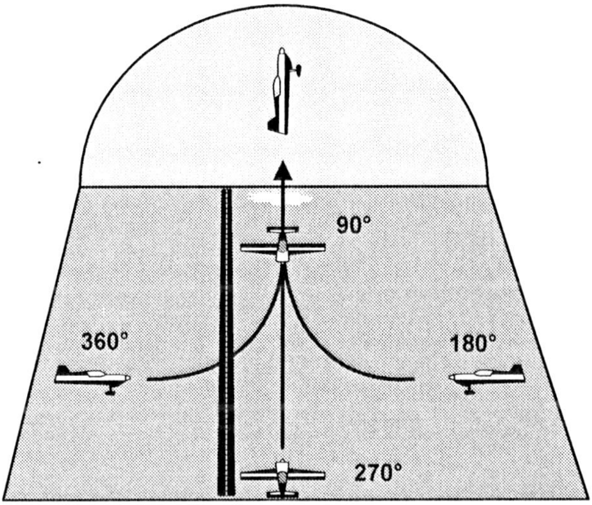

Another alternative is to fly using ground features that are more distant and can be seen nearer the horizon below the wing tip. When practising in your familiar local area, you can always arrange for such landmarks to be in the right place. You can fly a quarter, half, three quarter or full roll so that you always plan to stop on the same, landmark-oriented heading.

In Diagram 29-14 you could use the lake or the disappearing highway. Whenever you stopped rolling you should see a very clear picture and be able to interpret it in terms of under or over rotation. This picture assumes looking left and rolling right, a good combination.

If you were looking left and rolling left, you would have to swap the 90° and 270° captions on the diagram. Using this method of orientation, you should ideally look in the direction opposite to the roll, unless you have a high-winged monoplane such as a Decathlon. In this case it is better to look in the same direction as the roll.

Diagram 29-15 shows the view to the left from most low-wing monoplanes. It is very much like this, for example, in a Yak-55. If you plan to stop with this reference and have been rolling left, you will only see the lake at the very last second, as it pops out from being hidden by the wing.

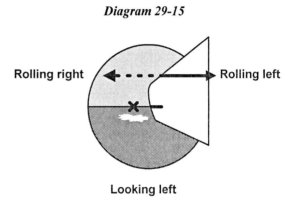

Diagram 29-15

Rolling right / Rolling left

Looking left

You would almost certainly over-rotate the roll if you were relying on seeing the lake before deciding to stop the roll. If you have been rolling to the right, you would have had a chance to pick up the visual reference much earlier. The chances of stopping on heading would be much greater. At slower rates of roll, you naturally have more time to pick up point features such as this. But if you are rolling at greater than 270° a second features start to blur and precise 'feature capture' is difficult. Did anyone tell you this would be easy?

Diagram 29-16 shows the same idea as before but with a slightly different wing configuration The pilot's head is aft of the wing trailing edge which is itself perpendicular to the fuselage longitudinal axis.

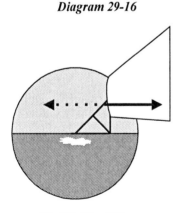

Diagram 29-16

Zlin 526, Giles 200

In this case, there is a much better chance of picking up the lake feature if rolling left and looking left at moderate roll rates.

Unfortunately the Giles can roll at over 400°/ sec. If you use full aileron, everything in the distance is a blur until you stop. In the more sedate old Zlins this would have been less of a problem. This slight advantage of wing configuration also applies in two-seat Pitts aircraft where the lower wing also sits ahead of the rear seat.

So much for visual methods of determining when to stop the roll. If you are held firmly in your seat with your shoulder straps, and you are old and have a stiff neck, and you are rolling at over 400°/sec, then none of the aforementioned is going to be of much use. But do not despair; there is another method which works with your eyes closed.

We all have a very sensitive balance system in our inner ear. We use it all the time to orientate ourselves about the three axes. Through it you are always aware of the direction gravity, whether it be the usual, vertical-down kind of gravity you get in normal terrestrial life or the local, any-direction gravity which we manufacture by centrifugal force while throwing ourselves around the sky for fun. Yes, remember, you are doing this for fun!

"Now then!", as they say in Yorkshire. This next bit needs the help of a friend and for you to hide your embarrassment. I've been through it lots of times in the Clubhouse and have not yet died from the strange looks I've generated from the great unwashed (straight and level pilots). Ask your friend (and you must know them well) to read out the following instructions and see what happens.

◆ Stand facing a blank wall (no windows), with your weight evenly divided between your two feet.

◆ Stretch out your arms so they are parallel to the ground with your palms facing forwards.

◆ Study the wall in front of you carefully and concentrate fully on the spot directly ahead.

◆ Empty your mind of everything except the location of this spot.

◆ Shut your eyes.

◆ Keep facing ahead and concentrating on the spot on the wall.

◆ Quickly turn through 90° so that your left arm is pointing directly at the memorised spot on the wall.

◆ Stand still!

Open your eyes and see where your left arm is actually pointing. I am sure it will be within 1° or 2° of the correct orientation. If it is not, try again. You just didn't settle yourself nor empty your mind enough before you turned. Once you have success through 90°, try a full 360° roll. You will find you can get very, very close every time. With practice, you can teach yourself to use this in-built 'inertial platform' to help you stop your rolls on heading.

To develop this skill in the air, try the following as a practice procedure. Fly directly towards your distant landmark (the lake in the pictures) in a shallow dive. Concentrate on that direction. Look at the left wing tip and, as you pull to the vertical, visualise that point moving to a position directly below your seat, under the belly of the aircraft. When you stop in the vertical, your bottom is pointing directly at the landmark. Open your field of view so you are not distracted visually by looking at a fixed point. Now roll quickly left and stop when your left wing tip is pointing at the same spot your bottom was a second ago. After you stop the roll, look to see that your left wing is pointing straight at the lake.

If you are looking left for a half roll, you must visualise the direction that your right shoulder points before you roll. For three quarters, you must visualise the point that was dead astern and will thus be directly above your head at the instant you start the roll. In each case, practice stopping by the inertial method and then confirm visually how close you are to the correct heading.

This use of the visual report, not to decide when to stop the roll but to confirm you have stopped in the right place, is very important. When you prepare a new sequence on the ground, use your local knowledge to create a mental picture of what precisely you expect to see at the stop of every vertical roll. When you confirm that these points are clicking into place regularly as the figures go by, you will gain great confidence.

With practice, you can harness this 'inertial' sense along with all the others you possess. When integrated with the available visual feedback it can work exceptionally well. The more mentally relaxed you are in your flying, the better you can harness this extra sense. If you get very stressed, your brain will start to 'load-shed' and this ability will be one of the first to desert you.

Further Development

I reasoned earlier in this chapter that rudder was not needed to stay vertical when rolling. This remains my view while the aircraft has good speed and is rolling relatively quickly. As speed and rate of rotation decay, however, just like with a child's spinning top, the forces of darkness (well, forces of instability at any rate) present themselves to take over control.

It is, of course, possible to gain such mastery over the vertical roll that you can continue to maintain a perfect vertical attitude while the aeroplane stops climbing and starts down backwards in a rolling tail slide. The torque of the engine will drive the rotation in this situation, and it can be assisted with aileron as well, and the result is what is now commonly called a torque roll.

As the aircraft becomes slow, the slipstream effect from the airflow around the fuselage will make itself more strongly felt. Also, there can be a side-force from the fully deflected aileron that tends to cause parasitic yaw. The balance of the various disturbing forces will vary from type to type, so I cannot cover all the alternatives here. But some rudder **will** be required to maintain the vertical while torque/aileron rolling at very low speeds.

If you are tempted to teach yourself to torque roll, the following tips might help.

Initially, fly a non-rolling vertical line until you are very slow. Then add aileron with the engine torque so that the roll rate is quite slow while the aircraft reverses direction. With this low roll rate, it will be much easier to get the correct rudder inputs to keep vertical.

If your aircraft has only outboard aileron, as in a regular 4-aileron Pitts, continued left aileron while sliding backwards will inhibit the roll to the left. In these aircraft you should change to full right aileron as the slide starts. The roll should accelerate quite quickly. If you have an aircraft with full span ailerons, like a CAP-232, the inboard bits, in the propwash, will work against the outboard bits that have the reverse flow. Initially the propwash dominates, so you can keep left aileron as the vertical direction reverses.

You will need to get out of your torque roll safely, without damaging the aeroplane's control surfaces. The lowest risk method of doing this is to maintain full throttle and apply full rudder. The aircraft will then fall off the vertical immediately. During this recovery, either hold the control column firmly in the centre, or put it fully into one corner or the other. The latter removes all risk of the control surfaces being thrown from one extreme to the other by the reverse airflow.

If you close the throttle while sliding backwards, you will suddenly start to slide backwards with much more speed, so this is a technique only for the most experienced of you.

Speaking from personal experience, the force exerted by the reverse airflow can be surprisingly great. It can for example, move the whole of the Pitts S2B elevator trim system completely to the fully nose-down setting just from the reverse flow over the trim tabs. After such a long slide, the changeover to forward flight, when it comes, can be very fast. In the same Pitts incident that the trim was self-operating, the aircraft changed over with such rapidity that the fuel from the bottom of the tank rushed to the top with enough force that it also popped out the rubber fuel cap. So take care!

Flying in Competition

If you are flying purely for fun, you will really enjoy vertical rolls. The problem is that you will tend always to roll in one direction, whichever you find easiest. The difference for a serious competition pilot is that he simply must be able to roll in either direction with equal facility.

In the relatively simple Sportsman sequences, a stall turn is occasionally followed by a quarter roll down. On the day of the contest there may well be cross wind considerations that strongly mitigate in favour of rolling in a particular direction. If you cannot do this with ease, then you are destined to have a bad flight. Not only will you be worrying about which way to roll, but your final positioning will probably be very poor. This quarter roll may be the only chance you had to counter the wind. You could easily end up 800 metres further away from the judges (or, worse, behind them) unless you can roll in the optimum direction.

In Intermediate the same quandary is apparent in quarter rolls up, while in Advanced there are ¾ rolls both up or down to add to the problem list. The only relief comes from half rolls, which can always be flown in the favoured direction. Until, of course, you have to design your Unlimited Free programme where there will be need for vertical opposition rolls on one line, so there can be absolutely no room for favouritism at the top level.

Energy Matters

The entry to a vertical up line almost always involves starting in very high speed level flight. In most aircraft, you will be flying level at a speed faster than you can sustain. If you continue level in this configuration, you must slow down. Therefore it is very important to minimise the amount of time you spend fast and level before pulling up. Do not hesitate too long. Get on with it. If you need to adjust position during a sequence, plan to do it during a low-speed section.

When rolling on the vertical down, the big question is where to have the throttle. Remember that in order to balance energy throughout a sequence, every opportunity to burn the maximum amount of fuel should be taken. As a general rule, then, power should be on, not off. But there are exceptions.

Firstly, if your aeroplane rolls really slowly, you may be at risk of exceeding V_{NE} if you roll for too long with power on. Alternatively, after the vertical down you may have to fly a figure that is more difficult to control at high speed, like level opposition rolls. It may be better to reduce power on the down line so that you exit slower. This can be a good tactic, but not if you subsequently have insufficient energy to complete the sequence above minimum height.

Another situation will occur if you are flying a relatively simple sequence in a very capable aircraft. For example, quite a few pilots now fly the Extra 300L in Intermediate contests and often they end up flying much too high. If the Intermediate sequence has been carefully designed to be flyable in a Stampe, then the Extra is going to take up too much space laterally and finish the sequence sub-optimally high without some energy squandering during the flight. Flying a vertical down line, and rolling to boot, with the throttle closed is an excellent way to dissipate surplus energy toward the end of a sequence.

CHAPTER 30

Positive Flick Rolls

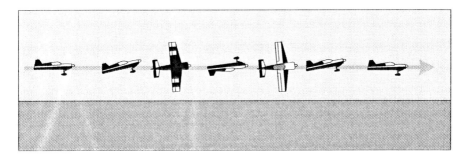

Flick rolls, which are also called snap rolls, came first. At one time in aviation history, this was the only way to roll the machine. Ailerons just didn't have the authority. Aileron development progressed, but even as late as the 1940s light aeroplanes were still in production where the primary directional control at sometimes had to be with the rudder. The ailerons generated so much adverse yaw that at low speed they could be used only to keep the wings level while you pointed the fuselage with your feet.

To roll any aircraft quickly requires a big difference in lift between left and right wings. Ailerons produce just such a lift differential, but in most aircraft, even today, there is another way of getting an even bigger rolling force than the ailerons can provide. This is by having at least one wing stalled.

If both wings are stalled, there can still be a major roll force, but there is also a huge increase in drag. With one wing stalled and one flying, the difference in lift is very large and the gross drag is the minimum you can get with such a high lift differential. Hence, this is the state that gives the fastest roll rate with relatively little energy loss. For this reason, I disagree with previous authors who have described the flick roll as a horizontal spin.

When spinning, you are not generally concerned about gross drag. You can have both wings stalled and still fly a perfectly fine spin. There are spin modes where you can alter the rate of rotation by changing elevator and aileron control inputs, and in doing so you are changing the depth of the stall on each wing and you may even un-stall one side of the aeroplane. But it is my definition of a spin entry that both wings are initially stalled and then a yaw is applied to start the autorotation. In a good flick roll, neither wing is stalled before the rudder is applied, but the resulting yaw quickly stalls one side only.

If you understand this difference between a spin and a flick, you will learn the optimum technique for flick-rolling your aeroplane much more quickly.

The Flight Manoeuvre

In level flight, the aircraft rapidly pitches nose up through about 10° to 15°, without any roll taking place at this stage. It then yaws, a wing stalls and drops, characterised by rapid roll acceleration. During the roll, the aircraft fuselage presents a small cone-angle about the flight path. After one full rotation the autorotation suddenly stops and the aircraft returns immediately to straight and level flight.

Ground References

During a level flick, the only sensible place to look is straight ahead. For a visual reference, use a distant landmark just below the horizon or a small cloud just above it. Use this to check your heading upon completion of the roll.

Technique

First, I will consider a level flick roll through 360°: one full rotation. Check your aircraft flight manual. Do not try to flick your aeroplane unless it is specifically authorized in the manual. If flicks are permitted, the manual will recommend an entry speed or a range of entry speeds. In the case of a range of speeds, I recommend you first start to practice towards the lower end of the range. For example, positive flicks are permitted from 90-140 mph in the Pitts S2A. On a first flight to learn to flick, I recommend using 100-110 mph as a target speed.

I must now digress to do some mathematics. I'll use the Pitts S2A as the basis for this illustration.

The 'stalling speed' given in the manual is 60 mph. This relates, of course, to the level, power off, 1g case. With power on this is reduced to about 55 mph. The entry speed I recommended earlier was 105 mph. Now, here come the equations:

$$\frac{105}{55} = 1.909 \quad \text{and} \quad (1.909)^2 = 3.64$$

Not too difficult. This means that a stall at 105 mph with power on will cause an instantaneous loading of 3.64g. You can make a similar calculation for your aeroplane and find the load factor for a stall at the chosen speed. The first part of learning good flick technique is to have a very consistent initial pitch-up. So the first part of the technique is just to do that.

A flick requires powerful control authority, to change the angle of attack and yaw the aeroplane quickly. For this reason they work better at a high power setting, when there is plenty of propwash over the tail. So it is best to slow to perhaps 20 mph below entry speed, then add power and initiate the flick as soon as the speed increases to the target.

Before doing this exercise, reset the G-meter to '1'. At the datum speed make a rapid application of aft elevator so that the nose of the aircraft pitches up about 10° to 15°. Much greater than this and the wings will reach critical alpha and both will stall, which is not required. Immediately release the back pressure and fly level again.

Check the G-meter to see the peak registered. With my figures, you would be aiming for 3.5g or just under (Diagram 30-1). Too much back stick and you would reach the 3.64 figure and stall both wings. Less than 3g and the alpha would not be high enough to initiate a good flick. If you pull back too slowly, the flight path will change as the aeroplane starts to climb. You want the flight path to stay level, so you must be quick.

Diagram 30-1

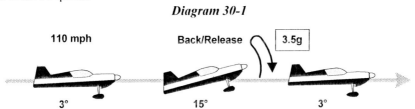

110 mph   Back/Release   3.5g

3°   15°   3°

Practice this back-release exercise over and over. Reset the G-meter each time. Make the pitch application as fast as you can, but do not exceed the 3.5g. As you do this, pay attention to the feel of your bottom on the seat. You will find that you feel the maximum load just after you reverse the control deflection. This slight lag is natural, due to the inertia of the aeroplane.

The exact moment that you feel heaviest in the seat is the actual split second that the wing has greatest angle of attack. Once you can consistently hit the 3.5g spot accurately, you are ready to try the next bit: adding the yaw.

Once you have started to move the control column back, you must rapidly apply full rudder to start the flick. You should reach maximum rudder travel just as the weight feels heaviest on your seat. The down-going wing will stall and a flick will

Diagram 30-2

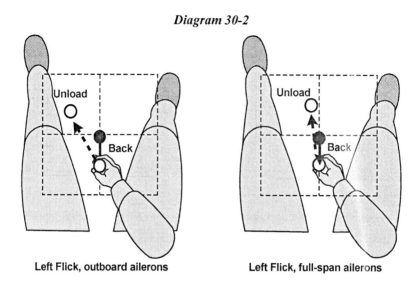

Left Flick, outboard ailerons   Left Flick, full-span ailerons

start, characterized by rapid roll acceleration. As soon as this happens, you should release the back pressure and unload by moving the control column smoothly forward.

With most aircraft you can assist the rotation by adding a small amount of aileron, on the same side as the rudder, as you unload. If you only have outboard ailerons, as in a Pitts Special, you can use perhaps two-thirds aileron deflection. In a monoplane with full-span ailerons, use only a small amount, maximum a quarter. Any more and the in-flick aileron may un-stall the down-going wing and slow the flick into a spiral.

These inputs are shown in Diagram 30-2. Notice that it is very important to pull back centrally, not with aileron on the same side as the rudder. During the roll, maintain full rudder and the unloaded elevator position. The forward elevator ensures a rapid rotation because of the angular momentum effect.

The two principal heavy lumps in the aircraft are the pilot and the engine. So the mass distribution is something like a weight training dumbbell with the centre of

Diagram 30-3

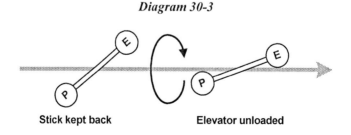

Stick kept back   Elevator unloaded

Diagram 30-4

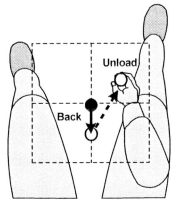

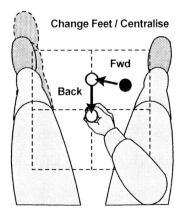

Right Flick, during roll   **Right Flick, recovery**

gravity between the large masses. When you unload the elevator during the flick, the 'cone angle' decreases and the weights come closer to the central axis of rotation (Diagram 30-3). This accelerates the roll, as when a skater spins on the ice and speeds up as she draws her arms close to her body.

While rotating, continue to look ahead to monitor the rotational progress. If the roll rate is high, as it should be, you will have to initiate recovery action somewhere in advance of 360°.

The optimum attitude to start the recovery will vary between types and you will discover this by trial and error. As a guide, it is likely to be somewhere between inverted and the 270° point.

Stop the roll by applying full opposite rudder and placing the control column central and even a little further forward than during the flick (Diagram 30-4). Then immediately centralize your feet and release the forward stick. Make sure you fly off with a level flight path. As you are now slower than before the flick, the nose will need to be a little higher relative to the horizon.

For those readers of a graphical bent, Diagram 30-5 shows the time/displacement for the rudder and the elevator during the whole manoeuvre. Note the delayed start of the rudder with relation to the elevator. Also, the instant of maximum alpha is after the elevator has started to return towards neutral.

The small increase in forward stick for the recovery is like a quick small jab and helps un-stall the wing to give a sharp stop. The elevator finishes further aft at the end of the roll because of the need to fly level at lower airspeed.

Diagram 30-5

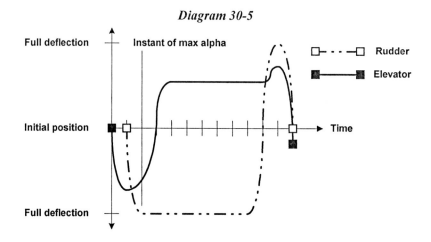

Error Analysis

There are a great many possible errors. I will list some of the more common and explain their effects. If you have problems getting a good flick, then this analysis may help find a solution.

Initiation

If you move the rudder first, rather than leading with the elevator, your heading will change before the nose rises. A flick will probably ensue, but you will generate a bigger initial heading change than if you follow my recommendations. This heading change will probably persist after you have stopped the flick.

If you are being judged in competition and use rudder first, then the judges are unlikely to see a clear pitch-up and you might well be accused of not flicking at all.

If you have not practiced the straight back-release 3.5g pull, you will probably use too much back stick in your initial enthusiasm (Diagram 30-6). Unfortunately, some flight manuals actually suggest you use full aft elevator control.

Diagram 30-6

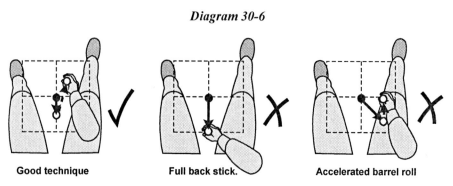

  Good technique   **Full back stick.**   **Accelerated barrel roll**

Doing this will cause a complete stall of both wings. With the added rudder, an autorotation will occur, but the rate of roll will be relatively slow and the energy loss through the manoeuvre will be excessive. The exit speed may be so slow that level flight is impossible after the recovery.

You may initiate the flick with the right amount of back stick, but then forget to unload. Again, the rate of rotation will be slow. You will probably not use enough forward stick to stop the roll and this may lead to over-rotation.

You must have a mental picture that moving the stick forward, unloading, is what really makes the flick roll go. Don't think of the back stick as the cause of the roll, just preparation for the unloading. Moving the stick backwards is like drawing a bow: it is only when you release it that the arrow flies. So it is with the flick.

Of course, you may not pull the stick back far enough to get a flick at all. In this case, when you apply the rudder, the aircraft will lurch sideways and nose-down, but will not roll much at all.

This is a very uncomfortable situation and you will recover from it by centralizing all the controls. A similar lurch will happen if you do actually have the correct back stick input but then unload too soon, before the rudder has had a chance to bite. This is simply the result of your hands working faster than your feet. When you apply full rudder with one foot, bring the other foot smartly back towards you so that it gives no resistance to the forward-going one.

When you apply the back stick, you may add aileron on the same side. The aeroplane will begin immediately to pitch and roll. This is in effect starting a pretty violent barrel roll. When you add the rudder, its secondary affect will add to the roll that has already started.

The aileron will delay, or even prevent, stalling of the down-going wing. The result will be at best a bad flick, at worst an accelerated barrel roll. The aircraft will fly a noticeably spiral path through the air. From inside, you will see the nose make a big circle around the horizon. Even if a bad flick does start, the aeroplane will have rolled perhaps 45° before stalling a wing and 'breaking' into the flick.

During the Flick

During the flick, even after a good initiation, you may inadvertently release the rudder somewhat. The flick will slow or even stop. The aircraft may continue to roll due to aileron, but the rapid autorotation will cease. Make sure you keep full rudder. Press hard against the stop until you decide it is time to recover.

You may unload too far forward. In a high-performance plane with a powerful elevator, you may transition into a negatively-loaded tumble. You will know this has happened if you feel yourself released from positive G and moved toward the side opposite to the rudder. When you recover after one rotation, the nose will be much lower than normal.

You may actually unload with some aileron on the opposite side from the rudder. Again, the aircraft may transition into a negatively-loaded rotation: this time an outside flick. The end result will be similar to that of the previous error.

Upon Recovery

You may just recover too early and stop short of the 360°. This is less likely than the opposite mistake. Just try again to get the timing perfect.

You will more likely recover too late. By the time you have effectively changed feet, the aircraft has overshot the wings level attitude. You will then be tempted to add opposite aileron to help with the stop, but this will actually prolong the roll as it hinders un-stalling the stalled wing. Next time recover earlier and keep the stick central (Diagram 30-7).

Diagram 30-7

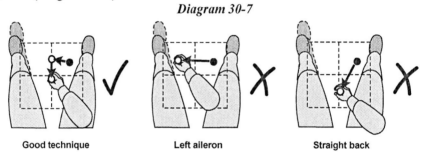

| Good technique | Left aileron | Straight back |

You may pull the stick back during the early stage of the recovery. This will also tend to inhibit un-stalling and will therefore lead to over-rotation. It may even prevent recovery completely in extreme circumstances. If this happens, revert to the emergency recovery action: close the throttle and let go of the stick.

Finally, you may keep the recovery rudder applied after the roll has stopped. If the elevator control is roughly neutral, this unwanted rudder input will simply yaw the aircraft and put it way out of balance. Uncomfortable but not life-threatening!

Further Development

Most specialist aerobatic aircraft have a range of flick entry speeds. In level flight, angle of attack is higher if airspeed is lower. For a good flick entry, however, the angle of attack is the same regardless of the airspeed. So the slower you are flying, the less will be the actual pitch-up at the start.

Diagram 30-8 shows some arbitrary speeds and angles. They are not prescriptive but give a good illustration of the principle. At 130 mph it needs at 12° change of attitude, while at 90 mph it needs only 7°.

Diagram 30-8

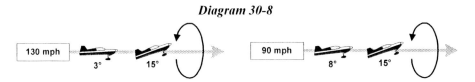

In competition, it is difficult to show the change of attitude that the judges want to see if you are very slow, so the movements must be exaggerated and the application of rudder delayed even more with respect to the start of the back stick.

Flick rolls consume energy. In some aircraft the maximum speed is a relatively low multiple of 'stalling' speed. The speed loss, even with quite good technique, may render a level recovery very difficult. In such cases, you can maintain speed through the figure if you perform it on a descending line rather than a level one.

Start on a fairly steep climbing line – one that is not sustainable. As the speed decays and you approach the stall, ease the control column forward to zero angle of attack. You can check this because the G-meter will read zero. As you float over the top of the bunt, you can be well below 'stalling speed' because you have no alpha (Diagram 30-9).

As you descend the airspeed will increase but G and alpha can both be close to zero. Watch the speed rise carefully and initiate the flick at a speed just a little slower than in the book. Because you have less than 1g, and therefore a very low angle of attack, the initial change of attitude should be large enough to reach the 'just sub-critical' alpha. When you stop the flick, continue with the descending line before smoothly coming level. If you have enough height, you can then repeat the whole process.

Diagram 30-9

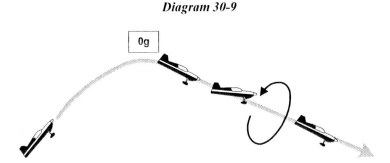

To Flick Left or Right?

Gliders are laterally symmetrical. That is to say that their aerodynamics are identical in left and right terms. Single-piston aircraft are asymmetrical because of the rotation of the propeller. When rolling with ailerons, the only noticeable engine/propeller effect is torque, which slightly assists the roll rate in one direction and opposes it in the other. But the difference is small.

During flick rolls the aircraft initially pitches rapidly. Because of this, the gyroscopic effects of the propeller cause much bigger differences between left and right rotations. I will describe the effects based on a Lycoming-engined aircraft with a propeller that turns clockwise when viewed from the cockpit. For anti-clockwise propellers, the opposite is true.

Diagram 30-10

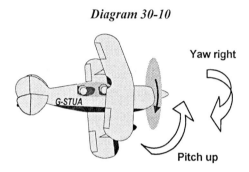

When you make the initial rapid pitch up, gyroscopic precession of the propeller causes the aircraft to yaw to the right (Diagram 30-10).

The bigger and quicker the pitch-up, the greater the gyroscopic effect will be. A good way to demonstrate this is to fly level with a little power at about 1.3 times V_{S1}. Then pull the stick quickly backwards until the wing buffets and stalls. Do nothing with your feet. Then immediately release the back pressure to un-stall the wing.

This will produce a 1.7g load, and so is not going to damage the aeroplane. When you do this the right wing will drop, because the aircraft will yaw right. If this wing-drop does not happen, then you probably have a very light, wooden propeller that produces relatively little gyroscopic force. If the left wing drops, you have a rigging problem.

Anyway, when you make the initial pitch up before starting a flick the aeroplane will go right a little. This plus full right rudder will yaw the aeroplane easily to the right making the flick entry very easy. It will be especially easy to the right if you over-do the back stick and pull back towards your elbow and so add some right aileron. Both these latter actions are, of course, bad technique!

It follows that if you want to flick the aeroplane to the left, it is better to use only the minimum back stick. This will limit the gyroscopic yaw. Otherwise a lot of left rudder authority is wasted just to overcome right yaw induced by the propeller. If you heave the stick a really long way back, it may be almost impossible to stall the left wing!

If you opt for the easy way out and flick right, the aircraft will show a big heading change at the start of the roll. Viewed from behind, it will 'jump' to the right quite a large amount during the roll because of the larger cone angle (Diagram 30-11).

If you choose to flick left, and persevere until you achieve good results, there will be much less heading change during the flick and a smaller cone angle with less sideways movement

Diagram 30-11

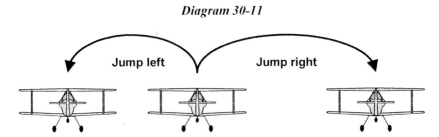

Jump left   Jump right

During a right flick, engine torque will oppose the roll and will assist the stop.

During a left flick, engine torque will assist the roll. It can make the rotation quicker than a similar flick to the right. It can also facilitate multiple flicks which would otherwise stop due to reducing speed and counter-acting torque. Beware, though, that at low speed and high power settings, this torque-assistance may make any flick more difficult to stop. You might find that you keep over-rotating to the left. One way to counter this is to momentarily retard the throttle as you apply the recovery actions.

Flying in Competition

The technique described above is ideally suited to the competition environment because it is designed to comply fully with the rather arcane judging criteria described in the rule books.

The most important thing to remember is that the first thing that the judge sees must be pitch, not yaw nor roll. Neither of these latter two should start until after the change of pitch attitude. Therefore there must always be some delay from the start of pitch-up to the application of rudder.

At low entry speeds the amount of pitch change you can show without actually stalling is limited. In this case, you must show the 'separation' between pitch and yaw/roll even more clearly.

In Intermediate competition, the repertoire includes full flicks on 45° diving lines as well as level ones. Although you should use a slower entry speed for these diving rolls, maybe 10 mph less than level, the main difference comes in the recovery.

In a level flick, it is the level-ness of the flight path that matters. Pitch attitudes before and after can and will be different as explained earlier. On a 45° down line, however, attitude before and after must both be exactly 45°.

If you use normal recovery technique, the descending line will be shallow after the flick. So when you stop this one you must use slightly more forward stick and keep it further forward to maintain the line after the flick as speed increases even more (Diagram 30-12).

The same applies to full flicks on a climbing 45° line, although this time the entry speed should be a little higher than for level, if the manual permits. The attitude before and after must be identical. A change in flight path does not matter. So you need to recover with a good amount of forward stick so that you are not steep after.

Also, after a climbing flick your airspeed will have decayed and control authority diminished. You must ensure you use a large opposite rudder input, not only to stop the rotation but also to regain and keep the correct heading.

Diagram 30-12

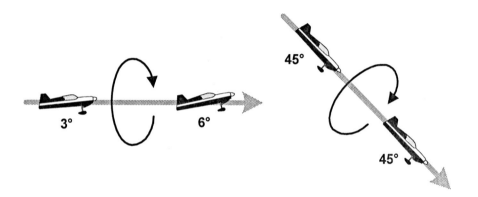

CHAPTER 31

Positive Half Flicks

The Positive Half Flick Roll merits a chapter of its own because it really is very different from a full flick on the same flight path. The initial conditions may be the same as for a full flick but the technique, especially the footwork, is quite different.

Flick rolls, in all their different forms and with all the possible entry attitudes, provide the aspiring aerobatic master with the greatest challenges of his craft. The half flick is the most delicate of these tasks. When flown well, it is a delight to behold, especially from inside the aeroplane. The sudden burst of activity on the controls, the blur of the world outside and the perfect stillness of a clean stop on heading provide immense satisfaction. The joy is a true reflection of the hours of frustration spent in perfecting the figure. Hours that are always needed simply because there is so much that can go wrong!

Before you try the academic, straight and level half flick detailed below, you might like to try a little exercise that will give you an idea of how a half flick can be fun.

Fly a climbing 45° line at full throttle. At about 20 or 30 mph above level 'stall speed' (check that this is below flick entry speed) quickly apply more back stick and full rudder. As soon as an autorotation starts, centralise all the controls. The incipient flick will stop and you will find yourself upside down at low speed. You can then gently pull through as though completing a loop of half-reverse Cuban.

Diagram 31-1

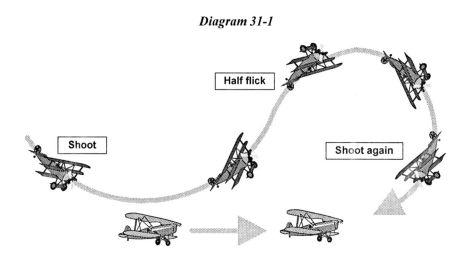

Diagram 31-1 shows how to use this in mock combat when you have a lot of overtaking speed!

The Flight Manoeuvre

The half flick from level flight starts in the same way as the full flick: pure pitch first followed by the sharp onset of a rapid autorotation, which is definitely not a spin. In the blink of an eye, the rotation stops as quickly as it starts and the aircraft once again perfectly level, but now inverted. It sounds simple. The appearance is deceptive.

Ground References

Distant landmark ahead, or line feature below; either works well, both is ideal.

Technique

The preparation and initiation are just the same as described earlier in "Positive Flick Rolls" on page 283. Bring the control column sharply back a controlled amount to gain high alpha and equally sharply apply rudder in the direction of the flick to stall one wing. Now the technique changes.

As soon as you feel the 'break' as the autorotation starts, or in some cases even before this, unload the elevator toward neutral and release the rudder. I mean you just to lift your foot momentarily from the pro-flick rudder once the rotation starts. No opposite rudder, just release.

Keep moving the control column forward and the rotation will stop. With good timing this will be wings level and inverted. As the rotation stops, re-apply the original pro-flick rudder to correct the heading change that has occurred during the initiation. The elevator rhythm is *"Back-Release-Stop"*. The rudder rhythm goes *"Left-Release-Left"* (or *"Right-Release-Right"*). The timing is about the same as if you say these words in normal speech. The half roll is that quick. If you choose to half flick to the left in the Lycoming-engined aircraft, engine torque will want to keep the flick going.

The initial heading change will be less than to the right but stopping will be less consistent. If you half flick with the engine, momentarily close the throttle after you have released the rudder. Re-apply the throttle once the rotation has stopped.

This gives the full mantra for a half flick with the engine. The controls go:

Stick-Foot, Release-Throttle Closed, Foot-Throttle Open.

This means:

- stick back and then rudder in
- release both controls and close the throttle
- re-apply the same rudder and open the throttle.

The final position of the elevator control is that required to fly level inverted at the residual airspeed.

The control inputs for rudder and elevator are shown in Diagram 31-2 in graphical format. There are small variations of detail between aircraft types, so please view this as illustrative rather than specific.

Note that the control inputs continue after the rotation stops. Also, you should realise that, after completion of the roll, you will need to keep the elevator forward to fly inverted and maintain some rudder to ensure that the heading remains good.

Diagram 31-2

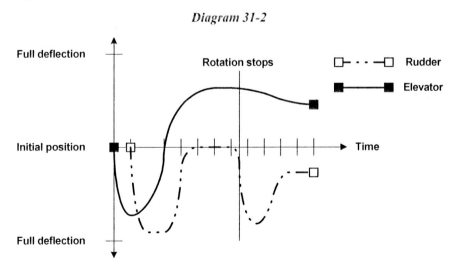

297

Error Analysis

Initiation

The errors associated with starting the figure are stalling fully and rolling into the flick. The causes of these, excessive back stick and in-roll aileron, are shown in Diagram 31-3.

The first is cured by pulling just far enough back to be effective at stalling one wing after the rudder is in. Recap on the Back-Release exercise described on page 285. Don't 'bury' the elevator and stall both wings.

Diagram 31-3

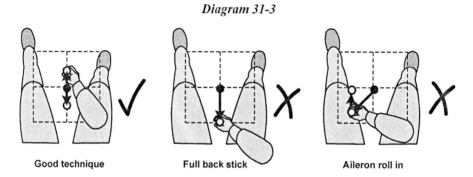

Good technique   Full back stick   Aileron roll in

'Rolling In' is seen as a bank angle being established with aileron before the actual 'snap' autorotation begins.

Avoid this by pulling back straight, or even very slightly away from the direction you are going to flick. For example, the natural tendency to pull very slightly towards your right elbow may help in getting a clean start to a left flick but will cause you to 'roll in' at the start of a right flick. Slow application of the rudder can also cause 'roll in' due to its secondary effect. If you apply the rudder quickly, this effect has no time to show itself.

Completion

The two big errors are over-rotation and change of heading. The first is easier to fix because it really revolves around timing. With practice, your timing will improve. The key elements of this timing are to avoid keeping the back stick and the initial rudder input for too long. Get in and get out as quickly as you can, as long as you do actually start the flick. It is, of course, possible to be so quick and slight with the control movements that no flick occurs at all.

Make sure that the control column goes far enough forward to actually make a stop. If you keep the stick back the flick will probably continue, albeit more slowly, even

Diagram 31-4

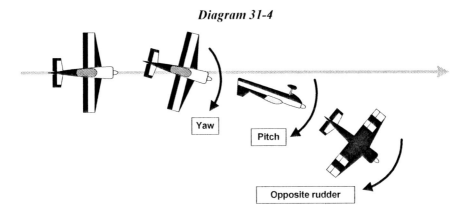

after you have released the pro-flick rudder. Use the power-off technique if you are flicking with the engine.

When you make a half flick to the right, in a Lycoming-engined aeroplane, you may get much better results if you use less than full rudder to start the flick. This is because the initial pitch-up actually yaws the aeroplane to the right gyroscopically. Only a little extra right rudder is then needed to start the flick. To the left, more rudder is needed, because you have to overcome the gyro first.

Your first attempts at a half flick will invariably show a large heading error when you stop (Diagram 31-4). This can easily be up to 45°. It will be greater when you flick against the torque of the engine (right with a Lycoming engine) because this direction is 'with' the gyroscopic yaw generated by the pitch up. The initial yaw, combined with extra pitch caused by having the stick back too long, then the use of opposite rudder to stop the flick, all add together to give the heading change. And, yes, you will make all these mistakes together.

The key points are to unload the back stick and rudder as soon as possible, so that the flick stops, and then to get hard on the same rudder afterwards to sort the heading. These points are illustrated in Diagram 31-5. I am not trying to imply that right flicks are always off heading and left ones are always straight, but you will get a better chance of staying on heading if you flick left with a clockwise propeller.

Diagram 31-5

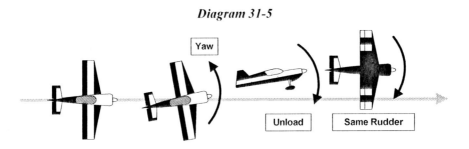

Further Development

Once you are fairly confident with the level variety, you can move on to try your half flicks on 45° climbing or descending lines. In Advanced competition you will have to perform these very accurately from time to time.

For a climbing flick, add 10 mph or so to your normal level entry speed. For a descending one, reduce the entry speed by the same amount.

The main difference in both cases is the need to finish accurately in the 45° attitude. When you fly level, it is your flight path that should be level afterwards, but on the 45°, it is your attitude that must be definitive.

To stop these half flicks accurately in the right attitude, you have to finish with the elevator control less far forward as you have been doing in the level ones (Diagram 31-6). The difference in attitude is only about 5° to 10°, but you have to make a real effort to change the final stick position you have previously learned to trust at the end of the level manoeuvre. Otherwise, you will be 'shallow after' on the down line or 'steep after' on the up line.

Diagram 31-6

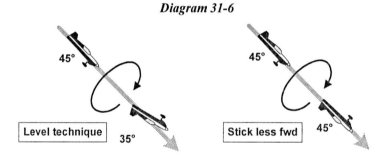

Flying in Competition

Wind Considerations

You can see from the earlier diagrams that when you make a half flick the aircraft jumps sideways even if it stays on heading. Even more important are the results of the likely heading error because of the wind. This is something to be borne in mind when flying the manoeuvre with a strong cross wind. It is always better to flick so that you 'jump' into the cross wind (Diagram 31-7).

This is especially important if the half flick is on the B-axis, being flown directly towards or away from the judges.

If you do this, any residual off-heading error will be masked because it is into the cross wind and your track will probably be straight even though your heading is

Diagram 31-7

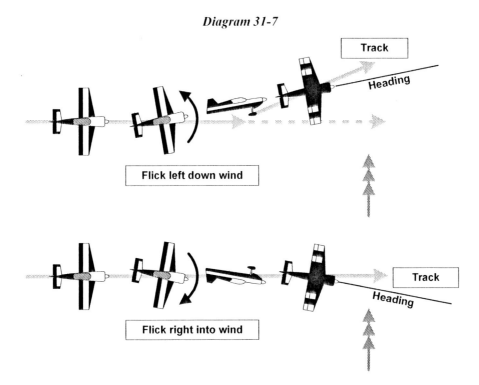

Track
Heading
Flick left down wind

Flick right into wind
Track
Heading

not. If you half flick down wind, then any remaining heading error will add to the wind drift and give the appearance of being much bigger than it really is.

If you successfully counter the natural heading change, the half flick usually finishes out of balance because you have re-applied a lot of rudder just as the flick stops.

This out-of-balance can make the next figure, a hesitation roll perhaps, more difficult than it should be. In some situations you can anticipate this by being off-heading before the half flick. Quite often you can do this without it being visible from the judging line.

Consider the combination in Diagram 31-8. After the half flick left you will normally be carrying quite a lot of left rudder.

Diagram 31-8

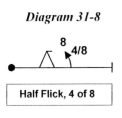

Half Flick, 4 of 8

This slide will tend to make the first part of the hesitation roll over-rotate and fish-tail a bit. In a level, centre-box situation, as long as you are not too close and high, you could afford to be a little off heading to the right before the flick. This would reduce, or eliminate the need for left rudder at the finish and the 4-of-8 would be easier and look better.

Sliding Setups

Sometimes the half flick comes immediately at the end of a looping segment.
Diagram 31-9 shows two possibilities. In
such instances, air speed is always low
and large heading changes are very likely
to arise using conventional technique.

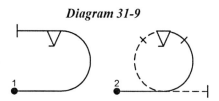

Diagram 31-9

You can achieve good results, however, by using a sliding technique to reduce the
amount of extra rudder needed to initiate the half flick.

Suppose you plan to half flick to the left at the top of the half loop. During the
looping segment, you should add right aileron, as if to make a heading change of
maybe 10° or 20° at the top. At the same time, add left rudder so that the wings stay
level throughout the half loop. By this method you will arrive at the apex of the
figure with the aeroplane sliding to the right in response to the left rudder.

You now add a little extra back stick for the flick entry but need only apply a small
amount of additional left rudder to stall the left wing and start the autorotation. The
heading change due to this small rudder input will also be small, and much more
easily corrected after the half flick has stopped.

Don't make the mistake of sliding with right rudder for a left-foot flick. You will
end up with a very big heading change. This 'opposite foot' slide is good to set up
a stall turn against the engine (page 203), but in that case you are looking to get a
180° heading change, not zero!

You can also use this 'same foot' sliding setup for a climbing half vertical flick,
provided the straight line before the flick is not so long that the slide dissipates.

Energy Matters

As before, flicks lose energy. All you can try to do by way of management is to
minimize this loss by good technique incorporating minimum back-stick.

CHAPTER 32

Inverted Spins

Over the years, inverted spins have had a generally bad press in aviation literature. This is a thoroughly undeserved and ill-founded reputation. One of the main problems is that pilots who have never even tried to do one talk about the subject as though they are experts. Bar talk gets passed on. They have scary, fatal episodes in movies.

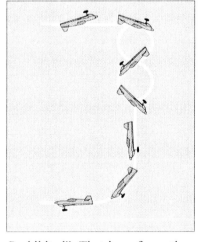

Most aircraft designers don't even want you to spin their aircraft upright. They have to have a test programme for upright spinning to get an airworthiness certificate, so this the test pilot does regularly. Then the placard goes up "Intentional Spins Prohibited". That is as far as they get at the factory.

Even some aircraft certified as 'fully aerobatic' still carry a prohibition on inverted spins, even though these impose no more stress on the aircraft than upright ones. Such a prohibition in the flight manual does not imply that, if spun inverted, the aircraft has a recovery problem and will kill you. A better conclusion would be that the factory did not want the expense of a full programme of trials to examine and prove a manoeuvre that they thought few people would ever want to do. The British-built Slingsby T67M is a classic example of a 'fully aerobatic' design that would be easily capable of competing in Intermediate contests but for its lack of clearance for inverted spins. Of course, the T67 can be spun inverted and recovered safely and consistently, but I guess this is meant to be a secret.

Diagram 32-1

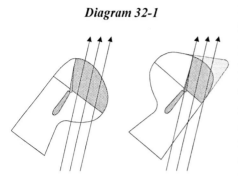

Fortunately there are still a good number of types out there that can legally be spun upside down, and I have had the pleasure of doing this in at least 16 of them, more if you divided the different categories of Pitts Special into more than two. In each and every case, I have found that a 'normal' recovery from any inverted spin is quicker and more definite than from the upright equivalent.

The reason for this is airflow over the rudder, which is invariably greater when inverted due to the tailplane configuration and thus gives more rudder authority. Diagram 32-1 shows how this manifests in a Pitts-style tail configuration.

The ghosted area shows how to get more rudder authority to stop upright spins. It is no coincidence that it looks similar to a CAP, Giles or Sukhoi rudder shape. Of course, with this rudder shape the control forces are higher and you need an aerodynamic horn balance which rather confounds the simple elegance of the Pitts shape. There is a roundabout for every swing!

The Flight Manoeuvre

In this chapter I will only deal academically with inverted spins entered from straight and level, inverted flight.

If you are a discerning reader, that last statement may have whetted your appetite to discover how else you might enter an inverted spin. One of the ways is to manipulate (or mishandle) a stall turn. Another is just to put the controls on from a level upright stall. An even more exotic affair is the *Eventail* (French word meaning 'fan' – the type you cool yourself with, not the person that is after your autograph) which is an inverted flat spin entered from a climbing 45° line. However, I digress. Back to the level inverted entry.

From the stall in level, inverted flight, the aeroplane yaws and a wing drops. If the yaw is induced with left rudder, the left wing drops toward the ground. The appearance to the pilot is of a roll to the right but, rest assured, the yaw is to the left. The aircraft spins. From the ground it appears just like an upright spin, except that the wheels are up and the canopy down.

After the requisite number of rotations, the yaw is stopped, the stall broken and normal flight resumes, albeit close to vertical down. Most mortals now pull to recover level again but this time upright. Competition pilots, however, have the option to push to recover once again in level inverted flight, now at high speed.

In upright spinning, we talk happily about spins to the left or right with no ambiguity. With inverted spins, the simple expressions 'left' and 'right' can cause confusion. This is because with left yaw we have right roll, and vice versa. It is thus common practice among experienced aerobatic pilots to refer to inverted spins as 'left foot' or 'right foot'.

Ground References

Try to be directly above a major line feature. To begin with, you will find it almost impossible to interpret what you see when you look at this feature during the spin. I still clearly remember my first 1¼ -turn inverted spin in competition.

It was an Intermediate event at Breighton, an old wartime airfield in the north of England. It was unfortunately blessed with a number of runways which criss-crossed in the middle of the 'box'. The inevitable happened and I lost track of which line was which once the spin started. I stopped perfectly aligned with the wrong runway and thus perfectly 90° off heading. This will also happen to you, have no doubt, albeit probably somewhere else in the world.

But you will soon begin to understand the picture. Once you are able to recognise the detail, you will find it easier to maintain orientation in an inverted spin than an upright one, because when upright the ground below is masked by the fuselage floor.

Technique

Half roll to inverted, close the throttle and fly level as the speed decreases. Maintain heading by looking up through the top of the canopy at the ground. Keep the wings level using your peripheral vision.

Keep increasing the high nose attitude by moving the elevator control further and further forward. When you feel the buffet associated with the stall, apply full rudder on the side you want to spin. Move the control column fully forward. Watch the line feature on the ground as the spin starts.

In some aircraft, the Pitts Specials for example, the layout, incidence and cross-section of the wings inhibits crisp drop of the wing at the inverted stall. Rotation is slow to start and the aircraft sinks noticeably.

In these aircraft, it helps to add quite a lot of in-spin aileron just a split second after you have applied the rudder. This helps to drop the wing more sharply. If you do this in a monoplane with full-span ailerons, however, it will have the effect of un-stalling the wing and will work counter to what you want. In these aircraft, keep the ailerons neutral throughout the spin. In this context, in-spin aileron means moving the aileron control to the opposite side to that which the rudder is applied.

Diagram 32-2

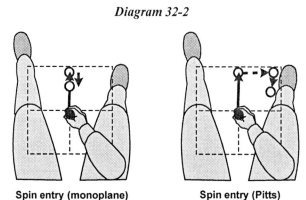

| Spin entry (monoplane) | Spin entry (Pitts) |

Diagram 32-2 shows the control inputs to enter a left foot inverted spin.

In most types, the spin will be fairly flat and oscillatory if the elevator control is kept fully forward. The spin is usually more steady, and the centre of rotation brought a little closer to the nose, if it is accelerated a little after about half a turn. To do this, bring the control column aft a small amount once the spin settles through 180°.

If the spin stops when you do this, you have pulled the stick too far back or relaxed the rudder pressure slightly. Try again with less unloading and make sure you keep full pressure with the pro-spin foot.

The recovery action from an inverted spin is best described as 'change feet and pull'. Recovery from the normal, slightly accelerated spin described above is very quick because of the extra rudder authority described. To stop an upright spin on heading it is customary to initiate recovery with 90° or more of the rotation still to go. Because inverted spin recovery is quicker, it should be left a little later. Sixty degrees is usually enough to stop an inverted spin unless it has been considerably flattened.

So, recover by applying full opposite rudder and immediately bring the control column centrally back. The amount of back stick needed will vary between types, so a 'standard' position cannot be specified. Your instructor or coach will tell you what works with your aeroplane, although this will soon become obvious with practice.

Further Development

There are differences between right foot and left foot spins. The main reason for this is gyroscopic precession from the propeller. With the usual clockwise-turning Lycoming engine, inverted spins with right foot will be flatter and those with left foot steeper (Diagram 32-3). This leads to my preference, when direction does not matter, for left foot spins as they recover marginally more quickly and stop closer to the vertical down.

Once pilots realise how straightforward inverted spins are, they gain a lot of confidence in the aeroplane. Knowledge and experience breed safety and justifiable confidence. With new students in the Pitts S2A, I often use an unconventional inverted spin at the end of the 'emergency recovery' flight.

In their initial training, pilots are taught that spinning is dangerous and to be avoided, and that stalling can easily lead to spinning unless you recover 'at the first sign'. It is not surprising, therefore, that new students are nervous about both stalling and spinning when they first start aerobatic training.

Diagram 32-3

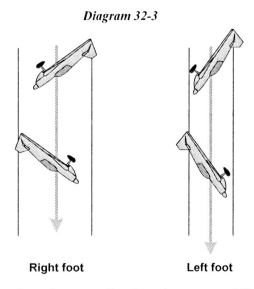

Right foot   **Left foot**

This fear has to be overcome if they are to approach new figures without undue apprehension. In reality, stalling and spinning, in approved aircraft, are not in-herently dangerous. What does occasionally kill the unwary is hitting the ground unexpectedly. If you know how to stall, spin and recover, and if you do so at a safe height, then the danger really does go away.

The cross-over spin demonstration goes like this. Close the throttle and approach the stall in level, upright flight. As the stall-buffet starts, put the control column smartly into the front left corner and apply full right rudder. Hold the controls on hard and look out of the top of the canopy.

After one rotation of inverted spin, let go of the stick and change feet. The spin stops immediately and after an economical pull-out to level the height loss is 800 feet. As part of the pre-spin patter, I explain exactly what I am going to do, point out the line feature below that we will be looking at during the spin and predict the height at which we will finish.

After this demo, the student doesn't always understand exactly what has happened, but they realise that doing 'the worst possible thing' with the controls at the point of stall is not actually 'mishandling', when you have the knowledge, but is a fun figure to fly. That this is possible repeatedly and with precision drives home the lesson.

Spinning is not dangerous; hitting the ground is.

Flying in Competition

As with their upright equivalents, inverted spins in competition always start from a level entry but offer differing recovery path options after the spin is stopped. Three variations on a one-turn inverted spin are shown in Diagram 32-4.

Diagram 32-4

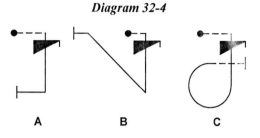

A   B   C

The most commonly encountered variants are those for one, 1¼ and 1½ turns. The really nice thing about inverted spins is that you can look at the ground directly below the aeroplane and can see exactly the centre of rotation.

Diagram 32-5

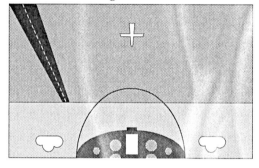

At a contest site, you can also see the runway(s) and box markers while you are spinning. As is the case with vertical rolls down, stopping on heading should be a relatively easy matter.

The direction you use for 1½ turns really doesn't matter as long as you can see the runway or markers when you approach the stopping heading. But for 1¼ direction matters a whole lot, because the two directions produce reciprocal exit headings, only one of which will be correct on any given day. Look at Diagram 32-5. You are flying inverted and approaching the centre-box cross for a 1¼ turn spin. The recovery is a pull to an upright finish and you want to end up flying towards the runway on your left.

To work out the direction of the spin, imagine you were to pull to vertical down and then aileron roll 1¼ so as to end pointing toward the runway. This would be rolling left. Likewise, in the spin the roll component must be to the left. So it is necessary to use right foot for the rudder. With a positive recovery, use the foot on the opposite side from the exit heading. If you were to recover by pushing to level inverted toward the runway, you would have to use left foot. With a negative recovery, use the foot on the same side as the exit heading.

Diagram 32-6

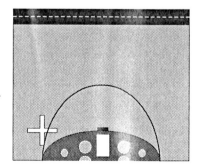

Diagram 32-6 is the picture you would see, after the 1¼ inverted spin with right foot, before you pull out from the vertical down.

Error Analysis

The primary error for any spin is to stop on the wrong heading. The solution is simply to keep practising. The more inverted spins you do, the better will be your spatial orientation during them. Consequently, your anticipation and recovery technique will become smoother and more consistent. Spins will then regularly stop on heading. It is just a matter of time, and timing.

Stopping in a true vertical down attitude presents further problems, similar to those described for positive spins. This is because of the relative wind effect, which is caused by the flight path still having a horizontal component during the first two turns of any spin. Thus, during the first two turns, the amount of back stick required to stop vertical varies, as in upright spins, depending on the recovery heading.

At the finish of a one-turn inverted spin, the aircraft will naturally adopt a flattish attitude. It will need a lot of back stick, possibly full deflection of the elevator control, to get to vertical down smartly.

After 1½ turns, the aeroplane naturally adopts a steeper attitude and only a small amount of aft elevator control will be required for the vertical. The biggest problem comes after 1¼, where not only do you need just the right amount of back stick, but you also need quite a lot of rudder to keep the wings level on the down line.

The right hand of the three pictures in Diagram 32-7 illustrates the problem. The entry line was left to right on the page and the pilot has performed a 1¼ spin with right foot. The aeroplane has stopped on heading but has weather-cocked into wind and has its right wing low. The situation is worsened by the application of full left rudder to stop the spin. Right rudder, the same side as used to start the spin, is needed to make the correction.

Diagram 32-7

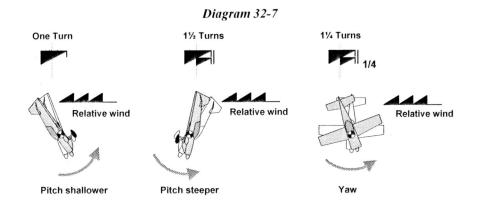

One Turn	1½ Turns	1¼ Turns
Relative wind	Relative wind	Relative wind
Pitch shallower	Pitch steeper	Yaw

It is possible to minimise this yaw error by using an advanced recovery technique suited to your aircraft type. Such modified spin recovery techniques are very valuable to the competition pilot, but should always be learned under instruction from someone with considerable type experience in high-level competition. Do not try to teach yourself such things on a type with which you are unfamiliar. I will describe two such techniques here: one for the Pitts Specials and one for a CAP-232. This will give you some idea of what is possible.

In the Pitts, you can stop the inverted spin with a smart application of back stick if the rudder is neutral. So instead of applying full opposite rudder to stop the 1¼ spin, just centralise your feet and apply aft stick until the spin stops. Then re-apply what was the pro-spin rudder to make sure the wings are level on the down line.

In the CAP-232 (and this works in a Giles G202 as well), you can stop the spin just with back stick even though the pro-spin rudder remains applied. To ensure that you have the elevator effectiveness for this, apply more than half throttle while there is still half a turn left to go. Then bring the control column centrally back smartly until the spin stops (almost fully back). Keep the pro-spin rudder applied so that the wings stay level at the finish. Relax the elevator once the rotation has stopped, to select a vertical down attitude.

CHAPTER 33

Inward Rolling Turns

The Rolling Turn is, without doubt, the most complex of the aerobatic figures that is neither driven by autorotation or gyroscopic forces. Eric Müller called it the *"absolute king in aerobatics"*; Neil Williams *"intricate and demanding"*.

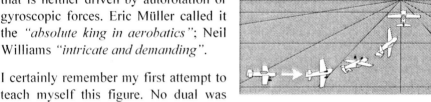

I certainly remember my first attempt to teach myself this figure. No dual was available, so I just had to read the book and then go try. My logbook still holds the exclamation *"First rolling turns!"* in the comments column, such was the landmark status of the day's flight. Needless to say, teaching myself was a slow process. That was nearly 20 years ago and I have now learned the best way to teach this subject, so maybe your progress will be quicker than mine.

There are several ways of describing a rolling turn. Traditional descriptions emphasise that this is a rolling manoeuvre to which you add some turning. So, while you roll you add an extra 'layer' of control inputs to make the aeroplane turn.

It therefore seems simple to deduce that if you can proficiently turn the aeroplane, and can also roll it, then you can reasonably expect to have a go at a respectable rolling turn. My alternative description is that the figure is half inside turn and half outside turn, with a constantly changing bank angle.

Missing from the first description is the word 'outside'. For roughly half of each turn you are going to be performing an accurate inverted turn with precisely varying bank angle. This makes it clear that a pre-requisite for starting to learn rolling turns is to be able to perform precise and consistent **inverted steep turns**

311

not just the much more familiar upright turns. Do not try to learn rolling turns until you can consistently fly inverted steep turns of constant bank angle with precision.

The Flight Manoeuvre

Rolling turns are also referred to as rolling circles. This actually implies a full 360° of heading change, which is not always the case.

The simplest defined figure consists of just one full 360° roll with 90° of turn, as illustrated in the heading picture. This 4:1 ratio of roll to turn is not unique. Ratios of 3:1 and 2:1 are quite common in Advanced or Unlimited competition sequences. These alternatives can be best visualised by thinking, respectively, of three or two rolls in a full horizontal circle.

The key points, academically, are that the aeroplane should always fly level throughout the turn. No going up nor down. Once started, neither the turn nor the roll should stop until the destination is reached.

The turn and roll should be 'evenly integrated', which basically means constant turn and roll rate, both in absolute terms and relative to each other. To achieve all these things, it is easier if you have (more or less) constant airspeed. You will then also achieve, excluding wind effects, a constant turn radius in relation to the ground.

Ground References

One of the key points of the figure is to exit on a precise heading. I've read a lot of aerobatic books, and all the authors are agreed on this aim. Unfortunately, none of them has really described how to achieve this, but this is something that I will make perfectly clear shortly.

A lot of emphasis has been placed on points near the horizon, at 45° and 90° relative to the start heading, as guiding landmarks. The trouble is, in no single rolling turn can you see both of these points at the really critical moments. Then again, you might just be able to arrange, in your local practice area, that you start in a spot and on a heading that gives you two such features.

But what if you are going to fly a full circle with four rolls? This is especially problematical if you are going to do this at a new contest site where you do not know the lie of the land and, even if you did, the likelihood of eight really good points being available in just the right places ... Need I go on? It simply does not work.

Look at Diagram 33-1, which is the lead picture for the chapter with some added annotation. At the start of the figure, you identify two lakes, one at 45° and one at 90° to the pilot's left.

While rolling through Positions 1 and 2 you can monitor the position of lake A and be sure to stop on heading. At Position 2 you can quickly look to your right and pick up lake B. So far so good. But lake B now moves down in your field of view and disappears completely under the nose of the aircraft at Position 3.

Just when you are most disorientated and need to know exactly how hard to push to keep the outside part of the turn going, you have no visual reference to guide you. So you do what you 'feel' is right and suddenly the horizon ahead is revealed as you stop rolling and only now, after the figure is over, can you be sure that you turned enough when upside down.

Diagram 33-1

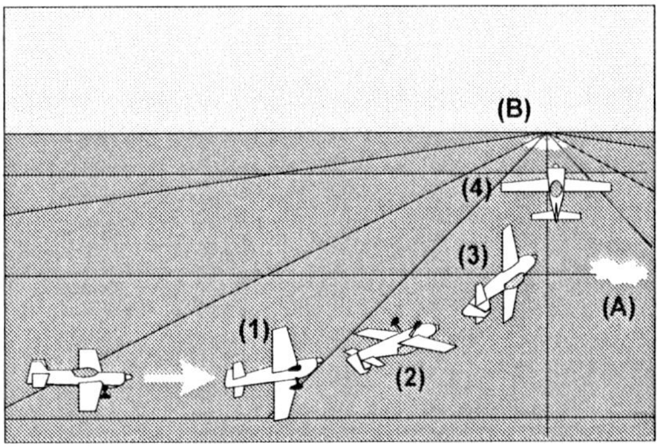

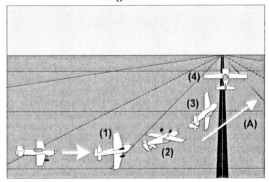

Diagram 33-2

In a full circle, even with the eight mythical landmarks, this loss of visual guidance happens four times.

If the rolling turn starts from level inverted flight, it is the 45° point that is lost to view. Whatever turn you do, you lose sight of one of the distant points at a critical moment.

Now look at Diagram 33-2. This time you have chosen a single line feature that is directly below you. It doesn't have to extend to the horizon, but a kilometre in each direction will be enough. You can watch the road while you roll to inverted at Position 2, and you can make a very good approximation to 45° as you pass inverted. The white arrow at A shows the direction. From here to Position 3, when the horizon ahead is obscured, you can continue to look at the same road. No need to cast rapidly about for a different object.

By the time you get to Position 3, you will be looking up over your right shoulder and you can tell just how much forward stick to use to keep the turn going on nicely. You will eventually, of course, lose sight of the road directly beneath the aircraft's belly, but by then you will know you have done exactly the right amount of turn because you will have been able to watch the road all the time except for the last 10° or so.

This also works with the road parallel to the start direction, and from this position you can fly a one-roll 90° turn (Diagram 33-3) or a two-roll 180° turn (Diagram 33-4) and still see/judge your heading accurately throughout.

Diagram 33-3

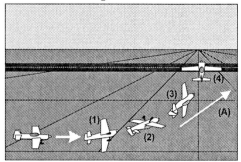

Diagram 33-5 is another set of pictures, showing the ground reference views through the same rolling turn as shown in Diagram 33-3. The white arrows show the heading relative to the road, respectively 22.5°, 45° and 67.5°.

Diagram 33-4

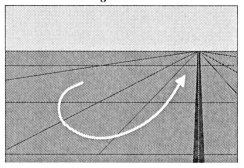

I have concentrated a lot here on where to look, before even starting on describing the technique. Hopefully this will give you a feel for the importance of the visual feedback needed for this figure.

The key matter of technique is to finish on heading. This is so much easier if you can also hit all the intermediate cardinal points. You will only do this if you pull and push the right amount each time the elevator control cycles back and forward, and use the rudder properly as well. The only way to be certain you are doing this right is to look where I have just described.

Diagram 33-5

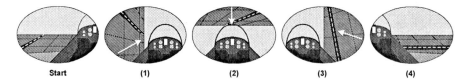

Start   (1)   (2)   (3)   (4)

Technique

The optimum entry speed for a rolling turn is equivalent to a slow cruising speed. This is usually around twice V_{S1}, typically 110-120 mph for a Pitts Special. If you start, or become, much slower than this, you will have only a small margin over the onset of an inadvertent flick roll as you go round the figure.

At higher speeds, the control forces become higher, G-forces accordingly increase a bit, and accuracy is more difficult. Also, the radius of the circle increases with speed, so you may find yourself taking up much more space than you had hoped.

Having set the entry speed in level flight, the next really important thing is to re-affirm to yourself the direction you want to turn. This might seem an obvious thing to say here, but you should always make this mental double-check before starting a roller. Some day in the future, you will be doing inward or outward rollers, starting from upright or inverted, turning left or right. In some cases, the entry control inputs are much less obvious than in the case of the start upright/roll inward figure described here. So this re-check of the turn direction is a very good habit to get in to and will ensure you always go in the planned direction.

Let's now say we are going to turn to our left. This means we are going to use left rudder at the start. We are also going to roll to the left and start in a positive sense with respect to the elevator.

The first control inputs, then, are some left rudder to start a skidding turn and some left aileron to start the roll. As with a straight and level roll, you must lift the nose with some back stick as you start rolling.

The view directly ahead through a one-roll, 90° turn to the left will look like Diagram 33-6. The individual pictures are just the same as for a straight roll, but you must imagine them stretched out across the horizon through a 90° arc. The control inputs required to achieve these pictures are analysed in the next series of illustrations.

Diagram 33-6

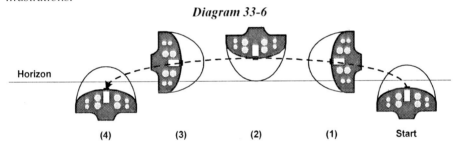

Horizon

| (4) | (3) | (2) | (1) | Start |

The pictures in Diagram 33-7 get you from the start to the first knife-edge position. As the bank angle changes, you must use various combinations of wing and fuselage lift to balance the aircraft weight.

Diagram 33-7

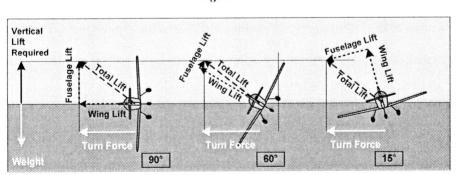

This is just as in a straight roll. But now, these two lift vectors must also provide the force required to keep the aeroplane turning. You can see from the 15° picture that when the wings are close to level, the turning force has to come primarily from fuselage lift; that is from left rudder application. By the time you have 60° of bank, however, the wing lift can provide both the turn force and the anti-gravity lift and there is a point close to this angle where no rudder is required at all.

However, at 90° of bank you have to provide all the anti-gravity lift from right rudder, while still using a smaller amount of back stick so that the wing lift keeps you turning. So, during these first 90°, you have pulled a little, pulled a lot and then relaxed to pull a bit less, while you have changed from a quite considerable left rudder input at the start, through neutral rudder, to a moderate amount of right rudder as you reach the knife-edge attitude.

As you roll beyond 90° (Diagram 33-8), you must quite quickly reduce the amount of back pressure as this will now start to bring the nose down. You must keep increasing the right rudder as the fuselage lift now begins to take over providing the turn force. This is typical of the 120° picture above.

At about 150° the use of right rudder is at its theoretical maximum and the elevator is theoretically neutral, about to become forward stick. At 180° there is still a lot of right rudder, but not as much as just before, as it now provides only the turn force while the vertical lift is provided by down elevator (forward stick).

Leaving the inverted attitude (Diagram 33-9), you start the outside, pushing, part of the turn. At 195° most of the turn force is still generated by the right rudder, but this is now tending to drag the nose down. So the forward stick must be increased to counter the bottom rudder. By about the 240° attitude, the rudder is again passing through neutral.

The forward stick is at a maximum, producing lift both for turning and to stay level. By the second knife-edge position, 270° of bank, you need left rudder for vertical lift and still a good bit of forward stick to keep the turn going.

Leaving the second knife edge attitude (Diagram 33-10), you rapidly reduce the forward stick and increase the left rudder, which reaches a maximum at 330°. By the time the wings become finally level, you will have back stick for the vertical lift and left rudder for the turn. To stop the roll and turn at the end of the figure, you must centralise the rudder and ailerons together.

You now know that, while you turn, you are using quite large rudder applications, sometimes to the right and sometimes to the left. As the secondary effect of rudder is roll, the left rudder applications will tend to speed up the roll rate, while the right rudder will oppose the roll. In order to maintain a constant roll rate, you must therefore modulate the aileron inputs to account for the rudder effects. The greatest aileron deflection would be at about 150° and the minimum at about 330°.

316

Diagram 33-8

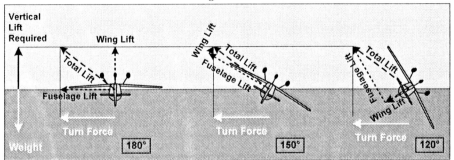

Diagram 33-9

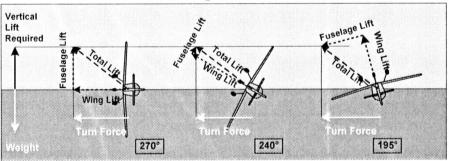

Diagram 33-10

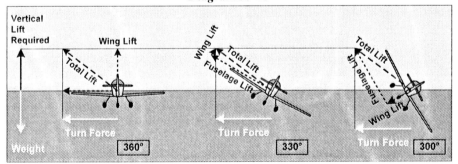

Error Analysis

The biggest overall tendency for inexperienced pilots is to rush through the figure and to work too hard. This makes the whole thing lack delicacy and rhythm. A key point in the early stages is to take your time, be delicate and precise, have a very quick, alert brain working in a relaxed, gentle body. You do not need to make big control deflections except occasionally with the rudder, and even then only very smoothly and progressively.

The most noticeable error during the main body of the figure is when the roll completely stops. This often happens when the opposing rudder is at its greatest. It also happens because of a 'human factors' cause: the pilot gets distracted from the roll rate by concentrating too hard on the task of finishing on heading. The solution, like most things, really only comes with practice. But you can help yourself progress by trying always to keep monitoring the roll rate through your peripheral vision while at the same time ensuring that the elevator and rudder inputs are sufficient to keep the turn going at the right pace. The roll rate is like the drone in a set of bagpipes, always there in the background and contributing greatly to the whole, but not the thing that demands your detailed attention.

Hitting the key intermediate directions and finishing accurately on the final heading are also very important because they are also very noticeable for an outside observer. The key technique here is to establish a steady rhythm and to avoid changes to it. It is also very important to look in the right place and to achieve symmetry, on the G-meter, between the amount you pull and the amount you push. You should finish with something like 2.5g on the meter both positive and negative. If you have +3.5g and -1.5g, then your rhythm is poor, you are pulling a lot harder than you are pushing and you will be turning more like 70°:20° than 45°:45°.

Another obvious error from outside occurs when the aeroplane climbs or dives instead of staying level. With inward rolling turns, the error usually manifests as a climb, while the descending error is more noticeable in outward rollers. The climb occurs because you apply the elevator too much, too early as you leave the wings level condition.

The optimum time for pulling, both to complete more turn and also to stay level, is between 60° and 90° of bank (Diagram 33-11). Similarly, the optimum time for pushing is between 240° and 270° of bank. If you pull significantly before reaching this angle you will climb noticeably.

The pictures in Diagram 33-12 illustrate clearly how the aeroplane will climb if you pull or push too much at around 30° or 210°. Climbing, of course, causes a reduction in airspeed. This means the rudder and elevator get lighter while the ailerons become less effective. Thus the whole rhythm is destroyed by this simple act, usually a result of being in a hurry to get it over with!

The last major error tendency is for the turn to slow or stop. This means most of the turn is being done by the pull and the push and not enough by the rudder. Just about everybody underestimates the amount of rudder needed when they first start to practice the figure.

When this is later pointed out, they do more with their feet but keep the same feel with their hand, so that it suddenly becomes likely that they turn a lot more than 90° in each full roll.

Diagram 33-11

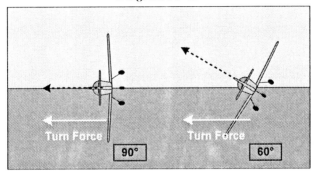

Diagram 33-12

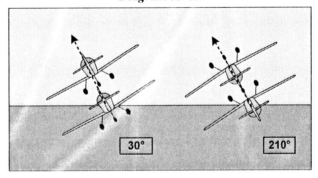

The most likely place for the turn to slow or stop during the first half roll is around the 150° point. Here the wing lift is minimum and the rudder input at its greatest. Especially in an aircraft with limited rudder authority, or heavy rudder load, there will be a tendency to insufficient fuselage lift.

To stay level, the compensation is to add more forward stick, increasing the negative wing lift. This keeps the plane level but reduces, or even eliminates, the turn force. This tendency is illustrated in Diagram 33-13 which shows, on the left, the correct forces and, on the right, the result of less fuselage lift and more wing lift.The turn force is greatly reduced. It could easily disappear altogether with just a little less rudder and a little more forward stick.

There is a similar problem at the 330° stage, which results in the turn stopping early and the final heading being considerably undershot. The diagram for this is at Diagram 33-14. It is the same as the previous illustration but with the aircraft almost back up the right way.

All in all, there is a huge amount that can go wrong. So you must expect progress to take some time. In the early stages, concentrate on building a rhythm with the

Diagram 33-13

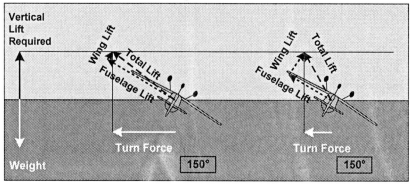

Diagram 33-14

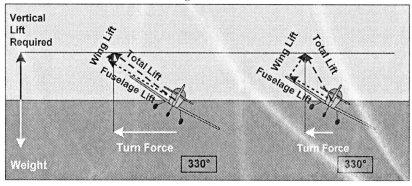

rudder and elevator inputs. Be steady and purposeful. Do not rush, and pay most attention to the steady change of heading as the roll progresses.

It is important to take your time and look hard to see where the errors are becoming apparent. To begin with, limit yourself to one roll and 90° of turn. Stop after each one and analyse what went right and what went wrong. Organise it so that you always finish in the same place and on the same heading relative to your ground line feature.

Make just a few repetitions and look for some small amount of progress in understanding and execution. Then stop and change to another exercise altogether before you become tired or overwrought mentally with this particularly confounding challenge. Remember, it is meant to be fun, not torture.

Further Development

The obvious next step after getting a grip on the basic rolling turn is to move the goal posts a bit and aim for a 120° heading change for each roll. This amounts to three full rolls in a circle. The principal difference is that you need to roll a tad more slowly and to pull, push and rudder just a little harder and longer at each individual application of these controls.

Diagram 33-15

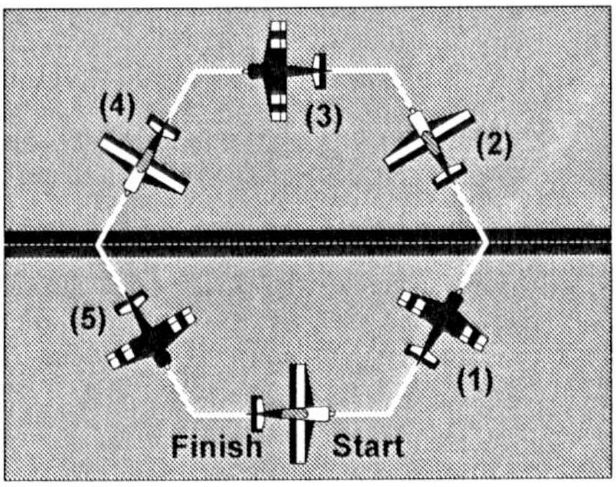

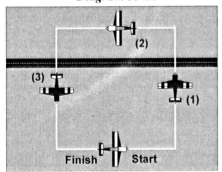

Visually, a 3-roll circle is probably the most difficult to keep up with as you go round. Again, it is important to fly over a line feature and to keep watching it for as much of the figure as you can. In this case, you have to visualize a hexagon on the ground and to see your headings in terms of being parallel to the six sides (Diagram 33-15).

A key point with this figure is the fact that you are parallel to the line feature inverted. Half way round the circle you must be upside down. The various sides that intersect the line feature at 60° are less easy to hit very accurately.

A simple rule of thumb is to be more than 45° at Point 1 and quite a bit past 90° at Point 2. Similarly, be noticeably more than 45° at Point 4 and a good bit past 90° at Point 5.

Diagram 33-16

This is a lot of numbers. Your task really is to find the best way for you, individually, to visualise the required headings. Try different ways and see what works best for you.

The 'headings' problem for a two-roll circle is much simpler (Diagram 33-16). It is easy to visualize the square pattern of key points. The difficulty arises in making enough turn angle while rolling very slowly. To do this figure well, you need an aeroplane with exceptionally good rudder control and wing lift capabilities.

The best I have flown in this respect is the CAP 232, but the relatively humble Pitts Special also has excellent fuselage lift characteristics. The Russian aircraft have always been a disappointment in this respect.

Flying in Competition

The first subject to cover here is the choice you have of where to start and finish, together with which way to roll/turn. The key factor is that you **must** finish on heading. Consequently, you must be able to guarantee visual contact with a line feature (usually the runway at the airfield concerned) as you come up to the end of the figure.

This means that with 90° and 180° turns, you must turn towards the runway (Diagram 33-17). You should position the sequence up to this point so that you can in fact turn this way without going over the dead line or behind the judges.

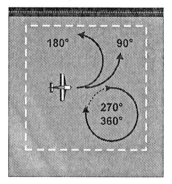

Diagram 33-17

For a 270° or 360° turn, it is best to start by turning away from the runway so that it will become visible again toward the end of the figure.

This consideration makes it clear that you must be able to perform rolling turns to left or right with equal dexterity. This pre-supposes that you can roll straight and level in either direction, and that you can perform precise upright and inverted steep turns in either direction. Your practice fuel bill has suddenly doubled.

This is always the principal factor as you move upward through the contest category structure: the repertoire increases at every step, **and** you have to be able to fly basic manoeuvres in either direction.

The second major subject under this heading is how your decisions on 'which way to turn' can be affected by wind conditions. But first we must talk about the effects of speed on radius. Let's assume no wind for a moment. At constant speed your perfect roller will produce a perfect circle in plan form. If you accelerate, or slow down, during the figure, the radius will change accordingly. This shown in Diagram 33-18.

Effectively, the change of speed, over a full 360° turn, will result in a sideways translation. In a cross wind, you can use this translation to compensate for the wind, if you plan the best way to turn.

Diagram 33-19 shows the paths over the ground of an accelerating turn. The still air condition is just that which was shown in Diagram 33-18. The other two pictures show a cross wind from the right relative to the start heading.

Turning into the wind gives a head wind when the aeroplane is slow, followed by a tail wind when it gets faster. The result is that the effects of the cross wind is actually increased. This will usually be a bad thing. Turning left, however, means that the aircraft will have the best airspeed when it is actually into the cross wind. Hence the acceleration effect can be used to counter the cross wind: usually a good thing.

Diagram 33-18

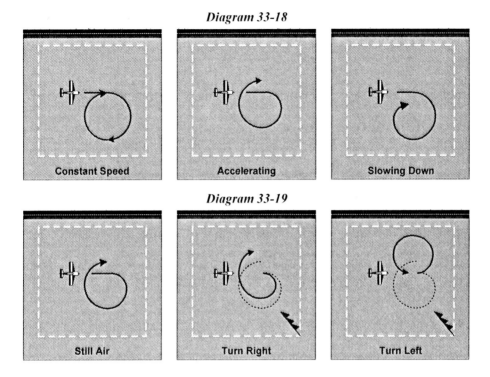

Diagram 33-19

Energy Matters

If started at high speed, a rolling turn will squander energy as the rudder work will cause very large amounts of drag (Diagram 33-20).

At the end of the roller, speed will have decayed and height will be unchanged. So I have to consider this to be bad sequence design, unless this is the end of the sequence and energy can be thrown away without fear of consequence. Even in this case, it is still not a good idea, as you will be low and any tendency to climb and descend will be much more obvious.

Diagram 33-20

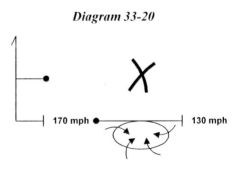

On the other hand, if you start a roller at low speed, for example after a half-loop, half roll combination, most aircraft will accelerate for at least a while (Diagram 33-21). It takes quite a long time to complete a full 360° rolling turn. If the controls are applied relatively gently, and if the cross wind is used to help inhibit the apparent increase in radius, most aircraft can gain significantly in airspeed and thus gain valuable energy. A design to make good use of this increased speed by climbing again, will result in a sequence with much less height loss overall.

Diagram 33-21

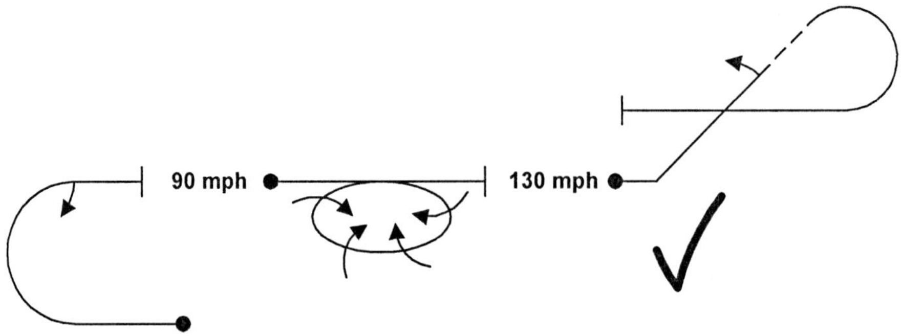

CHAPTER 34

Rolling Loops

Rolling in the top of a loop is a great exercise, not only for its own sake, but also to help develop spatial awareness. It is easier than the rolling turn, but shares the same principle of rolling axially while flying a circular flight path. Except now the circle is a vertical one rather than a horizontal one.

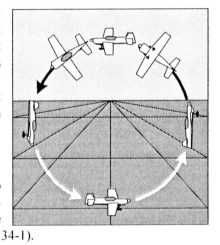

The Flight Manoeuvre

The concept is simple enough. A loop with some aileron rolling set symmetrically into the slow graceful arc as the aeroplane 'floats' over the top (Diagram 34-1).

The size of the loop and the time available for rolling will depend on the range of entry speeds that you can employ. The faster the entry speed and the higher the power-to-weight ratio, then the greater will be the looping radius and time.

Diagram 34-1

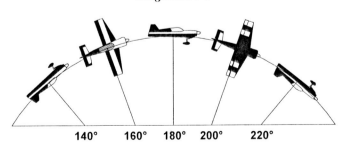

| 140° | 160° | 180° | 200° | 220° |

The number of rolls you can fit into this arc now depends on the aircraft's rate of roll. If you imagine a modern jet fighter, you can see that the time available over the top of the loop could be 10 seconds or more. With a roll rate of 360° per second, multiple rolls will be possible. At the other end of the scale, a vintage biplane might have only two or three seconds of 'float' and even one complete roll may be asking a lot in this time.

Despite these varying possibilities, the principles are the same and the control inputs will be similar. Initially, I shall consider only a single roll set into an 80° arc from 40° nose up to 40° nose down. The cardinal attitudes are shown in Diagram 34-1.

Ground References

The key here, as so often, is to fly parallel to a line feature and directly above it. As you approach the apex of the loop, you can put your head right back and look upward to locate the line feature as early as possible. As the aeroplane rolls, you should rotate your head so that you continue to look at the line feature below you.

The cockpit views in Diagram 34-2 equate to the attitudes in the earlier figure. The aircraft is a side-by-side two seater. Note that in the 160° attitude you have turned your head slightly to the right to get a good view of the line feature. The picture ahead at the top of the loop, the 180° attitude, is regular straight and level!

Diagram 34-2

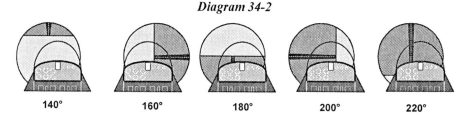

| 140° | 160° | 180° | 200° | 220° |

Technique

You will need to start the loop at a higher speed than normal, so that you can have a slightly bigger radius and better airspeed over the top. It is important not to float too early as you will then gain too much height and be very slow over the top. Low speed is not conducive to rapid rolling unless you have a very modern, carbon-winged monoplane.

Watch the wing tip until you are close to 45° climbing inverted, then rapidly look back above you to see the line feature as the horizon comes into view. When you estimate that you are about 40° nose up, apply full left aileron, with the elevator in the neutral position (see Chapter 3 and Chapter 10 for the definition of neutral point). Do nothing with the rudder at the first attempt. While you roll, the nose will continue to drop toward the horizon. Look to your right to confirm that the neutral elevator position is ensuring you stay on heading, parallel to the line feature. If you have a high performance machine and are rolling quickly, you may need a little right rudder (bottom rudder) to help bring the nose down a little quicker than under just the pure gravity drop.

Forecast ahead a little and try to make sure that the nose drops to the normal straight and level attitude as the wings come level after 180° of roll. This is the top of the loop. As you are floating with zero angle of attack, the only significant engine/ propeller force is the slipstream effect, so you may need a touch of right rudder to keep straight in this attitude. Keep rolling. If necessary, add a tiny bit of forward stick to keep the curve of the loop going. Otherwise keep the elevator at the neutral point.

The nose will continue to drop as you roll towards the second knife-edge position. If the nose does not drop fast enough, add a little left rudder to keep it on its way down.

As you come towards inverted, wings level at the end of the roll, resist the temptation to move the stick forward to hold the nose up. You want it to keep dropping. Just stop rolling as the wings come level and then add back stick to continue as in a normal loop. Remember to increase the pitch rate as you approach the end of the loop, to make an accelerate/stop segment.

Error Analysis

I will ignore the error that comes from the normal looping inputs, as these are dealt with elsewhere. The main things to think about are those that will go wrong during the rolling phase. The first problem is judging exactly when to start the roll, but this is not really critical unless you are in competition, so let's just say that your judgement will improve with practice.

The result of rolling too early is quite benign, in that you should just finish the roll level or just a little nose down. Starting the roll too late can result in finishing with the nose well down and lead to a bit of a rush or panic at the end (Diagram 34-3).

Diagram 34-3

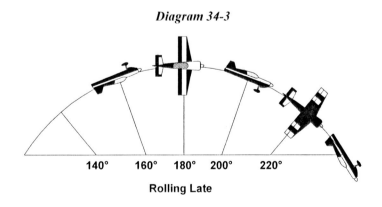

Rolling Late

Diagram 34-4

Back stick error   **Forward stick error**

When you start the roll, you had better use full aileron deflection unless you are in a very fast-rolling aeroplane. In this case, you may choose to use less than maximum. The most common error at this stage is to add some unwanted elevator, usually back-stick, as you put on the aileron. If you do this, you will notice the aeroplane go out of balance, with your body leaning toward the same side of the fuselage as the aileron input. You will also see the aeroplane go off heading relative to the line feature. Correct by adjusting the elevator position towards neutral.

If, by chance, you make the opposite error, stick too far forward when you roll, your body will go to the opposite side from the aileron and you will feel light on your seat (if not negative). Again, keep full aileron but make a small elevator adjustment backwards.

Both possible errors are illustrated in Diagram 34-4, showing the picture after 90° of roll.

At the stop, with the nose 40° or so below the horizon, it is sometimes difficult to actually be certain that you have stopped with the wings level. It is quite easy to under- or over-rotate. If you pull to complete the loop from this cock-eyed attitude, you will certainly find it hard to keep straight and will probably end up well off heading.

Diagram 34-5

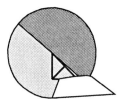

220°, wings level

It is thus a good idea as you stop to transfer your attention to the wing tip (Diagram 34-5) and see that it, or the sight if you have one, is pointing at the horizon, not above or below it. During the pull-out, of course, you should use small aileron adjustments to make the exit heading perfect.

Further Development

There are a large number of different loop/roll combinations that occur in competition flying. In most cases the principles of technique are the same. However, it is sometimes difficult to envisage how the various rolls should appear when symmetrically placed in the loop. Table 34-1 gives some examples; the third column details the exact attitude at the apex of the figure. The last of these four examples illustrates the area where technique changes.

Table 34-1 Attitude at the Apex of the Figure

Figure	Diagram	Apical Attitude
Inside/outside loop with half roll		First knife edge while rolling.
Loop with 4-point roll		Level, upright during second hesitation.
Inside/outside loop with three half rolls		Knife edge during the second half roll.
Outside loop down with 8-point roll		Level, upright during fourth hesitation

When the roll is at the bottom of a down-going loop, gravity no longer assists with the construction of the radius while rolling. So you must work during the roll to provide enough lift to maintain the curve.

If the loop without the roll would generate 5g at the bottom, then a perfect curve while rolling would require the aircraft to generate 5g of fuselage lift at the points where the wings are at right angles to the ground.

This is clearly asking a lot in the rudder authority department, as well as from the finesse of the pilot, but there are a few aircraft and artisans in the world who can appear to do it. Of course, such a figure also involves applications of large amounts of both positive and negative G in rapid succession and, for this reason alone, should come with a government health warning.

Thus, in these figures, there is a need for, alternately, large rudder inputs and large elevator inputs. There is a risk that you will get the timing wrong and end up with the rudder still 'on' at the same time that you are pulling or pushing.

The result will almost certainly be an inadvertent flick roll, which you must counter immediately by releasing both stick and rudder, followed by a return to normal flight and a quick bout of head scratching to try to work out which rudder was on at the wrong time and why?

Diagram 34-6

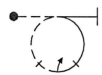

If you decide to try rolling loops of the down-going variety, you must be very careful about these excessively rapid changes in G-force.

The loop shown in Diagram 34-6 was part of the CIVA Unlimited Known sequence for 1995. At the bottom, either side of the half roll, the load went from about +6g to -6g. If you rolled very quickly, you would add the rotational effects to what was happening inside your skull. I think that year I suffered an injury from repeated practice of this loop, the sort of vertigo-inducing brain damage that you might get from boxing or a whiplash road accident. Fortunately, this effect was only temporary, but I learned a lot from it.

If I flew that figure now, I would roll slowly and make sure my head was very still, with my chin on my chest, during the G-reversal. I certainly would not practice it over and over again, nor submit it myself for an unknown programme in the hope of damaging a fellow competitor.

Flying in Competition

When considering hesitation rolls on page 216, I explained how it sometimes improves your scores to over- or under-rotate the knife edge points on a 4-point roll. The same consideration applies even if the hesitation is in a loop, not just in level flight.

Energy Matters

In the up-going loops, with rolls in them, there is very little more to say about energy management, other than that the small amount of aileron drag during the roll will cause the loss of more energy than in a normal loop.

With the down-going loops, there is much more energy loss because of the need for lots of fuselage lift at high speed. Therefore, you may not be able to return back to the starting height. If you can, then it will almost certainly be at a slower speed than you had at the start.

CHAPTER 35

Avalanches

Annette Carson, in the delightful *Flight Fantastic*, informs us that the first person attributed with inserting a flick roll into the top of a loop was American 'barnstormer' Earl Daugherty, flying a Curtiss Jenny in the early 1920s.

The name 'Avalanche' was coined in 1949 by British pilot Ranald Porteous, then chief test pilot of Auster Aircraft Limited, when he flew the same figure in the Farnborough Air Show. The Royal Air Force still calls it a 'Porteous Loop' in recognition of his performance.

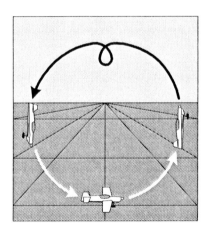

What was then the *avant garde* is now the norm, and every Intermediate competition pilot has this in his repertoire and a great many more besides enjoy the figure for its simple, low stress rotational delight.

The Flight Manoeuvre

The aim is a perfectly round loop with a precise, full 360° flick roll placed symmetrically about the apex.

The aeroplane must fly all the looping parts on the same axis, but it is inevitable during the flick that it will 'jump' sideways in the direction of the rudder used (Diagram 35-1, right rudder). So I cannot require that you stay in exactly the same vertical plane throughout

Ground References .

Diagram 35-1

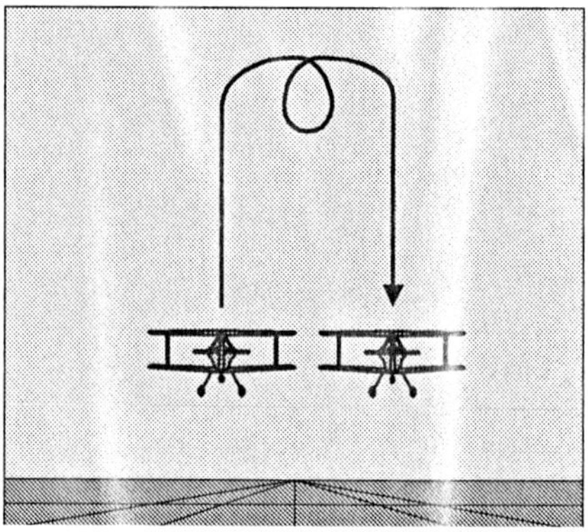

As in the rolling loop, always practice the avalanche directly over, and parallel to, a line feature.

Technique

The geometric aim is just as in the rolling loop, only now we must make a flick roll, not just use aileron. The entry requirements for this flick roll are just the same as for a level one. That is, enough speed to retain energy in order to exit the manoeuvre still flying, a high sub-critical angle of attack and, lastly, a rapid yaw brought about by maximum rudder deflection.

First you have to learn how to fly a loop so that you have adequate speed at the critical moment of flick entry. What you are looking for is a speed at which you can still pull 2g to 2.5g without stalling. This is 1.4 to 1.6 times power-on stalling speed. The best way to confirm this is just to fly a loop and to watch the G-meter as you go over the top. If your flight manual does not have a specific entry speed for this figure, use normal loop entry speed plus about 20 knots at first.

Start with a firm pull to 4g or 4.5g and then maintain this relatively high pitch rate through the vertical. As speed drops off, so will the reading on the accelerometer. Keep the back pressure on and try not to let the loading drop below 2g at the very top. If you can get 2.5g it will be better still. Of course, your 'no-flick loop' will not be anything like round (Diagram 35-2), but this does not matter. The flick roll will change the shape once you add it in.

Don't be surprised if you allow the load to fall below 2g when you first try. You do have to be quite firm with the elevator control. On the other hand, you might try too hard and end up getting buffet and then stall at some stage before you reach the top. If this happens, immediately release the back pressure to un-stall the wing and then roll to level as your recovery technique.

Diagram 35-2

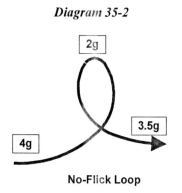

No-Flick Loop

Once you have done this strange loop a few times you will get the feel for maintaining speed up to the critical moment. You will be able to keep a high, but not stalling, alpha until initiation of the flick.

Now fly exactly the same loop again but, just as you approach 30° nose up inverted, apply full rudder and almost immediately unload the elevator control to just forward of neutral (Diagram 35-3). The unload is just the same as described for a level flick: add a little aileron on the same side as the rudder if you do not have full-span ailerons, but not too much.

If your timing of rudder and unload are just right, the aeroplane will autorotate rapidly. As this happens, you need to watch the horizon with your peripheral vision, so that you know when to stop, and the nose of the aeroplane to see the rate at which it is dropping earthward.

Diagram 35-3

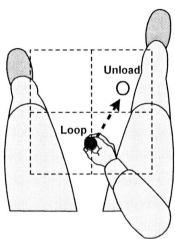

Right Flick, outboard ailerons

Stop the rotation by applying full opposite rudder and place the control column to the centre in both senses. You cannot use more forward stick to help with the stop because this will cause you to fly straight and lose the loop shape. As soon as the rotation stops, you will need to start applying back stick to keep the loop going.

Error Analysis

The first obvious error would be to start the flick too early, or too late. You really need to have a good guide to help you decide when the pitch attitude is just right. Normally, I urge you to judge this by looking at the wing tip. That is why I always like to have a sight there. But in this case, looking at the wing tip just as you start the flick will cause a great deal of disorientation. It is best to be looking ahead and up toward the horizon. This is where the sticky-tape recommendation bears repeating.

Diagram 35-4

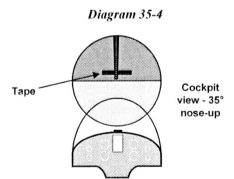

Tape

Cockpit
view - 35°
nose-up

Remember, we set this up so that you could fly a precise climbing inverted 45° line. Now, for the flick entry, the tape should be just below the horizon enabling you reliably to estimate approximately 35° nose up (Diagram 35-4).

The second most common mistake is to 'bury' the elevator. In other words, to pull the elevator control fully back.

This will stall both wings. An autorotation will certainly occur when you apply the rudder, but the rate of rotation will be sub-optimal and the gross drag on the airframe will be much larger than necessary. The aeroplane may well simply fall out of this attempt into a spin or, if the rotation does stop at the right time, be unable to sustain a looping shape until it has 'flopped' down and regained some speed.

The whole point of the 'no-flick' loop was to teach you the right amount of back stick to give a good, efficient flick. Resist the temptation to add loads more back stick just before you 'put the boot in'.

Occasionally, you might find that your hand gets ahead of your feet. You might be slow to apply the rudder and quick to unload. In this case, you will have insufficient alpha to start the flick and the result of the eventual rudder application will be a big 'lurch' but no real roll. Be quicker with the rudder next time, and delay unloading slightly so that the rudder has time to 'bite' first.

Stopping will not usually cause you any problems if you flick against the engine torque. In other words, stopping is easy if you flick right with a standard clockwise-rotating Lycoming engine. It might not give the quickest rotation this way, but at least the engine will be helping you to stop.

Diagram 35-5

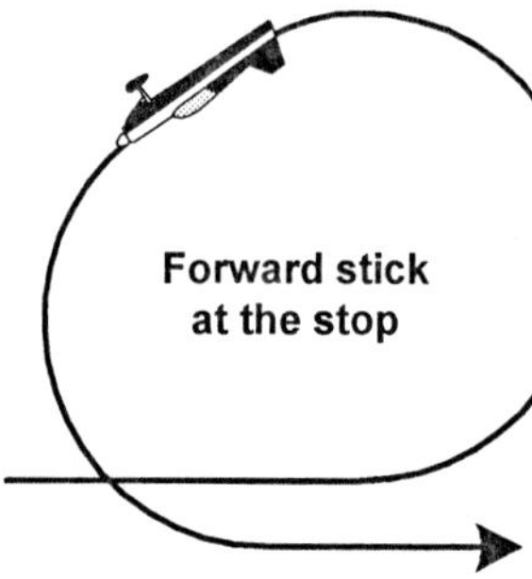

Forward stick at the stop

In a small aeroplane with a lot of torque, such as a Pitts Special, a flick to the left at low speed (and this is a low-speed flick) may be difficult to stop with power still on, especially as you cannot really add a lot of forward stick at the end of this flick because to do so would destroy the round shape of the loop (Diagram 35-5).

So if you want to practice an avalanche to the left in these aircraft, be ready to close the throttle at the point of recovery, and then to open it again once the rotation has stopped.

Further Development

Fortunately, nobody will ever ask you to do this:

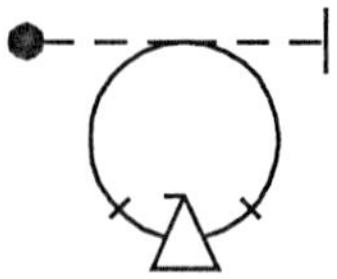

But these are all possible:

The double avalanche requires more energy at the point of entry, so it will be beyond the capability of lesser machines. If you have mastered the technique for the single flick, and can get consistently fast rotations, then it might just be a bit of fun to try the double. Start the loop with even more entry speed. Keep the loop small to retain as much of this speed as you can.

The avalanches with half or 1½ flicks present two extra problems. The first is just the physiological hassle of doing a half outside loop down. You need, obviously, to be quite comfortable with this kind of extreme bunt before trying it just after a potentially disorientating flick. The second problem is one of direction.

As with the level half flick, the stopping technique is quite different in that the rudder must be centralised early so that the rotation is barely more than an 'incipient' one, and then the pro-flick rudder must be re-applied as soon as the rotation stops in order to regain heading.

The 1½ flick has similar heading problems at the stop, although these can be minimised by early and pronounced unloading which limits the heading change induced at the start.

Flying in Competition

The main difference for the competition scene is that it is no longer enough for you to know, inside the aeroplane, that it has actually flicked. You have to convince those half-blind, incompetent judges two thousand feet below you and half a mile away that you actually flicked it. And remember, they are just crying out for the chance to say it was just a 'pull-and-roll' cheat or an 'accelerated barrel' or simply that it 'didn't flick'.

Here, then, is one time (and there are not many) that it is a positive advantage to be flying an aeroplane that generally has a low rate of roll. Because when it flicks, it will go round much faster than is actually possible with ailerons alone at low speed. Consequently the panel of critics will have to grudgingly accept that it was indeed a flick, even if they were unable to see with any great accuracy the precise details of the entry conditions.

If you have a shiny new Scruggs Industries Carbon Wundastunta, that rolls with aileron alone at 500° per second, then the flick is going to be hard to distinguish from the cheat. So now you are going to have to be especially careful to show all the required elements of change of attitude at the start of the roll.

This means that those on the ground must be able to discern a very sharp pitch change of about 10°, with no parasitic roll, just before the rudder goes in and the flick 'breaks' (Diagram 35-6). But this 10° must not put you over-critical on both wings or you will end up with a 'buried' article. So you must ease off just enough during the half second or so before the initiation that a quick 'jolt' of the stick will

Diagram 35-6

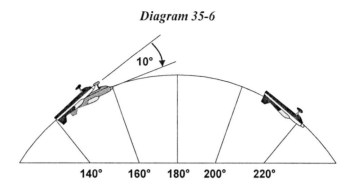

show the pitch without stalling. From then on, all is much as before. In the picture above, the '10°' angle shown is actually closer to 20°.

As you look at the page, the apparent distance of the plane, if it was real size, is probably closer than most aircraft in an actual contest. The judges have to notice a pitch change that may be less than half that pictured. This is why you have to be pedantic about showing the incidence change.

By the way, I don't really mean everything I say about judges … I am occasionally one myself, of course: eagle eyed, sharp of brain, fair of conscience and, usually, paying attention.

Energy Matters

Flicks always gobble up energy, even if you are proficient in technique and keep such loss to a minimum. If you are able to finish the avalanche with a nice round shape, back at exactly the same height that you started it, then you are going to be slower than when you started. Expect something like a 20 knot deficit.

If you finish at the same speed as you started, you have either lost height or you are flying a machine with more specific excess thrust than anything I've had the privilege of handling.

Better Aerobatics

Part Five

Advanced and Unlimited Figures

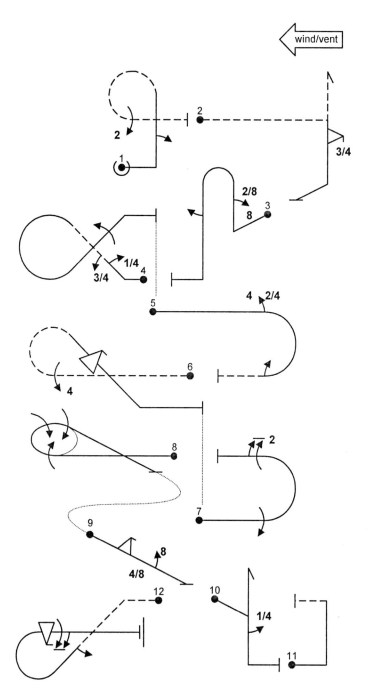

wind/vent

British Aerobatic Association (BAeA)
Advanced Known Compulsory Sequence 2003

CHAPTER 36

Positive Flick Roll Fractions

The heading picture shows a vertical Three Quarter Positive Flick to the left, descending and climbing. This chapter deals with the various fractions that might be encountered in Advanced and Unlimited competition sequences. Positive half flicks have already been detailed, so there will not be a great deal more to say about them here, other than to place them into context with the other fractions that come up from time to time.

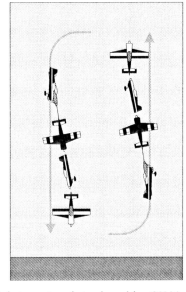

The 'others' are ¾ and 1¼ flicks, the former being most common because it is permitted in Advanced (downwards) and Unlimited (up and down) Unknowns. The longer variety has appeared in Unlimited Known programmes for some years, but is now also much included in the shorter Free Programmes that are the result of the Bonus Points system introduced by CIVA in time for the 1998 WAC at Trencin, Slovakia.

The Flight Manoeuvre

Not content with the classic flick roll, we now want to stretch ourselves a bit more and get to grips with serious fractions of flicks on precisely defined vertical lines. If you are asking yourself why on earth would anyone want to spend good time and money on such an arcane matter, then read no further. You have a life. You are not an aerobatic anorak, nor a connoisseur. You are just a normal person. If, however, you **do** want to read on, you are indeed an unusual individual. All serious competitive aerobatic pilots are unusual. Not in the strange sense, but in the sense that there are not so many of us about.

Technique

By the time you reach this stage of the book, you should be well familiar with the requirements of a good flick roll entry. All I will say again here is that you must try to move your hands and feet very quickly indeed. But not so fast that you overdo the movement nor that you lose the accuracy.

Entry speeds need to be considered in more detail, as they vary from the 'standard' level entry speed. If your entry speed level is 'X' knots, then on a 45° down line it should be 'X-10' knots and on a vertical down line probably 'X -20' knots. The real reason for this is that you have to make bigger initial pitch changes because you are starting from lower alpha, zero in the case of the vertical. Thus you probably need a 15° change of attitude to start a vertical flick down in contrast to a 5° attitude change when level. Remember, in level flight at modest airspeed you probably already have 10° of the 15° 'in the bank' so to speak.

Also, when vertical down the aeroplane is relatively stable in pitch. If you were to make a sudden pitch change and then let go, the angle would tend quickly to reduce, due to both static stability of the aeroplane plus a component of gravity. A last reason for a lower entry speed is that the descending flight path adds kinetic energy to balance that lost due to the excess drag, so running out of speed during the flick is never a consideration, whereas the mechanical and physiological stresses of autorotation at high speed are worth a thought.

On the 45° and vertical up lines, the situation is radically changed. Speed will be lost due to the altitude gain as well as through the extra drag. To facilitate a viable exit airspeed, you just have to start at higher-than-level speed. Ten knots extra will probably be enough for the 45° line; for the vertical up line, initiate as close as you can to the maximum speed allowed for the type you are flying.

On the vertical up, stability is reduced somewhat because the effect of gravity is destabilizing. Once you make a quick pitch change it will stay there, or even get bigger. This is fortunate, because it means that at this very high entry speed, you do not need quite such a big stick movement to get the right alpha as you would on the down line.

For half flicks, there is no time to unload. For ¾ flicks, there is almost enough time, but there is no real need because of the stop conditions which I shall explain shortly. For full flicks and 1¼ flicks, unloading is very important.

For the fractions, that is anything other than a full 360° rotation, the biggest problem is stopping on heading. Each different amount of rotation requires different elevator and rudder positions at the stop. First, I should explain why this is so.

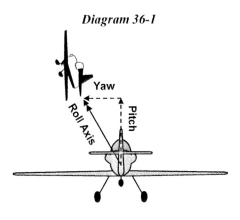

Diagram 36-1

During the initiation of the flick, you first pitch and then yaw the aeroplane. As a result, the axis of rotation is displaced up and to the side of the original flight path.

In Diagram 36-1 you can see the result of a ¾ flick to the left with no stop correction. To get the aeroplane back into the correct attitude (so that you see it from exactly rear-end on) the pilot must re-apply some back stick and right rudder.

Diagram 36-2 shows the same ¾ flick to the left, on a down line. The two views show the trajectory and attitude as seen from side-on and front-on axes. You can see that, as before, to regain vertical down at the stop requires right rudder and back stick. This correction remains regardless of the direction of flight: up, down or wherever.

Diagram 36-2

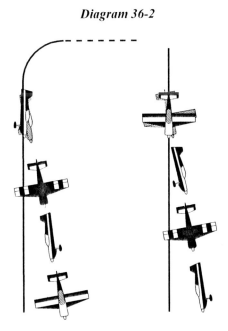

You can extend this series of drawings to work out the control inputs required at the stop for all flicks from ½ to 1¼.

When you fly a normal full flick level, you do not really think of these stopping problems because the actions are both opposite to that used at initiation: opposite rudder and forward stick, just like a traditional spin recovery.

Consequently this full flick recovery comes very naturally. In all the others, at least one of the stopping control inputs is the same as those for starting. This takes a lot of practice to master, and you need to work hard during preparation on the ground to get the right actions drilled into your head.

To simplify matters for you, Table 36-1 covers all the possibilities. It pays to study this so that you know the correct inputs without having to work them out from scratch each time you fly the figure. This is a bit like the old way of learning multiplication through reciting tables. Notice that no two stop conditions are the same.

Table 36-1

Extent of Rotation	Symbol	Stopping Rudder	Stopping Elevator
Half (½)		Same (as initiation)	Back (same)
Three-quarters (¾)	3/4	Opposite	Back (same)
Full		Opposite	Forward (opposite)
One-and-a-quarter (1¼)	1/4	Same	Forward (opposite)

If you ignore the 'back-forward' wording in column four above, and just go with the 'same-opposite' idea, then the table applies equally to negative flicks, which are covered in detail in Chapter 39.

Error Analysis

These fractions suffer from all the other initiation errors described earlier, so I won't go through them all in detail here. The key points really are generating just the right amount of pitch-up and exquisite timing with the rudder. Also, the faster you can make these inputs, without losing precision, the better will be the final result. Slow application of either control results in a bigger divergence from the original flight direction before the rotation starts.

With fractions such as these, a big pitch or heading change at the beginning leads through to a major heading or pitch error at the end.

As with all flicks, stopping the rotation exactly on target is a matter of timing and practice. Over-rotation is most likely on half and 1¼ flicks where the stopping rudder is the same as the initiation rudder. Because you cannot really use full opposite rudder to stop the flick (it will cause a really serious heading error), the stop is likely to be hesitant, wobbly or just simply over. If this happens regularly, and especially if you are flicking 'with' the engine (left with a Lycoming) then you can improve the sharpness of the stop by closing the throttle momentarily as you move the elevator in the recovery.

You will inevitably have pitch and yaw errors at the stops until you have really mastered the subtlety of getting stick and rudder into just the right spots at the finish. With the ¾ and 1¼ particularly, you can get a very big yaw error because you used too much back stick at the start, so be careful to limit the initial pitch change to just what is required, no more. In aircraft with a particularly powerful rudder, such as the CAP-232, full rudder is not required to get the flick going. With the short fractions, therefore, you can be a little miserly with the rudder input and thereby minimise the errors at the end. For example, with a ¾ left, less rudder at the start means less back stick at the end.

Flying in Competition

You should practice all fractions of flicks in either direction. Only this way will you ultimately be able to cater for all possible wind conditions. This is an ideal situation to aim at, so you will have to decide for yourself just how much fuel you are prepared to burn seeking such perfection. Highest on the priority list here should be the ¾ vertical up and down, because they have potentially the greatest disaster factor if you do them the 'wrong' way and perhaps also exit the box as a result.

The other important thing to realise is that judges pay much more attention to your attitude at the end of a flick than at the beginning. There is no logical reason for this; it is just the way it is. Maybe it's because they know that stopping errors are likely and so look hard for them. Consequently, they are less discerning in the short time just before you start.

Whatever the reason, you can learn to exploit this fact by employing some subtle attitude mismanagement on occasions. A short word for 'attitude mismanagement' is 'cheating', but I prefer to think of it in terms of a good performance rather than an ethically dubious process.

Consider a vertical ¾ flick on the up line:

Look at this aeroplane: Can you tell if the wings are level?

No. It could look like this from the left:

Now another one: Can you tell if this one is vertical in pitch?

No. It could be like this from the side:

The point I am trying to make here is that there are some things the judges can see, and therefore downgrade for, and some things they cannot.

In the first case above, you could be a little left wing high before a half flick to the left and lose no marks. At the stop, you would need much less left rudder to regain vertical and so would be much better placed to execute a stall turn or, especially, a tail slide. In the second case, you could be a bit positive before a ¾ flick and thus be able to stop wings level with much less opposite rudder and much less side slip. This would make a Humpty at low speed much easier to get round comfortably. If it was a ¾ flick down, you could be negative before the initiation.

In both cases, you would almost certainly stop much closer to the vertical in both axes, which is just what the judges are expecting to find fault with.

Cheating like this is not something you can always do the same way. It depends on exactly where in the box, and on which axis, the different figures are flown. So it is something to work out in the planning stage: not so difficult for a known sequence that is the same all year, but quite difficult for an unknown that you have only a day or less to fully commit to heart.

CHAPTER 37

Outward Rolling Turns

I began Chapter 33 on inward rolling turns by quoting Eric Müller's description of them: *"The absolute king in aerobatics."* Well, there are good kings and bad kings. For reasons that will become clear later, the outward roller is for most pilots the 'bad' king. This is an undeserved reputation.

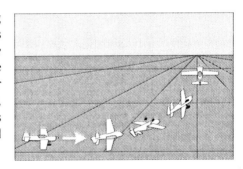

In principle, Outward Rolling Turns differ from inward ones only in the direction of roll. Apart from this, the geometry of the flight path is identical. Energy and performance considerations are also identical. Yet only in 2003 were they accepted by CIVA as appropriate for international Advanced competition, having been previously classified as Unlimited. In the UK, a single outward roll in a 90° turn has always been part of the Intermediate repertoire. I remember flying one in the Unknown at the UK Nationals in 1985. I don't suppose I did it very well, but the point is it was there.

So why, I wonder, has there been such a discrepancy between the status of inward and outward rollers in differing national and international rules?

I think the answer lies in the perceived risk of height loss. When you first start to learn outward rollers, using an adaptation of the technique you use for inward ones, you will almost certainly end up losing height, possibly quite dramatically. This is because you have not really appreciated, or had explained to you, the subtle differences that cause this problem. Once you understand these differences, you will find it much easier to get round without the associated plummet.

The Flight Manoeuvre

The aeroplane executes a level turn and at the same time rolls continuously with aileron in the opposite direction. The aircraft in the lead picture is turning left (based on its original upright position) while rolling right. As with inward rollers, the par configuration is to have one full roll for every 90° of turn. The other possibilities of three or two rolls in a horizontal circle are also quite common.

Ground References

As with the inward rollers, you should fly relative to a straight line feature on the ground below. Similarly, you should work hard to look mostly at this line feature throughout the figure, with only occasional reference to the view directly ahead.

In the illustration, Diagram 37-1, you are starting flying towards a main road which crosses your track at a right angle. At the end of the figure, you will be parallel to the road and just the other side of it. At points (1), (2), (3) and (4) you have turned, respectively, 22.5°, 45°, 67.5° and 90°.

Diagram 37-1

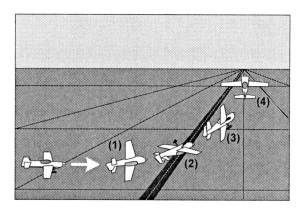

The cockpit views you see as you go round this turn are shown in Diagram 37-2. In the three middle pictures, the white arrow shows your direction of flight across the ground, relative to the road. Remember, the aeroplane is rolling right.

Following on with another full roll, Diagram 37-3 is the next set of pictures.

Diagram 37-2

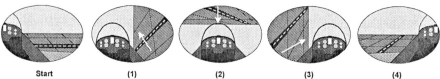

| Start | (1) | (2) | (3) | (4) |

Diagram 37-3

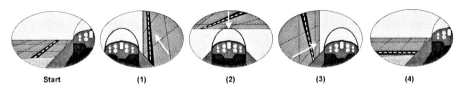

| Start | (1) | (2) | (3) | (4) |

Technique

Entry speed should be just the same as for the inside roller, but I recommend you start with the nose higher by 5° or 10°. This will help counter the initial tendency to lose height. You must then fix firmly in your mind the direction of turn. This is the side you are going to apply rudder when you start.

It is always wise to think clearly about the turn direction and the rudder input before you start. I will describe the situation for turning left and rolling right, and will show the various lift diagrams for this exercise.

So you start by applying some left rudder to initiate a flat turn and then almost immediately you apply aileron in the opposite direction. The first time you do this it will feel really strange. It is a very counter-intuitive thing to do.

As soon as you get to a significant bank angle, wing lift begins to oppose the turn, so you rapidly need a big increase in left rudder to generate sufficient fuselage lift to make sure it keeps going the right way (Diagram 37-4). And you must unload the elevator toward neutral to help with this.

You will see from the 15° and 60° pictures that the left rudder really has to dominate in the early phases if you are to keep the turn going. By the time you get to 90° you can begin to relax the rudder, but you must keep the turn going with forward stick.

As you reach 120° you must get the rudder back to just about neutral, as the wing lift will now meet the needs both to turn and to stay level (Diagram 37-5).

Diagram 37-4

345

Diagram 37-5

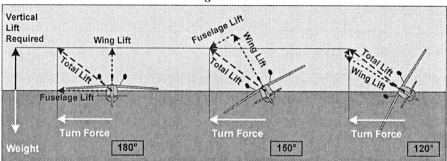

Diagram 37-6

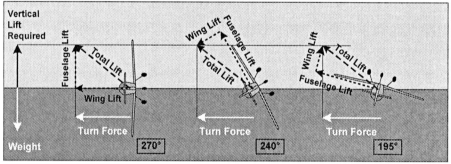

Diagram 37-7

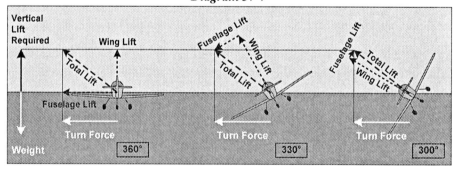

The control inputs here are just like an inverted steep turn. To determine exactly how much to push at this stage, you must be looking at the line feature below. You can then ensure that you have enough forward stick to get you through 45° of turn by the time you have completed a half roll. By 150° you must introduce some right rudder while keeping a fair push going. By 180°, only the right rudder is keeping you turning, while the forward stick is just as in straight and level inverted.

As you leave wings level inverted (Diagram 37-6), you must rapidly increase the right rudder as, again, the wing lift starts to oppose the turn. At 240° the fuselage

346

lift must be maximum and the elevator becoming slightly positive. At 270° you must still have right rudder for fuselage lift and now you are relying on back stick to keep the turn going.

When leaving the second knife-edge position, you must release the right rudder or it will strongly oppose the turn (Diagram 37-7). Use increasingly more back stick to both turn and keep the nose up. At 300° the rudder should be neutral and all the lift coming from the wings. From there to wings level, you will need to reintroduce left rudder and reduce the elevator until you reach the normal level state.

Error Analysis

In this figure, as in the inward rollers, you gradually cycle the elevator back and forward, and the rudder left and right, to make the turn while rolling. In the inward rollers, each change brings in a control that tends to hold the nose up against gravity.

Diagram 37-8

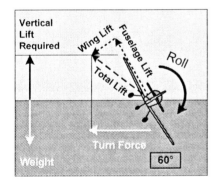

The main difference in the outward roller is that as you change from left to right, forward to back, each time you are adding a control movement that will cause the nose to go down.

Look at the 60° attitude again (Diagram 37-8). You have just changed from positive wing lift to negative. If you are short of rudder authority and try to keep the turn going with more forward stick the nose will go down sharply. So you must work really hard with the rudder and resist the temptation to start pushing too much, too soon.

At the 150° position, you are just beginning to add right rudder after having used left rudder to the extreme (Diagram 37-9).

As you change, you are adding bottom rudder. Doing so too quickly or too early will result in the nose going down when it should be going up. Similar problems occur in the second half of the figure at both the 240° and 330° positions.

In Chapter 17 on rolling straight and level, I used Eric Müller's term 'sacred circle' for

Diagram 37-9

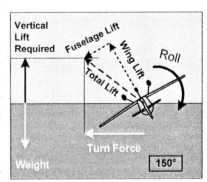

the path drawn by the nose of the aircraft during the roll. In rolling turns, a similar idea can be followed through, only this time it is a curve not a circle.

Diagram 37-10 is a picture that shows the views directly over the nose during the outward roller described above. Note that at Positions 1 and 3 the nose is above the horizon. If it was below the horizon, you would not be generating enough fuselage lift to fly level.

Diagram 37-10

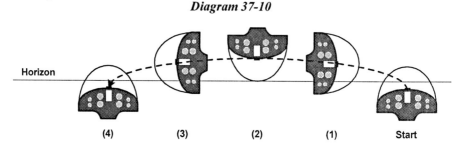

| (4) | (3) | (2) | (1) | Start |

Diagram 37-11 shows the 'sacred circle and curves' as drawn by Müller. In his inward roller, he has the nose above the horizon in knife edge. This will give the required fuselage lift. But in his curve for outward rollers, Eric has the nose below the horizon in knife edge. This cannot keep you level.

Diagram 37-11

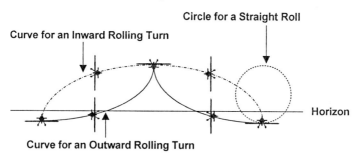

Circle for a Straight Roll

Curve for an Inward Rolling Turn

Horizon

Curve for an Outward Rolling Turn

A theoretical 'sacred curve' for an outward roller would in fact look like Diagram 37-12. The problem with the theory, as shown in Diagram 37-4 to Diagram 37-7, is that to achieve this profile you need absolutely massive amounts of fuselage lift from 30° to 60° of bank, and this is just not available in most aircraft. It is really, really difficult to get the nose to rise **and** turn at the same time.

What actually happens during the first quarter of the figure is that the nose stays roughly level, as in Müller's curve, or even goes down a bit. This is one manoeuvre where the theoretically perfect is almost unobtainable. The answer is to give yourself some leeway by starting with the nose higher than is actually necessary for

Diagram 37-12

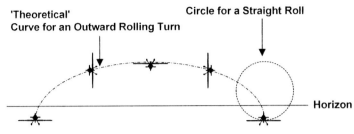

Diagram 37-13

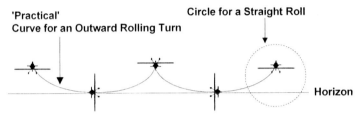

level flight. This means you are actually climbing a bit before the entry, but this is a benign error and it only needs to be for a very short time.

So Diagram 37-13 is a practical 'sacred curve' for an outward roller. The high nose position at each point when the wings are level helps to maintain height without quite such extreme use of the rudder. It balances the knife-edge points where you cannot keep the nose up. The cockpit views are shown in Diagram 37-14.

The turn rate is not perfectly constant, but this is the hardest error of all to detect – much harder than the really obvious descending segments that result from starting with too low a nose position.

As in many parts of aerobatics, especially if you are flying in competition, it is not necessary to try to be perfect but just to be better than everyone else. So when flying the outward rolling turn, always make that little extra effort to have the nose high with the wings level and allow it to go a little bit lower in knife edge.

Diagram 37-14

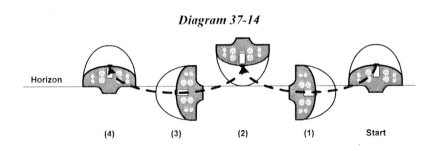

Another significant difference between inward and outward rollers is the optimum time for turning. This is when the rudder input is smallest. At this time the wing lift, by far the more efficient form, is providing both vertical lift and turn force. In another 'practical' solution to a difficult problem, you can turn a little bit more quickly during these periods to cover for turning not quite enough when the rudder is in full cry.

Diagram 37-15 shows both sorts of roller, one below the other. The optimum turning segments, related to bank angle, are shown shaded. Note that for the inward roller, these segments are the 30° preceding knife-edge, while in the outward roller they are the 30° after knife edge.

Diagram 37-15

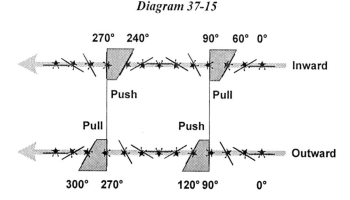

Perhaps the last thing to mention here is another aspect of the 'new' rudder being on the bottom side each time you change feet. Because adding this 'bottom' rudder will bring the nose down, you will be reluctant to use it. You may well hold on to the 'top' rudder for too long. If you do this, you will stop the turn altogether. Once you are through knife edge, you must relinquish your hold on the top rudder, but be sure to bring the bottom rudder in slowly, little by little until the wings next become level.

As with inward rollers, your rudder inputs will sometimes be pro-roll and sometimes anti. Remember that this will vary the roll rate unless you modulate your aileron inputs to compensate. Whenever rudder and aileron are on the same side, you must reduce the aileron input a little, and vice versa.

Heading errors occur whenever you do not maintain just the right turn rate for the established roll. As with inward rollers, the way to ensure you hit the heading is to look in the right place: **not** at points on the horizon, but at the line feature directly below you.

Further Development

It is fun, and immensely challenging, to learn the outward roller starting from straight and level inverted. The difficulty lies in getting your head round the control inputs needed to start. Of course, these are just the same as in the second half of the figure when started from upright. Your brain, however, is less accustomed to working things out when you are upside down so the puzzle increases in magnitude.

Let's just recap on what happens during the half of the outward roller that goes from inverted to upright.

The rolling bit is just like the second half of a straight and level roll. But while rolling upright you have to turn through 45° in the direction opposite to the roll. In all your rolling practice up until now, you have been working over and over again to learn to roll straight. And one of the most obvious errors in straight rolls is the 'dishing out' that occurs at the end because you released the forward stick too early.

So what you now have to learn is how to 'dish out' on purpose through exactly 45°. As this is something you have been desperately trying to avoid up until now, it is not surprising that there is a small mental block about doing it on purpose. Nevertheless, this is what you have to do.

Fly level inverted and put the nose 5° or 10° higher than really necessary. As always when starting a roller, think rudder first. Look at the ground below and decide which way you want the nose to turn. Use that rudder. For an outward roller from inverted, use aileron on the same side as the rudder and then start to pull slowly back (Diagram 37-16).

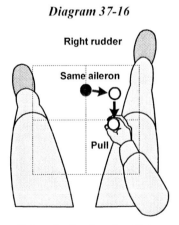

Diagram 37-16

Right rudder

Same aileron

Pull

Outward roller, from inverted

Initially use a great deal of rudder and have the elevator neutral by about 30° (bank) after the start. Keep lots of rudder through to about 60° when you can begin to reduce that as you also add in a little back stick to keep turning. By 90° all the turn is with back stick and rudder is just holding up the nose.

Once started, you should then be back in the groove established by practising starting from upright.

Flying in Competition

All the considerations regarding wind correction and which way to turn are as discussed for inward rollers.

It is worth repeating that to win a contest you do not have to get 10 out of 10 for every figure, just more than the other pilots. Outward rollers are difficult co-ordination exercises and generally give the judges lots of opportunities to downgrade. To do better than the rest, you have to learn to avoid the big obvious mistakes, such as finishing off heading or, especially on outward rollers, noticeably descending.

To solve the first problem, make sure you practice using a line feature below you. In the competition, focus on the runway or, if there are any, the box markers, to keep a constant review of your heading.

To make sure you don't descend all the time, be sure to have the nose high each time the wings are level and just a little lower in each knife edge position.

Energy Matters

Because there are a few points around the circle where you need even more rudder than for an inward roller, the outward roller loses just a little more energy. So to maintain constant airspeed, a higher power setting is usually required.

Otherwise, the inward roller considerations apply.

CHAPTER 38

Tail Slides

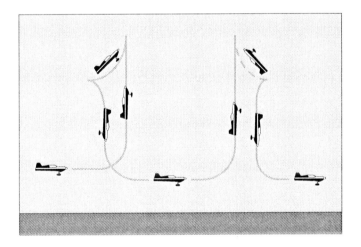

What flies backwards? Helicopters, Harriers, my avian favourite Humming Birds and, of course, aerobatic pilots. Maybe it should have been *"Who flies backwards?"* ... whatever. And perhaps it is not actually flying, but falling. But it certainly is a delicate manoeuvre requiring a high degree of precision.

From my own personal point of view, it has also been the most frequent curse-generator during Unlimited competition flying, wherein I have flown too many different types of aircraft and never really got to know any one of them really well enough to be certain of getting it just perfect every time.

Airmanship

A successful tail slide is going to expose the primary flight controls of your aeroplane to reverse airflow. This may be prohibited by your flight manual.

353

If so, don't do it.

If you are going to fly these figures, you must understand how the control stops for all three flight controls work on your aircraft. Most modern aerobatic aircraft have push rods to operate the ailerons and elevator. In this configuration, the aileron and elevator stops are usually incorporated into the mechanism near the base of the control column. They almost certainly have a cable-operated rudder, in which case the rudder stops are usually built into the hinge mechanism on or near the stern post.

If your aircraft has cable-operated controls and the stops are at the control column end of the cables, then you must not perform any figure that might give significant reverse airflow, because the control hinge mechanism is almost sure to get damaged.

Even with the modern systems described above, some damage may occur if the controls are allowed to move rapidly from full deflection one way to the other. When subject to reverse airflow, the control column should be held very firmly to prevent 'snatching' by the aerodynamic forces generated when flying backwards.

The Flight Manoeuvre

All civilian aeroplanes are unstable going backwards. I wanted to say 'all aeroplanes' but some modern military types leave this point open to discussion. I will ignore such things from now on. If you are not sure what 'unstable going backwards' means in real life, then get hold of one of those darts they use in the dart-board game and throw it backwards. In no time at all it will flip over so that it is going forwards. You just can't make it go backwards for any length of time at all.

Diagram 38-1

Canopy
Up

Canopy
Down

Aeroplanes are just like this, with the exception that you can make them go backwards a little bit longer, but still not really very far or very fast.

As you can see from the title picture, there are two types of tail slide. In the first, the aeroplane slides backwards and falls 'canopy-up', which is the same as saying 'wheels-down'. The second type (Diagram 38-1) occurs when the fall is 'canopy-down' or 'wheels-up'. In either case, when the aircraft slides backwards it should do so with wings level and no rolling motion.

The figure starts with a vertical line. On the way up, there may be some vertical rolling to do. Then you just keep going up until the aircraft stops. It then starts to slide backwards. After going backwards for a fuselage length or so (if you get it right) the aeroplane quickly 'changes ends' by pitching through vertical down. The wings stay level and the aeroplane does not roll. The nose carries through to the other side in a pendulum motion which you can either oppose or exaggerate depending on your mood.

Before long, you settle into the vertical down, and a flick or aileron roll, or both before returning back to level flight (pull or push, as your heart desires!).

Ground References

It's good to have a landmark on the horizon off the wing tip when you pull up. In the diagrams that follow I have chosen a (non-nuclear) power station. You might also arrange for a line feature below.

Technique

The tail slide starts with the decision as to which type you are going to do. Only then should you pull (or push) to the vertical from level flight. This part of the figure is just like a stall turn or a humpty-bump. This should, by now, be nothing new to you. For completeness, however, let me just remind you of the pitch feel diagram for pulling to the vertical (Diagram 38-2). This will make sure that each element of the figure will be precisely defined.

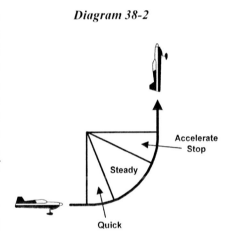

Diagram 38-2

Be careful when you 'accelerate-stop' that you do not go past the vertical and then 'bobble' back to the true attitude.

Once you are set in the vertical, and have finished any rolling you need to accomplish on the way up, you need to adjust the pitch attitude ever so slightly so that the fall, when it comes, is in the direction you want. For a canopy-up slide you need to be just a little positive, for canopy-down negative (Diagram 38-3).

Having set the attitude you now need to reduce the engine and propeller forces as much as you can. Obviously, this means closing the throttle, but there are a number of ways to do even this simple task.

If you close the throttle quickly, your footwork will not be able to keep pace accurately. With a Lycoming engine, you will yaw right. You will see this by the left wing appearing to rise up. If, on the other hand, you are too slow in closing the throttle, the left wing will try to go down. The best compromise is probably to be reasonably quick, but not to slam it closed uncontrollably.

355

Diagram 38-3

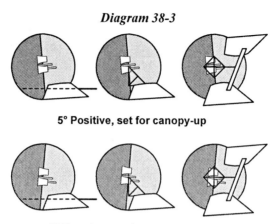

5° Positive, set for canopy-up

5° Negative, set for canopy-down

Your aim should be to get the power off and then have the aeroplane perfectly wings level with no sideslip.

Once the power is off the aeroplane will quickly lose all airspeed. At this stage try to make no control inputs at all, as you must not disturb the fine balance you have created. Hold the controls firmly, though, because once you start to slide you must not let the reverse airflow move the control surfaces as it would like.

You now need to detect the precise moment when the plane starts to go backwards. I have yet to find an Air Speed Indicator that has negative numbers, so this is where the wool comes into its own.

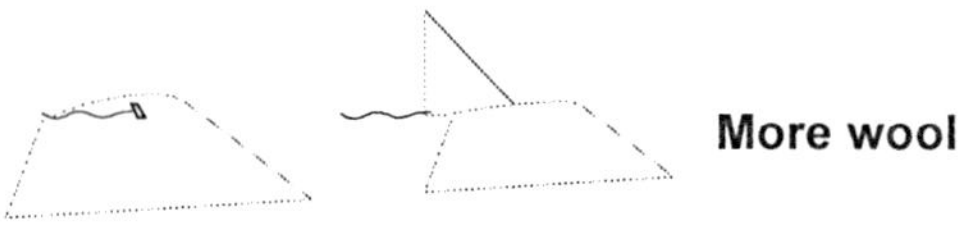

"What wool?" you might well ask.

If you are going to practice sliding, you must have a visual indication of the reverse airflow. Diagram 38-4 shows how I have it mounted on my Pitts.

When you are going fast forwards, the wool streams out behind. As you get very slow, the airflow becomes more disturbed by the propwash and the wool gets floppy and begins to wave a little. As the airflow reverses, so does the wool. The timing is precise and obvious.

Diagram 38-4

Fast   **Slow**   **Backwards**

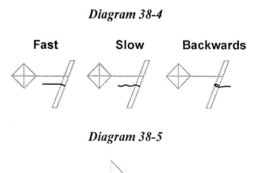

Diagram 38-5

More wool

Other ways of attaching the wool are shown in Diagram 38-5. If you just have a flat wing surface to work with, you can fix the wool to the skin with propeller tape. On a strut or a sight, you can simply tie it on. I've seen and flown a number of aircraft with various different weights of string attached to them, and they all seem to be stiffer and slower to react than knitting wool. In the extreme, I've also seen little mechanical weather vanes made of little bits of steel or aluminium pivoted somewhere on a sighting frame, but I must say this seems un-necessarily complicated, not to mention drag and weight implications.

So, now you know exactly when the aircraft starts to slide backwards. Once this has started, you should move the elevator control fully forwards (canopy down) or fully back (canopy up) to make doubly sure that the fall is in the planned direction.

The further you slide backwards, the faster will you be travelling and the more violent will be the changing of ends when it occurs. After a long slide, the pendulum effect will be strong and the nose will swing a long way past vertical down. Don't worry about this, just use aileron as necessary to damp down any rolling tendencies you detect. The nose will soon come down again to the vertical.

Diagram 38-6

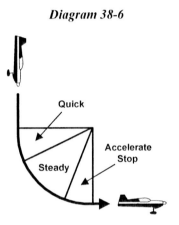

As soon as you establish the vertical down, add power and then recover to level flight. During the pull-out, remember to use the three-section pitch feel pattern shown in Diagram 38-6.

Error Analysis

If you are absolutely vertical in pitch, in other words if you don't cheat, there is a 50:50 chance the aeroplane will fall the wrong way. So you have to cheat a bit, but getting just the right amount takes some practice and coaching.

Diagram 38-7

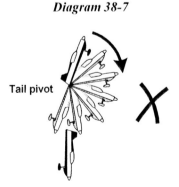

If at first you cheat too much, you will perform a Tail Pivot, not a Tail Slide, although the difference may not be particularly obvious from the cockpit (Diagram 38-7). You see, it is very difficult from inside the aeroplane to tell how much 'apparent' slide there has been.

I say apparent, because it may well seem quite a long way from inside, while the outside observer hardly notices you go backwards at all. Perception is sometimes delusion. This is another situation where a friend on the ground with a radio can give very valuable critique, so that you can improve your perception.

A Tail Pivot occurs when the aeroplane does not slide backwards at all. At the end of the pivot, there will be little pendulum effect, and this absence of swing-through is the best guide to not really having slid at all.

To be sure of sliding at least half a fuselage length, you must be that little bit closer to vertical. If you realise just in time that you are too far off the vertical to slide properly, you may save the day by adding elevator in the opposite direction for that normally required for the type of slide you have set up for.

Reverse Elevator Control

Diagram 38-8

If you were planning to fall through canopy up, you would expect to use back stick during the slide. If you are too positive at the crucial moment, however, you will just perform the tail pivot if you apply back stick. If you apply full forward stick you might just generate enough force from the reverse flow over the elevator to hold the nose up for a bit of a slide.

Diagram 38-8 shows just this situation. Notice how the forward stick, when flying backwards, will tend to make the nose pitch up with respect to the pilot's normal view.

Reverse Rudder Control

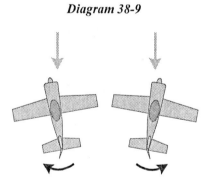

Diagram 38-9

If, when you get to the point of sliding backwards, your wings are not level, or if you are carrying a bit of rudder and side-slipping, then the slide will be poor. It will have a large amount of yaw as well as, or instead of, pitch when it falls through. If the error is only small, however, it may be possible to save the figure by applying full rudder during the backwards movement and thus generate a bit of opposing yaw.

To counter the error in this way, you have to work out the correct rudder and, as you are going backwards at the time, the rudder control laws are reversed. So, to yaw to the right needs left rudder and vice versa.

This is all very confusing, and you will not react correctly in the heat of the moment unless you have an easy rule of thumb to fall back on. The rule is this:

"Rudder on the side of the lower wing".

Diagram 38-9 shows two aircraft sliding backwards and 10° off the vertical . The left one has the left wing low and is being saved by left rudder; the right one is the opposite case. Hopefully, this simple correction will become relatively easy to remember, or even automatic, after a good bit of practice. Just remember, if you see a wing slightly low on the way back, put on full rudder that side to save the day.

Residual Torque/Slipstream

After you have closed the throttle there will still be some residual torque and slipstream effects. The torque you will naturally counter with aileron and is generally small enough not to cause problems.

The slipstream effect will continue to induce yaw to the left (Lycoming engine). If you counter this with right rudder there is a risk of slipping to the left upsetting the fine balance.

You can help avoid this by having the left wing just a little bit high just as you close the throttle. During the remaining vertical climb, the residual slipstream will gently level the wings for the slide and you can keep off the dangerous rudder pedals.

Diagram 38-10

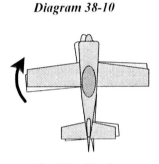

Rapid throttle closure

Conversely, if you notice, as you are about to close the throttle, that the left wing is a little low, you can try to save the day by waiting until the vertical speed is very low and then closing the throttle very quickly. This will have the effect of raising the left wing slightly as the slipstream effect suddenly disappears (Diagram 38-10).

Further Development

The normal recovery from a tail slide is by way of the vertical down attitude, as in a stall turn. This is actually a required part of the figure in competition sequences based on the FAI Aerobatic Catalogue figures. In air shows, or in Freestyle competition, you can, of course, do other things as you see fit. To save height, or to change positioning alternative exit strategies are possible.

One obvious option is to recover onto a descending, angled line, perhaps 45° down, but maybe 30° if you want to make more distance across the ground during the recovery (Diagram 38-11).

On this line you can aileron or flick roll, depending on how much energy you want to build or destroy. With sufficient power/weight ratio in your aeroplane, you can even choose to fly off level after the change-over, by exaggerating the pendulum effect, then adding full power at the right time.

Diagram 38-11

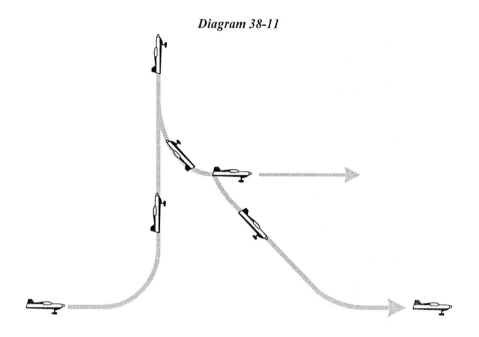

Another, even more sporting recovery is via a flat spin (Diagram 38-12). In the situation shown this happens to be of the inverted variety after a canopy-up slide. Entry to the spin would be full power and full forward stick during the pendulum, then full right rudder. As the spin rotation starts, add full right aileron.

"Flat Spins" on page 373 deals with recovery options at this stage!

Diagram 38-12

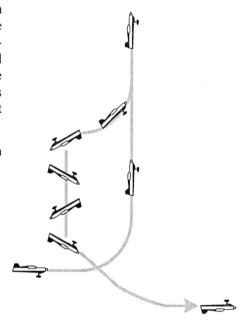

CHAPTER 39

Negative Flick Rolls

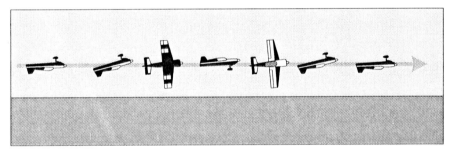

In Chapter 30 on positive flick rolls, I went on a bit about the concept of flick rolls; about how they are not 'horizontal spins'; about how important it is not to 'bury' the damn thing with too much elevator; about the importance of unloading to accelerate the autorotation. Everything from that argument is equally valid for flicks with negative angle of attack.

Negative Flicks do not enter the competition repertoire until the Unlimited level. Consequently, less experienced pilots are often deterred from learning the figure even though it is quite possible for any Intermediate category aircraft that is cleared for inverted spinning. To get a small insight into the world of the negative flick, you can try a quite simple and benign exercise based on the regular straight and level roll. All you need to do is this:

♦ Fly your aeroplane straight and level at really quite a slow speed. A good demonstration speed in the Pitts S2A is 90 mph, which is about 1.5 times V_{S1}. You can approximate a speed for your own aircraft based on a similar ratio, as long as it is less than any quoted flight manual speed for a negative flick roll. Because you are so slow, you will naturally be starting with the nose very high and a low power setting.

- Now start a straight and level roll to the left, adding a little power for the extra drag. Keep the nose high as you roll. As you come towards inverted, you will be applying quite a lot of right rudder for the reversed adverse yaw and you will also be moving the control column quite a long way forward to keep the nose high and thus maintain height.

- Just exaggerate the forward stick and the right rudder a little more and suddenly, as if developing a mind of its own, the aeroplane will 'break' into a faster rotation. If you immediately release all the controls, you can easily stop wings level, erect and with the nose maybe a little below the horizon to get some speed back.

You have just experienced your first negative flick roll. In this case, a half flick from inverted to upright. As with inverted spins, the direction of roll in a negative flick is opposite to the rudder causing it. Your initial aileron roll to the left has been converted to a flick roll with right foot and forward stick, which also happens to roll to the left.

The Flight Manoeuvre

In level inverted flight, the aircraft rapidly pitches nose up through about 10° to 15°, without any roll taking place at this stage. It then yaws, a wing stalls and autorotation starts.

During the roll, the aircraft fuselage presents a small cone-angle about the flight path. After one full rotation the autorotation suddenly stops and the aircraft returns immediately to straight and level inverted flight.

Ground References

The horizon will be visible ahead of you, along with all the intervening terrain as you look up toward the top of the canopy. The best visual reference is a major line feature disappearing into the distance ahead. You should fly directly over, and parallel to, the feature.

Technique

Your first attempts at the negative flick roll should be started from straight and level inverted. Your entry speed, of course, should be as per the flight manual. This will usually be between 1.4 and 1.7 times V_{S1}.

To fly level at this speed will not take full power, or anything like it, yet the initiation of the flick will be made quicker and easier with more power applied. So you should add power immediately before the initiation or should be accelerating level from even lower speed with a correspondingly high power setting.

To begin the negative flick, first you must quickly establish a high, but not over-critical negative alpha. For positive flicks, I described a simple 'back-release' exercise which ought to achieve about 3g as quickly as possible but without stalling the wings. You should do the same kind of exercise inverted, in order to gain some consistency in applying the right amount of rapid forward stick (Diagram 39-1).

Diagram 39-1

Once you are consistent with this rapid push, you can add the yawing element. With a normal Lycoming engine aircraft, you will find this easier if you use left foot when you first begin to learn. This is because the gyroscopic precession associated with rapid negative pitching produces a yawing motion to the left. Thus adding left rudder will be very effective in stalling a wing. If you used right rudder, then quite a lot of the rudder effectiveness would be lost in simply overcoming the gyroscopic effect.

So you push quickly, centrally forward to create the high negative alpha and after just a very short delay, you apply full left rudder. If the angle of attack is right and the rudder well timed, the flick roll will start easily.

The big advantage of learning the negative flick, as opposed to the positive one, is that you can practice this pitch/yaw initiation and then immediately release the controls as the flick starts. The aeroplane will then quite naturally come right way up. You can stop the figure upright after half a flick and quickly review your technique.

You should do this half flick exercise until your flick initiation is consistent and effective. Then you can go on to the next phase of the technique which is to accelerate and sustain the autorotation through the full 360°.

To accomplish the full negative flick, you must unload the forward elevator once the flick has started (Diagram 39-2). This will accelerate the roll, just as with the positive flick, and result in less overall drag. Thus you will achieve a fast roll rate in an energy-efficient way, compared with those that just keep the stick fully forward.

As with the positive flick, the exact stick position when you unload will depend somewhat on the aileron configuration of your aeroplane. With only outboard ailerons, as in a Pitts Special, it will be useful to apply some in-spin aileron.

If you have full-span ailerons, such in-spin aileron will almost certainly un-stall the stalled wing and lead to an accelerated barrel roll. So look at the two pictures in Diagram 39-2 and use the technique that is most appropriate for your aeroplane.

During the rotation, make sure you keep your left foot held hard against the rudder stop. **Do not let the aerodynamic forces on the rudder, nor the movement of your body out of the seat, cause you to reduce the rudder input.**

Diagram 39-2

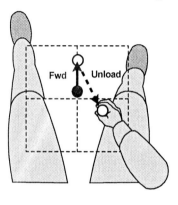
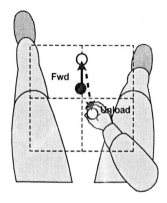

Left Foot Flick,
outboard ailerons

Left Foot Flick,
full-span ailerons

Watch the horizon ahead. When you have perhaps 120° to go, change to full right rudder and bring the control column even further back, and central, to make the recovery (Diagram 39-3).

As the flick stops, move the stick centrally forward again to regain level inverted flight. Now look up to double-check your heading, which should be the same as before you started.

The line feature should be nicely lined up with your fuselage. If not, see which rudder is needed to fix the heading.

Diagram 39-3

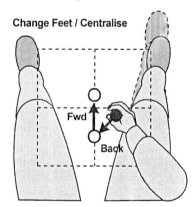

Left Foot Flick, recovery

You will probably find that you should have used more right rudder to stop the flick and get the heading sorted out all in one go.

Diagram 39-4 is a graphical representation of the elevator and rudder control inputs.

Diagram 39-4

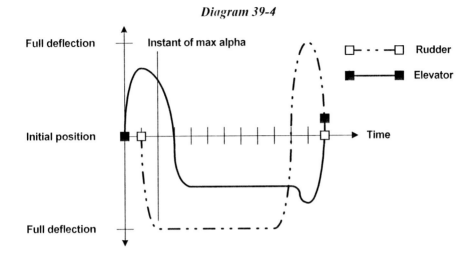

Error Analysis

Initiation

Make sure you lead with the elevator. Do not move the rudder first, nor even at the same time as the elevator, but after just a slight delay. Ruddering too soon will give an excessive heading change, as the aeroplane will yaw more than necessary before autorotation starts.

Do not add right aileron until you start to unload, otherwise the aeroplane will 'roll in' to the flick. Particularly, avoid pushing the control column straight to the front right corner (Diagram 39-5). This will cause a major 'roll in' and if you keep the stick there throughout the roll, you will rotate slowly and lose much more speed than you would with good technique.

Diagram 39-5

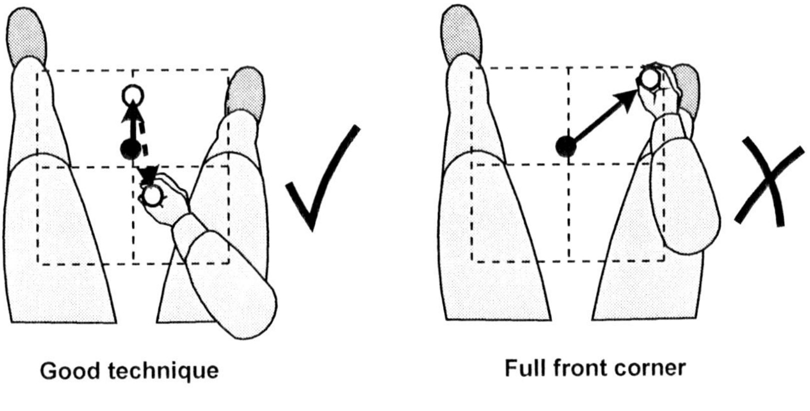

Good technique   **Full front corner**

During the Flick

Do not release the rudder. Work really hard to maintain foot pressure against the negative G loading. If you have full rudder and the flick slows or stops, then you have the stick too far back, or too much in-flick aileron.

Recovery

To recover properly, you must not apply out-spin aileron; Diagram 39-6, centre picture. If you do, and it is quasi-natural to apply left aileron to help stop a right roll, then you will almost certainly over-rotate. This error would be even more pronounced if you were flicking initially with right foot and thus had engine torque assisting the roll element.

Diagram 39-6

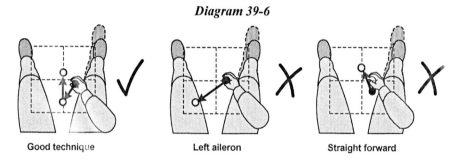

| Good technique | Left aileron | Straight forward |

You must apply opposite rudder and **more back stick**. In a high performance aeroplane, like an Edge 540 or Sukhoi, you should have unloaded the elevator control to aft of neutral during the flick. It is quite easy then to make the mistake of moving the stick straight forward to somewhere near neutral as you apply the recovery rudder (see the right hand picture of Diagram 39-6).

In these highly responsive aircraft, what you have just in fact done is ask the plane to change a negative flick into a knife-edge tumble with right foot. This is a gyroscopic-driven manoeuvre, and you will find it very disorientating for this to suddenly happen when you expected the flick to stop.

I had personal experience of this transition a number of times when I converted from the Yak 55M to the Sukhoi 26MX. It was only when I trained with Xavier Delapparent in France, and it happened with him watching, that I learned what I was doing wrong.

It seemed pretty life-threatening at the time, especially on a down 45° line started at less than 2,000 feet. So I was glad to learn that it was a simple matter of **more stick back** during the recovery that prevented the problem every time.

As ever, to recover from this loss of control, close the throttle, let go of the stick and apply opposite rudder once again. In this instance, this would mean left rudder – the one you initially started the flick with.

Commitment

The biggest single cause of failed negative flicks is lack of commitment at the point of initiation. It is understandable that at first you will be apprehensive about what is going to happen, and about the physiological effects of the forces you are going to experience. Rest assured that the whole affair is much worse if the flick does not start properly. A negative-G 'lurch' – when no flick occurs – or accelerated barrel roll both produce far more uncomfortable bodily forces than a proper flick roll.

The key elements, therefore, are to make sure that you have control inputs at the start that are both fast and of the right amplitude. Holding back, for whatever inadvertent psychological reason, will always hurt more than a good flick, which also brings a lot of satisfaction.

Understand the technique. Go for it as though you mean it.

Further Development

For positive flicks, I have devoted Chapter 36 to explaining the different techniques for fractions of rolls from ½ to 1¼. Most of the ideas have direct read-across to negative flicks so I will just summarize a few salient points here.

During the flick, the axis of rotation is changed in both pitch and yaw from that which existed as a flight path the instant before. To stop the fraction and regain the original attitude requires different elevator and rudder control positions depending on the extent of the rotation achieved (Table 39-1). As with positive flicks, only the full 360° rotation finishes with both opposite rudder and opposite elevator.

These different stopping corrections for different amounts of rotation must become second nature if you are to complete all the varying options cleanly in competition. The only way to gain this level of control and precision is through constant practice. Such flights will be more useful if you have a ground observer to confirm the errors of geometry that you think you see from inside the aeroplane.

For negative flicks on climbing or descending lines, you should modify the entry speed, as compared to level flight, just as for the same positive flicks. Generally, the steeper the down line, the slower should be the flick initiation speed and vice versa.

Table 39-1

Extent of Rotation	Symbol	Stopping Rudder	Stopping Elevator
Half (½)		Same (as initiation)	Forward (same)
Three-quarters (¾)	3/4	Opposite	Forward (same)
Full		Opposite	Back (opposite)
One-and-a-quarter (1¼)	1/4	Same	Back (opposite)

CHAPTER 40

Ming Vases

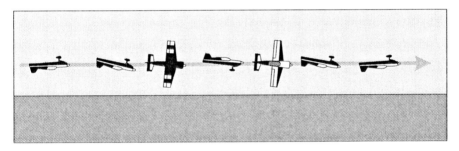

The title of this chapter is somewhat cryptic. Its origin lies in Eric Müller's book *Flight Unlimited*. He considers entering a positive flick roll from inverted flight a barbaric display of bad taste, *"... rather like taking a Ming Vase and using it as a mallet."*

So, here we are concerned with any flick roll entered from a line which has an angle of attack opposite to that intrinsic to the flick: positive from inverted, or negative from upright. Whether or not you agree with Eric's stance on the suitability of these manoeuvres, they **can** be done and they **are** called for in many Unlimited unknown sequences.

As these esoteric flicks carry a little higher co-efficient then their more natural versions, some pilots actually include them in their short Free programmes when they are seeking to add maximum K to a basic figure. So to consider yourself a complete pilot you must be able to fly them from time to time.

The Flight Manoeuvre

Flying level inverted, the aircraft pitches rapidly with the nose going down toward the ground. It then yaws and autorotation starts. After one full roll, the aeroplane is again inverted and stops rolling to fly off level. The aircraft could have been flying straight and level, upright. It would then have pitched down toward the ground and performed a level negative flick. Similarly, it could have been on a climbing or descending 45° line, upright or inverted (Diagram 40-1).

The key thing about the flick in each case is that initially the nose would pitch down toward the ground. In regular flick rolls performed on lines of the same loading, the nose always goes up, away from the ground when the first pitch input is applied.

Diagram 40-1

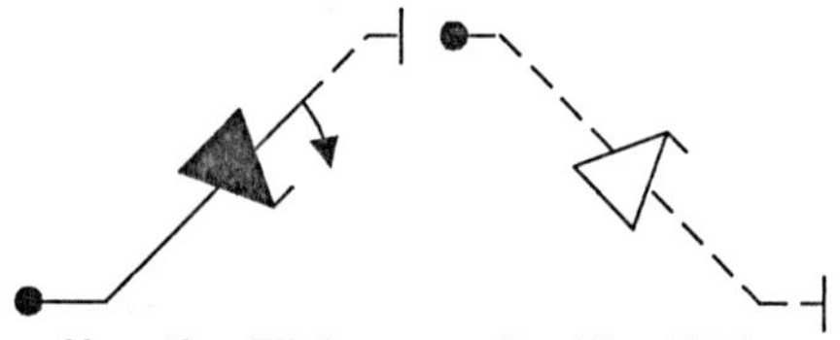

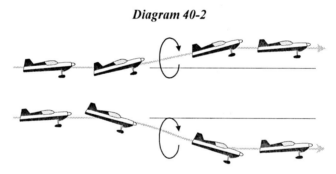

Negative Flick   **Positive Flick**
Positive Line   **Negative Line**

In a normal flick, there is always a small increase in height with a correctly flown figure. This is kept small, however, by the relatively small pitch change and the fact that you are moving against gravity (Diagram 40-2).

Conversely, during a Ming Vase, the height loss is greater than the previous small gain. This change of height will be noticeable if the figure is flown at low level, or if the technique is slow or laboured. Once again, commitment to the figure is an essential ingredient of success.

Diagram 40-2

Ground References

As for flicks on normally-loaded lines.

Technique

The technique is largely the same as has been previously described for classic flick rolls. The principle difference involves the amount of pitch required on initiation.

Diagram 40-3 shows the different geometry at the initiation of two types of flick roll from level flight. When a positive flick is started, the initial pitch change may be as small as 10°, because the wing is already positively loaded to counter gravity.

Diagram 40-3

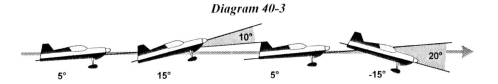

To start a negative flick from the same attitude, however, requires the wing to have a high negative alpha and consequently a much greater initial pitch change. This will be approximately double what is necessary for the normal flick in this situation.

After this initial pitch, the technique is to rudder and then unload as for a normal flick. Be aware, though, that the large initial pitch change means that for any fraction of a flick, the attitude error on stopping will also be greater.

The situation in the vertical, up or down, is slightly different. On these lines, some residual angle of attack will persist for a while after you have set the vertical attitude. See "'Hitting' the Vertical" on page 42. This will then decay, but it is likely that the alpha will not be entirely zero when the flick is started. It will, however, be much smaller than on a level or 45° line and so the difference between normal flicks and 'Ming Vases' is a bit less in these vertical situations.

Error Analysis

Because the initial pitch is towards the ground, the very same direction that gravity is pulling, there is much more tendency for the flight path to change than in a normal flick.

To minimize this undesired property, you must be as quick as you possibly can in applying the elevator. Also, to allow time for the big pitch change to occur, you must delay the onset of rudder application just a little more than normal. You might call this 'increasing the separation' of the pitch and yaw controls. Without this separation, the start of the flick will not be clear from the view of the audience.

Because of the increased size of the pitch change, it is even more important not to delay unloading the initial elevator when the flick starts to rotate. Unloading quicker than normal can thus help reduce the amount of attitude error when you stop the flick. This is especially important for fractions and multiples such as 1½.

These figures are very difficult to perform well if your aircraft has a forward centre of gravity, because of the reluctance of the aircraft to pitch rapidly. This is especially noticeable in tandem two-seaters when flown solo, unless there is a ballast system to help keep the balance point well aft.

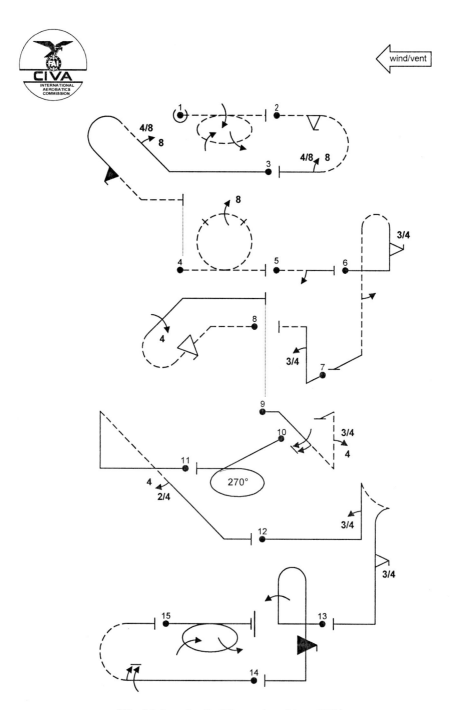

wind/vent

World Aerobatic Championships, 1994
Unlimited Unknown Sequence

Better Aerobatics

Part Six

Freestyle Figures

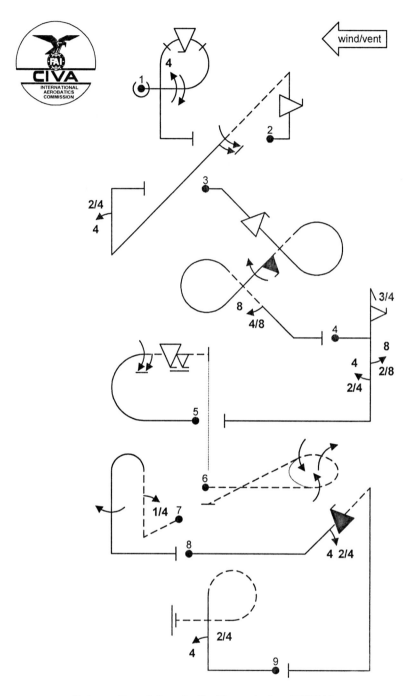

wind/vent

International Aerobatic Commission (CIVA)
Unlimited Known Compulsory (Qualification Programme) 2003

CHAPTER 41

Flat Spins

A flat spin is nothing supernatural. It does not hold any mystery, nor is it temperamental. It is simply a predictable development of a normal spin and all the normal rules of autorotation continue to apply.

Flat spins can be flown upright or inverted, and they are always flatter when power is applied than when gliding. The degree of 'flatness' is strongly effected by gyroscopic effects when power is on, so the direction of yaw is quite important in getting the best results.

With a Lycoming engine, it is best to use left rudder when upright and right rudder when inverted (Diagram 41-1).

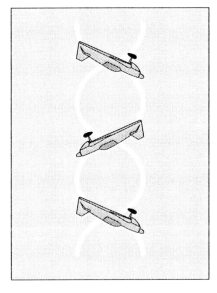

A developed flat spin by accident is very unlikely thing. Mishandled recovery from a normal spin, or 'botching' a vertical turn-around figure, can produce some exciting inadvertent spins, but these are more likely to be accelerated normal spins than developed flat ones. A good flat spin is something you have to work at.

Once you have learned the technique and become accustomed to the feelings induced, performing flat spins generates a great deal of satisfaction, knowing that you have overcome all the myths and misunderstandings surrounding the manoeuvre.

The Flight Manoeuvre

There are several different ways of entering a flat spin. You can develop a normal spin or modify a stall turn. Alternatively you could decay a climbing flick roll ... and so on.

I will describe a couple of these later.

Diagram 41-1

The main characteristic of the spin once developed is a high nose attitude, in some cases with the aeroplane completely flat or even with the nose above the horizon.

The rate of rotation is moderate at best, not really fast, while the height loss per turn is much less than for a normal spin. For example, I once flew an upright flat spin at a demonstration over the beach 'airport' at Birkdale Sands, near Southport on the west coast of northern England. I started the spin from a stall turn at 4,000 feet and started recovery at 2,000 feet. The spectators counted 14 turns.

Left rudder   **Right rudder**

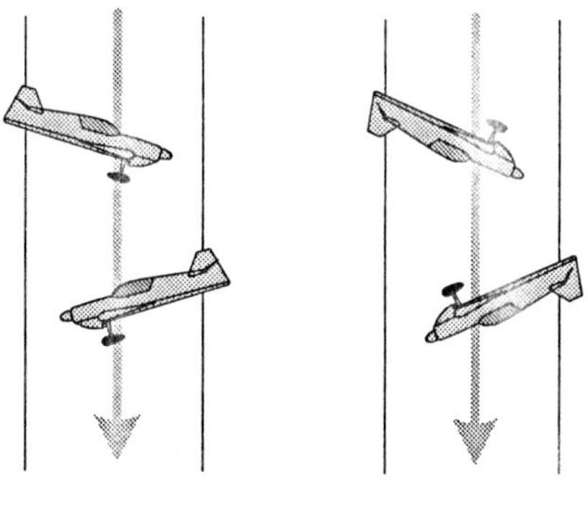

Ground References

In an upright flat spin, you can't see the ground unless you have a large clear polycarbonate floor panel. Inverted, you will have a very clear view of the ground through the canopy. If you watch the centre of rotation on the ground, you can maintain your orientation and it is useful to have a runway or other strong line feature directly below you.

If you cannot see the ground and, instead, look at the horizon rushing past the nose, you will probably become quickly dizzy or disorientated. In an upright spin, therefore, it is probably best to study the altimeter quite closely and just keep a peripheral view of the juxtaposition of nose and horizon.

Technique

Entering the Upright Flat Spin

To begin with, I will assume you are entering a flat spin by modifying a normal spin. The principal control movement to make the spin flatter is out-spin aileron. For an upright flat spin in a Lycoming-engined aeroplane with a clockwise turning propeller (seen from inside) you should spin with left rudder.

Diagram 41-2 Right aileron in a left spin

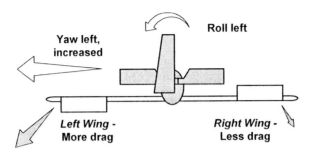

Diagram 41-2 shows the primary effect of adding out-spin aileron – right aileron in a left upright spin. The down-going left aileron increases further the angle of attack on that side. So the drag increases on that side also. Conversely, on the right side the drag is reduced.

The overall effect is to greatly increase the yaw couple acting on the aeroplane. The increased rate of yaw causes a greater gyroscopic force in pitch from the propeller and this makes the nose rise.

Diagram 41-3

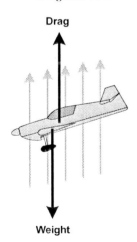

Adding power will provide both more propeller rpm, giving more nose up gyro, and more airflow over the elevator which will also raise the nose. With the flattening attitude and the increasing yaw rate, the roll component of the spin appears to reduce. Drag is very high, so rate of descent is low (Diagram 41-3).

It follows that aircraft with powerful elevators and big or heavy propellers will spin flatter than those with smaller elevators and lighter propellers. Another factor that greatly effects the flatness of the spin is centre of gravity position.

When the direction of flight is mostly straight down and rotating fast, there is a balance between the, almost vertical, drag and the actually vertical weight. The couple produced tends to lower the nose. The further aft the centre of gravity position, the smaller is this nose-down force and hence the greater is the power of the gyro and elevator to lift the nose.

For this reason, two seat aircraft invariably spin flatter with two people on board than with one. I do not know of a powered aerobatic aeroplane where the second occupant moves the centre of gravity forward.

Once the spin has flattened it can be further accelerated in some aircraft by unloading the elevator a small amount. This sequence of control inputs is shown in Diagram 41-4. Remember that for the best effect, full power should be applied at the same time as the out-spin aileron.

The optimum position of aileron and elevator varies a little between aircraft types, so you will have to experiment a little to find the best combination for your aircraft and its weight distribution.

Recovery

I have flown considerable numbers of flat spins in the following aircraft: Pitts S1 and S2 series, Yak-52, Yak-55, Sukhoi-26 and -29, Giles G202 and CAP-232. In every one of these types, recovery from a flat spin is quicker and more positive with power on. These aircraft have very powerful rudder and elevator controls whose effectiveness is greatly improved by the increased slipstream that is apparent with full power applied. In each case, this increase in rudder and elevator authority is far greater than the difference in gyroscopic forces with power on and off.

Previous authors have held back from recommending the power-on recovery technique, but I know from personal conversation that they themselves know about it, understand it and, more importantly, actually use it.

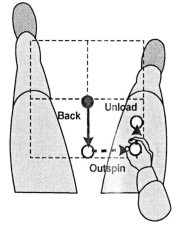

Diagram 41-4

Left Spin, out-spin aileron

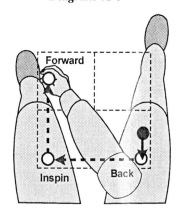

Diagram 41-5

**Recovery -
Right rudder, inspin aileron,
forward stick**

There is no reason why such knowledge should be kept a trade secret among 'Unlimited' pilots, but I suspect the real reason for always recommending 'throttle closed' recoveries is a mixture of conservatism and fear of litigation.

When you recover from an intentional spin, the correct control inputs will always work. They will almost certainly work better with power on. The wrong inputs will not recover from a spin. The wrong inputs with power on will make the lack of recovery even more certain.

My intention with this book is to give you the correct technique that will recover, so I have no fear of also recommending that you use power to help when it will definitely do so.

The control movements for recovery from an upright flat spin to the left are shown in Diagram 41-5.

First you apply full right rudder. Then you move the stick back, left and forward. There must be three distinct stick movements and they should be made without rushing so that all three actions have time to work.

You must not go directly from the start position to the finish position without visiting the other two stations on the way.

If you make this recovery with power on, in one of the aircraft I have listed at the start of this section, the spin will stop in less than one rotation; normally in about half a turn. If you do the same but with the throttle closed, the recovery will take longer: perhaps two or three turns depending on just how flat and fast it was rotating.

This is because, in order to stop rotating, the nose has to go down. After a developed flat spin the aircraft has almost no forward speed. With just an idling slipstream there is little the elevator can do. You just have to wait for the nose to go down under gravity as the rudder and in-spin aileron slowly overcome the yaw couple. As the nose drops, the spin will speed up before it finally stops.

With power on, the rudder is quicker at overcoming the yaw and so the nose-up gyro also reduces quickly. With full-span ailerons, the increased slipstream also boosts the anti-yaw effects of the in-spin aileron. Lastly, the now-more-effective elevator is able to force the nose down quickly.

Entering the Inverted Flat Spin

To convert a normal inverted spin into a flat one, the same principles are applied as for an upright flat spin: out-spin aileron, power and some unloading.

For best effect in the Lycoming-powered aeroplane, you should start the inverted spin with right rudder. This will produce yaw to the right and roll to the left. Because the aeroplane is rolling left, out-spin aileron is actually right aileron, the same side as the rudder. Have a look at Diagram 41-7 to see this explained. Make sure you can sort out in your head which is the pilot's right and left! The control movements for the inverted flat spin entry are shown in the left side of Diagram 41-7. Remember that you should add power to increase the gyro and elevator effects once the out-spin aileron is applied.

Diagram 41-6   Right aileron in a right-foot inverted spin

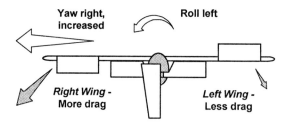

Diagram 41-7

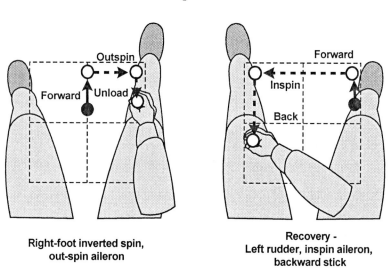

Right-foot inverted spin,
out-spin aileron

Recovery -
Left rudder, inspin aileron,
backward stick

Recovery

For all the same reasons as with the upright spin, recovery is quicker with the power left on. The control movements are shown in the right side of Diagram 41-7. Once again, be sure to make three distinct movements with the control column. Do not go straight from the start position to the end position. Go via both front corners, and don't rush.

Other Entries

If you want to enter a flat spin without going through a normal spin first, it is best to conjure up a situation where the aeroplane has little or no horizontal speed.

For an upright spin, you can make a very good entry from a stall turn. A normal stall turn, with the engine, uses the same foot as an upright flat spin. Fly the stall turn quite normally, except that you should not apply the forward stick that normally counters the gyroscopic effect during the turn. As the nose drops toward vertical down, the aeroplane will take a positive angle of attack.

Maintain full left rudder and apply full back stick as the nose swings through vertical down. As the spin starts apply full right aileron. Once the spin is established unload the elevator a little.

For an inverted spin, fly vertically upward and then use aft elevator to ease the aeroplane gently onto its back at the very top of the line.

This is similar in effect to the top of a Humpty Bump. As the aeroplane reaches a level inverted attitude, you want it to drop straight down, so reduce power to encourage a lot of sink. Immediately then apply full forward stick and full right rudder. As the spin starts, add power back on and full right aileron. Once the rotation is established, unload with a little back stick.

Alternatively, fly a canopy-up tail slide. Add full forward stick in the pendulum, together with right rudder and aileron. Watch your oil pressure!

Further Development

The Eventail

Eventail is a French word meaning fan and was coined by Xavier Delapparent for a figure which is fundamentally an inverted flat spin performed on a climbing 45° line.

If you do this on an axis flying towards your audience, they will see the top of the aeroplane as it pivots rapidly in yaw in the direction opposite to a normal stall turn. If the aeroplane and the technique are just right it is possible to conjure two complete rotations and finish perfectly vertical down right in front of the crowd/judges (Diagram 41-8).

The simplest way to initiate the Eventail is with rapid application of full forward stick, full right rudder and partial left aileron from a climbing inverted line of about 45° or a little less.

After half a turn of negative flick apply full right aileron to transition into a flatter attitude. The rotation should accelerate markedly and pitch more steeply nose up. If the aeroplane has a sufficiently well aft centre of gravity, then two rotations of the flat spin are possible. With a more forward centre of gravity and steeper initial climb angle, the rotational energy may dissipate earlier.

Diagram 41-8
Double Eventail (with audience!)

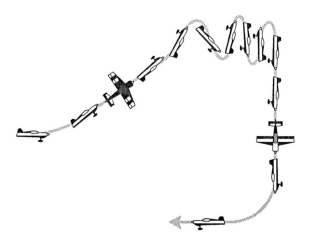

Recovery is quite complex. Initially, with about 180° to go (that is with the nose pointing upwards) you should reduce power momentarily to reduce a little the gyroscopic force. Then as the nose drops to vertical for the last time, apply full power again and full left rudder, moving the control column through both front corners to full left and almost fully aft as well. Centralise everything as the rotation stops.

If you are flying this figure for fun at height, you can maintain the full pro-spin controls and transition from the Eventail into a very dynamic flat inverted spin with a vertically down trajectory. If you think you might be going to do this, don't drink any fizzy stuff before you go!

Energy Matters

Flat spins destroy energy like almost nothing else. There is nothing you can do about this, except recover with minimum height loss and burn petrol as soon thereafter as possible. This is another benefit of the power-on recovery. It is quicker, loses less height and starts rebuilding energy sooner.

CHAPTER 42

Knife-Edge Spins and Tumbling

A knife-edge spin is not really a spin as we know it. It is definitely not a classic autorotation and the wings are not stalled. But the aeroplane does fall vertically down (almost) and rotate as it descends; so what is it really doing?

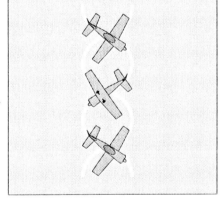

Actually, it is a completely new kind of rotation – rapid pitch rotation, or tumbling.

You can also tumble the aircraft on lines other than straight down. These are sometimes given other names to suit the situation: *'Ruade'*, *'Cap Lomcovac'* and so on.

All current Final Freestyle programmes include numerous versions of this type of manoeuvre. Stress on the body is relatively low, because of the low entry speeds, although the strange motion does initially take some getting used to; it is so unnatural. However, the tumble is gyroscopically driven, so stress on the engine, especially the crankshaft, is high!

Other authors, notably Xavier Delapparent, have written quite extensively on these matters, so I plan not to repeat here all that has been said before. If you want to learn more and more in this area, then I recommend you get hold of a copy of Xavier's book on the *Four-Minute Freestyle*.

However, I feel compelled to include the basic ideas and theory here, knowing how frustrating it would be for you to want to know and not to be able to track down another reference work.

The Flight Manoeuvre

Knife-Edge Spin

Look at the aeroplane in Diagram 42-1. Imagine it just falling to earth, on its side without any rotation. Gravity and built-in stability will combine to make the aeroplane yaw to the right to become vertical in attitude as well as flight path. It will try to come wings level.

This is just what happens if you stop a stall turn with the nose just a bit off to one side.

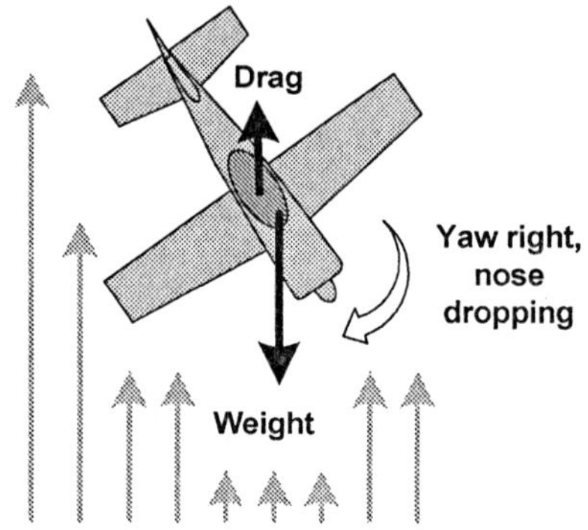

If we now apply full rudder, let's say to the left, the aeroplane will still fall without rotating, as long as you maintain zero angle of attack. Depending on the authority of your rudder, your centre of gravity position and your power setting, the angle of the fuselage to the vertical can be larger or smaller. With some modern aircraft the angle can be quite noticeable.

Diagram 42-1

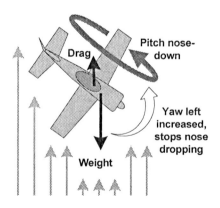

Diagram 42-9

If you now add forward stick, the aeroplane will start to pitch. With high engine rpm, this pitch will also generate a large gyroscopic force which will assist the left rudder in holding the nose up against gravity.

So you now have an aeroplane falling in knife edge, with the fuselage maybe 45° from vertical in yaw and rotating 'nose-down' with respect to the pilot due to the forward stick; a knife-edge 'spin' (Diagram 42-9).

Tumbles

As I said above, the knife-edge rotation, gyroscopically enhanced, that you have learned to fly almost vertically down, can also be flown on other lines. In this case it seems even less sensible to call the manoeuvre a spin and so I will group this family of tricks under the general heading of tumbling. It is rather like the

Diagram 42-2

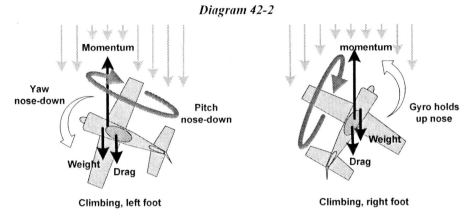

Climbing, left foot   Climbing, right foot

aeroplane doing a rapid somersault, pitching forward rapidly around the pivot axis of the wing while otherwise flying a bit sideways.

This appears to be a very un-natural thing for the aeroplane to do, and it is equally difficult to hand-fly in the bar afterwards. Our wrists just do not have the right joints.

Going vertically down was reasonably easy to describe and understand. Next easiest is probably vertical up. On this climbing line you can tumble with left rudder or right, but always with forward stick. (Diagram 42-2).

Tumbles can also be flown on 45° lines, up or down and also level. Diagram 42-3 illustrates a level tumble with left foot, if you imagine looking down on the aeroplane from directly above.

Diagram 42-3

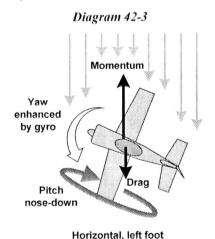

Horizontal, left foot

For all these tumbles to work well, aircraft centre of gravity position is very critical. The drag induced is very large, so entry speeds cannot be too slow or the line cannot be maintained.

As the entry speed increases, however, so does the stability of the aircraft. So it becomes more reluctant to follow the large yaw changes demanded by the rudder and gyro.

The further aft the centre of gravity, the less stable the aeroplane becomes in yaw, so the better it tumbles. This is another situation where a tandem two-seater really benefits from a ballast system when flown solo, or tumbling may be impossible.

Ground References

For the knife-edge spin, a big line feature right below you is essential. Big, because you need to start quite high. Once you are on your way down, big will become much bigger at quite an alarming rate. This is a great way to lose height.

For tumbling much is the same, but as you have forward momentum you can look towards fixed points further away as well.

Technique

Knife-Edge Spin, Stall Turn Entry

The simplest entry is from a stall turn with the engine (Lycoming = left foot as ever). Fly a perfect stall turn up to the point of changing feet to stop the yaw. Don't change feet. Make the nose swing through to about 45° past vertical. If your aeroplane has a particularly aft centre of gravity you may find it wants to go right through to fuselage level, right wing low. This is too far and will make the start of the rotation very difficult because of insufficient roll control, so you may be advised to throttle back a little as you swing through vertical down.

With the nose in this odd, 45° attitude, smoothly apply forward elevator to start the pitching motion. As you move the stick forward, you must use aileron to keep the wings in the vertical plane, or you will soon gather an angle of attack and start a negative flick roll. The aileron position required varies between types, but is usually just a little left of centre (Diagram 42-4).

If you have the aileron too far left, the aeroplane will roll left and assume a positive angle of attack, despite the forward stick. It will enter a rapid positive flick roll to the left. If you have the aileron central or slightly to the

Diagram 42-4

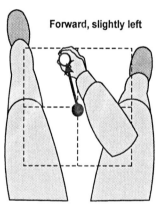

Forward, slightly left

Knife-Edge Spin

right, the aeroplane will roll right into a negative angle of attack and will start a flick roll with left yaw and right roll.

Your task with the ailerons is to balance the aircraft between these two departure modes so that it falls straight downwards. It's a bit like balancing a pencil on the tip of your finger; it takes practice.

Vertical Tumbles

Tumbles on vertical up lines are best entered at maximum negative flick speed.

With left foot, gravity and gyro will work together to bring the nose down as you pitch forward. So you can expect the fuselage to become parallel to the ground quite quickly, but you will be rewarded with a very dynamic tumble. With right foot, you need to establish a fair bit of yaw before adding the forward stick.

Gravity will want to bring the nose down, but slipstream effect and gyro will both want to hold it up. The result can be a more sedate, but better sustained and controlled tumble than with left foot.

Other Lines

As you change the entry line through 45° up to level, then to 45° down, you should reduce the entry speed, just as you would for a flick roll entry.

If speed is high initially on a climbing 45° line, you can start aileron rolling left and then transition to a tumble by adding rudder, forward stick and reducing the aileron input as the speed reduces. A similar transition can be flown on level or descending lines if you are careful to observe maximum flick speed limitations.

When performing all these tumbles, the most difficult part of the technique is to maintain the correct aileron position that will keep the aeroplane in knife-edge. Rather like the way a tail slide eventually changes ends, a tumble will invariably decay into a flick roll. If you want to learn real mastery of this figure, you should strive to perfect just a single rotation with the ability to stop precisely in the same attitude you started. This is much harder than to simply allow the decaying process to take its course.

The French term for a tumble, usually on a climbing 45° line, is a *Ruade*. This translates best as a mule-kick, which is illustrative of the rudder input. No-one has better control of the figure than Delapparent.

In the CAP-231Ex he flew in the Breitling competitions in the early-90s, he would fly two consecutive *ruades*, with a stop between them, on a climbing 45° line, finishing with a hammerhead-style pivot to the right to get back to vertical down.

In his later Sukhoi 31 display, he would fly level, parallel to the crowd and fly an alternating series of single *ruades* and aileron rolls; complete control at all times.

These precise stops probably appeared less dynamic to the layman than a continuous two or three tumbles decaying into a flick roll. But to those who understood what he was doing, the extent of control and timing was exceptional. If you ever get a chance to see Xavier fly, take it.

Recovery

Recovery is always the same: opposite rudder and stick centrally back. Unless you are really confident on your type's recovery characteristics, it is sensible to reduce the power initially to cut down on the gyroscopic effects before applying the recovery controls.

Energy Matters

You lose a lot. Just make sure you have a plan for getting it back fairly soon.

CHAPTER 43

Half Flick Combinations

The Krysta Loop

In the search for geometric perfection that is the basis for *Aresti*-style figures, the half flick always presents a major challenge because of the almost inevitable, unwanted heading change. But the artistic side of Freestyle flying aims always to break away from the strictures of formal geometry, or at least from its predictability. So an original mind sometimes works in a non-intuitive

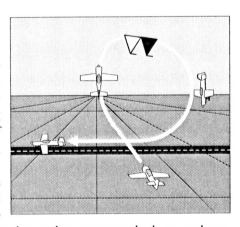

manner and comes across something that makes everyone look up and say, *"How did he do that?"*.

A classic example of this was the rather special 'Avalanche' flown in 1958 by Vilém Krysta, a member of the Czech team at the Lockheed trophy that year. A loop with a flick roll in the top was by then well known. The challenge of the figure was to make it round, symmetrical and to finish perfectly on heading. Then along came Krysta and somehow he managed, during the flick, to get exactly 90° off. What's more, he could then do it again and use another 90° heading change to get back onto the original axis. But how could he fly a flick roll and, quite sweetly, change heading by 90° while the aeroplane was in seemingly normal autorotation?

Krysta was sadly killed in a flying accident in 1959, and it was several more years before this riddle was solved. The flick roll in the Krysta Loop was actually two half flick rolls, one positive and one negative, with different rudder inputs but therefore with a continuous 360° rolling appearance in a constant direction. It was almost impossible to detect the change in elevator and rudder half-way through the roll. Krysta had hit upon the idea of exploiting the very heading change that everyone else was fighting. He was forcing a 45° heading change with his half positive flick and then compounding it by another 45° in the same direction by changing feet halfway through. Brilliant; and actually not particularly difficult to fly once you understand the concept and can fly both positive and negative flicks normally.

Technique

For orientation, it is best to be flying towards a line feature, at right angles, as shown in the heading picture. Entry speed and the technique are the same as for an avalanche up to the point of initiating the roll. Because the aim is to exploit the natural heading change, it is best to start the positive half flick with the rudder that adds to the natural gyroscopic yaw associated with the back stick. In the standard Lycoming engined aeroplane this means you should use right rudder.

Start the roll with a quick application of back stick and full right rudder (Diagram 43-1). As soon as the flick 'breaks', and autorotation starts, begin to move the control column forward, both accelerating the flick and preparing to change to negative. As you approach 180° of roll (you will be back upright with the sky above your head) change as quick as you can to full left rudder and push full forward stick. The rotation, which started to slow just a little when you came off the right rudder, will kick again as the left rudder bites and you will soon find yourself coming once again to the inverted attitude.

To stop the roll, re-apply right rudder and bring the control column centrally back so that you can also continue with the temporarily forgotten looping manoeuvre. As the rotation stops, look quickly to the line feature now on your right. You can adjust the exact amount and duration of the right, stopping, rudder so that it also brings you exactly parallel to the highway.

Diagram 43-1

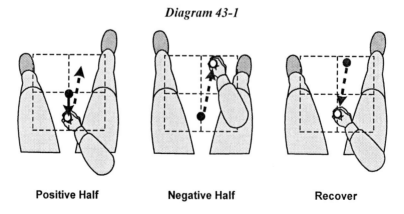

| Positive Half | Negative Half | Recover |

Diagram 43-2

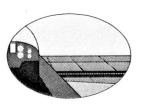
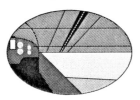
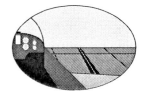

| **Start** | **Inverted after stop** | **Finish** |

Diagram 43-2 shows some cockpit views. The centre picture is what you should see as you stop the half negative flick. In order to get the full 90° heading change, the flick rotation must not be too fast. In some respects, this figure is much easier in the 1950s or 1960s type aircraft. It was invented in a classic Zlin 226, and it works very well in a two-seat Pitts Special.

In today's very high performance aircraft you have to find a technique that allows for a slower roll-rate during the flick than you normally strive for. If the roll is too fast, the aeroplane's yaw inertia prevents you from getting the exit heading easily. If you are able to force it round with really brute rudder effects, then it is very punishing for the body and airframe alike.

The best approach to this problem seems to be to fly a very big loop and have what would normally be 'too slow' a speed at the top. This way it is possible to conjure a slower roll and execute the heading change with much less stress and strain.

Further Development

When you string two loops, one after the other, you can plan to finish in the opposite direction to which you started, or you can end up going the same way. In the first case, you just do the same thing over again for the second loop. For the

Diagram 43-3

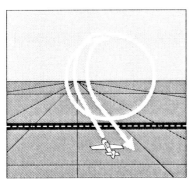
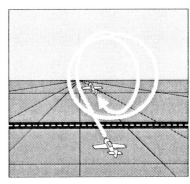

| **Right/Left, Right/Left** | **Right/Left, Left/Right** |

389

latter, to really 'quarter the orange', you must roll in the opposite direction for the second flick (Diagram 43-3).

Energy Matters

In one of the classic older aircraft, especially a biplane, you must expect to lose a lot of energy through the loop.

If you modify the exit radius of the first loop to give you good entry speed for the second, you must expect to be lower at the end than at the start. You can defeat this somewhat by having a really fast entry for the first loop and making it quite big. This might allow enough height loss on the way down to get fast enough for the second. You will only find out with practice what your aeroplane can do.

Modern Unlimited aircraft tend to have much greater power/weight ratios and can replace energy almost as fast as you can squander it. This has enabled further extension of the Krysta discovery into the flick-rolling turn.

Flick Rolling Turns

In a normal rolling turn, you must be careful not to have a large angle of attack and a lot of rudder at the same time. Failure to observe this precaution may well result in your smooth aileron roll rapidly changing to a flick. If you do this in a competition flight, you will be most displeased and the judges will rub their hands with glee as they award you another 'egg'.

But this is Freestyle now and you can do what you like. What I am about to describe is probably the most absurd way to fly and is certainly one that consumes copious amounts of Avgas to no other purpose than to go round in circles. But it is fun.

Technique

You had best start at just about maximum flick-rolling speed and with maximum power. You then just initiate a half positive flick to the right but without any intention of keeping straight. So you can be generous with the back stick and the rudder (Diagram 43-4).

If you have a lot of slipstream and full-span ailerons, only the outer part of the wing will be stalling and the inner part flying normally. So you can, abnormally, use right aileron as well. A combination of part-flick, part-aileron roll will keep the maximum roll rate going faster and longer than a pure flick alone.

As the roll progresses, maintain the right aileron but begin the process of reversing the elevator and the rudder together. You should aim to hit full forward stick and left rudder just as the wings become level. This is the same as in the Krysta loop, but you are starting the positive flick upright and the negative phase from inverted.

Diagram 43-4

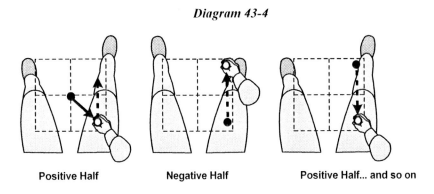

| Positive Half | Negative Half | Positive Half... and so on |

As the aeroplane comes back upright again, it is time to re-apply the back stick and right rudder, all the time keeping the right aileron input.

How long you can keep this going is a personal matter. If you do more than three rotations, however, be wary when you stop because it may well seem to your inner ear that straight and level is neither. In such cases, a quick roll to the left, the opposite direction, can help with your re-orientation. It is probably obvious at this stage that you should not do this sort of thing at other than high level until you have become extremely proficient.

A few years ago we had a charity event at my flying club, raising money for handicapped children. Paul Bonhomme flew for an hour in a Sukhoi 26, I think, to see how many loops he could do. My contribution was to fly a flick-rolling circle around the airfield perimeter, in a Yak-55M, so that someone below could count the number of rolls I could fit into one circumnavigation. This was perhaps more disorientating than an hour of loops, but it was over and done with a bit quicker. The total was 48 rolls, plus one back the other way for the benefit of the inner ear!

On another such charity day I flew two inverted ILS approaches at RAF Benson, Oxfordshire, in a Slingsby T67. But that is another story ...

Further Developments

The technique described above results in what is in effect an **inward** flick rolling turn. If you start upright but begin with a negative half flick, and go on to make it positive as you pass inverted, you will fly an **outward** flick rolling turn. This is breaking a great many Ming Vases in rapid succession, but what the heck! Just watch the altimeter! Unless you have the nose quite high, and a great deal of thrust, the only way this figure can go is down.

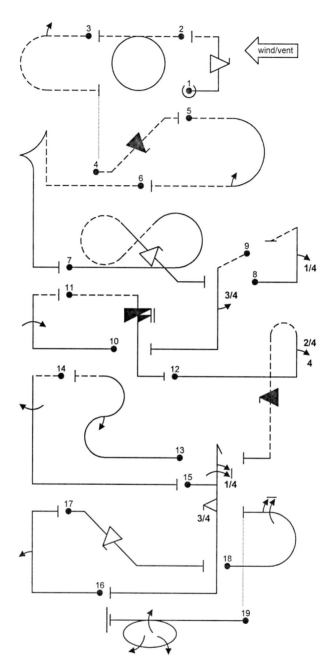

European Aerobatic Championship
Ravenna, Italy, 1983
Known Compulsory Sequence

Better Aerobatics

Part Seven

Competition Flying

Aerobatic Drawing Software

In the late 1980s, when office desk-top computing first started to become available, I was intrigued to see what could be done to get rid of the pencil and calculator from the arcane art of drawing aerobatic sequence diagrams in the Aresti style. Of course, it was possible to make drawings using early drawing software packages, but the time taken was enormous because of the amazing number of different shapes that you had to construct.

After a couple of frustrating years I discovered a new software package that had just come onto the UK market, called Visio 2. I never saw Visio 1, which probably only surfaced in the USA.

The key thing about Visio was that it enabled you to store Master Shapes in a Stencil, so that you could use them over and over again. In this respect, it was just like the Aerobatic Catalogue, which had all the basic drawings in book form and you then used and adapted them as necessary.

Visio also gave you access, as a programmer, to the geometry of each shape in an algebraic form, so that you could manipulate the lines and curves mathematically, without having to be an artist. This was ideal for making the interface more wide in its appeal to potential users.

With Visio 3, it became possible to add special custom properties to individual shapes and make inventory-like arithmetic calculations. So it became possible to associate figures with their relevant catalogue numbers and K-factors, to list them and to add them. It also became feasible then to write Visual Basic sub-routines that would carry out repetitive tasks, such as adding the total K for a sequence, checking the Free Programme criteria, making the judging sheet and so on.

After much midnight oil was consumed, development of the system reached the stage where it could be used by any moderately computer-literate aerobatic pilot and, more importantly, could actually speed up the process of designing and checking sequences.

By the late 1990s, this software system was recognised internationally, both by CIVA and, in 1997, by a special IAC President's Award.

Visio is now a Microsoft standard product and the aerobatic software has reached version 6. At the time of writing, details of the software can be found on the worldwide web at: www.worldaerobatics.com/Aresti6.

All of the line drawings in this book were made using Visio 4 and Aresti 6 on a Dell laptop computer.

CHAPTER 44

Sequence Construction

Designing a sequence for a competition programme is a complex technical task, but it also has its artistic side. The first requirement is a sound understanding of the FAI Aerobatic Catalogue, which I described briefly in Chapter 4.

Second comes knowledge of the repertoire appropriate to the level of complexity demanded for the occasion, whether it be a Sportsman Known programme for next year or an Advanced Unknown to be flown the next day at a World Championship.

Thirdly is a profound understanding of the capabilities of the aeroplanes that will be taking part, especially their perform-ance limitations.

Lastly, and most difficult to define, is the need to be able to shape the sequence as a whole so that it flows in a pleasing way, makes use of the available space and gives opportunities for making the wind 'disappear'.

I have gained a lot of pleasure from designing sequences over the years. I have also learned a great deal in the process. My first efforts, Intermediate Free programmes for myself, in the late 1980s, did not always turn out very well. But I persevered and improved.

Once I became the CIVA Delegate for the United Kingdom, I started submitting proposals for international Advanced and, later, Unlimited known programmes. Looking back over recent years, I have gained a lot of satisfaction from seeing my sequences flown at every international Advanced contest since 1997, and from actually flying my own at the 2002 European Unlimited Championship. Thankfully, I can pass on some of this slowly accumulated knowledge here.

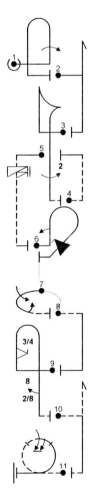

Design for Performance and Energy

Most sequences will be flown by a wide variety of aircraft, the exceptions being personal Free Programmes and any sequence at a one-design contest. It is a basic tenet of fairness in multi-type competition that the compulsory sequences, Knowns and Unknowns, should test the pilot not the aeroplane.

Any sequence must be flyable by the minimum aircraft that is taking part without a forced break to gain height and with the prospect of being able to score well in each figure.

Design for Performance

By all means make figure 1 require a high entry speed. But thereafter ask only what is practical bearing in mind what has just happened. Don't try to design 'impossible' figures, or force flick rolls at dangerously high speeds; these are not good tests of the pilot's ability, only his recklessness.

After longish periods of negative G, allow time for recovery before requiring a long pull; putting pilots to sleep is not your job either. And, of course, don't have any sustained negative at all if any of the aeroplanes involved are devoid of inverted fuel and oil systems.

Design for Energy

There are a number of principles which must always be exploited in compulsory sequence design if you are not to penalise unfairly the minimum aircraft. Here are some of them.

♦ Do not force very high-speed flight except before figure 1.

♦ Never force the pilot to close the throttle and slow down.

♦ Avoid repeated rolling on vertical down lines.

♦ Build in good periods of level, accelerating flight.

♦ Allow speed loss by climbing before spin entries.

♦ Do not force prolonged stretches of high speed level flight between figures.

Diagram 44-1

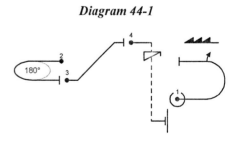

I suppose I should give some examples. Diagram 44-1 is from a Sportsman Known programme. The numbers 1 to 4 are illustrative only; the sequence is important. Imagine it is being flown by a clipped-wing Cub and by an Extra 300. Between the Immelmann and the 180 turn, speed can be pursued relentlessly by the Cub pilot. The turn forces cross wind correction – perhaps more than really ideal for the Extra pilot, especially if he too has been accelerating at full power.

At the end of the turn, the 45° up line gives the Cub pilot the chance to squeeze every last drop of height out of his remaining speed before the spin entry. He will probably gain a good 500 feet. It does the same for the Extra pilot but if he has been at full power, he will climb about 1,500 feet and have a big problem putting the spin at centre box.

This combination will force the Extra pilot, if he is thinking properly, to throttle back after the Immelmann and fly only slowly through the turn. He will actually have to make his aeroplane fly more like a Cub to keep good positioning.

Here (Diagram 44-2) are two alternative segments of Intermediate programme. Now we have a Decathlon competing against the Extra 300. In the left-hand sequence, the Split-S results in a high exit speed and is followed by a transit to the right end of the box for the stall turn. During this transit, the Decathlon will slow down.

At the top of the stall turn, it might get back to its original height or just a little higher. Because of its slow roll rate, the Decathlon will lose height on the stall turn, even more on the pushed Humpty, which it will again exit at very high speed. The speed will be lost once again on the dash to the left end of the box to pull up for the half Cuban. Because of the now slower entry speed, the half Cuban will also be a height loser.

Even if you could sustain a high speed between figures 3 and 4, you could not use the excess speed to gain back height. Making the looping section of the half Cuban very large would cause it to be very pointed in shape because you would be very slow into wind at the top.

In the Extra 300, you could gain height doing this short series.

Diagram 44-2

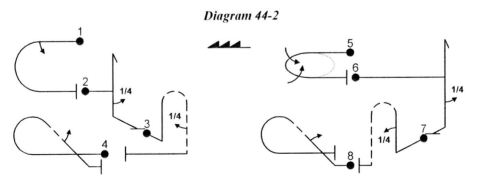

In the right hand sequence, there is time to accelerate to optimum speed for the rolling turn. At the end of the roller, there is time to accelerate again to get maximum level speed for the stall turn. The length of the up line is not important, so the Decathlon can score well even from a minimum entry speed. At the top of the stall turn the Decathlon will be a good 500 feet higher than it was at the same point of left-hand sequence.

The level high speed cross-box line after the ¼ roll down need be held for only the minimum time before starting the humpty. If a lot of cross wind correction was required, it could have been partly accomplished during the roller. The down line of the Humpty is plain so also need be held for only the minimum time; just long enough to get entry speed for the reverse half Cuban which, again, can be entered without delay.

The height loss for the Decathlon in the second set is probably 1,000 feet less than in the first set. The Extra pilot, in the second set, will be drawing much longer vertical lines than the Decathlon. He will be exposed to the head wind during the stall turn and the Humpty for much longer and will start the reverse half Cuban further down wind and going faster than his more performance-challenged colleague.

There is a good chance he will go out of the box during the half-reverse Cuban, so he has positioning issues to think about that will counter any advantage he may have been expecting from performance issues alone.

Here, sequence design has taken away all the performance advantage of the Extra pilot. The Decathlon pilot can compete on skill alone, and may even have an advantage if there is a strong head wind. As a matter of added interest, the total K for the badly designed section is 60K, while for the better design, the difficulty is 69K. The second option is therefore a more technical challenge for a good Intermediate pilot, while not being any help at all to the rich guy with the Extra!

Design for Known Programmes

Apart from performance and energy matters, what other issues are there around design for Known sequences?

The most important realisation is that the sequence must still present difficulties at the end of the season as well as at the beginning. Such difficulties can only really come from changes in external conditions, because everything the pilot is doing in the cockpit will be very well understood by then. So we are really talking about including in the sequence a lot of things that are changed considerably in different wind conditions.

Reducing the quantity and careful placing of cross wind correctors is one such opportunity. Another is the inclusion of a good number of looping shapes and 45° lines. These require different techniques from the pilot in different wind conditions.

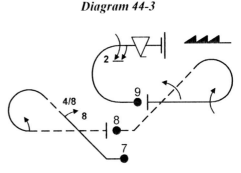

Diagram 44-3

Diagram 44-3 shows an extract from the Advanced Qualifying programme for the 2002 World Championship. During the flying of the programme there were some quite strong and variable winds. The alternating 45° lines combined with into-wind and down wind looping segments made it very difficult to fly really good basic shapes, with the rolls centred and so on.

In calm conditions, it would have been much easier to get right. Additionally, high performance aircraft tended to climb throughout this section and go out of the box on figure 7. Quite often, the finish of the sequence was much higher than optimum for judging the flick because pilots did not 'hold back' their powerful machines. This was a challenging sequence throughout the season, just because of these last three figures which actually appear deceptively unchallenging.

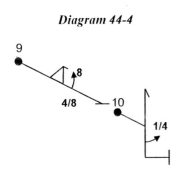

Diagram 44-4

A stall turn, with the wings parallel to the main axis, is also a good idea. In strong wind conditions this might be bridged considerably unless the turn is done with the nose into the wind. This might be particularly difficult if there are strong head and cross wind components, as the stall turn may show best if executed against the engine. Similarly, a half flick on the B-axis always presents better in a strong wind if performed with up wind rudder.

So this also gives the challenge of using different techniques on different days.

Diagram 44-4 shows another Advanced Known segment. The half flick, 4/8 figure takes up quite a lot of space on the B-axis. If there is a strong on-judge or off-judge wind, it must be flown into this wind to stay in the box. If there is also a healthy head wind component, the half flick really should be done with the into-wind foot. So the 4/8 must also be practised in either direction. Then it may be better to stall turn against the engine to avoid losing points for 'flying over' the top. There is no performance challenge here, it can all be flown by a Pitts S2A, but there is a great deal to work out technically on the day of the contest flight.

Design for Free Programmes

In the Compulsory programmes, Known and Unknown, each pilot pits his flying skill against the others. The Free Programme is different, because here he pits his sequence design skill as well. This is a skill that is exercised solely on the ground and which can be honed over the long winter months by careful thought and study. It should be one reason why you are reading this chapter. Whilst it is quite possible to arrive at a good sequence by copying one flown by someone else in a similar aircraft type, it is much more satisfying to win in one you have created from scratch entirely by yourself. So here are some ideas that might encourage and help you.

Choice of Figures

Choose figures that have the least complicated judging criteria. The two figures in Diagram 44-5 have the same total of 21K.

The avalanche has a great many judging criteria. The judge is going to be a very busy bunny and he is going to find a lot of things wrong. Some of his opinions and down-grades, for example how many points to take off for an 'egg-shaped' loop, are subjective and undefined. For the humpty, things are

Diagram 44-5

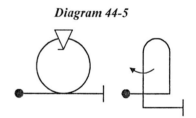

quite different. Be vertical up and down, centre the roll and stop on heading and there is very little left to really take points off for. The next two figures (Diagram 44-6) both total 20K.

Once again, the second option has much more chance of getting a good score, because of having a smaller number of key judging points. It is generally a good idea to avoid 45° lines, as judges seldom agree about what is steep and what is shallow. Also, the appearance of 45° lines changes a lot in different wind conditions and judges are not as adept at making allowances for this as they are with vertical lines.

Diagram 44-6

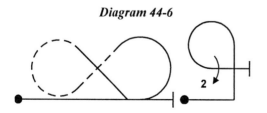

One implication of avoiding 45° lines is that, in a 15 figure Advanced sequence anyway, you will have to choose more vertical figures that incorporate high ranges of negative G. In such a sequence, you will have to take care when training not to overdo the negative and get too many bad headaches!

The lowest score in a sequence often comes from the rolling turn, such is the plethora of criteria for this figure. If the rest of your design is sound, it is therefore a good idea to keep the K invested in your roller to the minimum.

Diagram 44-7

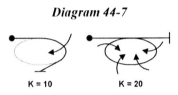

K = 10   K = 20

Here (Diagram 44-7) the difference in K is 10. If you might get a score of 8 for the simple turn, you might expect to get 6 for the longer one. This represents a difference of 20 points on the final score.

In an Advanced Free programme at a closely-fought contest, this represents 2/3 of a percent and might make a difference of two or three places among competitive pilots.

Choice of Figure 1

By all means start with a high speed figure with lots of vertical penetration, but avoid the temptation to vest it with a disproportionate amount of K. If you make figure 1 over-complicated, you make the judges' job harder. You also give them more opportunities to take points away, which they will do with pleasure.

Diagram 44-8

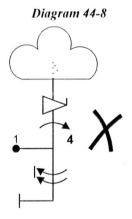

A relatively low score for figure 1 is not the way to get really good scores for subsequent manoeuvres. The judges will sub-consciously set your 'average' mark somewhere near your first score. They shouldn't do this, of course, but they are human, just as you are.

If you fly anywhere other than Arizona, there is a good chance there will be some cloud around, and this may interfere with your flight at the top of the box. The rules allow for the sequence to be flown with an un-penalized break if the ceiling is between 800 metres and the 'top of the box +50 metres'.

In these circumstances, you will probably want to get the top of figure 1 close to the cloud base, without going into it. This is not a good place for a stall turn (Diagram 44-8) where you must continue upwards until all speed is lost. Much better to have a Humpty Bump where you can pull early over the top if the cloud gets too close.

The Big Picture

In Diagram 44-9 you will see plan and elevation views of the 1,000 metres square aerobatic 'box' of sky used for all formal competitions. The elevation view has 100 metres, 200 metres and 1,500 feet above ground lines to show some of the lower limits typically used for safety at decreasing levels of pilot experience.

The best part of the box to fly in is the white central core. The light grey segments are OK, but not ideal, while the darker grey areas really are on the 'avoid if at all possible' list.

Diagram 44-9

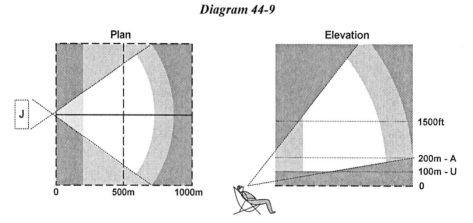

I know, simply staying in the box is hard enough. Why on earth try to make it even harder by having preferences inside this restricted space? As you can easily understand from the arc-shaped segments, it is all to do with giving the judges a good chance to see you without twisting their necks too much left and right or falling backwards off the chairs.

More seriously, in these different extreme parts of the box, the judge will be watching your aircraft from angles or distances that make it very difficult to judge attitude accurately. They will think they see inaccuracies even if there are none.

Remember, what the judge sees is not important. It is what he **thinks he sees** that is crucial.

If you fly an aircraft at the lower end of the performance scale, you will be used to starting sequences quite high and finishing near, but hopefully not below, the lower limit. In this case it is really important that you start somewhat distant from the judging line and then get closer as you descend.

This concept is illustrated in the left picture of Diagram 44-10, which is predicated on a 1,200 foot minimum height. As the sequence progresses and the aircraft gets

Diagram 44-10

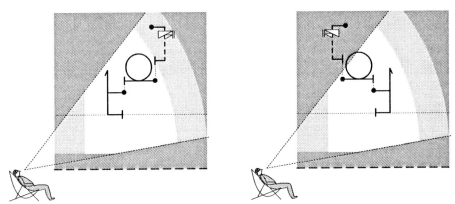

lower, the pilot is bringing the performance closer to the judges. The angle of the judge's sight line does not change much.

Each figure is presented optimally in terms of height and range. In the right hand picture, even though all the manoeuvres are well inside the box, the judge's sight line has changed a great deal. His perception of the aircraft shape is constantly changing. He is having to think about your positioning, rather than being blissfully unaware of it. This awkward presentation should not, but will, lose marks.

When you are designing your sequence, you should consider its overall structure and the likely height for each figure. Then you must build in elements that will allow you always to be at the optimum range for your height at any particular time. Design the overall shape of the sequence so that you have the best possible chance of staying in the white area; certainly you must have a very good probability of getting the last figure in this area so that the judges are able to see that you have flown according to plan.

Cross Wind Correctors

In just the right wind conditions, you could fly a sequence that had only main-axis figures. As you slowly lost height, the wind would kindly drift you slowly closer to the judging line and you would finish the last figure in perfect position. If ever this happens to you, just look off your left wing tip and there you will see a large pig keeping perfect formation.

In the real world you have to design a sequence that can be well presented in conditions that include a strong on-judge or off-judge wind.

At a major international competition recently, I found myself one morning in the role of Jury member responsible for monitoring the weather. The Free programmes were being flown and there was a strong, but just within limits, off-judge wind component. After a number of pilots from different countries had flown, doing their best to stay in the box and finish close to the judges, the Team Manager from a large East-European country tried very hard to persuade the Contest Director to stop the flying and move the judges' position by 90° so that the strong cross wind component would become a strong head wind component with much less across. The Contest Director and Chief Judge wanted to keep things moving, so the box orientation did not change.

When it came time for the first pilot from the objecting nation to fly, I understood their concern. He had the first 8 figures of a 15 figure sequence with no cross wind correctors. He would have to start very high and almost right over the judges heads to have any chance of staying inside the far boundary by the time he got to figure 9. Needless to say, he did not have a very happy flight. The day of the competition is just too late to think about such things.

To counter a strong cross wind, at any rate in the Intermediate and Advanced categories, you need to have a wind correcting figure at the rate of about 1 in 5. Diagram 44-11 is an example of such a sequence at Advanced level. This programme was my friend Kester Scrope's silver-medal flight in a French-built G202 at the Advanced World Championship in 2002.

The first four figures of the sequence are all vertical shapes with simple judging criteria. The down-going rolls are not good for energy conservation, but ensure that there are no rotational heading errors.

The G202 is very low drag and can actually sustain the high speeds generated on these down lines and convert them back to height again. The accelerating period between figures 5 and 6 restores some energy and then it is time to counter the wind. Figures 7 to 11 are a little more risky in terms of judging downgrades, but we should have convinced the judges with figures 1 to 4 that this is a good flight. Figure 11 gives the next chance to counter the wind, so that we can place 12, 13 and 14 in just the right place. The rolling turn is kept to a low coefficient and it is put at the end where it cannot have any influence over later grades.

Because there are two correctors in this sequence (ignore figure 15) they can be used to add to each other in a strong cross wind, or they can be flown opposite in light winds so that they cancel each other out.

In shorter sequences there may only be room for one cross box corrector. You have to accept this cross-box movement even on a still-air day when you really don't need it. Having to take it can be detrimental to your presentation when there is no wind to correct for. But there is even a design trick for this situation, whereby you can build in a single correction phase that can have a variable outcome.

Diagram 44-11

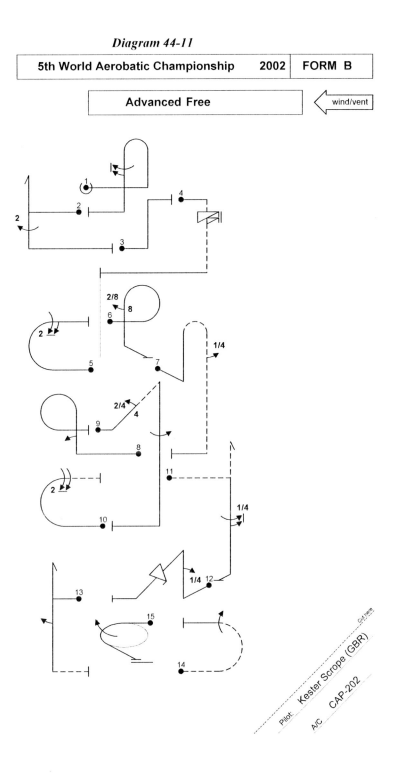

5th World Aerobatic Championship	2002	FORM B

Advanced Free wind/vent

Pilot: Kester Scrope (GBR)
A/C CAP-202

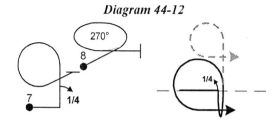

Diagram 44-12

One way to achieve the 'no-correction' correction is to use a 270° turn (rolling turn at the higher levels) as the second figure in the combination. An example is shown in Diagram 44-12. By changing the start point and the radius of the 270° turn, you can finish the combination with a correction in either direction, or of course no correction at all.

Sequence Cards

You should always have a sequence card mounted on the instrument panel in clear view when you fly a sequence. Nine times out of ten you will not need to look at it, but on the tenth occasion it is essential. When this need arises, it is really important that you can gather the information you need quickly.

Even if you don't refer to it in flight, drawing the sequence card will have helped you to learn the sequence by involving other parts of your brain than just those concerned with reading. Diagram 44-13 is an abbreviated example.

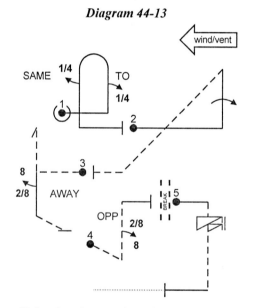

Diagram 44-13

My first recommendation is always to have the wind drawn from the same side of the form. Don't change it for different conditions or judging positions. You always need to be able to tell 'into wind' with a single glance, not a double take.

My second is not to use 'Left' and 'Right' as roll direction indicators. The wind conditions are not always as you plan and you may find that your pre-flight planning needs a change at the last second. Use 'TO' or 'AWAY' to indicate the direction to move the control column in roll, relative to the direction you want to use on the B-axis. For the second roll, that gets you back on the main axis, use 'SAME' or 'OPP(OSITE)' and remember what you did a moment before.

CHAPTER **45**

Ground Preparation

For those among you who are gardeners, this chapter title refers to preparation **on** the ground, not preparation **of** the ground.

Setting the Aim

Every aerobatic flight, from the very first lesson to the winning Unknown at a National Championship, must have an aim.

The total that you can learn or achieve on any particular flight is small. The activity into which you are about to launch is complex and physically demanding. It is also immensely intellectually demanding and this is probably of more significance than the physical challenge.

In a busy environment like an aeroplane cockpit, the brain is constantly performing routine functions as well as trying to learn new things. There is a very strict limit to how much new stuff it can actually absorb before it becomes 'full'. Full that is in terms of short-term retention.

After this stage, any new information can only be assimilated at the expense of something learned earlier. There is absolutely no point in continuing with a lesson, particularly, after this stage. This applies whether the lesson is self-taught or under dual instruction.

Under competition stress, the brain is a very fragile instrument. It has to maintain concentration while monitoring an absolutely enormous number of different external stimuli. As long as all goes to plan, it will cope. If, on the other hand, it suddenly detects an unexpected error or, even worse, comes up against a totally blank space, it can rapidly become an inert grey mass performing only rudimentary life-support functions. This is a layman's way of saying that all your carefully laid plans can suddenly fall around you like a collapsing house of cards leaving you with no real alternative to simply landing with an embarrassed look on your face.

So, this aim must be limited and achieveable. Along with the aim must go a plan of how to achieve it.

Making a Plan

... for a Learning Flight

Before you get airborne, you must have a plan of what exercises you are going to fly, in which order and in which place(s). If you are flying solo, you must know this; if you are flying dual you must agree it.

Then you must stick pretty closely to the plan. Only by doing so will you be able to measure your achievement against the aim and thereby monitor your progress.

When flying any particular single exercise, such as a one-turn spin, or a positive half flick, you should not aim for, nor expect, perfection. For the first one or two repetitions, you should aim just to appreciate the errors you are making. For the next two or three attempts, you should concentrate on making some improvement in fixing those technical errors. If after half a dozen figures you have definitely seen an improvement, then you have achieved the aim and should stop that exercise.

If at this stage you have not seen any improvement, then you should also stop. Because you have not really analysed the errors well enough, you are now getting tired and any more failures will lead to loss of confidence as well. Take a short breather and try again with a different planned exercise, or simply go home, land and think about it. Seek assistance if necessary concerning your technique, re-read the book, whatever. Just make a mental note not to keep banging your head against a proverbial brick wall while flying. It is just too costly a hobby to get nothing out of a long flight.

Over the last 13 years, I have accumulated something over 2,000 hours of teaching aerobatics in a Pitts S2A. The average flight duration is probably 30 to 35 minutes, no more. This, on average, is about the length of time that the brain can work, take in new ideas and make progress. After this time performance deteriorates, both that of the student and of the instructor. You may be able to extend the duration if you are flying a low-performance non-specialist aircraft such as a Cessna 152 Aerobat or a Robin 2160. But the extra time consumed will not be time that the brain has spent learning aerobatics; it will just have been climbing for height and transit flying.

... for a Performance

Learning the Sequence

There are a number of ways of learning the sequence on the ground. The first and simplest of these is to look at it on a piece of paper. But you need to do more than just that if you are really to 'learn the script'.

One very good aid is to draw the sequence, at first slowly and then faster, over and over again. By using the hand you are exercising another part of the brain that is not employed in just reading or studying. Then you can bring the voice into play and speak the sequence out loud. Another bit of brain brought to the task. All these things you must do without making a mistake. They must be flawless. So start slowly and then build up the speed to real time and then faster still.

Rehearsal

Lastly there is the 'dance'; originally made famous, or perhaps infamous, by Ladi Bezak, winner of the first ever World Aerobatic Championship in 1960.

This is an idiosyncratic and deeply personal way of rehearsing a sequence that involves walking about in a square, simulating wings and control inputs with the arms and hands, making precise head movements to be always looking in the right place and generally pirouetting around and looking quite strange. Again, this can be done at low and high speeds, but must always be flawless.

You must practice success, not failure. If this all sounds a strange way for an otherwise rational human being to perform, fear not. All world champions have done it before you. Would you expect a Shakespearean actor to have a go at Hamlet without a rehearsal?

At the Aeroplane

Pre-flight your aeroplane before the briefing or rehearsal. Once you walk out to the machine, you don't need any distractions that you could have found earlier. Never rely on anyone else to pre-flight the aeroplane for you, not even to adjust the rudder pedals or harness; especially not to refuel the aeroplane and thus check the fuel cap is closed. If you want this to be right, and no distraction, you should do it yourself.

If you are at a competition, prepare early. You must not rush, because to do so destroys concentration. But you must not be late nor delay your fellow competitors either. So you simply must plan ahead and allow time for things to go wrong. Then, if they don't go wrong, you will have a few serene moments for meditation before you launch.

In the last few minutes before take-off, keep yourself to yourself. Don't be concerned to watch the errors or imperfections of the other competitors. That is the job of the judges. Your job is simply to do your best. The most difficult thing at this time is to maintain your concentration and your confidence. You need both.

Technique and Focus

I have seen many skilful pilots turn in disappointing performances at the competition. I have done it myself far more often than I would wish. It is one thing to fly with good technique. You will have good results in training and good feedback from your coach. It is another problem to maintain the mental focus required at the actual contest that will enable the good technique to come through the barrier of psychological stress that comes from being on a big stage.

Focus is the ability to overcome stress through the application of concentration and confidence. This is the area of sports psychology, in which I cannot profess to be an expert. It is my responsibility, however, to get you to realize the importance of focus to a successful competitive career. I will confess that there have been many times when loss of focus has let me down, but there are also occasions that shine bright in my memory when I have succeeded in maintaining focus and brought home the trophies.

One such occurred at the UK Nationals in 1999. The last programme was the second Unknown and I was leading going into this round. Therefore it was my privilege to fly the last flight of the main contest. It was a clear sunny day and the judges had been out on the line for several hours. I am sure they were all looking forward to a nice cup of tea after this last flight.

I prepared in my normal way and strapped into my G202 with both concentration and confidence intact. It was my usual routine to set the electric elevator trim to the contest setting before each flight, using the stick-top buttons, and then to pull the circuit breaker so that there would be no inadvertent trim selection once airborne. On this occasion, I found, just seconds before take-off that the trim had run to fully aft and the button on the stick top was stuck so that I could not move the trim to its regular place.

I had to go back to the hangar and try to fix it. There is no way you can fly an Unlimited sequence with the trim set fully aft! I made the radio calls, taxied back, shut down, got out and sought technical assistance. The judges would have to wait for their tea. They would hate me and give me rotten scores! Somehow I must not think that way. I must just patiently get the snag fixed, not worry about the time, be serene yet focused. It took about 20 minutes to solve the sticky switch, set the trim in the right place and isolate the system from further potential problems. It seemed more like a day and a half in my state of arousal.

Somehow I managed to hold it all together. I flew the sequence neatly enough. The judges did not hate me, though they did really appreciate that late cup of tea. I won the trophy.

I cannot describe to you how I managed to overcome the stress of that afternoon. I cannot write in words what went through my head. But it was the day for me when 'focus' really came to mean something tangible, and I have been seeking to retain it ever since. There is a book that will help more in this area, and I recommend it to you all. It is *Peak Performance for Aerobatics* by Fred DeLacerda.

CHAPTER 46

Entering the Box

The one single thing you can do to give you the greatest chance of doing your best is to start in the right place, at the right height and speed. Yet this simple skill is one of the most neglected aspects of contest aerobatic coaching. I know this for two reasons: first, it was a long time before anyone told me how to do it and, second, my judging experiences at domestic

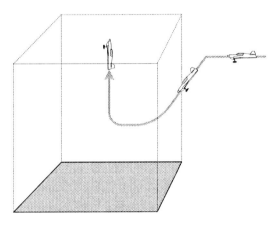

contests have proved how few contestants know how to do it.

I certainly hadn't learned how to do it properly when I attended my first Unlimited World Championship in Oklahoma in 1996. At the split second that I pulled up for figure 1, I knew I was too far into the box and that positioning of the next two or three figures was going to be difficult. This was sufficient distraction for me to make a bit of a mess of the vertical flick and any chance I had of 'doing my best' at that event went overboard right there.

Here are some of the essential ingredients for starting right.

* Plan the whole flight from wheels off to wheels on, not just the bit in the middle.

* Measure the actual, not forecast wind.

* Know exactly where you are all the time when approaching the box.

♦   Know how to establish the energy required to finish the sequence.

♦   Make best use of any permitted warm-up figures.

♦   Make the wing-rocks work for you, not against you.

I will discuss each of these topics in turn. The basis for this will be a competition flight from take-off to figure 1, flown direct into the box from take-off. If you fly in a contest and have to make an airborne hold, you must do the wind-checking at 2,000 feet in the hold, not in the box during the climb.

The Plan

Diagram 46-1

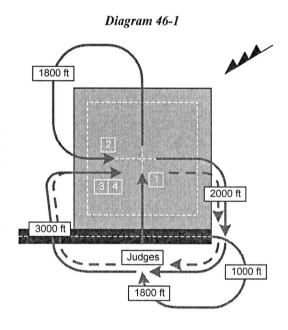

Your plan for the flight must begin on the runway on take-off. It must include which ways to turn, how to check the wind, the height and speed to climb to, the warm-up figures you are going to do and how you are going to wing-rock before figure 1. Diagram 46-1 shows an example of such a plan, which I will go on to describe in more detail. I'll also assume a centre-box figure 1 which requires a high speed start. You will learn to make similar plans for occasions when figure 1 starts slow, or in another spot.

Wind Checks

The first wind check, of course, is before take-off. In this case, there is a cross wind from the left. After take off, turn right through 270° and climb to 1,800 feet. This is roughly half way between the bottom of the box and the top for an Unlimited flight. Climb as quickly as you can, then when level throttle back to stay at best climb speed (ie not very fast) for the wind checks. This gets you to the Position 1. Fly across the box from behind the judges, into the on-judge wind component, and measure your drift to the left caused by the head wind on the main axis.

Leave the box and make a 270° turn left, still at 1,800 feet and, say, 90 knots, to reposition onto the main axis. You are now at Position 2. Fly parallel to the runway at low speed to check the on-judge drift. Leave the box and turn right, climbing through 2,000 feet to 3,000.

Down wind, check the trim is set for zero G. Stay at a slow datum speed, say 100 knots once you reach the top of the climb. Fly a slightly angled right base, into the on-judge wind to reduce ground speed, looking at the box. Judge when to turn onto the main axis based on your observation of the on-judge component.

Warm-Up Figures

Turn in toward the box, still at just 100 knots. When you guess the time is right, lower the nose, add full power and dive at 45°, nose slightly left of the axis to counter the on-judge component. You are now at Position 3. Look at the judges line to confirm your relative position. Come level at the figure 1 entry speed and pull up for the warm-up Humpty (Catalogue 8.1.1). On the way down from the humpty, assess the effect of the head and cross wind components on the figure.

After the Humpty do the first of the permitted two half rolls. Stay inverted long enough to check the oil pressure (inverted system working) and then roll back upright. Turn right and follow the same down wind track back to the 3,000 feet start position (dashed line now). Re-tighten the ratchet on the lap strap and set the shoulder strap to optimum.

Start

When you turn onto the main axis for the last time, adjust the positioning if necessary based on the perceptions from the warm-up run-in. This time, as the nose hits 45° down carry out three wing rocks to the right, looking at the judges position each time to monitor your relative position. You are now at Position 4. Pull level at entry speed and execute figure 1 without delay.

Key Points

The key points are:

♦ Stay close to the box.

♦ Use the wind to reduce ground speed during the wind checks and when making the precision approach to the box. Less ground speed equals more accuracy.

♦ Use the warm-up run to exactly replicate the starting run, minus the wing rocks.

♦ Look at the judges during the wing rocks.

♦ Do not check the altimeter at the base of the dive. It lags much too much to be accurate. Determine your energy by the height and speed before the dive.

411

Energy

You get to practice known sequences a lot. So it should not be a problem to arrive at the optimum energy balance for the flight. The best plan is the one that gets all the way through without busting the height minimum, but does actually get you close to it at the lowest points of the programme. Flying higher than necessary is not a winning strategy.

The best way to ensure repeatability in the sequence is to define the energy at the start by your height and speed when you are slow, before any dive that might be needed for figure 1. You cannot measure energy accurately by having a target speed and height at the end of the dive. Both parameters are changing too quickly and the altimeter is surprisingly inaccurate in a dive due to lag.

Always set your energy by adjusting the height that you turn into the box from base leg, while always keeping the same approach speed of around 100 mph or 100 knots.

Positioning

While you are turning, throughout the plan, you will have a good view of the box, as long as you stay close to it. Once on the final run-in, you will only be able to see the box accurately while diving or wing-rocking. So the run-in line must be just long enough to embody those two functions and no longer. Time and again I see Sportsman and Intermediate pilots dive too early and enter the box flying level for 5, 10 seconds or more. All this time they are losing energy, because they are slowing down level, and cannot see the judges. They invariably pull up for figure 1 much too early.

The two key elements to positioning are running in on base leg, not extended finals, and leaving any dive as late as possible.

Base Leg

The actual position and angle of the base leg will vary depending on the wind strength and the actual optimum box position of figure 1.

Diagram 46-2 shows three possible approaches, one each for a left-box, centre-box and right-box figure 1. Note that these lines represent tracks over the ground, so on a day with a particularly strong wind, the headings used should allow for drift as noted during the wind checks.

Notice how close to the box the base legs are when the start is in the centre or right box. The next thing to illustrate is the diving portions, to show where you will be pointing at while doing the wing rocks.

Diagram 46-2

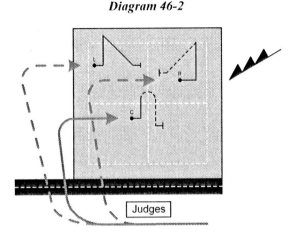

Diagram 46-3 shows three approaches, two to a start height of about 500 metres, one somewhat lower. These are 45° lines which assume that attitude and no head wind. On a windy day the flight paths would actually appear steeper. In each case, even in a 45° dive for a left-box start, the aiming point is well into the 1,000-metre box, or even beyond it. It is not necessary to go much more than 500 metres down wind of the box, even for a left-box start on a day with no wind.

Diagram 46-3

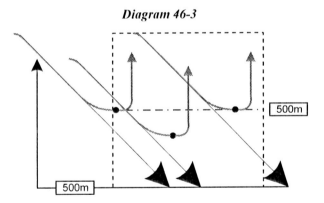

Warm Up Figures

In Advanced and Unlimited competitions, under international rules, you are allowed to fly one of three warm-up figures plus two half aileron rolls prior to starting the sequence. In domestic events, and in lower categories, you may be restricted to just the two half rolls or something different altogether.

If you are allowed warm-up figures, you should take them and use them as practice for starting figure 1 in the right place. For a diving start, I have already described how to do this. But what if it is a slow start?

Diagram 46-4

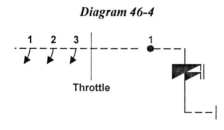

Throttle

Let's say that the first figure is an inverted spin. You are going to have to do three wing rocks, close the throttle and fly level to the stall (Diagram 46-4). To simulate this on the warm-up run through the box, you can fly in slow, upright, making a mental note of when to do the first two wing rocks based on what you can see below and beside you. Then you can roll inverted (the first half roll) in place of the third wing rock and close the throttle. You will now be able to see the box just as you will for the proper start. Instead of stalling, re-apply power and roll upright (the second half roll allowed) and as you do so look down and check exactly where you would have been for the spin entry. Then dive and do any other permitted warm-up figure.

Next time round you can apply what you learned from this dummy run to get the spin exactly in the right place.

Wing Rocks

Wing Rocks also go by the name of 'Wing Dips', though you could be excused for thinking that had something to do with barbecued chicken. They are the universal means of indicating the start and finish of a programme, or in fact any interruption thereto. The definition of a wing rock is that the aeroplane must quickly adopt a bank angle in excess of 45° and then return to wings level. Three of these manoeuvres must be flown in reasonably quick succession each time the signal is given.

Flight Path

There is no defined flight path for the aeroplane while the wing dips are being executed. They can be performed on a level, climbing or descending line. It is quite acceptable to have the first one or two level and then finish climbing or descending. It really is up to you to decide how to do them for the particular sequence you are about to fly.

For less experienced pilots in lower performing aeroplanes, my usual recommendation is to do two rocks level, then set the 45° diving line for the start and then finish with the third rock before coming level for figure 1. Of course, if figure 1 was a Spin or a Split-S, then diving is not going to happen. In this case all three wing rocks could be level. I have even seen some more ostentatious pilots do their wing dips climbing, although this does not really give you a very good view of the box and I don't recommend it.

414

On days when there is a strong cross wind, all three of the wing rocks can be started with the nose offset into wind to ensure a flight path straight down the main axis. The heading can be made correct as the wings come level for the third time. Other than this cross wind correction, your heading should not change during the dips, or your start position will be rather indeterminate to say the least. This is no simple task, so it is worth saying a couple of words about wing rock technique.

Technique

Level

Diagram 46-5

If you are going to fly straight and level with, even momentarily, 45° of bank you'd best be reminded of what is needed to do so.

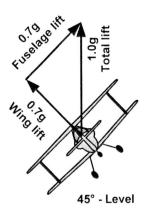

To get 1g of vertical lift at 45° of bank you need to generate 0.7g of fuselage lift by using top rudder, but also only 0.7g of wing lift (Diagram 46-5). So as the wing goes down you must move the control column slightly forward, or at least release some back pressure to avoid going off-heading to the side of the lower wing.

45° - Level

The generation of the fuselage lift also creates a lot of drag, so you need to add power to compensate if you are to maintain a constant airspeed. In some aircraft, adverse yaw helps by reducing the required rudder input

If you don't release the back stick pressure and if you don't add enough rudder, you will go off heading and descend. In order to compensate for these heading changes, some less experienced pilots decide that they will do their wing dips in alternate directions, left and right.

This works to a degree, but has two inherent problems. Firstly, there are an odd number of dips, so it cannot really work properly. Secondly, the more cynical judges will see the alternating wing rocks and immediately conclude that the pilot cannot do them straight. If he can't do straight wing rocks, what chance has he of doing a straight roll? Need I say more? You must learn to do all three wing dips to the same side without losing heading.

This will also give the added benefit of being able to look at the judges each time the wing is down and in this way you can make a much better judgement of your rate of progress toward the correct starting position. And because the wing rocks can be spaced out a bit, you do not have to rush this critical judgement.

You can see from Diagram 46-5 that, with a wing rock to the left, too much back stick will make you turn left. Adverse yaw from the right aileron during the roll back will also be in this direction. So, when you return to the wings-level attitude at the end of each wing dip, you will need to apply an extra helping of 'top' rudder.

Diving

Diagram 46-6

If you are dipping and diving, then things become quite a bit easier, because you don't have to generate the total 1g.

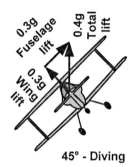

Typically, in an accelerating dive, you might have only 0.4g or less (Diagram 46-6). Now you can wing dip with the stick even further forward and using much less rudder.

Of these, the forward stick is the most important to remember as it is what really keeps you straight.

The steeper the dive, the easier the straight wing rocks become and the greater is the final speed you can attain.

416

CHAPTER 47

Wind Correction

Aerobatic competition is often compared with ice skating. We have a similar series of compulsory and freestyle programmes, we have a standard 'arena' and we have a panel of blind and prejudiced judges. Maybe that last bit is just in ice skating.

I have often used this analogy myself when outlining the basic system of competition to lay people. Then I just have to emphasize that the really big difference is that the ice does not move, while the sky does. Move that is, relative to the judges. Just think how nice it must be to be an Olympic ice skater. They have a warm-up rink they can practice on all morning before the big show in the afternoon. And they can practice in the full knowledge that their timing and positioning will be just the same 'on the day' as on every other occasion. Some luxury that. If you want another good analogy, ask how easy it would be to demonstrate all your kayaking skills if you had to stay beside one spot on the bank of a fast flowing river.

The aerobatic performer has always to consider the wind. Each time he flies any particular sequence it will be different in timing and technique from the last occasion, because the wind will be different. Of course, I am not pointing out all these difficulties by way of complaint, just to demonstrate that the accomplished aerobatic competitor can really be justified in feeling superior!

I remember on one very windy day we were flying a British contest at Peterborough with a tremendous off-judge wind. Most pilots were getting into all sorts of bother and were being blown a huge distance until they were becoming very difficult to see. As a result the positioning scores were very poor indeed and the figure grades were little better as the judges struggled to see what was happening so far away.

When my time came to fly, I was determined to do better. If necessary I would fly way off heading just to stay close to the judges. As an extra help, there was a 180° inverted turn as figure 8. By flying this into the cross wind and by using lots of top rudder, I could widen out the radius to be really quite big. The turn would take a long time to complete, and probably not score too well, but it was only 5K. Positioning, at Advanced and with no corner judges, was worth 40K.

My figures were far from perfect, but I won the sequence, most likely because the judges were so pleased to see an aeroplane close up. I only got one comment on the judging sheets for positioning. It read, *"A little close after Figure 8"*. How good it was to read that remark!

Main Axis Wind

Most figures are flown predominantly on the main axis. Flying the same sequence on different days requires only that you think about the time spent between consecutive figures when flying into the wind or down wind. This will enable you to put each figure in the correct place in relation to the judges' left and right fields of view. All looping figures have to be adjusted for these differing winds, of course, but I have described how to do this in earlier chapters.

On windy days, it is always necessary to work just that little bit quicker when travelling down wind. It is also wise to fly your 45° lines a little steep. You will occasionally be spending a little time flying on the B-axis, so that the main axis wind becomes a cross wind, in which case the following techniques come into play.

Secondary Axis Wind

More often than not, there is a cross wind component blowing you either on- or off-judge. To counter this problem you must look further than simply adjusting the shape of figures or the time spent level between them. Without some form of cross wind compensation you will quite rapidly become either a dot in the distance or a nuisance directly overhead the judges.

One kilometre is 0.54 nautical miles. If you start right at the back of the box and fly straight lines up and down the box in a 16 knot cross wind (the maximum allowed under CIVA Regulations), you will be over the judge's heads in just over two minutes. To stay in a smaller area, so as to be neither too close nor too far away, you should incorporate some major cross-box travel every minute (three figures) or so. Alternatively, you have to find another way of correcting for the wind. Doing nothing simply is not an option.

There are three things that make staying in the box possible. Unless you happen to have the luxury of a still-air day, every flight will probably have to exploit at least two of the three. They are, in order of intuitiveness:

- b-axis figures
- flying off-heading, and
- sliding.

B-axis figures were dealt with primarily in Chapter 44, so here I will be concerned only with the other two.

Flying Off Heading

Flying off heading, crabbing, drifting, call it what you may, is flying in contravention of the judging criteria. It deserves to be penalised by having points taken off the grades awarded for the figures. But judges can only take points off for errors they think they see, so many times you can fly off heading and get away with it. This gives a lot of opportunities for wind correction without penalty.

In extreme situations, you might even choose to fly a bit off-heading and take the penalty rather than be disqualified by a deadline infringement, but you should never get to such an extreme if you think wind correction, and apply it, right from the start.

You can fly off heading and get away with it in two situations:

- your elevation from a judging sight-line point of view is relatively low, or
- you are travelling toward or away from the judges some way on their left or right.

All you have to do to make enough cross wind correction is fly perhaps 10° off heading for every straight and level part of the sequence.

Judge Elevation	*Diagram 47-1*

What then is a suitably low elevation angle where you can get away with a judicious bit of crabbing? Probably something like 40°.

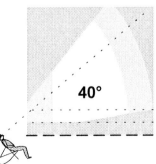

At this angle or lower, the judge is seeing more of the side of the aircraft and less of the bottom. You can see from Diagram 47-1 that this gives you quite a big area to play in. As long as you correct right from the start of the sequence and stay in this area you are very unlikely to be seen.

Judge Azimuth

When you are actually on the B-axis but compensating for the main axis wind, you can fly off heading as long as you are not in the centre, going directly toward or away from the judges. Of the two aeroplanes in the plan view Diagram 47-2, one is on heading but blowing with the wind toward the centre, while the other is 10° off heading and tracking straight across the box. This 'cheating' will not be seen by the judges.

Diagram 47-2

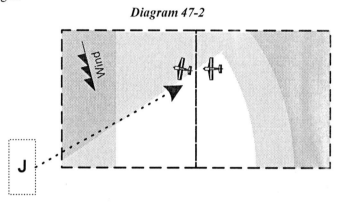

A good time to apply the heading error, when you can easily understand its effect is in downward looping segments. For example, pulling out from a stall turn.

Apply a very small amount of aileron toward the side that the wind is coming from. As you come level you will have a 5° or 10° heading error that will counter the wind. Diagram 47-3 shows this from the viewpoint of looking vertically down.

Diagram 47-3

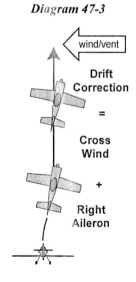

If you subsequently start another looping segment, you must again roll 5° or 10° to the right so that you have the wings in the right attitude by the time you get to the vertical. On the way down, re-apply the into-wind aileron to set off another small heading change.

As long as you keep making small corrections in this way you can keep just the right distance from the judging line. You will never be faced with suddenly needing a big heading change because you have been making the wind disappear from figure 1.

If you are flying a whole loop, you should only drift at the beginning and the end, not over the top. When you are at the highest point of the loop, the judges' sight line is more elevated and the error can be more easily seen.

In Diagram 47-4, follow the pictures from 1 to 5. From vertical up to vertical down, fly the loop on heading and accept a small amount of travel toward the left. Before the entry and at the exit, be off heading to the right to get back the distance lost over the top.

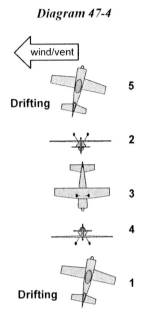

Diagram 47-4

Sliding

Sliding as a method of wind correction is a development of flying off-heading. Simply stated, it is the technique of generating side force while flying figures with perfectly normal attitudes. Side force, from rudder application, in turn generates fuselage lift which is very inefficient, so it also produces quite a lot of drag. For this reason it should be used sparingly and only when crabbing will be noticed.

Whereas crabbing is done in horizontal flight, sliding is always started during looping segments. It can be carried into straight lines but not sustained indefinitely along them without a small bank angle. To understand about sliding, you must first consider a flat turn.

If you apply left rudder and a little right aileron to stop any roll, you can make a flat turn to the left in most aeroplanes. The responsiveness in flat turning depends on the position of the fuselage lift centre of pressure relative to the aircraft centre of gravity position. This centre of pressure is always behind the centre of gravity. This gives the aeroplane its directional stability. But if the centre of pressure is close to the centre of gravity then the moment from the rudder side force is greater and so the aeroplane turns.

To counter a flat turn, and convert it into a side slip, you bank the aeroplane in the opposite direction from the turn. The two turning moments then cancel each other out and you are left with a straight side slip caused by the rudder side force (Diagram 47-5).

Diagram 47-5

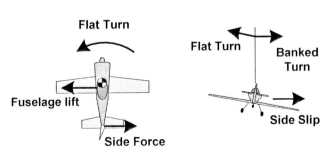

To apply side slip you have to apply a bank angle. While this may be noticed if done when flying level, the small change is almost impossible to detect when applied during a looping segment.

Imagine pulling out from a vertical down line (Diagram 47-6). If, when you pulled, you added a little right aileron and kept the aircraft balanced, it would head off to the right by a few degrees. This is, in fact what you would do to make a wind correction by flying off heading. But if you now simultaneously add some left rudder, you will correct the heading change and produce a side slip to the right.

As you reached wings level, the amount of slide would be equivalent to the amount of rudder and aileron applied. So would the increase in drag.

This kind of slide can be applied throughout a looping manoeuvre. In a horizontal eight you have two ¾ loops and can slide all round both of them provided you have enough power. Thus you can be constantly combating the wind whenever you are looping. Once you stop and hit a straight line, whether it is level or vertical, you cannot sustain the slide without a bank error which might be detected. But you will carry some sideways momentum into the line and this will degrade only slowly.

This same technique was described in Chapter 21 on the stall turns as a way of facilitating a turn against the engine or in an aircraft with a forward centre of gravity. It can also be applied when pushing in an outside looping segment, except now the rudder must be applied on the same side as the aileron to produce the slip (Diagram 47-7).

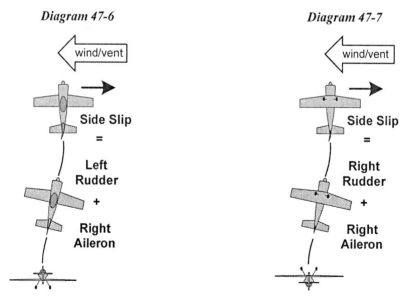

Diagram 47-6	*Diagram 47-7*
wind/vent	wind/vent
Side Slip	**Side Slip**
=	=
Left Rudder	**Right Rudder**
+	+
Right Aileron	**Right Aileron**

CHAPTER 48

Judging

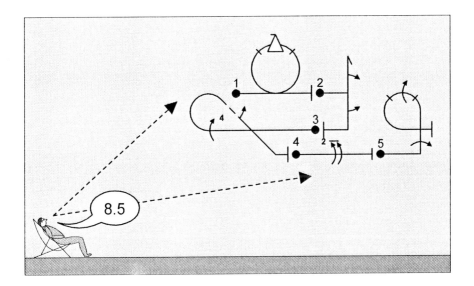

If you want to do well in aerobatic competition you just have to know about judging. And your knowledge must be quite extensive. You need to know not only the judging criteria and the system of grading figures, but also how the judge goes about his job, what is easy for him and what is hard, what he can see and what he cannot see.

Lastly, you need to understand that what he actually sees and what he thinks he sees are not necessarily the same. This is the realm of the optical illusion, and it has many applications in competition flying.

I can explain a lot of the technical, and a few of the psychological, points here, but not everything. To learn more for yourself, so that you can become a more successful competitor, you must volunteer and get yourself as much judging experience as time will allow. This can be an especially useful way of spending a weekend when there is a contest on at which you cannot fly but can at least help out. Not only will you learn many things of use to you later as a pilot; you will also earn the gratitude of the organisers and abuse of the contestants. This is the natural order of things and nothing else should be expected.

Do not expect thanks from pilots when you judge!

The Judging System

The judge is supposed to assume that you are going to fly a perfect figure. When you start, you have a maximum grade of 10 in the bank. As you proceed through the different elements of the figure, the judge notes inaccuracies and deducts marks at a rate of half a point for every 2.5° of error detected.

When the figure is complete, and before you start the next one, the judge has to call out to his scribe the result of his mental arithmetic so that each figure can be graded from 0 to 10 in intervals of 0.5. This seems reasonably simple, but in practice it isn't.

What the Judge is looking for

For each figure that comes along, the judge must have a mental model against which to compare your performance. This model will contain a number of different elements, depending on how complex are the figure and the judging criteria. As each element comes along, he will assess its accuracy, determine the extent of any errors, calculate how many points to take off, work out a running total (counting down from 10) and then look at the next element. This is quite a high workload, even for a relatively simple figure.

Table 48-1 is an example of the thought processes for a vanilla humpty. This is one of the simplest figures, but there are six opportunities for downgrading.

Table 48-1

Figure	#	Element	Criterion	Action
8.1.1	1	Entry Line	Level?	Downgrade
	2	Radius In	Size	Set Standard
	3	Up Line	Vertical?	Downgrade
	4	Top Radius	Constant?	Downgrade
	5	Down Line	Vertical?	Downgrade
	6	Radius Out	Compare with #2?	Downgrade

For each of the 'Downgrade' actions in the last column, the judge has to evaluate the size of any error and deduct a point or two from the maximum, then carry this downgrade forward in his head, adding the others on until the end of the figure. With just five adjudication points, this is a reasonable task.

In this next example (Table 48-2), I have just added two rolling elements, but the judging criteria have jumped from 6 to 22!.

Table 48-2

Figure	#	Element	Criterion	Action
8.1.1 +	1	Entry Line	Level?	Downgrade
9.1.1.4 +	2	Radius In	Size	Set Standard
9.4.5.2	3		Vertical?	Downgrade
	4	Up Line (1)	Length	Set Standard
	5		Constant Rate?	Downgrade
	6		Barrelled?	Downgrade
	7	Roll	Stop Heading?	Downgrade
	8		Vertical?	Downgrade
	9	Up Line (2)	Length As #4?	Downgrade
	10	Top Radius	Constant?	Downgrade
	11		Vertical?	Downgrade
	12	Down Line (1)	Length	Set Standard
	13		Constant Rate?	Downgrade
	14		Barrelled?	Downgrade
	15	Quarter Roll (1)	Stop Heading?	Downgrade
	16	Hesitation	Duration?	Downgrade
	17		Constant Rate?	Downgrade
	18		Barrelled?	Downgrade
	19	Quarter Roll (2)	Stop Heading?	Downgrade
	20		Vertical?	Downgrade
	21	Down Line (2)	Length As #12?	Downgrade
	22	Radius Out	Compare with #2	Downgrade

You can see that this is now becoming a very big task in terms of evaluating all the errors and carrying a total of deductions forward to be subtracted from 10 at the end of the figure. You have to start asking whether it is reasonable to expect a regular guy to be able to do this, accurately and consistently, while watching upwards of 50 flights a day.

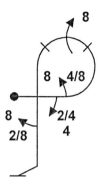

Diagram 48-1

Diagram 48-1 is a figure from the Unlimited first unknown in the British Nationals in 2001. This figure was actually nominated by one of the competitors. It has 16 different rolling fractions, each of which has in theory three judging criteria, plus 11 hesitations. There are also the usual criteria for radii and straight lines. Altogether it has around 40 different elements that should be measured by eye in real time.

Load Shedding

This complexity is too much for each element to be accurately judged in all its detail in real time. So we have to conclude that some load-shedding must go on in the judge's brain in order to reduce the size of the task to something manageable. This load-shedding may be conscious or sub-conscious; more likely the latter. But it must happen.

For example, consider the 8-point roll in the top of the P-loop. The judge will pay a fair amount of attention to determining exactly when the roll starts. He will also carefully count out the hesitations to himself to make sure there are actually eight points. This is important because a total of seven or nine would merit a hard zero. But it is probably not really feasible for him to accurately assess the number of degrees each of the eight roll sections actually covers, to compare each one with the required 45° and to determine a downgrade for each one and add it to the running total.

So it may be reasonable for a pilot to assume that as long as he starts and finishes the roll at roughly the correct part of the loop and does in fact make eight roll stops without a really big error, he will have done quite well.

This deduction does at least give the pilot the confidence to attack the figure with the understanding that it is still possible to get a reasonable score. My average score for this figure from all judges was 71%, equivalent to 14.5° total error through the whole figure. If no deductions at all were made for the overall shape and lines, this score means that in all the rolling elements they detected an average stopping error (14.5/16) of less than 1°. If the shape was a little poor and the vertical slightly off, these errors alone might account for, say 1.5 points off. This would leave only 1.4 marks off for roll stops, or a total error of 7.5° in 16 roll elements.

I do not claim to be able to fly that accurately, so I just have to conclude that, in a complex figure, quite close is actually close enough. Load shedding is clearly in operation here. You need to learn to look at the figures you are going to fly, consider how load-shedding might apply to each one, and then take care to fly the really important elements carefully. But you need not be overawed by the apparent complexity of the whole thing.

Judging Clarity

I use the term 'Judging Clarity' here as a way of describing a style of flying that results from considering the judges' workload and their likely load shedding proclivities. I mean to imply that if you know the elements in a figure that the judge is most likely to be concentrating on, you can fly in such a way as to make those key points very clear. Other parts of the judging criteria, which may actually get less of the judge's attention, can then either be ignored, modified or just load-shed in turn by the pilot's brain.

Corners

As an extremely simple example, consider the combination in Diagram 48-2. When you fly off the top of the 45° up line, your actual pitch attitude change is only going to be about 25° because of the high nose attitude needed for the spin. You are going to fly for only a very short time before the spin entry, so you will be going very slow. Yet the radius at the top of the figure

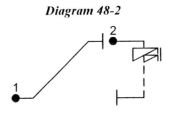

Diagram 48-2

is really meant to be the same as at the bottom – quite large in view of the higher speed there.

But if you make the top radius as big, and have only 25° of attitude change, it will be difficult for the judge to see whether this is actually a push-off or whether you have just become shallow because of the low speed and lack of attention. In other words, the judge will find it difficult to tell exactly when to stop judging your 45° attitude and look for a level flight path.

The answer is to make the pitch change at the top very quickly, so that there is a definite end to the 45° line, followed by an early spin entry.

The clarity of your finish to the 45° line and start to the spin will make the transition look sharp. Because he has had no difficulty seeing the various key points he will find it easy to judge. You might get a small downgrade for the tight top radius, but the overall score will be better than if the judge thinks your line got very shallow because the end of it was not clear.

Here is the start of a figure that begins with a half vertical roll up (Diagram 48-3). We'll just consider the sequence of events to the end of the line segment after the half roll.

Diagram 48-3

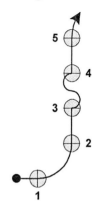

The judge needs to be certain exactly when the figure starts (1), so the first point of emphasis is how clearly you 'break' the horizontal line at the start. You must have a very quick 'pop' to start the pull-up. This does not mean a lot of G, just a very quick onset of G. Then the judge must clearly see the point at which you judge yourself to be vertical (2), because he has to both assess how close you are to vertical and to start measuring the length of line before the start of the half roll (3).

If the transition from pull-up to vertical line is not really clear, the judge will not really know when to make either of these two important judgements. So you need to make an 'accelerate/stop' move just as you come to vertical up, as shown in the pitch feel diagrams that accompany many of the earlier chapters.

Diagram 48-4

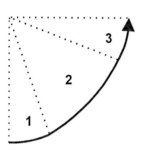

The curve in Diagram 48-4 has three segments: Quick, Steady and Accelerate/Stop. The radius is not constant, but this is very difficult for the judge to detect. Instead of noting this error, he simply sees a quarter loop, with very clear ends, that turns precisely into a good vertical.

He sees no errors and makes no downgrade because he is now measuring the line length and the details of the roll; all thoughts of the constancy of the radius have been shed. The figure looks precise because it is clearly presented. Some might think it looks 'aggressive' but in reality it is just clear and easy to see the different elements of the basic shape. Similarly, the start of the upper looping segment (5) must be very clear so that the distance from (4) to (5) can be seen.

Another pilot may fly just as accurately, but if the judge is not exactly sure when the curve stops and the vertical line begins, he won't be quite so sure that it is as accurate and he will perceive a difficulty in measuring the vertical line lengths. Consequently, the figure will look less clear and he will interpret that as less accurate.

When going around corners, it is not necessary to pull a lot of G, just to modulate the pull so that the start and end are clear. You should try to develop this style of flying that makes very clear the key points of the geometry of the basic shape. Learn to apply its principles to all the figures you fly, whatever the extent of the looping segments or the length of the straight lines.

Rolls

Roll rate is not a criterion for judging aileron rolls. A slow roll and a fast roll should, if otherwise equal, get equal scores. But often we see that quicker rolls seem to get better scores. There are two reasons.

The first is purely to do with technique. If you have an aeroplane that rolls slowly and your elevator technique is flawed, there is likely to be a significant loss of height and heading at the end. With a quicker rolling aircraft, the same amount of ham-fistedness is likely to result in a smaller error simply because of the shorter time available for angular deviations to occur.

The second reason happens, however, even with very good rolls by both pilots but in a situation where the judge is very busy. If the aeroplane rolls slowly, the judge has time to consider elements of the judging criteria that are internal to the roll. He is especially likely to see changes of roll rate. If the roll is quick, the time for those internal judgements is reduced because of the overwhelming need to judge the stopping attitude and the things that immediately follow, such as balanced line lengths or the shape of looping segments.

Diagram 48-5

So for clarity, and to actually put up the judge's workload to suit your situation, you will probably get better results if you always roll as fast as you can. The only exception to this is when the stop of the roll is immediately followed by a looping segment with no line before it (as in Diagram 48-5).

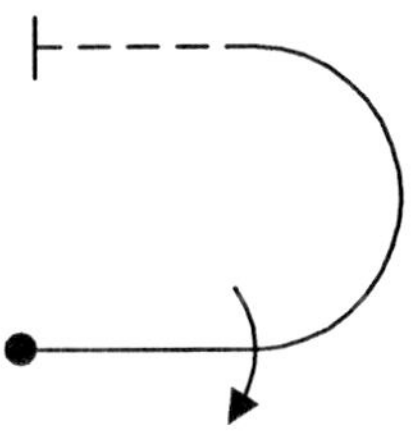

If you roll exceptionally quickly here, it is more likely that there will be an appearance of a line before the half loop up, simply because you have to hesitate slightly to make sure the wings really are level before you start to pull. If you roll a little more slowly, you will be able to anticipate wings level before you actually get there and will be able to make your 'pop' start to the loop without any semblance of a line.

If the roll in Diagram 48-5 had been a 4-point roll, you would have to have distinct pauses between the hesitations. Make sure you do not make an equal hesitation after the fourth stop, because this will be seen as a line.

Judging Perception

You now appreciate that the judge has an enormous number of things to look for, and that he cannot possibly see them all. This is particularly true of very complex figures and less so for simple ones. But there is another set of conditions that make it very difficult for the judge to be exactly sure of the precise attitude of the aeroplane.

Because we fly in a three dimensional space, the judge's sight line is constantly moving, he is seeing different aspects of the aircraft from different angles and at different distances. He has always to try to evaluate the attitudes against a hypothetical set of straight lines which he tries to envisage in all three axes. But the picture of the aeroplane is changed by perspective and parallax, light and shade.

The result of this is that there are some errors that are easy to see and some that are very difficult. For example, if you are flying straight towards the judging line, it will be very difficult for the judge to tell if you are climbing or descending a little, but it will be really obvious if you are just a little bit off heading. If you fly low through the box from right to left, it will be easy to tell if you are level, but difficult to tell if you are off heading. When you are looping, the aspect of the aeroplane seen by the judge is constantly changing. Again, he will find it difficult to pick up small errors in heading during these phases. When you fly a 45° climbing line down wind past the judges, their angle of view changes and the pitch attitude of the aircraft appears to change even though it is held perfectly constant.

Once you know how these perceptions appear from the judging line, you will start to understand the optical illusions from which the judges suffer. You can then fly intentionally inaccurately, either to obtain a better situation from a technique viewpoint, or to present a picture which is more like that the judge is expecting to see. Some might call this 'cheating', I prefer to think of it as a gloss on an otherwise flat performance.

Flight Path 'Cheating'

Here is a snippet from a Sportsman sequence (Diagram 48-6).

Diagram 48-6

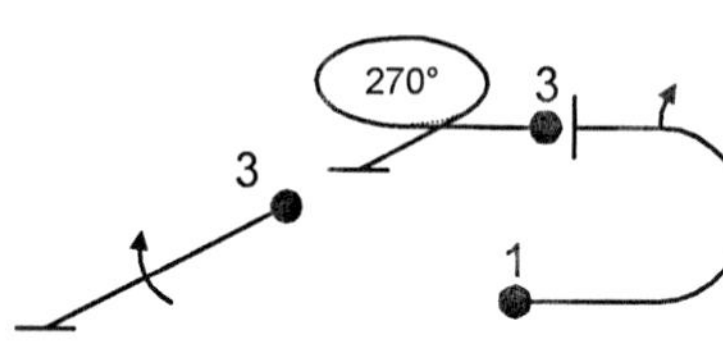

Assume you are flying a low powered aircraft and that you are going to finish the roll going towards the judges. After the Immelmann you will be slow. During the 270 turn, you will not be able to accelerate very much. Then you are faced with a roll from low speed for which you probably have insufficient aileron or rudder effectiveness. But all is not lost.

During the section of the turn where you are going away from the judges, they will not be able to judge your flight path accurately; bank angle yes, flight path no. So you can lower the nose for a bit here and gain a little more speed. At the back of the turn you must again be level, but as you get towards the end of it the judges will be seeing you head on. Just lower the nose a little again. As you fly directly towards the judges keep descending slightly, gaining speed, and fly the whole roll on heading but descending slightly. It will not be noticed.

Attitude 'Cheating'

I gave one example of attitude 'gloss' in Chapter 22 on hesitation rolls, based on the illusion given when flying past the judging line with 90° of bank. Here is another example to do with pitch attitude.

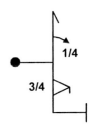

Diagram 48-7

Consider the stall turn in Diagram 48-7. Assume it is flown directly in front of the judges. After the quarter vertical roll, which you do to the left, the judges are looking directly at the bottom of the aircraft. After the turn, as you start on the down line, they cannot really be sure of your pitch attitude.

So, knowing that one of the major difficulties of the 3/4 flick is to finish wings level, you can anticipate and avoid the error by being slightly negative in the down line. When you add the back stick for the flick, this will bring you vertical and so you will have a good chance of stopping wings level.

Similarly, you can be slightly positive down before a negative flick in this situation. If you pull up with the judges seeing only the side of the aeroplane, you can be left wing high before a left half positive flick and, once more, improve the chance of having just the right attitude after you stop the roll.

Heading 'Cheating'

All judges know that fractions of flicks are likely to show attitude/heading errors at the end. This is something that they will not load shed. They also know that there are key elements to the initiation of the flick that they must watch for: the sudden 10° or 15° increase in alpha; the rapid roll acceleration that indicates the start of autorotation (the 'break').

Once the flick is complete, they must make a quick calculation based on their observation of these key points, and then move on. The less critical parts of the manoeuvre may not be so well imprinted on their minds. One such less-easily remembered element is the precise attitude just before you initiated the flick. You may have been slightly off-heading or not quite wings level, but if you had a good initiation and finished in the correct attitude, this earlier indiscretion may be forgotten or made light of, especially if your competitors had notable errors at the finish.

The conclusion is that you can afford to be a little inaccurate, on purpose, before a flick fraction if this small error will help you to finish with no error.

Here is a classic example from the Advanced World Championships in 1998. The figure concerned is shown in Diagram 48-8. The 1½ flick at low speed is notoriously difficult to stop on heading. The following multiple roll is also likely to produce a heading error in the same direction as the flick. This figure was the British nomination for the first Unknown sequence.

Diagram 48-8

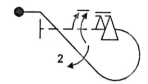

A large percentage of the less experienced pilots finished the figure well off-heading. This was quite noticeable to the judges and the heading penalty was also carried forward to the next figure in the sequence (Diagram 48-9, Picture 1). More experienced pilots, however, had no such problems. The main reason for their improved performance could be seen when observing along the main axis, but not from the seating position of the judges.

Diagram 48-9

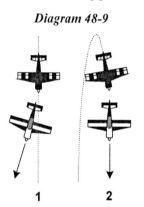

1   2

The best technique for this figure is to intentionally make a heading error during the long looping segment. The direction of this error must be to the right if you are going to flick with left rudder. So, during the pull, you add a little right aileron so that you arrive at the top with a 10° error (Diagram 48-9, Picture 2).

This is very difficult for the judges to see when the figure is positioned on reasonable low sight line elevation, neither too close nor too high.

The natural error from the flick is then likely to bring you back onto the right heading, with little residual sideslip so that it is easy to fly the aileron roll and finish perfectly on heading.

Conclusion

Aerobatics is primarily about learning to fly accurately and safely in all attitudes. It has purity of form. When you fly for your own appreciation, you are truly in pursuit of perfection.

Flying in competition is made impure by the fallacies of human perception. To be successful in this arena you have to learn to fly beyond the pure ideal and into a realm of performance where illusion becomes the main challenge. The pilot who wins may not be the one who flew most accurately, but he will be the one who appears to have flown most accurately.

One hundred percent accuracy with 75% clarity leaves you with a score of 75%. Ninety percent accuracy with 90% clarity gives you a winning margin at 81%. To win, you don't have to be perfect; you just have to appear better than the others.

An atmospheric into-sun shot of three aircraft operated by the author in June 2000:
Pitts S2A, CAP G202 and CAP 232. *Ed Hicks*

Printed in the United Kingdom
by Lightning Source UK Ltd.
106437UKS00001BC/21

9 780954 481407